WEEDS OF THE NORTHEAST

Weeds
OF THE
Northeast

RICHARD H. UVA

JOSEPH C. NEAL

JOSEPH M. DiTOMASO

COMSTOCK PUBLISHING ASSOCIATES A DIVISION OF

CORNELL UNIVERSITY PRESS | ITHACA AND LONDON

First published 1997 by Cornell University Press
First printing, Cornell Paperbacks, 1997

Printed in South Korea

Library of Congress Cataloging-in-Publication Data

Uva, Richard H. (Richard Hart), 1969–
    Weeds of the Northeast / Richard H. Uva, Joseph C. Neal, and Joseph M. DiTomaso.
        p.   cm.
    Includes bibliographical references (p.   ) and index.
    ISBN 978-0-8014-8334-9 (pbk : alk. paper)
    1. Weeds—Northeastern States—Identification.   2. Weeds—Canada, Eastern—
Identification.   I. Neal, Joseph C. (Joseph Crowell)   II. DiTomaso, Joseph M.
III. Title.
QK118.U93   1997
581.6'52—dc20   96-36434

Cornell University Press strives to use environmentally responsible suppliers and materials to the fullest extent possible in the publishing of its books. Such materials include vegetable-based, low-VOC inks, and acid-free papers that are recycled, totally chlorine-free, or partly composed of nonwood fibers. For further information, visit our website at www.cornellpress.cornell.edu.

Paperback printing   10   9   8

CONTENTS

Acknowledgments   vii

About This Book   1

How to Identify a Weed   4

Shortcut Identification Tables   5

    Table 1. Weeds with thorns, spines, or sharp prickles   5
    Table 2. Weeds with square stems (or angled or winged so as to appear square)   6
    Table 3. Weeds with whorled or seemingly whorled leaves   6
    Table 4. Weeds that exude milky sap from fresh roots, stems, and/or foliage   7
    Table 5. Weeds with an ocrea (a papery sheath that encloses the stem at the nodes)   7
    Table 6. Weeds with palmately compound or seemingly palmately compound leaves   8
    Table 7. Weeds with dissected or seemingly dissected leaves   8

Vegetative Key to the Weeds   9

Spore Producers   18

    Bryophyta   18
    Equisetaceae (Horsetail Family)   22

Monocots   24

    Commelinaceae (Spiderwort Family)   24
    Cyperaceae (Sedge Family)   26
    Juncaceae (Rush Family)   28
    Liliaceae (Lily Family)   30
    Poaceae = Gramineae (Grass Family)   34

Dicots   88

    Aizoaceae (Carpetweed Family)   88
    Amaranthaceae (Amaranth Family)   90
    Apiaceae = Umbelliferae (Carrot Family)   98
    Asclepiadaceae (Milkweed Family)   102
    Asteraceae = Compositae (Aster Family)   106
    Brassicaceae = Cruciferae (Mustard Family)   168
    Campanulaceae (Bellflower Family)   188
    Caryophyllaceae (Pink Family)   190
    Chenopodiaceae (Goosefoot Family)   204
    Convolvulaceae (Morningglory Family)   208
    Cucurbitaceae (Gourd Family)   218
    Dipsacaceae (Teasel Family)   220
    Euphorbiaceae (Spurge Family)   222
    Fabaceae = Leguminosae (Pea or Bean Family)   228
    Geraniaceae (Geranium Family)   242
    Lamiaceae = Labiatae (Mint Family)   246
    Lythraceae (Loosestrife Family)   254

Malvaceae (Mallow Family) 256
Onagraceae (Eveningprimrose Family) 264
Oxalidaceae (Woodsorrel Family) 266
Phytolaccaceae (Pokeweed Family) 268
Plantaginaceae (Plantain Family) 270
Polygonaceae (Smartweed Family) 274
Portulacaceae (Purslane Family) 288
Primulaceae (Primrose Family) 290
Ranunculaceae (Buttercup Family) 294
Rosaceae (Rose Family) 296
Rubiaceae (Madder Family) 300
Scrophulariaceae (Figwort Family) 304
Solanaceae (Nightshade Family) 312
Urticaceae (Nettle Family) 320
Violaceae (Violet Family) 322

Woody Plants   **326**
Anacardiaceae (Cashew Family) 326
Bignoniaceae (Trumpetcreeper Family) 330
Caprifoliaceae (Honeysuckle Family) 332
Celastraceae (Stafftree Family) 336
Liliaceae (Lily Family) 338
Ranunculaceae (Buttercup Family) 340
Rosaceae (Rose Family) 342
Simaroubaceae (Quassia Family) 346
Solanaceae (Nightshade Family) 348
Vitaceae (Grape Family) 350

Hardwood Seedlings   **354**

Comparison Tables   **363**
Table 8. Comparison of pigweeds and amaranths 363
Table 9. Comparison of weedy species in the carrot family (Apiaceae) 364
Table 10. Comparison of 4 members of the aster family that have finely
   dissected leaves 365
Table 11. Comparison of sowthistles and prickly lettuce 366
Table 12. Comparison of bindweeds and wild buckwheat 368
Table 13. Comparison of wild cucumber and burcucumber 369
Table 14. Comparison of trifoliolate (3 leaflets) legumes and woodsorrel 370
Table 15. Comparison of broadleaf plantain and blackseed plantain 372
Table 16. Comparison of selected speedwell species 373
Table 17. Comparison of groundcherry and nightshade species 374

Glossary   **375**
Bibliography   **385**
Index   **389**
About the Authors   **397**

The Grass Identification Table appears on a foldout at the back of the book.

ACKNOWLEDGMENTS

The following individuals generously contributed their time and expertise to the development of this manual. They gave us information on the status of weed species throughout the Northeast and in various cropping systems, offered tips on how to identify important weeds, reviewed the proposed layout and content of the book, and lent us photographs. We thank them all for their support and advice.

In particular we thank Andrew F. Senesac, Weed Science Specialist for Cornell Cooperative Extension at the Long Island Horticultural Research Laboratory, Riverhead, N.Y. From inception to completion of the book, Dr. Senesac gave unstintingly of his time, expertise, and encouragement. He also provided numerous photographs. His contributions on the taxonomy and ecology of the genus *Amaranthus* and many of the mustards (family Brassicaceae) were especially valuable. Additionally, through the results of his weed scouting program, he made us aware of many species whose importance in the Northeast is increasing.

Edward Cope, Extension Botanist (systematic botany) at the L. H. Bailey Hortorium, Cornell University, assisted us often with the identification of unknown weeds, helped resolve the taxonomy of confusing genera, and offered advice on the vegetative key. Jeffrey Derr, Horticultural Crops Weed Scientist, Virginia Polytechnic Institute and State University, generously advised us on the weed species found in the southern portion of the region covered and contributed several photographs. Larry Kuhns, Pennsylvania State University, provided information on weeds of noncrop land, Christmas tree plantations, nurseries, and landscapes, and in particular on mile-a-minute weed. William Curran, also of Pennsylvania State University, advised us on the economically important weeds of agronomic crops in the Northeast and lent us several photographs. Bradley Majek, Rutgers University, provided advice and guidance on the economically important weeds of fruit, vegetable, and agronomic crops. Prasanta Bhowmik, University of Massachusetts, supplied advice on the weeds of turfgrass and agronomic crops in New England. Robin Bellinder, Cornell University, offered guidance on weeds of vegetable crops in the Northeast. Russell Hahn, Cornell University, advised us on weeds of agronomic crops in the Northeast. Other scientists who gave us information and advice are Betty Marose, University of Maryland, Euel Coats, Mississippi State University (Virginia buttonweed and southern crabgrass), David Yarborough, University of Maine, and Nate Hartwig, Pennsylvania State University.

Additionally, we are grateful for the assistance of the following people in bringing this book to completion. We thank Margo Quinto for her painstakingly detailed copyediting, Joseph Gilmore for the excellent layouts of the color pages, and Richard Rosenbaum, Cornell University Press, for text design and layout. We especially thank Helene Maddux, Cornell University Press, for developmental editing and overall project management, including shepherding the book through the production process.

We thank the Ciba-Geigy Corporation for allowing us to reprint many drawings from their books *Grass Weeds 1* and *2, Monocot Weeds 3,* and *Dicot Weeds 1.* We are also grateful to The Scotts Company for permitting us to use drawings from the *Scotts Guide to the Identification of Grasses.* Bente Starcke King, formerly scientific illustrator for the L. H. Bailey Hortorium at Cornell University, drew illustrations for the book, as did Richard Uva.

We thank the following organizations for funding the research and development that resulted in this book. Without their support, the book would not have been written.

Cornell University College of Agriculture and Life Sciences

Genesee Fingerlakes Nursery and Landscape Association

Golf Course Superintendents Association of New England

Massachusetts Turf and Lawn Grass Association, Inc.

Nassau-Suffolk Landscape Gardeners Association

New York State Integrated Pest Management Program

New York State Turfgrass Association

Northeastern Weed Science Society

Pennsylvania Christmas Tree Growers Association

Pennsylvania Foundation for Ornamental Horticulture

Virginia Nurserymen's Association, Inc.

R. H. U.
J. C. N.
J. M. D.

WEEDS OF THE NORTHEAST

ABOUT THIS BOOK

Weeds of the Northeast is a practical guide to the identification of common and economically important weeds of the northeastern United States and southern Canada. It is also a reference book for those aspects of weed biology and ecology important to weed management. Relying on vegetative rather than floral characteristics for identification, this up-to-date manual describes 299 weed species that infest agronomic and horticultural crops, turfgrass areas, nurseries, gardens, and noncrop areas such as landscapes and roadsides. In compiling the species list, we defined the Northeast as the region south to Virginia, north to Maine and southeastern Canada, and west to Wisconsin. The weeds included are those that decrease crop yields or quality, reduce the aesthetics or functionality of landscapes and turfgrass areas, or adversely affect human or animal health. Also included are species with the potential to spread and infest more acreage and crops than they do now, as well as species considered crops in some areas and weeds in others. For example, orchardgrass and timothy are often cut for forage yet are highly competitive weeds in orchards and reduced-tillage areas. Similarly, red maple is a desirable landscape tree, but its seedlings are a constant aggravation in mulched landscape beds.

The book contains several tools for identifying weeds. Specimens with unusual vegetative characteristics, such as thorns, square stems, whorled leaves, milky sap, an ocrea, palmately compound leaves, or dissected leaves, can be rapidly identified using the shortcut identification tables (pp. 5–8). For weedy grasses, the grass identification table at the back of the book provides diagnostic information in an easy-to-use tabular key. The main tool for identifying an unknown specimen, however, is the dichotomous key to all the species described in the book. This key, unlike those found in most identification manuals, relies on vegetative characters, such as leaf orientation, lobes on the leaf margin, and presence and placement of hairs, rather than on floral characters to separate the species. The vegetative key and the diagnostic tables are each designed to narrow the choices to a few possible species. The identity of the specimen can then be confirmed by reading the descriptions of the species and comparing the specimen with the drawings and photographs.

The species descriptions are organized into four main groups: nonflowering or spore-producing plants, monocots (including grasses and grass-like weeds), herbaceous broadleaf (dicot) weeds, and woody weeds. Within each main group, the weeds are presented in alphabetical order by family name, genus, and species. The species descriptions provide a wealth of information in a condensed format: what the weed looks like at various stages of growth, how it propagates and spreads, the crops or management systems in which it is common, its geographic distribution, whether it is toxic to humans or livestock, and more. Accompanying each description are drawings and color photographs of identifying characteristics, seeds, and early and late stages of growth.

To facilitate both easy access to information about a species and easy comparison among species, we have presented the species descriptions in a standardized format, as shown on the facing page. The common and scientific names and the five-letter Bayer code (a standardized abbreviation and computer code) are from the Weed Science Society of America's *Composite List of Weeds*. For species not listed in that publication, we have adopted the common and scientific names in Gleason and Cronquist's *Manual of Vascular Plants of Northeastern United States and Adjacent Canada*, 2nd ed. Key characteristics for identification, dispersal, or management, as well as those of general importance are in boldface type. Following the species descriptions are tables designed to assist in the comparison of similar species and an illustrated glossary.

Although we diligently reviewed the book for accuracy, as with all human endeavors mistakes can occur. If you notice an error or have important information to add, please write to Joseph C. Neal, Department of Horticultural Science, Box 7609, North Carolina State University, Raleigh, NC 27695-7609.

Format and content of a species description

Common name (*Scientific name*) [Bayer code]
Synonyms

GENERAL DESCRIPTION: A summary of the weed's life cycle, growth habit, size, and special characteristics, including poisonous compounds and effects.

PROPAGATION / PHENOLOGY: How the weed propagates and spreads, when plants emerge, and what climatic or other factors affect germination, growth, and development (when information is available).

SEEDLING: A description of the seedling or of the emerging shoots of perennial weeds.

MATURE PLANT: A description of the vegetative characteristics of mature plants.

ROOTS AND UNDERGROUND STRUCTURES: A description of underground structures, with particular attention to vegetative propagules of perennial weeds.

FLOWERS AND FRUIT: A description of the flowers, fruit, and seeds, as well as the season(s) of occurrence.

POSTSENESCENCE CHARACTERISTICS: A description of the weed in the dormant season and any persistent characteristics of dead or dormant plants that may be useful in identification.

HABITAT: A description of the environs in which the weed is frequently found and of cropping systems, soil types, and management inputs that affect its distribution and spread.

DISTRIBUTION: Information on where the weed occurs in North America and (when available) where it is a serious problem.

SIMILAR SPECIES: Descriptions of species that resemble the weed, whether related to it or not. For each similar species, if there is a full description elsewhere in the book, or if the species is described in a table, only the common name is listed. If there is no full description, the scientific name and Bayer code are provided in the description of the species it most closely resembles.

HOW TO IDENTIFY A WEED

When trying to identify an unknown weed, start first with the list of characters in the shortcut identification tables. If these obvious characteristics are not present, or you are still not sure of the weed's identity, use the vegetative key or the grass identification table to narrow the choices. When the key or tables have eliminated all but a few species, read the descriptions of each of those species and compare the illustrations with your specimen before deciding on the weed's identity.

The vegetative key is organized in typical dichotomous fashion, with two choices (same numbers) at each juncture. **Consider both choices before moving on to the next pair of choices.** This key differs from most dichotomous keys in several ways. First, it is based on vegetative characters rather than floral characters. Second, it is designed to narrow your choices—not separate individual species. Third, because we recognize that it is easy to make "wrong turns" in an identification key, many species appear in several different parts of the key, even though technically they do not belong at some of those points. For example, birdseye pearlwort (*Sagina procumbens*) occurs at three points in the key: with the nonflowering plants, because it is often mistaken for a moss; with the flowering plants that have whorled leaves, because although its leaves are actually opposite, they can appear to be whorled when the axillary buds sprout; and with the flowering plants that have opposite leaves, its correct place. Some plants may have alternate and opposite leaves at different growth stages. These species appear in each relevant part of the key.

It may take some practice to learn how to use the key. We suggest you start with a species you know before trying to identify an unknown one. If your unknown specimen doesn't fit the descriptions, go back to the key and search for a "wrong turn"; if none is apparent, it may be that the weed is not in the book, since we could not include every species that might occur in the Northeast. If you cannot positively identify your specimen, send a sample to your state cooperative extension office for identification.

SHORTCUT IDENTIFICATION TABLES

The first step in identifying an unknown weed is to determine whether it has certain unusual vegetative characteristics: thorns, square stems, whorled leaves, milky sap, an ocrea, palmately compound leaves, or dissected leaves. The following tables contain species that have one or more of these diagnostic features. Using these tables you can quickly eliminate possible species and may be able to identify your specimen without referring to the key, especially if the species appears in more than one table. You can confirm your identification by reading the species description, on the page listed.

Table 1. Weeds with thorns, spines, or sharp prickles

Location of thorns, spines, or sharp prickles	Common name	Scientific name	Described on page
On fruit only	longspine sandbur	*Cenchrus longispinus*	40
	beggarticks	*Bidens* spp.	122
	common cocklebur	*Xanthium strumarium*	166
	burcucumber	*Sicyos angulatus*	218
	wild cucumber	*Echinocystis lobata*	218
	jimsonweed	*Datura stramonium*	312
On stem at leaf base only	spiny amaranth	*Amaranthus spinosus*	96
	spiny cocklebur	*Xanthium spinosum*	166
	prickly sida	*Sida spinosa*	262
On leaves, stems, flower heads, and/or fruit	common burdock	*Arctium minus*	114
	musk thistle	*Carduus nutans*	124
	Canada thistle	*Cirsium arvense*	132
	bull thistle	*Cirsium vulgare*	134
	prickly lettuce	*Lactuca serriola*	150
	perennial sowthistle	*Sonchus arvensis*	158
	annual sowthistle	*Sonchus oleraceus*	160
	spiny sowthistle	*Sonchus asper*	160, 366
	wild mustard[1]	*Brassica kaber*	170
	common teasel	*Dipsacus fullonum*	220
	mile-a-minute	*Polygonum perfoliatum*	282
	catchweed bedstraw	*Galium aparine*	302
	horsenettle	*Solanum carolinense*	316
	greenbriar, catbriar	*Smilax* spp.	338
	multiflora rose	*Rosa multiflora*	342
	brambles	*Rubus* spp.	344
	honey locust	*Gleditsia triacanthos*	356
	black locust	*Robinia pseudoacacia*	356

[1] Stiff hairs may be prickly.

Table 2. Weeds with square stems (or angled or winged so as to appear square)

Common name	Scientific name	Described on page
field horsetail	*Equisetum arvense*	22
beggarticks	*Bidens* spp.	122
little starwort	*Stellaria graminea*	200
common teasel	*Dipsacus fullonum*	220
ground ivy[1]	*Glechoma hederacea*	246
henbit[1]	*Lamium amplexicaule*	248
purple (or red) deadnettle[1]	*Lamium purpureum*	248
spotted deadnettle[1]	*Lamium maculatum*	248
healall[1]	*Prunella vulgaris*	250
creeping thyme[1]	*Thymus serpyllum*	252
scarlet pimpernel	*Anagallis arvensis*	290
bedstraws	*Galium* spp.	302
stinging nettle	*Urtica dioica*	320

[1] In the mint family (Lamiaceae = Labiatae).

Table 3. Weeds with whorled or seemingly whorled leaves

Leaf arrangement	Common name	Scientific name	Described on page
Whorled leaves	carpetweed	*Mollugo verticillata*	88
	corn spurry	*Spergula arvensis*	194
	purple loosestrife[1]	*Lythrum salicaria*	254
	scarlet pimpernel[2]	*Anagallis arvensis*	290
	bedstraws	*Galium* spp.	302
Other leaf arrangements that appear to be whorled	field horsetail[3]	*Equisetum arvense*	22
	birdseye pearlwort	*Sagina procumbens* (opposite)	194
	knawel	*Scleranthus annuus* (opposite)	196
	leafy spurge	*Euphorbia esula* (alternate)	224
	cypress spurge	*Euphorbia cyparissias* (alternate)	224
	toadflaxes	*Linaria* spp. (alternate)	304

[1] Leaves may be opposite or whorled.
[2] Leaves opposite or occasionally in whorls of 3.
[3] Stems are actually whorled; leaves are scale-like structures.

Table 4. Weeds that exude milky sap from fresh roots, stems, and/or foliage

Common name	Scientific name	Described on page
common milkweed	*Asclepias syriaca*	102
hemp dogbane	*Apocynum cannabinum*	102
chicory	*Cichorium intybus*	130
hawkweeds	*Hieracium* spp.	148
common catsear	*Hypochoeris radicata*	148
prickly lettuce	*Lactuca serriola*	150
sowthistles	*Sonchus* spp.	158, 160
dandelion	*Taraxacum officinale*	162
salsifies	*Tragopogon* spp.	164
common Venus' looking-glass	*Triodanis perfoliata*	188
small Venus' looking-glass	*Triodanis biflora*	188
cypress spurge	*Euphorbia cyparissias*	224
leafy spurge	*Euphorbia esula*	224
prostrate spurge	*Euphorbia humistrata*	226
spotted spurge	*Euphorbia maculata*	226
nodding spurge	*Euphorbia nutans*	226
Norway maple	*Acer platanoides*	354
white mulberry	*Morus alba* (young shoots only)	358

Table 5. Weeds with an ocrea (a papery sheath that encloses the stem at the nodes)

Common name	Scientific name	Described on page
prostrate knotweed	*Polygonum aviculare*	274
wild buckwheat	*Polygonum convolvulus*	276
Japanese knotweed	*Polygonum cuspidatum*	278
Pennsylvania smartweed	*Polygonum pensylvanicum*	280
ladysthumb	*Polygonum persicaria*	280
mile-a-minute	*Polygonum perfoliatum*	282
red sorrel	*Rumex acetosella*	284
curly dock	*Rumex crispus*	286
broadleaf dock	*Rumex obtusifolius*	286

Table 6. Weeds with palmately compound or seemingly palmately compound leaves

Leaf arrangement	Common name	Scientific name	Described on page
With 3 leaflets	birdsfoot trefoil	*Lotus corniculatus*	228
	hop clover	*Trifolium aureum*	228
	large hop clover	*Trifolium campestre*	228
	black medic	*Medicago lupulina*	230
	kudzu	*Pueraria lobata*	232
	rabbitfoot clover	*Trifolium arvense*	234
	white clover	*Trifolium repens*	236
	strawberry clover	*Trifolium fragiferum*	236
	alsike	*Trifolium hybridum*	236
	red clover	*Trifolium pratense*	236
	woodsorrels	*Oxalis* spp.	266
	buttercups	*Ranunculus* spp.	294
	wild strawberry	*Fragaria virginiana*	296
	Indian mock-strawberry	*Duchesnea indica*	296
	rough cinquefoil	*Potentilla norvegica*	298
	poison-ivy	*Toxicodendron radicans*	328
	poison-oak	*Toxicodendron toxicarium*	328
	virgin's bower	*Clematis virginiana*	340
	brambles	*Rubus* spp.	344
	bittersweet nightshade	*Solanum dulcamara*	348
With 4 or more leaflets	oldfield cinquefoil	*Potentilla simplex*	298
	common cinquefoil	*Potentilla canadensis*	298
	silvery cinquefoil	*Potentilla argentea*	298
	sulfur cinquefoil	*Potentilla recta*	298
	brambles	*Rubus* spp.	344
	Virginia-creeper	*Parthenocissus quinquefolia*	350

Table 7. Weeds with dissected or seemingly dissected leaves

Common name	Scientific name	Described on page
poison-hemlock	*Conium maculatum*	98
spotted waterhemlock	*Cicuta maculata*	98
wild carrot	*Daucus carota*	100
common yarrow	*Achillea millefolium*	106
common ragweed	*Ambrosia artemisiifolia*	108
chamomiles	*Anthemis* spp.	112
mugwort	*Artemisia vulgaris*	116
spotted knapweed	*Centaurea maculosa*	126
dogfennel	*Eupatorium capillifolium*	140
pineapple-weed	*Matricaria matricarioides*	152
tumble mustard	*Sisymbrium altissimum*	184

VEGETATIVE KEY TO THE WEEDS

1. Spore producers: liverworts, mosses, and horsetails (*Equisetum* spp.) . . . . Part A
1. Flower and seed producers:
    2. Stems herbaceous:
        3. Grasses and grass-like species: monocots (leaves usually parallel-veined, with bases sheathing the stem) . . . . Part B
        3. Broadleaf species: dicots (leaves usually with branched veins) . . . . Part C
    2. Stems woody: shrubs, woody vines, trees, brambles, and saplings . . . . Part D

Part A. Spore producers: liverworts, mosses, and horsetails (*Equisetum* spp.)

1. Hollow erect jointed stems . . . . **field horsetail** and **scouringrush**, p. 22
1. Mat-forming . . . . **liverworts**, p. 18
                                            mosses, p. 20
                            birdseye pearlwort (a flowering plant often mistaken for a moss), p. 194

Part B. Grasses and grass-like species: monocots (leaves usually parallel-veined, with bases sheathing the stem)

1. Leaves relatively broad, often ovate or lanceolate (habit and leaves reminiscent of a dicot) . . . . **dayflowers**, p. 24
1. Leaves narrow, often basal (habit and leaves reminiscent of a grass):
    2. Stems 3-angled, sharply triangular in cross section . . . . **sedges**, p. 26
    2. Stems roundish or sometimes flattened:
        3. From a bulb . . . . **onion** and **garlic**, p. 30
                                  star-of-Bethlehem, p. 32
        3. From fibrous roots, rhizomes, or stolons:
            4. Leaves hollow and round, stem-like . . . . **rushes**, p. 28
            4. Leaves flat:
                5. Leaves folded in the bud:
                    6. Short auricles present . . . . **perennial ryegrass**, p. 58
                    6. Auricles absent:
                        7. Ligule a fringe of hairs . . . . **sandburs**, p. 40
                                      bermudagrass, p. 42
                      7. Ligule membranous:
                        8. Blade with a prow- (boat-) shaped tip . . . . **bluegrasses**, p. 78
                                roughstalk bluegrass, p. 80
                      8. Blade tip otherwise . . . . **bluestems** and **broomsedge**, p. 34
                                  orchardgrass, p. 44
                                    goosegrass, p. 50
                                perennial ryegrass, p. 58
                5. Leaves rolled in the bud:
                    9. Ligule absent . . . . **slender rush**, p. 28
                                    barnyardgrass, p. 48

9. Ligule present (considered present even if very small):
   10. Ligule a fringe of hairs . . . . **witchgrass,** p. 64

                                                  fall panicum, p. 66

                                   wild-proso millet, p. 68

                                          common reed, p. 76

                                             giant reed, p. 76

                                                  foxtails, p. 82

   10. Ligule membranous:
      11. Auricles present . . . . **quackgrass,** p. 52

                                             tall fescue, p. 54

                                      Italian ryegrass, p. 58

      11. Auricles absent:
         12. Upper surface of blade hairy . . . . **downy brome,** p. 38

                                        large crabgrass, p. 46

                              common velvetgrass, p. 56

         12. Upper surface of blade mostly hairless or hairy only near the
            ligule region . . . . **oats,** p. 36

                                             cheat, p. 38

                                      crabgrasses, p. 46

                                           tall fescue, p. 54

                                    wirestem muhly, p. 60

                              creeping bentgrass, p. 62

                                      nimblewill, p. 62

  dallisgrass, knotgrass, and **fringeleaf paspalum,** p. 70

                                  reed canarygrass, p. 72

                                             timothy, p. 74

                                  colonial bentgrass, p. 80

                                      shattercane, p. 84

                                      johnsongrass, p. 86

Part C. Broadleaf species: dicots (leaves usually with branched veins)

1. Lower leaves opposite or whorled (2 or more leaves per node):
  2. Lower leaves or all leaves whorled:
    3. Stems square . . . . **scarlet pimpernel** (leaves opposite or in whorls of 3), p. 290

                                               bedstraws, p. 302

    3. Stems rounded:
      4. Plants prostrate . . . . **carpetweed,** p. 88

         birdseye pearlwort (leaves opposite, axillary shoots
                         give appearance of whorled), p. 194

        knawel (leaves opposite, axillary shoots give appearance of whorled), p. 196

      4. Plants erect . . . . **corn spurry,** p. 194

        purple loosestrife (leaves may be opposite or whorled), p. 254

        toadflaxes (leaves mostly alternate, lower leaves
                        may be opposite or whorled), p. 304

  2. Lower leaves opposite:
    5. Stems square (in cross section):
      6. Leaves with spines on the midrib, leaf surfaces wrinkled . . . .
      . . . . **common teasel** (stems square or round), p. 220

      6. Leaves without spines, not conspicuously wrinkled:
        7. Leaf margins entire or nearly so . . . . **little starwort,** p. 200

                                              healall, p. 250

creeping thyme, p. 252

scarlet pimpernel (leaves opposite or
in whorls of 3), p. 290

7. Leaf margins regularly toothed or lobed:
    8. Stipules present . . . . stinging nettle, p. 320
    8. Stipules absent . . . . ground ivy, p. 246

henbit and deadnettles, p. 248

5. Stems rounded, ridged, or angled but not square:
  9. Stems erect:
    10. Leaves compound . . . . spanishneedles and beggarticks, p. 122
    10. Leaves simple:
      11. Leaf margin entire:
        12. Fresh foliage exudes a milky sap when cut . . . .
        . . . . hemp dogbane, p. 102

common milkweed, p. 102

nodding spurge, p. 226

        12. Fresh foliage does not exude a milky sap when cut . . . .
        . . . . corn cockle, p. 190

field chickweed, p. 192

campions and catchflies, p. 198

purple loosestrife, p. 254

toadflaxes (leaves mostly alternate, lower leaves
may be opposite or whorled), p. 304

      11. Leaf margin lobed or toothed . . . . common ragweed, p. 108

giant ragweed, p. 110

nodding beggarticks, p. 122

galinsogas, p. 142

common teasel (stems square or round), p. 220

copperleafs, p. 222

hairy willowweed, p. 254

9. Stems prostrate, sprawling, ascending, or vine-like (many are common turf
weeds):
    13. Upper surface of leaf blade smooth or nearly hairless:
      14. Habit vine-like, stems twining . . . . swallowworts, p. 104

virgin's bower, p. 340

      14. Habit low, prostrate, ascending (common turf weeds):
        15. Foliage exudes a milky sap when cut . . . . spurges, p. 226
        15. Foliage does not exude a milky sap when cut:
          16. Leaves on vegetative stems <5 mm wide . . . .
          . . . . birdseye pearlwort, p. 194

red sandspurry, p. 194

knawel, p. 196

oldfield toadflax (leaves mostly alternate, lower leaves
may be opposite or whorled), p. 304

          16. Leaves on vegetative stems >5 mm wide . . . .
          . . . . field chickweed, p. 192

thymeleaf speedwell, p. 192

common chickweed, p. 202

common purslane, p. 288

moneywort, p. 292

Virginia buttonweed and poorjoe, p. 300

purslane speedwell, p. 308

13. Upper surface of leaf blade hairy or rough (hairs may be small—use lens):
    17. Upper leaves alternate on flowering stems . . . . **speedwells,** p. 308
                                                       slender speedwell, p. 310
    17. Upper leaves opposite on flowering stems . . . . **eclipta,** p. 138
                                                      chickweeds, p. 192
                                   thymeleaf sandwort, p. 202
                                                poorjoe, p. 300
                                     Florida pusley, p. 300
                           germander speedwell, p. 310

1. Lower leaves alternate (1 leaf per node), or a basal rosette present, or plant yellow, with "leafless," thread-like, twining stems:
    18. Plant yellow, stems "leafless," thread-like, and twining . . . . **dodders,** p. 212
    18. Plant otherwise, leaves alternate or in a basal rosette:
        19. Leaves or stems with spines or prickles:
            20. Spines at the leaf bases or nodes only . . . . **Russian thistle,** p. 90
                                           spiny amaranth, p. 96
                                     spiny cocklebur, p. 166
                                         prickly sida, p. 262
            20. Spines in other locations:
                21. Fresh foliage exudes a white sap when cut . . . . **prickly lettuce,** p. 150
                                         perennial sowthistle, p. 158
                                 spiny sowthistle, pp. 160, 366
                                       annual sowthistle, p. 160
                21. Fresh foliage does not exude a white sap when cut . . . **musk thistle,** p. 124
                                         Canada thistle, p. 132
                                           bull thistle, p. 134
                                   common teasel, p. 220
                                       horsenettle, p. 316
        19. Leaves and stems unarmed:
            22. Leaves compound or leaves simple and cut or lobed >75% of the way to the midrib:
                23. Leaves compound (with distinct leaflets):
                    24. Leaves with 3 leaflets:
                        25. Individual leaflets with a prominent indentation at the tip (heart-shaped) . . . . **woodsorrels,** p. 266
                      25. Individual leaflets rounded or pointed at the tip:
                            26. Leaf margins with many prominent teeth . . . .
                                 . . . . **buttercups,** p. 294
                                 Indian mock-strawberry, p. 296
                                     wild strawberry, p. 296
                                     rough cinquefoil, p. 298
                            26. Leaf margins entire or nearly so:
                                27. Plant a sprawling or ascending vine . . . . . . **kudzu,** p. 232
                                   bittersweet nightshade, p. 348
                              27. Habit otherwise . . . . **birdsfoot trefoil,** p. 228
                             clovers and **hop clovers,** pp. 228, 234, 236
                                     black medic, p. 230
                                 rabbitfoot clover, p. 234
                         bittersweet nightshade, p. 348
            24. Leaves with 4 or more leaflets:
                28. Leaves pinnately compound . . . . . . **spotted waterhemlock,** p. 98
                                     poison-hemlock, p. 98

giant hogweed, p. 98

wild carrot, p. 100

bittercresses (leaves simple but easily mistaken for compound), p. 174

yellow fieldcress, p. 182

birdsfoot trefoil, p. 228

vetches, p. 238

trailing crownvetch, p. 240

filarees, p. 242

28. Leaves palmately compound . . . . **buttercups,** p. 294

cinquefoils, p. 298

23. Leaves simple and cut or lobed >75% of the way to the midrib:

    29. Leaves palmately cut, about as wide as long . . . .

    . . . . **ivyleaf morningglory,** p. 214

geraniums, p. 244

Venice mallow, p. 258

musk mallow, p. 258

buttercups, p. 294

cinquefoils, p. 298

    29. Leaves pinnately cut, longer than wide:

        30. Leaves dissected . . . . **yarrow,** p. 106

chamomiles, p. 112

dogfennel, p. 140

pineapple-weed, p. 152

bittercresses, p. 174

        30. Leaves pinnatifid, lyrate, or lacerate . . . **common ragweed,** p. 108

mugwort, p. 116

knapweed and **cornflower,** p. 126

chicory, p..130

dandelion, p. 162

yellow rocket, p. 168

shepherd's-purse, p. 172

bittercresses, p. 174

field pepperweed, p. 176

Virginia pepperweed, p. 178

wild radish, p. 180

yellowcress and **fieldcress,** p. 182

mustards, p. 184

cutleaf eveningprimrose, p. 264

bittersweet nightshade, p. 348

22. Leaves simple, cut or lobed <75% of the way to the midrib:

    31. Ocrea present:

        32. Habit prostrate and mat-forming; leaves 1–3 cm long . . . .

        . . . . **prostrate knotweed,** p. 274

        32. Habit otherwise:

            33. Plant a vine . . . . **wild buckwheat,** p. 276

mile-a-minute, p. 282

            33. Plant not a vine . . . . **Japanese knotweed,** p. 278

smartweeds and **ladysthumb,** p. 280

red sorrel, p. 284

docks, p. 286

ocrea

31. Ocrea absent:
    34. Plant a vine . . . . **hedge bindweed,** p. 208
                                          field bindweed, p. 210
                                     morningglories, p. 214
                                     wild cucumber, p. 218
                                     burcucumber, p. 218
                         bittersweet nightshade, p. 348
    34. Plant not vine-like:
        35. Margins of lower leaves entire or nearly so, leaves unlobed:
           36. Upper leaf surface distinctly hairy (hairs conspicuous):
               37. Hairs on erect stem and flower clusters black . . . .
               . . . . **hawkweeds,** p. 148
               37. Hairs whitish . . . . **cornflower** and **knapweed,** p. 126
                                     horseweed, p. 136
                                     cudweed, p. 144
                                     pussytoes, p. 144
                               common mullein, p. 306
                       clammy groundcherry, p. 314
           36. Upperleaf surface not hairy, only sparsely hairy, or hairs
               small and inconspicuous:
               38. Leaf blades lanceolate or linear (blade > 3 times longer
                   than wide):
                   39. Basal rosette present . . . . **asters,** p. 118
                                   horseweed, p. 136
                                    salsifies, p. 164
                      common eveningprimrose, p. 264
                                   plantains, p. 270
                       smooth groundcherry, p. 314
               39. Basal rosette absent . . . .
               . . . .**dayflowers** (actually monocots), p. 24
                                     asters, p. 118
                                   horseweed, p. 136
                                   salsifies, p. 164
                                     kochia, p. 206
                                     spurges, p. 224
                      common eveningprimrose, p. 264
                                   toadflaxes, p. 304
                       smooth groundcherry, p. 314
               38. Leaf blades rounded, oblong, or ovate (blade < 3 times
                   longer than wide):
                   40. Lower leaves with dense white-woolly hairs on
                     underside; blades large (often about 50 cm long and
                     40 cm wide) . . . . **common burdock,** p. 114
                   40. Lower leaves not densely hairy on underside; blades
                   smaller:
                     41. Basal rosette present . . . . . . **English daisy,** p. 120
                                     plantains, p. 272
                     41. Basal rosette absent:
                        42. Plant prostrate . . . . **prostrate pigweed,** p. 92
                               common purslane, p. 288
                        42. Plant erect or ascending:
                           43. Leaves with distinct petioles and netted

venation . . . . **tumble pigweed,** p. 90

pigweeds and **amaranths,** p. 94

common pokeweed, p. 268

smooth groundcherry, p. 314

black nightshade, p. 318

bittersweet nightshade, p. 348

43. Leaves lacking distinct petioles; leaf bases form a sheath around the stem; parallel venation (broadleaf-like monocots) . . . .

. . **dayflowers** (actually monocots), p. 24

35. Margins of lower leaves toothed and/or lower leaves lobed or cut:

44. Basal rosette present, or basal leaves present, or plant developed from a basal rosette:

45. Leaf margin with rounded or pointed indentations extending 25–75% of the way to the midrib:

46. Fresh foliage exudes a milky sap when cut . . . .

. . . . **chicory,** p. 130

common catsear, p. 148

dandelion, p. 162

46. Fresh foliage does not exude a milky sap when cut . . .

. . . . **cornflower,** p. 126

oxeye daisy, p. 128

horseweed, p. 136

yellow rocket, p. 168

wild mustard, p. 170

shepherd's-purse, p. 172

bittercresses, p. 174

wild radish, p. 180

yellowcress and **fieldcress,** p. 182

mustards, p. 184

cutleaf eveningprimrose, p. 264

moth mullein, p. 306

45. Leaf margin with rounded or pointed indentations extending <25% of the way to the midrib:

47. Erect "stems" bear flowers only, no leaves (scapose) . . . . **English daisy,** p. 120

cornflower, p. 126

dandelion, p. 162

plantains, p. 272

violets, p. 324

47. Erect stems leafy . . . . **common burdock,** p. 114

oxeye daisy, p. 128

horseweed, p. 136

fleabanes, p. 136

purple cudweed, p. 144

field pepperweed, p. 176

Virginia pepperweed, p. 178

pennycresses, p. 186

common mallow, p. 260

eveningprimroses, p. 264

moth mullein, p. 306

field violet, p. 322

44. Basal rosette absent:
    48. Leaf margin with rounded or pointed indentations
        extending 25–75% of the way to the
        midrib . . . . **oxeye daisy,** p. 128
                                                 horseweed, p. 136
                         common groundsel, p. 154
                                musk mallow, p. 258
                              common mallow, p. 260
                cutleaf eveningprimrose, p. 264
                                      jimsonweed, p. 312
    48. Leaf margin with rounded or pointed indentations
        extending <25% of the way to the midrib:
        49. Leaves of the middle portions of the stem with
            prominent petioles . . . . **horseweed,** p. 136
                                     rough fleabane, p. 136
               sunflower and **Jerusalem artichoke,** p. 146
                            common cocklebur, p. 166
                     common lambsquarters, p. 204
                                    copperleafs, p. 222
                                      velvetleaf, p. 256
                                  musk mallow, p. 258
                              common mallow, p. 260
                                      prickly sida, p. 262
                                groundcherries, p. 314
                                  nightshades, p. 318
                          violets and **pansies,** p. 322
        49. Leaves of the middle portions of the stem sessile or
            nearly sessile . . . . **oxeye daisy,** p. 128
                                      fleabanes, p. 136
                            Canada goldenrod, p. 156
                          field pepperweed, p. 176
                       Virginia pepperweed, p. 178
                Venus' looking-glasses, p. 188
                        hairy willowweed, p. 254
                       eveningprimroses, p. 264

Part D. Stems woody: shrubs, woody vines, trees, brambles, and saplings

1. Leaves simple:
  2. Plant a vine or vine-like:
    3. Leaves alternate:
      4. Stems with spines or prickles . . . . **briars,** p. 338
      4. Stems unarmed . . . . **bittersweets,** p. 336
                                bittersweet nightshade, p. 348
                                      wild grapes, p. 352
    3. Leaves opposite . . . . **Japanese honeysuckle,** p. 332
  2. Plant a shrub or tree:
    5. Leaves alternate:
      6. Ocrea present . . . .
      . . . . **Japanese knotweed** (herbaceous, often mistaken as woody), p. 278
      6. Ocrea absent . . . . **white mulberry,** p. 358

common cottonwood, p. 360

black cherry, p. 360

common chokecherry, p. 360

5. Leaves opposite . . . . **Tatarian honeysuckle,** p. 334

red maple, p. 354

Norway maple, p. 354

1. Leaves compound:
   7. Plant a vine:
      8. Leaves alternate:
         9. Prickles present . . . . **brambles,** p. 344
         9. Prickles absent:
            10. Leaflets 3 per leaf . . . . **poison-ivy** and **poison-oak,** p. 328
            10. Leaflets 5 or more . . . . **trumpetcreeper,** p. 330

            Virginia-creeper, p. 350
      8. Leaves opposite . . . . **virgin's bower,** p. 340
   7. Plant a shrub or tree:
      11. Leaflets 5 or fewer . . . . **poison-oak,** p. 328

      box elder, p. 354

      ashes, p. 358

      11. Leaflets 6 or more:
         12. Leaflet margins entire or sparsely or minutely toothed . . . . **dwarf sumac,** p. 326

         poison-sumac, p. 326

         tree-of-heaven, p. 346

         black locust, p. 356

         honey locust, p. 356

         ashes, p. 358

         12. Leaflet margins conspicuously toothed:
            13. Thorns or prickles present . . . . **multiflora rose,** p. 342
            13. Thorns or prickles absent . . . .**sumacs,** p. 326

            ashes, p. 358

Liverworts

GENERAL DESCRIPTION: **Branching moss-like** primitive plants that **grow flat on the ground**.

REPRODUCTIVE CHARACTERISTICS: Reproduction occurs **vegetatively and by spores. Small bud-like branches (gemmae)** are produced in cup-like structures on the surface of the plant. Drops of rain fall into these cups and mechanically detach and disperse the gemmae. This appears to be the more important means of dispersal in nursery and greenhouse crops. Stalked umbrella-like structures contain spore-producing reproductive organs that, at maturity, release the spores.

MATURE PLANT: Most weedy liverworts are thallose **(lobed or ribbon-like)**. They lack distinct axes, leaves, and stems.

ROOTS AND UNDERGROUND STRUCTURES: Attached to the soil by root-like structures (rhizoids).

IMPORTANT SPECIES: *Marchantia polymorpha* **L.** is a common weed of container-grown nursery crops and also occurs in irrigated turfgrass and landscapes, and in excessively moist areas. Its tissues are dull green, forked or lobed, and ribbon-like, with prominently sunken midribs. Individuals may grow to 12 cm or more in length. Several plants growing together can form a mat. *Lunularia cruciata* **(L.) Dumort.** has crescent-shaped cup-like structures (gemmae receptacles), unlike *Marchantia polymorpha*, which has round receptacles. In the northeastern United States, *Lunularia cruciata* is found only in greenhouses.

POSTSENESCENCE CHARACTERISTICS: None of note.

HABITAT: Liverworts are weeds in container crops, greenhouses, and irrigated turfgrass. They grow on **excessively moist soil**, as well as on rocks and tree bark. Liverworts require moister conditions than mosses.

DISTRIBUTION: Several species occur throughout the United States.

Liverwort foliage
with gemmae
cup structures

A. Senesac

Liverwort habit

A. Senesac

Liverwort fruiting structures

A. Senesac

19

Mosses

GENERAL DESCRIPTION: **Primitive mat-forming** plants usually found on shady moist surfaces. **Most mosses are perennial.**

REPRODUCTIVE CHARACTERISTICS: Mats spread **both vegetatively**, crowding out other species, **and by airborne, desiccation-resistant spores.** Capsules containing the spores are produced at the tips of the leafy shoots on leafless stalks. Spores are released and dispersed by air. Those that land on moist surfaces absorb water and germinate to form protonema (minute branching filaments).

MATURE PLANT: Leaves are small, usually only a few millimeters long, lack petioles, and are often awl-shaped. They are arranged spirally on slender stems. Dense mats or patches of moss plants may hold considerable amounts of water by capillary action.

ROOTS AND UNDERGROUND STRUCTURES: Root-like structures (rhizoids) develop at the base of the leafy stems and absorb water and salts from the soil. True conductive tissue is absent, and many species absorb water through the surfaces of the stems and leaves.

IMPORTANT SPECIES: **Silver thread or silvery bryum (*Bryum argenteum* L.)** grows in **many diverse habitats**—for example, on dry, compact soils, sandy areas, and waste places. It is a common weedy moss in paths, turfgrass, golf greens, between bricks of walks, and in the cracks of sidewalks. Crowded overlapping leaves at the ends of stems give the stem a smooth cylindric shape. Mature leaves are white (lack chlorophyll) and give this moss its bright silvery gray appearance.

POSTSENESCENCE CHARACTERISTICS: None of note.

HABITAT: Mosses are most **often found in shady, moist sites**, but **many species are adapted to a variety of site conditions.** They are frequently weeds in irrigated turfgrass (particularly golf greens and shady lawns), container-grown crops, greenhouses, and perennial crops such as tree fruit, where the soil is undisturbed.

DISTRIBUTION: Many species occur throughout the United States.

SIMILAR SPECIES: **Birdseye pearlwort** is a mat-forming moss-like broadleaf weed often found in golf course greens, container-grown crops, between stones or bricks on paths, and other habitats similar to those of mosses. Its erect flower-stalks resemble the leafless stalks subtending the spore-bearing capsules of mosses, but they bear small white flowers or seed capsules. Unlike mosses, birdseye pearlwort has a fibrous root system and awl-shaped leaves that are opposite and approximately 1.5 cm in length.

Moss (partially cut out) in golf green

J. Neal

R. Uva

Moss with fruiting capsules

Algal crust in golf green

J. Neal

Field horsetail (*Equisetum arvense* L.) [EQUAR]

Synonyms: common horsetail, horsetail fern, meadow-pine, pine-grass, foxtail-rush, scouring-rush, bottle-brush, horsepipes, snake-grass

GENERAL DESCRIPTION: A primitive, **rhizomatous perennial with 2 stem forms**: an **erect leafless cone-bearing stem**, which emerges in early spring, and a later-emerging **vegetative stem** with whorls of leafless branches at the nodes, giving the plant a bottle-brush appearance. Vegetative stems grow erect or prostrate at the base with an ascending tip.

REPRODUCTIVE CHARACTERISTICS: Reproduction is primarily by **creeping rhizomes** that bear tubers. Reproduction by spores is also possible but probably not significant in agricultural systems. At the ends of fertile unbranched stems, cones, 0.5–3.5 cm long, produce thousands of minute spores from mid-April to May. The fertile stems soon wither and die, giving way to the vegetative branched stems. Of primary concern are the rhizomes, which, along with starch-filled tubers, are easily spread by cultivation, in topsoil, and in infested balled and burlaped nursery crops.

MATURE PLANT: **In the spring, the fertile stems are whitish, succulent, unbranched, and bear a terminal cone.** They grow to 30 cm or more in height and are approximately 8 mm thick. The fertile stems have dark, toothed sheaths (modified leaves) at the nodes (14–20 mm long). The teeth (5–9 mm long) are attached and form a tube around the stem. Fertile stems wither and dessicate soon after the spores are shed. **Vegetative stems emerge after the fertile stems have withered.** They are **green, hollow, grooved**, and grow **erect** or prostrate at the base with an ascending tip to 10–50 cm or more in height and 1.5–5 mm thick. **Branches grow in whorls from the middle and upper nodes** of the stem and are attached below the toothed sheaths. Branches are 3- or 4-angled, unbranched or sparsely branched. Stems and branches are coated with hard silica deposits. Leaves are small, scale-like, and black-tipped; 8–12 are joined into a sheath or tube around the stem at the nodes.

ROOTS AND UNDERGROUND STRUCTURES: **Extensive rhizome system** can grow to a depth of 1.5 m below the soil surface. Rhizomes are forked, have a dark felt-like coating, and bear small tubers.

POSTSENESCENCE CHARACTERISTICS: Vegetative stems die at the end of the growing season, turn black, and, by late autumn, are not generally found.

HABITAT: Field horsetail is a common weed of landscapes, orchards, and nursery crops. It grows on many different soils but does particularly well on sandy soils, on neutral or slightly basic soils, and in areas where the water table is high and soil drainage is poor. It is also found in low meadows, pastures, small fruit crops, roadsides, woodlands, and embankments. Field horsetail is **resistant to most herbicides used in agriculture**.

DISTRIBUTION: Found throughout the United States and Canada.

SIMILAR SPECIES: **Scouringrush (*Equisetum hyemale* L., EQUHY)** is found only in wet areas and can be distinguished by its evergreen stems that lack, or have very few, branches throughout the growing season.

Field horsetail habit

Field horsetail fruiting stalks

Scouringrush habit

Field horsetail in squash

Asiatic dayflower (*Commelina communis* L.) [COMCO]

Synonym: common dayflower

GENERAL DESCRIPTION: An **annual monocot** that **resembles a dicot**. It initially grows erect but with time takes on a creeping or somewhat ascending habit. Stems are light green, somewhat succulent, branched, and root at the nodes.

PROPAGATION / PHENOLOGY: Propagation is generally **by seed**. Vegetative reproduction is possible when stems fragment and root at the nodes to form colonies.

SEEDLING: The first leaf blade is oblong to oval with a rounded point; **veins in the leaf are parallel**. Later leaves are lanceolate. Blades are generally wider than those of the grasses.

MATURE PLANT: Stems grow up to 50 cm tall and 80 cm long and are swollen at the nodes, appearing jointed. **Stems and leaves are thick and fleshy. Leaves lack petioles and are simple**, lanceolate to lance-ovate, rarely ovate, pointed at the apex and rounded at the base, and often hairy on the upper and lower surfaces. Blades are 3–5 times as long (5–12 cm) as wide (1.5–4 cm) and have **smooth margins and parallel veins. Sheaths at the base of the blade clasp the stem**, forming a 1–2 cm long tube. Hairs are often present at the base of the blade where the sheath opens.

ROOTS AND UNDERGROUND STRUCTURES: Fibrous root system. Where they touch the ground, **stems root at the nodes**.

FLOWERS AND FRUIT: Flowers, produced from July through September in small clusters (cymes) in the leaf axils, are enclosed by a clasping, folded, green, leaf-like bract. Flowers have **2 larger blue petals above and 1 smaller white petal below**. Each flower lasts only a day. The spathe (1.5–3 cm long) has dark green veins, is separated at the base, and is on a long flower-stalk (1–7 cm) arising from the leaf axils. Fruit are 2-celled capsules, usually with 2 seeds per cell. Seeds are 2.5–4.5 mm long, brown, pitted, flat on one side and rounded on the other.

POSTSENESCENCE CHARACTERISTICS: Foliage and stems are very susceptible to frost and do not persist.

HABITAT: Asiatic dayflower is primarily a weed of landscapes and field and container nurseries. Usually found growing on moist, rich soil in shady areas, it does not tolerate cultivation or mowing.

DISTRIBUTION: Originally native to Asia, it has escaped cultivation to become a weed in the eastern half of the United States.

SIMILAR SPECIES: **Spreading dayflower (*Commelina diffusa* Burm.f., COMDI)** is an annual with a reclining or creeping growth habit. It is found in turf areas and is most common in the southeastern and south-central United States. Unlike that of Asiatic dayflower, the **reduced flower petal is blue, not white. Erect dayflower (*Commelina erecta* L.)** is usually found on sandy sites and is differentiated by its perennial life cycle and erect growth habit. In addition, erect dayflower's **leaf-like bracts are fused** at the base.

Asiatic dayflower habit

J. Neal

J. Neal

Asiatic dayflower flower

J. Neal

Asiatic dayflower seedling

J. DiTomaso

Asiatic dayflower seeds, 4.3 mm

Yellow nutsedge (*Cyperus esculentus* L.) [CYPES]

Synonyms: yellow nut-grass, nut sedge, chufa, northern nut-grass, earth almond

GENERAL DESCRIPTION: A **perennial with 3-angled stems, long grass-like leaves,** yellowish green foliage, and 1–2 cm long **tubers** at the ends of **rhizomes**. Flowers are in spikelets at the ends of the stems.

PROPAGATION / PHENOLOGY: **Reproduction is primarily by tubers**, although viable seeds can also be produced. Tubers sprout and seedlings emerge from May until mid-July. **Rhizomes** can also spread the weed. Dormant tubers may remain viable for 10 or more years and are easily spread by cultivation, in topsoil, and with nursery stock.

SEEDLING: Seedlings are not often found. When present, seedlings are **very grass-like** but soon develop the characteristic **3-sided (triangular in cross section) base**.

MATURE PLANT: Leaves are flat and shiny or have parallel veins that form grooves and ridges. **Yellow-green blades are narrow** (3–8 mm wide) **and grass-like**. Leaves are produced at the base of the plant in groups of 3, forming a sheath around the stem. Flowering stems are erect, unbranched, **triangular in cross section**, smooth, yellow-green, and generally solitary.

ROOTS AND UNDERGROUND STRUCTURES: **Rhizomes and tubers are present.** Tubers are 1–2 cm long, rounded, ridged or scaled, white at first, turning brown and then black. Tubers are produced at the end of rhizomes beginning in late June and continuing into autumn. A single plant may produce hundreds or several thousand in a season. Most tubers are found in the first 15 cm of the soil. They require a chilling period to break dormancy. After germination, tubers produce a primary basal bulb 1–2 cm beneath the soil surface; the bulb develops fibrous roots, then rhizomes, secondary basal bulbs, and tubers.

FLOWERS AND FRUIT: Individual flowers are inconspicuous, similar to those of grasses, and are organized into yellowish or brownish spikelets, 1–3 cm long and flattened. They are present from July to September. Spikelets occur at the ends of stems in terminal umbel-like clusters. Bracts below the flower clusters are leaf-like and often longer than the flower cluster. The single seed is enclosed within a 3-angled, yellowish brown, elliptic fruit (achene). Achenes are 1.5 mm long.

POSTSENESCENCE CHARACTERISTICS: In late summer, foliage may become yellow to reddish brown owing to a common rust disease. Foliage and the rhizomes die with the first killing frost. Only the tubers overwinter.

HABITAT: Yellow nutsedge is a weed of most agricultural, horticultural, and nursery crops as well as turfgrass and landscapes. It is found growing in many soil types and exposures but is most common on well-drained, sandy soils or damp to wet sites. Infestations often start in wet areas, then spread.

DISTRIBUTION: Found throughout North America.

SIMILAR SPECIES: **Purple nutsedge (*Cyperus rotundus* L., CYPRO)** has dark green leaves and stems and reddish brown or purple spikelets, whereas yellow nutsedge has yellow-green leaves and stems and yellowish or brown spikelets. Purple nutsedge develops **tubers along the length of the rhizomes**; yellow nutsedge tubers form only at the tips. Although nutsedge may resemble grasses, grasses do not produce leaves in groups of 3 and do not have tubers or 3-angled stems.

Yellow nutsedge habit

R. Uva

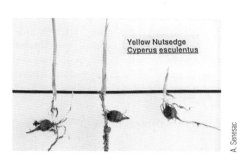

Yellow Nutsedge
Cyperus esculentus

A. Senesac

Sprouting yellow nutsedge tubers

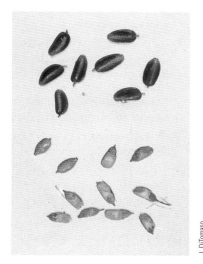

J. DiTomaso

Nutsedge nutlets: *top*, yellow,
1.4 mm; *bottom*, purple, 1.0 mm

J. Neal

Nutsedge leaf tips: *left*, yellow; *right*,
purple

J. Neal

Nutsedge flower heads: *left*, purple; *right*, yellow

27

Slender rush (*Juncus tenuis* Willd.) [IUNTE]

Synonyms: path rush, field rush, slender yard rush, wire-grass, poverty rush

GENERAL DESCRIPTION: A **clump-forming**, grass-like **perennial** (15–60 cm tall), with **narrow, wiry, rounded stems**.

PROPAGATION / PHENOLOGY: Reproduction is both vegetative and **by seed**.

SEEDLING: Seedlings are very small with slender **grass-like leaves** only 1 mm wide. **Whitish auricles** (1–3.5 mm long) are present at the junction of the leaf blade and sheath.

MATURE PLANT: **Stems are round, hollow, wiry, and dark green. Leaves are basal and flat, inwardly rolled at the margins to almost rounded** (0.5–2 mm wide). Sheaths cover 1/3–1/2 the height of the stem and have thin, dry, papery margins with a pair of papery ligule-like auricles at the junction of the blade and sheath. Ligules are absent.

ROOTS AND UNDERGROUND STRUCTURES: **Fibrous roots** are present at the nodes of **short rhizomes**.

FLOWERS AND FRUIT: Flowers occur from June through August and are produced in clusters (cymes) near the ends of the stems. Two (1–10 cm long) **leaf-like bracts often extend beyond the flower cluster**. Flowers are small, greenish brown (2.8–5 mm long), with lanceolate sepals and petals (3 each). Fruit are egg-shaped capsules (2.6–4.2 mm long) that split into 3 sections at maturity. Seeds are small (0.5 mm or smaller in length) and orange-brown.

POSTSENESCENCE CHARACTERISTICS: Plant often turns brown at top. Wiry, erect stems may persist throughout the winter.

HABITAT: Slender rush is a weed of turfgrass, landscapes, and nursery crops, especially along paths and in gravel or stone driveways and roads. It also grows in pastures, meadows, and waste places, on both moist and dry sites. It is particularly successful in compacted soils.

DISTRIBUTION: Found throughout the United States and southern Canada.

SIMILAR SPECIES: Other rushes can also be weedy. Rushes can be distinguished from the grasses and sedges by their round stems and the presence of sepals and petals.

Slender rush flower heads

Slender rush habit
Bente Starcke King

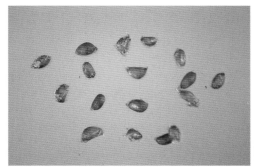

Slender rush seeds, 0.4 mm

Wild garlic (*Allium vineale* L.) [ALLVI]

Synonyms: field garlic, scallions, wild onion, crow garlic

GENERAL DESCRIPTION: A **bulbous perennial** with grass-like leaves that emerge in the early spring. All plant parts have a **strong scent of garlic or onion** when crushed. The stems are unbranched (30 cm to 1 m high), usually producing a cluster of tiny aerial bulbs at the top of the stems in place of the flowers, or red-purple, pink, or white to green flowers. In areas under stress from repeated mowing or cultivation, the foliage is more slender and does not produce flower-stalks or aerial bulblets.

PROPAGATION / PHENOLOGY: Reproduction is **by aerial bulblets** and **underground bulblets**, but **rarely by seed**. Plants grow rapidly in early spring to summer, produce flowers in May and June, then senesce.

SEEDLING: Seedlings are **grass-like with hollow, hairless leaves** that are round in cross section.

MATURE PLANT: **Basal leaves arise from the bulb. Leaves are linear**, grooved above, 15–60 cm long and 2–10 mm wide, **smooth, round, and hollow. Foliage has the scent of garlic or onion. Flowering stems are solid**, unbranched, smooth, erect, and leafless above; they become stiff with age.

ROOTS AND UNDERGROUND STRUCTURES: Fibrous roots are attached to the bottom of a rounded to egg-shaped bulb (1–2 cm in diameter). The **bulbs have a papery outer coating** often with distinctive puzzle-like cell architecture. **Bulblets** form at the base of the larger bulbs. Some are soft and germinate in the first autumn; others are hard and remain dormant over the winter, germinating the following spring or 1–5 years later.

FLOWERS AND FRUIT: **Flowers or bulblets are produced in May and June at the top of the stems in globe-shaped umbels** that are surrounded by a single 1-parted papery sheath-like spathe. **Aerial bulblets are often produced** at the top of the stem **in place of flowers** and **develop long tail-like green leaves**. Flowers, when present, are red-purple or pink, sometimes white or greenish and on long pedicels (0.5–2.5 cm). They do not generally produce seed in the northeastern United States. Fruit contain 2 seeds and are produced in egg-shaped 3-parted capsules at the end of the stems above the short bracts (2–3.5 mm long), with 2 seeds per cell. Seeds (3 mm long) are flattened, black, and wrinkled.

POSTSENESCENCE CHARACTERISTICS: Plants die back in the summer, but the leafless stalks, bearing the capsule, may remain.

HABITAT: Wild garlic is a weed of turfgrass, nursery crops, landscapes, winter wheat, and other cereal crops. In wheat, the heads of aerial bulblets easily shatter during harvest, contaminating the flour and giving it a garlicky odor and flavor. When grazed in pastures, wild garlic can impart a garlicky odor and flavor to beef and dairy products. Wild garlic usually grows on rich soils but can tolerate a wide range of soil conditions.

DISTRIBUTION: Found throughout the eastern half of the United States.

SIMILAR SPECIES: **Wild onion (*Allium canadense* L., ALLCA)** is similar except the leaves **are flat in cross section, not hollow**, and the **bulb has a fibrous, net-veined outer coating**, unlike the thin membranous outer coating of wild garlic. Wild onion has a 3-parted spathe below the flower cluster and does not produce hard dormant bulbs. Its habitats are similar to those of wild garlic.

R. Uva

Wild garlic foliage and bulbs

J. Neal

Wild garlic habit

R. Uva

Wild garlic bulblets

J. DiTomaso

Left, wild onion seeds, 3.0 mm;
right, wild garlic seeds, 3.1 mm

Star-of-Bethlehem (*Ornithogalum umbellatum* L.) [OTGUM]

Synonyms: summer snow-flake, star-flower

GENERAL DESCRIPTION: A **bulbous perennial** frequently sold commercially as a spring-flowering ornamental. It has escaped cultivation and can grow as tufts in lawns and landscapes in the early spring. All parts of the plant are **poisonous** if ingested.

PROPAGATION / PHENOLOGY: Reproduction is primarily **by small bulbs (bulblets)** formed around the base of the parent bulb. Bulbs are renewed each year. Seed production is rare but has been reported in North America. Young plants are noticeable in turf in early spring before the first mowing and in late spring in landscape beds.

SEEDLING: **Rare** in North America.

MATURE PLANT: Basal leaves are linear, and flowering stems are up to 30 cm high and leafless (scapes). The **grass-like leaves** (10–30 cm long by 2–6 mm wide) are fleshy and dark green, with a **whitish grooved midrib**, similar to crocus.

ROOTS AND UNDERGROUND STRUCTURES: Ovate **bulbs** grow in clumps and are subtended by a fibrous root system.

FLOWERS AND FRUIT: **Flowers**, present from April through June, are **bright waxy white** (occasionally bluish) on branched, open, clusters (corymbiform racemes) at the end of leafless flower-stalks. The 6 petals (tepals) are lanceolate-oblong (1.5–2 cm long) and white above with a distinctive green stripe underneath. Seed pods are present in mid to late spring. Fruit are 3-lobed, egg-shaped capsules containing several seeds. Seeds are black, somewhat egg-shaped (1.5 mm long), and have a granular surface.

POSTSENESCENCE CHARACTERISTICS: Plants die back to a bulb soon after setting seed in early summer.

HABITAT: Star-of-Bethlehem has escaped cultivation and is a weed of turfgrass and landscapes, often found in and around old flower gardens. It is less common in meadows, along roads, and in waste areas. **Early-season maturation and senescence enable this weed to escape most control measures.**

DISTRIBUTION: Common in the northern United States, the Piedmont region of the southern states, and Canada.

SIMILAR SPECIES: Several bulbous cultivated flowering plants resemble star-of-Bethlehem, but few have escaped to become weedy.

Mature star-of-Bethlehem plants and bulbs

R. Uva

R. Uva

Star-of-Bethlehem flowers

R. Uva

Emerging star-of-Bethlehem shoots

33

Broomsedge (*Andropogon virginicus* L.) [ANOVI]

Synonyms: beard-grass, whiskey grass, broomsedge bluestem, sedge grass

GENERAL DESCRIPTION: A **clump-forming perennial grass** with erect branching, flowering stems (50 cm to 1 m high). Most commonly recognized in the dormant stage: as persistent tan clumps of dried leaves and stems.

PROPAGATION / PHENOLOGY: Reproduction is **both vegetative and by seed**. Seedlings emerge in late spring or early summer. Clumps enlarge by **short rhizomes**.

SEEDLING: Young **leaves are folded in bud**, and the **sheaths are strongly compressed** (flattened). The **ligule is membranous** but fringed **with hairs** on the upper margin. **Hairs** are present at the junction of the blade and sheath.

MATURE PLANT: Foliage is smooth or sparsely hairy and often has a whitish or bluish cast on the surface. Leaves are folded in the bud, auricles are absent, and the ligule is 1 mm long and membranous, with a fringe of hairs on the upper margin. Stems are slightly flattened, often with long soft hairs at the uppermost nodes, and branched in the upper part. Blades are folded (keeled) near the base, linear (10–30 cm long by 2–8 mm wide), and sharply pointed at the apex. The upper surface of the blade may be hairy toward the base and along the margins in the region of the ligule. Sheaths are compressed (flattened) and smooth but may be hairy along the margins. The collar is narrow, hairy at the edges, and divided by the midvein.

ROOTS AND UNDERGROUND STRUCTURES: Densely fibrous root system from **short rhizomes**.

FLOWERS AND FRUIT: Flowering occurs from July through September. The **conspicuously silky-haired inflorescence** is produced along the upper half of the stem in the sheathed axils of the upper leaves. Spikelets are in racemes in groups of 2–4 (2–4 cm long). Two spikelets are present at each point of attachment, one sessile (fertile) with a long awn (2–4 cm), the other stalked (sterile) and lacking an awn.

POSTSENESCENCE CHARACTERISTICS: **In the fall, plants turn reddish tan** and stems become stiff, **persisting well into winter**. The hairy racemes of the spikelets are easily recognizable when the stiff stems blow in the wind.

HABITAT: Broomsedge is a weed of low-maintenance pasture, turfgrass, nursery crops, and other perennial crops. It is usually found in open, sunny locations on low-fertility and drought-prone soils, particularly unmanaged meadows, roadsides, and waste areas.

DISTRIBUTION: Found in California and throughout the eastern half of the United States, but not common in the northern New England states.

SIMILAR SPECIES: **Little bluestem (*Andropogon scoparius* Michx., ANOSC =** *Schizachyrium scoparium* (Michx.) Nash) is very similar, but its flower clusters (racemes of spikelets) are solitary, whereas those of broomsedge are in groups of 2 or more. **Big bluestem (*Andropogon gerardii* Vitman)** is generally larger than broomsedge (to 2 m in height) and has a longer raceme of stalked spikelets (5–10 cm).

Broomsedge habit (dormant)

J. Neal

Broomsedge collar region
Ciba-Geigy Corporation

Juvenile broomsedge

J. Neal

Broomsedge fruit

J. Neal

Little bluestem collar region
Ciba-Geigy Corporation

J. DiTomaso

Broomsedge seed, 3.5 mm (including lemma)

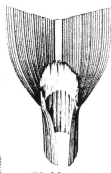

Big bluestem collar region
Ciba-Geigy Corporation

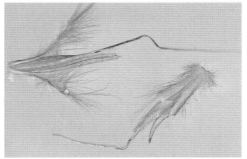

J. DiTomaso

Left, little bluestem seed, 8.0 mm (including lemma); *right*, big bluestem seed, 6.5 mm (including lemma)

35

Wild oat (*Avena fatua* L.) [AVEFA]

Synonyms: wheat oats, oat-grass, flax-grass

GENERAL DESCRIPTION: An **annual grass** with stout, **erect stems** to 1 m in height. It can grow solitary or in a tuft.

PROPAGATION / PHENOLOGY: Reproduction is **by seed. Cool, moist conditions promote germination**, which occurs primarily in the spring. Tillers are produced 2–4 weeks after emergence. Seeds fall to the ground as they ripen, usually before crop harvest.

SEEDLING: **Leaves are rolled in the bud. Auricles are absent**, and **ligules are membranous**, large, whitish, and pointed. Leaves may be smooth or hairy. Hairs, when present, are both small and large; larger hairs are sparse.

MATURE PLANT: Leaves are rolled in bud, and auricles are absent. Ligules (2–6 mm long) are membranous, rounded, and torn at the top (lacerate). Blades are linear, not keeled (7–40 cm long by 4–18 mm wide), rough to the touch, and taper to a pointed tip. Blades are often hairy near the ligule and on the margins near the base. Sheaths are compressed and vary from smooth to occasionally sparsely hairy. Collars are sparsely hairy at the edges. Stems are smooth and erect.

ROOTS AND UNDERGROUND STRUCTURES: Extensive fibrous root system.

FLOWERS AND FRUIT: Flowers from July to September. **Spikelets are in a loose, open, drooping, panicle** (15–40 cm long and up to 20 cm wide). Spikelets are nodding, and the florets (1–3 cm long) have a twisted, angled, dorsal awn (3–4 cm long) that straightens and twists with changes in humidity. A single plant can produce 100–150 seeds.

POSTSENESCENCE CHARACTERISTICS: Flowering stems persist. Long glumes (1–2 cm) will remain on spikelets for an extended period.

HABITAT: Wild oat is a weed of agronomic crops, especially spring cereals, as well as of vegetables, nursery crops, and landscapes. Found on heavy clay and clay-loam soils, it prefers cool climates and moist soil and often grows on the lower, moister regions of agricultural fields.

DISTRIBUTION: Most common in the western United States and in the northern Great Plains of the Midwest. Occasionally a weed as far east as New York.

SIMILAR SPECIES: The bent awns of wild oat can distinguish it from cultivated **oat** (***Avena sativa* L., AVESA**), which has straight awns or none at all. In addition, the panicles of wild oat are looser and wider than those of oat.

C. Elmore

Wild oat habit

Wild oat collar region
Ciba-Geigy Corporation

J. DiTomaso

Wild oat seed head

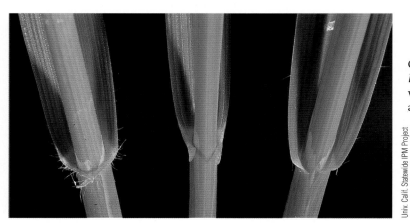

Univ. Calif. Statewide IPM Project

Collar region,
left to right:
wild barley, wheat,
and wild oat

Downy brome (*Bromus tectorum* L.) [BROTE]

Synonyms: downy chess, cheatgrass, downy brome-grass, slender chess, early chess, drooping brome, wall brome

GENERAL DESCRIPTION: A **summer or winter annual**, 10–60 cm in height, that ranges in habit from **clump-forming and erect to spreading**.

PROPAGATION / PHENOLOGY: Reproduction is **by seed**; seeds germinate in early to midspring and in late summer to midautumn.

SEEDLING: The first leaf blade is linear (8 cm long by 2 mm wide) and opens perpendicular to the ground. **Leaves are rolled in the bud, lack auricles**, and have a **membranous ligule** (1 mm long) that is delicately fringed at the top. **Young leaf blades are twisted and appear to be spiraling upward.** Blades have **soft, short, dense hairs** (<1 mm) on both surfaces. Rounded sheaths have similar hairs and are whitish with a tinge of red at the base.

MATURE PLANT: Leaves and ligule are similar to those of the seedling. **Blades** are flat, **hairy** on both surfaces, and sharply pointed (3–21 cm long by 2–6 mm wide). **Sheaths** are rounded, **hairy**, and have prominent pinkish veins.

ROOTS AND UNDERGROUND STRUCTURES: The **root system is fibrous**. Downy brome does not root at the nodes.

FLOWERS AND FRUIT: Flowers are produced between May and July. The seedhead is a drooping, dense, soft, purplish panicle (4–18 cm long). Spikelets are 3–8 flowered (1–2.5 cm long) with long awns (10–18 mm). The seed is grooved, yellow to reddish brown, and 6–8 mm long.

POSTSENESCENCE CHARACTERISTICS: The characteristic drooping seedhead may persist.

HABITAT: Found on dry, sandy or gravelly soil in meadows, pastures, and wasteland, downy brome is a weed of turf, nurseries, landscapes, pastures, winter grains, and agricultural crops. It is a major weed of rangeland in the western United States.

DISTRIBUTION: Found throughout the United States, except the Southeast.

SIMILAR SPECIES: **Cheat or chess (*Bromus secalinus* L., BROSE)** is smooth or with occasional hairs on the blades and the lower sheaths. The awns of cheat are shorter (3–5 mm long) than those of downy brome. **Common velvetgrass** has a coat of dense hairs on the blades and leaves, but differs from downy brome in that the back of the ligule is hairy in mature plants, sheaths are compressed, and the blades of young plants are not twisted.

Downy brome habit

R. Uva

Downy brome
collar region
Ciba-Geigy Corporation

Cheat
collar region
Ciba-Geigy Corporation

R. Uva

Downy brome seedling

R. Uva

Downy brome hairy leaf

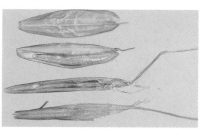

J. DiTomaso

Top, cheat seeds, 7.5 mm (to tip of lemma); *bottom*, downy brome seeds, 10.5 mm (to tip of lemma)

39

Longspine sandbur (*Cenchrus longispinus* (Hack.) Fern.) [CCHPA]

Synonyms: bear-grass, bur-grass, hedgehog-grass

GENERAL DESCRIPTION: A coarse-textured, light green, clump-forming **summer annual** with prostrate or ascending tillers (20–40 cm tall, occasionally to 80 cm), which root at the lower nodes and terminate with a spike of **spiny burs**.

PROPAGATION / PHENOLOGY: Reproduction is **by seed**; seedlings emerge in the spring and early summer. The spiny burs are dispersed by sticking to the skin and fur of animals and to shoes and clothing. The dried burs can also float on water.

SEEDLING: **Leaves are folded in the bud. Ligule is a fringe of hairs**, 0.7–1.7 mm long. The **blade is rough**, sometimes sparsely hairy with long hairs at the base near the ligule and collar. The **sheath is smooth** (glabrous) **with finely hairy margins, compressed** (flattened), and often tinged red. The collar is narrow but distinct and lighter in color. Tillers initially ascend but become more prostrate with age and mowing. Lower node of tillers can develop adventitious roots.

MATURE PLANT: **Tillers elongate in radial (or pinwheel) fashion** from the crown. Flowering stalks are coarse and wiry, with swollen nodes. **Vegetative characteristics are similar to those of seedling plants.** Mature leaf blades are light green, 6–18 cm long by 3–8 mm wide, flattened, and sometimes coiled. Leaf sheaths are strongly compressed, and the collar is broad. Lower stems become maroon with age.

ROOTS AND UNDERGROUND STRUCTURES: A fibrous root system from the crown, with adventitious roots developing at the lower nodes of the tillers.

FLOWERS AND FRUIT: Tillers terminate in a spike-like raceme of flowers and **bur-like fruit**. Plants flower over an extended period of time, between July and September (longer if weather permits). Each spike has 6–15 burs (involucre). Each bur is rounded to egg-shaped (globose to ovate), 6–10 mm in diameter, with short hairs.

POSTSENESCENCE CHARACTERISTICS: Late in the season, the lower foliage turns straw-colored, and the stems are reddish to maroon. The entire **plant, including the burs, turns straw-colored after frost**. The wiry stems and spiny burs can persist through the winter. The burs may remain on or near the soil surface through the next summer.

HABITAT: Usually found on sandy soils, but can survive in a variety of soil types. A common turfgrass weed in the southeastern United States and occasionally a weed of cultivated crops.

DISTRIBUTION: Longspine sandbur and **field sandbur (*Cenchrus incertus* M.A. Curtis, CCHIN** = *Cenchrus pauciflorus* Benth.) are most common along the coastal Southeast but have been reported as far north as Massachusetts and west to California. Locally a problem in the Midwest, north-central states, and Great Lakes region.

SIMILAR SPECIES: Seedlings may **resemble other species with hairy ligules**, particularly **foxtails** and **fall panicum**. However, foxtails and panicums are rolled in the bud, whereas sandbur is folded. There are **several weedy species of sandbur**. Many are very similar to longspine sandbur and are differentiated primarily by the shape of the burs. **Field sandbur** is also a common summer annual or, in some locations, a short-lived perennial weed. It can be distinguished from longspine sandbur by its burs, which are ovoid (less rounded) and smaller (3–4 mm wide).

Longspine sandbur inflorescence

J. Neal

Field sandbur
collar region

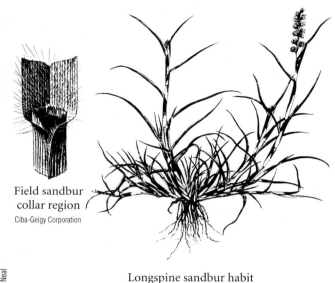

Longspine sandbur habit
Regina O. Hughes, USDA

Longspine
sandbur seedling

J. Neal

Longspine sandbur habit

J. Neal

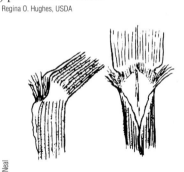

Longspine sandbur
collar region
Regina O. Hughes, USDA

Longspine sandbur ligule
and collar

J. Neal

Longspine sandbur seed, 9 mm
(including spines)

J. DiTomaso

41

Bermudagrass (*Cynodon dactylon* (L.) Pers.) [CYNDA]

Synonyms: *Capriola dactylon*, scutch-grass, dogs-tooth-grass, wire grass, couch grass

GENERAL DESCRIPTION: A **wiry perennial** with **spreading rhizomes and stolons**. The **leaves are gray-green to bluish green**. Bermudagrass has a spreading, prostrate to ascending habit, forming dense mats when mowed, but it may grow erect (10–30 cm tall) in unmowed areas. In the southern United States and transition zones, bermudagrass is a valuable lawn and pasture grass, but its competitiveness has made it a formidable weed in most crops from New Jersey south.

PROPAGATION / PHENOLOGY: Reproduction is **primarily by stolons and rhizomes** and less commonly by seed.

SEEDLING: **Leaves are rolled in the bud, auricles are absent**, and the **ligule is a row of hairs** (0.5 mm long). **Blades are smooth** on both surfaces, **relatively short and narrow**, with slightly rough margins. **Sheaths are green and smooth. Collars** are narrow, white, **smooth on the youngest seedlings** only, but **hairy on older seedlings**.

MATURE PLANT: **Ligule is similar to that of seedlings. Leaves** are flat, with **a ring of white hairs in the collar** region. Blades are linear-lanceolate, relatively short (5–16 cm long by 2–5 mm wide), and smooth or with hairs toward the base of the blade. **Margins are slightly rough. Sheaths** are **strongly compressed** and smooth or with **a few hairs** (1–3 mm long) **in the collar** region.

ROOTS AND UNDERGROUND STRUCTURES: Flattened **stolons are abundant**, with shoots arising from the axils of brownish leaf sheaths. **Rhizomes** are hard, scaly, and sharp, forming a dense sod. Roots are present at the nodes of both stolons and rhizomes.

FLOWERS AND FRUIT: Flowers are present in July and August. The **seedhead** consists of **3–7 finger-like spikes** about 4 cm long (3–10 cm) **radiating from a central point at the terminal end of the stems**. Flattened spikelets are in 2 rows on one side of the spike. Each spikelet produces 1 seed (1.5 mm long).

POSTSENESCENCE CHARACTERISTICS: Plants become dormant with frost. Straw-colored foliage persists through the winter and into spring.

HABITAT: Bermudagrass is a weed of most crops but is most troublesome in perennial crops, as well as turfgrasses and landscapes. It tolerates a wide range of soil and site conditions, including drought.

DISTRIBUTION: Found throughout the southern United States, north to southern New Jersey and occasionally farther north.

SIMILAR SPECIES: **Nimblewill** has a similar gray-green color, coarse-textured appearance, and habitat. However, it grows more erect and is considerably less competitive than bermudagrass. In addition, it is more cold-tolerant and consequently is found at higher latitudes in the Northeast.

Bermudagrass habit, showing stolons

J. Neal

Bermudagrass collar region
Ciba-Geigy Corporation

Bermudagrass stolon

J. Neal

Bermudagrass inflorescence

J. Neal

Bermudagrass seeds, 1.7 mm

J. DiTomaso

Orchardgrass (*Dactylis glomerata* L.) [DACGL]

Synonyms: cocksfoot, cock's foot

GENERAL DESCRIPTION: A **clump-forming perennial** that can grow to over 1 m in height but can tolerate mowing.

PROPAGATION / PHENOLOGY: Reproduction is **by seed. Crown enlarges by tillering.**

SEEDLING: The first leaf blade opens perpendicular to the ground. **Leaves are folded in the bud, lack auricles, and have a finely toothed membranous ligule** (3–5 mm long). **Blades are long** (7–12 cm long and 1.3–2.3 mm wide), smooth on both surfaces and on the margins, light green, strongly keeled, and folded near the ligule. **Sheaths are flattened and keeled**, smooth, whitish at the base, and loosely appressed to the stems.

MATURE PLANT: **Leaves are similar to those of the seedlings. Ligules are somewhat longer in mature plants** (5–7 mm). **Blades are bluish green, very long** (7–30 cm long by 3–8 mm wide), and somewhat rough on the surfaces and margins. Blades are strongly keeled and V-shaped in cross section. **Sheaths are strongly compressed** and keeled, and the collar is broad and prominent.

ROOTS AND UNDERGROUND STRUCTURES: Root system is very dense and fibrous. Orchardgrass does not produce rhizomes.

FLOWERS AND FRUIT: Flowers occur from late spring through midsummer. The **seedhead is a stiff, branched panicle**, 5–20 cm in length. Spikelets are fan-shaped and appear densely crowded and sessile in 1-sided clusters. Awns, if present, may be to 2 mm long.

POSTSENESCENCE CHARACTERISTICS: A perennial grass that remains green year-round.

HABITAT: Orchardgrass is a forage grass but is also a weed of turf, landscapes, nursery crops, and other perennial horticultural crops. It tolerates partial shade to full sunlight and is found in fields, disturbed sites, and roadsides.

DISTRIBUTION: Occurs throughout much of North America, excluding the Florida peninsula.

SIMILAR SPECIES: **Goosegrass** has similar folded sheaths; however, orchardgrass has a large membranous ligule, whereas goosegrass has a smaller membranous ligule (≤2 mm) that is cleft in the center.

Orchardgrass habit

A. Senesac

Orchardgrass
collar region
The Scotts Company

J. Neal

Orchardgrass ligule and collar

J. DiTomaso

Orchardgrass inflorescences

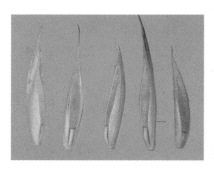

J. DiTomaso

Orchardgrass seeds, 8 mm

Large crabgrass (*Digitaria sanguinalis* (L.) Scop.) [DIGSA]

Synonym: hairy crabgrass

GENERAL DESCRIPTION: A **summer annual** that can grow **prostrate** and spreading **or ascending** to 1 m in height.

PROPAGATION / PHENOLOGY: Reproduction is **by seed**; seeds germinate from mid-spring through late summer. Vegetative spread can occur by rooting stems, but it is not considered an important means of propagation.

SEEDLING: The first leaf blade is lanceolate to linear, about 3–4 times longer than wide, and opens parallel to the ground. Crabgrass seedlings are upright. Leaves are linear with tapered leaf tips, about 10 times longer than wide (5–12 cm long by 4–10 mm wide). **Leaves are rolled in the bud, lack auricles,** and have a **jagged membranous ligule. Stiff hairs on the blade and sheath are at a 90° angle to the plant surface.** The collar is broad with long hairs at the margin.

MATURE PLANT: **Leaves and ligule are similar to those of seedlings. Blades** are about 12 times longer than wide (3–20 cm long by 3–14 mm wide) and have **hairs on both surfaces and on the sheath.** More mature plants have **compressed sheaths.** Tillering begins after the 4–5 true-leaf stage (late spring, early summer). Tiller internodes elongate later in the season (mid to late summer). **Elongated stems root at the nodes.** On maturing plants, older sheaths and leaves may turn dark red or maroon.

ROOTS AND UNDERGROUND STRUCTURES: Roots are fibrous, with adventitious roots arising from the nodes of elongated tillers.

FLOWERS AND FRUIT: Flowers occur in mid to late summer. The **seedhead commonly consists of 3–5(–13) spikes clustered at the top of stems.** Spikelets are elliptic and in 2 rows along the spike. Each spikelet contains a single shiny, yellow-brown seed (2–3 mm long).

POSTSENESCENCE CHARACTERISTICS: Large crabgrass dies with the first killing frost and appears as brown patches in an otherwise green lawn. It is recognized by long wire-like "stems" and seedheads that persist well into the winter.

HABITAT: Large crabgrass is a common weed of most agronomic and horticultural crops as well as turf and landscapes. It can tolerate poor, dry conditions but is found in nearly every soil type and crop. It is also common along roads and in waste areas.

DISTRIBUTION: Common throughout the United States and other temperate and tropical regions of the world.

SIMILAR SPECIES: **Smooth crabgrass (*Digitaria ischaemum* Schreb. *ex* Muhl., DIGIS)** is similar to large crabgrass but has few hairs on the blade and sheath and is generally smaller. **Southern crabgrass (*Digitaria ciliaris* (Retz.) Koel., DIGSP)** has hairs on the sheaths but lacks hairs on the blades and is more common in the southeastern than in the northeastern United States.

Large crabgrass habit (more than 10 tillers) in mulch

Large crabgrass seedlings

Large crabgrass seedling
(2 tillers)

Large crabgrass collar region
Ciba-Geigy Corporation

Smooth crabgrass seedhead

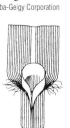

Smooth crabgrass
collar region
Ciba-Geigy Corporation

Smooth crabgrass seedling
(1 tiller)

Southern crabgrass
collar region
Ciba-Geigy Corporation

Left to right: southern crabgrass seeds, 2.8 mm (with lemma); smooth crabgrass seeds, 1.9 mm (with lemma); and large crabgrass seeds, 2.6 mm (with lemma)

47

Barnyardgrass (*Echinochloa crus-galli* (L.) Beauv.) [ECHCG]

Synonyms: watergrass, cockspur grass, panic-grass, summergrass, billion dollargrass

GENERAL DESCRIPTION: A **summer annual** with erect, thick **clump-forming** stems (1.5 m tall). In turf, plants grow prostrate to produce a mat-like rosette.

PROPAGATION / PHENOLOGY: Reproduction is **by seed**; seeds germinate in early spring to midsummer.

SEEDLING: The first leaf blade is linear and opens parallel to the ground. **Leaves are rolled in the bud, lack auricles,** and **have no ligule.** Blades are 7–14 cm long and 3–5 mm wide, smooth on both surfaces, with rough margins. Sheaths are somewhat compressed, tinted maroon toward the base, and usually smooth but occasionally with hairs at the base. The collar is green and smooth.

MATURE PLANT: **Leaves are similar to those of seedlings,** and **ligules are absent.** Blades are about 10–20 cm long by 5–20 mm wide, lack hairs, and are smooth to somewhat rough on both surfaces. The **midvein is distinct** and keeled in the basal portions of the leaf. **Sheaths are open, compressed,** and smooth, but sometimes have a tuft of short hair at the base. The collar is whitish, broad, and smooth.

ROOTS AND UNDERGROUND STRUCTURES: **Roots are fibrous** and shallow. Tillers often form adventitious roots where they touch the soil.

FLOWERS AND FRUIT: Flowering occurs from July through September. The **seedhead is a coarsely branched green to purplish panicle.** Spikelets are single-seeded, barbed along the nerves, and can have a long terminal awn (2–10 mm). The length of the awns varies among biotypes. The seed is shiny, oval (3–4 mm long), and brownish, with longitudinal ridges.

POSTSENESCENCE CHARACTERISTICS: Plants are killed by the first frost. The large thick stems and fan shape of tillers remain well into winter.

HABITAT: Barnyardgrass is a very common weed in irrigated crops, including turf, landscape, nursery, and agricultural crops. It is **usually found on moist, rich soils** and is common in cultivated areas, ditches, and waste places.

DISTRIBUTION: Found throughout much of the United States, Canada, and Mexico.

SIMILAR SPECIES: **Johnsongrass** and **fall panicum** have coarse-textured foliage and may resemble barnyardgrass in their mature forms, but both johnsongrass and fall panicum have a distinct ligule.

R. Uva

Barnyardgrass habit

R. Uva

Barnyardgrass seedling

Barnyardgrass inflorescence

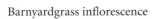

J. Neal

Barnyardgrass
collar region
Ciba-Geigy Corporation

J. DiTomaso

Barnyardgrass seeds, 3.5 mm
(largest, with lemma)

49

Goosegrass (*Eleusine indica* (L.) Gaertn.) [ELEIN]

Synonyms: silver crabgrass, wire-grass, yard-grass, crowfoot-grass, crows foot grass, bullgrass

GENERAL DESCRIPTION: A **summer annual** that usually produces a **prostrate, mat-like rosette** with stems radiating from a central point but can grow erect to 60 cm in height. The **flattened leaf sheaths in the rosette** are **whitish to silvery**, hence the common synonym silver crabgrass.

PROPAGATION / PHENOLOGY: Reproduction is **by seed**; seeds germinate in early to midsummer when soil temperatures are above 18°C (65°F). **Goosegrass usually germinates 2–3 weeks later than crabgrass.**

SEEDLING: The first leaf blade is about 3–5 times longer than wide and opens parallel to the ground. **Leaves are folded in the bud, lack auricles, and have a short, membranous, unevenly toothed ligule (≤1 mm) that is cleft in the center.** Blades are 2–4.5 cm long and 3–5 mm wide, smooth on both surfaces, strongly folded along the midrib, and have distinct individual veins. **Sheaths are smooth, prominently compressed, and light green to white at the base.** The collar is broad and hairless.

MATURE PLANT: **Leaves are similar to those of seedlings.** The **ligule is membranous** (1–2 mm long) and **cleft in the center**. Blades are **folded along the midvein** (5–20 cm long by 3–6 mm wide), **smooth** or occasionally sparsely hairy on both surfaces, and have rough margins. The loosely overlapping **sheaths are smooth** to sparsely hairy toward the ligule and **whitish at the base**. The **collar is broad, white**, and sparsely hairy at the edges.

ROOTS AND UNDERGROUND STRUCTURES: The **root system is fibrous**. Goosegrass does not root at the nodes.

FLOWERS AND FRUIT: Flowers are produced from June through September. Seedheads mature in late summer through early autumn but persist into winter. **Seedheads consist of 2–6(–10) spikes in clusters at the top of stems. Spikelets are flattened in 2 rows** along the spike and contain 3–6 reddish brown to black seeds (1–1.8 mm long).

POSTSENESCENCE CHARACTERISTICS: Goosegrass dies after the first hard frost. Characteristic flat tillers radiating from a central point and seedheads persist well into winter.

HABITAT: Goosegrass is a common weed of turf, nursery, landscape, and agricultural crops. It is also found in gardens, roadsides, and waste areas on most soil types. **It tolerates close mowing, compacted soils, and drought.**

DISTRIBUTION: Found throughout the southern United States, extending northward to Massachusetts, North Dakota, Utah, and along the West Coast.

SIMILAR SPECIES: **Crabgrass** is similar in overall growth habit (mat-forming rosette in turf), but leaves are rolled in the bud, whereas goosegrass leaves are folded in the bud. **Orchardgrass** is a perennial with strongly compressed sheaths and leaves folded in the bud, but it has a much larger ligule (5–7 mm) than goosegrass.

Goosegrass habit

A. Senesac

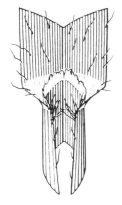

Goosegrass
collar region
Ciba-Geigy Corporation

A. Senesac

Goosegrass seedhead

R. Uva

Goosegrass seedling

J. DiTomaso

Goosegrass spikelet and seeds, 1.7 mm

51

Quackgrass (*Elytrigia repens* (L.) Nevski) [AGRRE]

Synonyms: *Agropyron repens*, quitch grass, couch grass, wheat-grass, shelly-grass, knot-grass, devils-grass, scutch-grass, quick grass

GENERAL DESCRIPTION: A **rhizomatous perennial** that generally grows erect (1.2 m high), bending at the nodes. It can tolerate mowing.

PROPAGATION / PHENOLOGY: Reproduction is **by seeds and rhizomes**.

SEEDLING: The first leaf blade is narrow, about 90 times longer than wide, and opens perpendicular to the ground. **Leaves are rolled in the bud; auricles are present** but may be undeveloped and difficult to see on very young seedlings. The **ligule is membranous and very short (0.4 mm long)**. Blades are 10–20 cm long and 2–2.5 mm wide, hairy to smooth on the upper surface, and smooth on the lower surface. **Sheaths can also be hairy or smooth.** When present, hairs are short (<0.5 mm); they are most numerous on the lower parts of very young seedlings but are most obvious on the blade and sheath of the first leaf. The collar is whitish and divided by prominent veins.

MATURE PLANT: **Leaves are rolled in the bud; auricles are narrow, slender, and clasp the stem.** The **ligule is membranous and very short (<1 mm)**. Blades are 4–30 cm long and 3–10 mm wide, flat, hairy to smooth on the upper surface and smooth on the lower surface. **Sheaths are rounded and smooth, but those near the base of the plant may have short hairs.** The collar is broad.

ROOTS AND UNDERGROUND STRUCTURES: Fibrous roots arise at the nodes of the **long, sharp-tipped rhizomes**.

FLOWERS AND FRUIT: Plants flower in June and July. The **seedhead is a long spike** (5–20 cm). Spikelets are 4–6 seeded and 1–1.5 cm long, arranged in 2 rows along the axis. Awns are usually present and are 0.5–10 mm long.

POSTSENESCENCE CHARACTERISTICS: This perennial grass remains green year-round.

HABITAT: Quackgrass is a weed of most agronomic and horticultural crops as well as turf, nurseries, and landscapes. It grows in cultivated fertile soil, areas where reduced tillage is practiced, and waste areas.

DISTRIBUTION: Found throughout much of the northern United States and Canada, except South Carolina and Florida west to southern Arizona.

SIMILAR SPECIES: **Tall fescue** and the **ryegrasses** are similar to quackgrass but lack elongated rhizomes and grow in clumps.

Quackgrass habit in corn

Quackgrass
collar region
Ciba-Geigy Corporation

J. Neal

Quackgrass rhizome

J. Neal

Quackgrass inflorescence

J. Neal

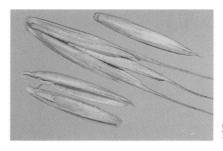

Quackgrass seeds, 9 mm (including lemma)

J. DiTomaso

53

Tall fescue (*Festuca arundinacea* Schreb.) [FESAR]

Synonyms: Festuca elatior, alata fescue, reed fescue, coarse fescue

GENERAL DESCRIPTION: A dark green **clump-forming perennial forage and turfgrass** that has escaped cultivation. **Leaves are broader** and generally grow more rapidly than leaves of more desirable turfgrasses; blades are at a 45° angle from the soil. In unmowed areas, tall fescue can grow to 1.5 m tall. **Many strains of tall fescue contain endophytes** that can be toxic to livestock.

PROPAGATION / PHENOLOGY: Reproduction is **by seed. Clumps enlarge by tillering**.

SEEDLING: The first leaf blade is long and narrow. **Leaves are rolled in the bud, auricles are absent**, and the **ligule is membranous and short**. Blades are 9–13 cm long and 1–2 mm wide, glossy on the lower surface, smooth and hairless throughout. **Blades have conspicuous parallel veins** and taper slowly to the apex. Sheaths are smooth and reddish at the base, round to slightly compressed. **Ligules are short** (1 mm long) and **membranous**. The collar is whitish and divided in the center by the midrib.

MATURE PLANT: **Leaves are rolled in the bud; auricles are short and blunt with a fringe of marginal hairs.** Ligule is similar to that of seedlings. Blades are 10–60 cm long and much wider (4–12 mm wide) than in the seedling stage. Leaves are dark green with occasional hairs on the basal portion of the upper surface of the leaf. **Margins are rough**, and the **blades are coarse and thick**, with dull surfaces and **prominent veins above** and a **glossy surface beneath**. Sheaths are round and lack hairs. The **collar is broad.**

ROOTS AND UNDERGROUND STRUCTURES: **Root system is fibrous**; rhizomes are not produced.

FLOWERS AND FRUIT: Flowers appear in early to midsummer. Seedheads mature and persist until autumn. The **seedhead is a loose or a compressed panicle**, 10–40 cm in length. Spikelets are 1–1.8 cm long with 3–8 seeds per spikelet. Awns, if present, are 0.3–4 mm long. Seedheads often lay flat in turf and are not injured by mowing.

POSTSENESCENCE CHARACTERISTICS: This perennial grass stays green year-round.

HABITAT: Tall fescue is a weed of turf, nurseries, landscapes, orchards, and reduced-tillage crops. It may also be found in fields, dry waste areas, and less commonly in cultivated crops. Cultivars of tall fescue are used as forage and turfgrasses.

DISTRIBUTION: Found throughout the United States.

SIMILAR SPECIES: **Quackgrass** and **ryegrasses** are similar to tall fescue; however, quackgrass has long clasping auricles and rhizomes that produce a spreading growth habit. Ryegrasses have claw-like auricles, whereas those of tall fescue, if present, are blunt and short. Tall fescue has dark green, coarse-textured foliage unlike quackgrass and ryegrasses.

Tall fescue habit in turf

J. Neal

Tall fescue
collar region
Ciba-Geigy Corporation

Tall fescue inflorescence

J. Neal

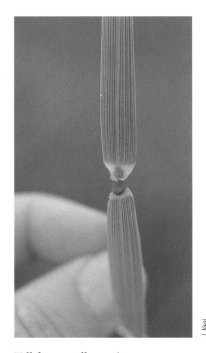

J. Neal

Tall fescue collar region

J. DiTomaso

Tall fescue seeds, 7 mm

55

Common velvetgrass (*Holcus lanatus* L.) [HOLLA]

Synonym: velvet-grass

GENERAL DESCRIPTION: A **clump-forming perennial** with **grayish green velvety foliage**. It may grow prostrate in turf or erect to 1 m tall.

PROPAGATION / PHENOLOGY: Reproduction is **by seed. Clumps enlarge rapidly by aggressive tillering**.

SEEDLING: The first leaf blade opens perpendicular to the ground. **Leaves are rolled in the bud, lack auricles, and have a membranous ligule (1.5 mm)**, jagged at the top. **Blades** are 3.5–9 cm long and 1 mm wide and **covered with short hairs** (<0.5 mm long) **on both surfaces. Sheaths are slightly compressed, with short hairs** at a 90° angle to the surface. The hairs are less noticeable as they progress up the plant. The base of the sheath and the collar are white.

MATURE PLANT: **Leaves are similar to those of seedlings, but the ligule is somewhat larger** (1–4 mm) **and hairy on the back surface. Blades** are 4–20 cm long and 4–10 mm wide, pale green, flat, covered with **dense soft hairs. Sheaths are also velvety hairy**, pink-nerved, compressed, and slightly keeled, with margins open almost to the base. Collars are hairy and narrow.

ROOTS AND UNDERGROUND STRUCTURES: **Root system is fibrous.**

FLOWERS AND FRUIT: Flowers occur from June through August. **Seedheads are soft-hairy, grayish, purple-tinged panicles** (5–15 cm long and 1–8 cm wide) **produced on hairy stems**. At maturity, panicles dry to a light tan color. Spikelets are 2-seeded (4 mm long) with an awn (1–2 mm) on the second floret. The awn becomes curved or hooked when dry.

POSTSENESCENCE CHARACTERISTICS: As older leaves senesce in autumn and winter, portions of the clumps turn yellow, but some leaves remain green.

HABITAT: Common velvetgrass is a weed of low-maintenance turf, forage crops, and orchards. It often grows on damp, rich soil in open areas of meadows, fields, and roadsides. In addition to moist, poorly drained, and acidic soils, it can tolerate a wide range of other conditions, including drought.

DISTRIBUTION: Common on the West Coast and in the eastern United States extending from Virginia to Mississippi, and into Ohio, Indiana, and Illinois. Not as common in the extreme northern states.

SIMILAR SPECIES: The dense coating of velvety soft hairs on the blade and sheath of common velvetgrass easily distinguishes it from most other grasses, except **downy brome**. However, mature downy brome is an annual that lacks hairs on the back of the ligule. In addition, leaves of young common velvetgrass are not twisted.

Common velvetgrass habit in turf

Common velvetgrass
collar region
Ciba-Geigy Corporation

J. Neal

Common velvetgrass
inflorescence

J. Neal

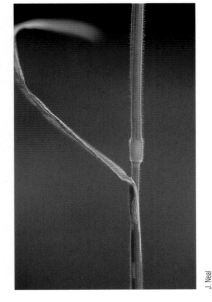

J. Neal

Common velvetgrass hairy stem

J. DiTomaso

Common velvetgrass seeds,
2.5 mm (largest)

Italian ryegrass (*Lolium multiflorum* Lam.) [LOLMU]

Synonyms: *Lolium italicum*, annual ryegrass, Australian rye

GENERAL DESCRIPTION: An **erect clump-forming winter annual** reaching 1 m in height, but will tolerate close mowing.

PROPAGATION / PHENOLOGY: Reproduction is **by seed**; seeds germinate from early to late spring and late summer into midautumn.

SEEDLING: The first leaf blade is long and narrow, oriented perpendicular with the soil surface. **Leaves are rolled in the bud; auricles are usually present but may be absent on very young seedlings, and the ligule is membranous (2 mm long).** Blades are about 50 times as long as wide (10–14 cm long by 2–3 mm wide), lack hairs, and have prominently raised veins. Sheaths are also smooth and often are reddish at the base.

MATURE PLANT: **Auricles are narrow, long, and claw-like. Blades** are long and tapered (6–20 cm long and 4–10 mm wide), **glossy below and rough above**, with prominent veins and smooth margins. Sheaths are rounded, and the collar is broad.

ROOTS AND UNDERGROUND STRUCTURES: The **root system is fibrous**. Stems do not root at the nodes.

FLOWERS AND FRUIT: The **seedhead is a terminal spike** (10–40 cm long). The **spikelets are placed alternately along the flowering stem**. Each spikelet is 1.5–2.5 cm long and consists of 10–20 florets and **long awns** (5–8 mm). Spikelets contain only 1 glume.

POSTSENESCENCE CHARACTERISTICS: Senescence occurs in warm, dry weather, usually after seed maturation. Foliage turns yellow, then straw-colored.

HABITAT: Italian ryegrass is a weed of grain, turf, nursery, and other cool-season or perennial crops. It is also found in waste areas and cultivated crops in most soil types.

DISTRIBUTION: Occurs throughout the United States.

SIMILAR SPECIES: **Perennial ryegrass (*Lolium perenne* L., LOLPE)** is shorter (30–60 cm tall), has small or malformed auricles, has spikelets with 6–10 florets, and is a **perennial. Awns are often absent or greatly reduced.** Italian ryegrass is more robust in habit than perennial ryegrass. **Quackgrass** also has awns and a seedhead that can look similar to that of ryegrass. However, quackgrass is a rhizomatous perennial with spikelets subtended by 2 basal bracts (glumes), whereas all species of ryegrass have only 1 basal bract.

Italian ryegrass
collar region
Ciba-Geigy Corporation

Perennial ryegrass
collar region
Ciba-Geigy Corporation

J. Neal

Italian ryegrass
inflorescence

J. Neal

Italian (annual) ryegrass habit

J. Neal

Perennial ryegrass inflorescence

J. DiTomaso

Left, Italian ryegrass seeds,
6.5 mm (not including awn);
right, perennial ryegrass
seeds (without awn), 6.0 mm

59

Wirestem muhly (*Muhlenbergia frondosa* (Poir.) Fern.) [MUHFR]

Synonyms: *Muhlenbergia commutata*, *Muhlenbergia mexicana*, mexican drop-seed, satin-grass, wood-grass, knot-root-grass

GENERAL DESCRIPTION: A **rhizomatous perennial** that is erect (1 m tall) to sprawling, or prostrate. Plants can appear bushy and top-heavy.

PROPAGATION / PHENOLOGY: Reproduction is **by creeping rhizomes and by seeds**, which germinate in early to late spring.

SEEDLING: Seedlings are flat, rough to the touch, and have short blades. **Leaves are rolled in the bud; auricles are absent, and ligules are membranous (0.8–1.5 mm long) and torn or jagged across the top.**

MATURE PLANT: **Leaves and ligule are similar to those of the seedling. Stems are branched and stiff, with a wiry appearance.** Internodes are smooth and shiny. **Blades are short** (10 cm long by 3–7 mm wide) and **flat**, lack hairs, and have rough margins. **Sheaths** also lack hairs; they are rounded and **shorter than the stem internodes.** The base of the stem bends abruptly and touches the ground, often rooting at the lower nodes.

ROOTS AND UNDERGROUND STRUCTURES: **Fibrous roots** are present at the lower stem nodes and the nodes of **short, thick, scaly rhizomes.**

FLOWERS AND FRUIT: Flowers are produced from August to October. **Spikelets are very small** (3 mm) and are produced **in condensed panicles** located at the terminal end of the stems and from the leaf sheaths. Panicles are 3–10 cm long and 0.5–1 cm wide. Terminal panicles are slightly longer than the upper leaf blades; axillary panicles are smaller than the terminal panicles and may be partially covered by the leaf sheath. Spikelets are soft and green or brown to purplish, and, when present, awns are slender (2–7 mm long).

POSTSENESCENCE CHARACTERISTICS: Short, wiry leaves and stems remain intact throughout the winter with the remnants of seedheads still attached within the sheaths.

HABITAT: Wirestem muhly is a weed of nursery crops, orchards, vegetables, landscapes, and occasionally agronomic crops. It also grows in waste areas, roadsides, ditches, and stream banks, often on moist, rich soils.

DISTRIBUTION: Found throughout the northeastern United States, west to North Dakota, and south to Georgia and Texas.

SIMILAR SPECIES: Can resemble **nimblewill**, although wirestem muhly is more robust, up to 2–3 times as tall. Also, nimblewill lacks scaly rhizomes.

Wirestem muhly emerging from rhizome

W. Curran

R. Uva

Wirestem muhly foliage

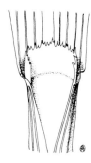

Wirestem muhly
collar region
Bente Starcke King

R. Uva

Wirestem muhly roots and rhizome

J. DiTomaso

Wirestem muhly seeds, 2.5 mm
(not including awn)

Nimblewill (*Muhlenbergia schreberi* J.F. Gmel.) [MUHSC]

Synonyms: wire-grass, drop-seed

GENERAL DESCRIPTION: A mat-forming, **stoloniferous, coarse-textured perennial. The foliage is grayish green.** Stems are erect when young but become branched with age, spreading and bending, and rooting at the nodes. Tips of developed blades strongly arch toward the soil. In unmowed areas, nimblewill grows from 20 to 60 cm high.

PROPAGATION / PHENOLOGY: Reproduction is from **seeds and stolons**.

SEEDLING: The first leaf blade is linear, tapering gradually to a point, about 5 times longer than wide. It opens parallel to the soil surface and eventually arches downward. **Leaves are rolled in the bud; auricles are absent, and the ligule is membranous, very short (<0.5 mm)**, and toothed across the top. **Blades are 2.5 cm long and 1–2.1 mm wide**, smooth throughout. **Sheaths are smooth, slightly compressed**, and have prominent dark green veins. The collar is white.

MATURE PLANT: **Leaves and ligules are similar to those of the seedling. Blades are short** (2–8 cm long by 2–4 mm wide) **compared with blades of many other grasses** and smooth, except for a few hairs near the ligule. **Sheaths are compressed**, membranous along the margins, and loosely appressed to the stems. The collar is smooth, with long hairs on the edges.

ROOTS AND UNDERGROUND STRUCTURES: Horizontal stems **(stolons) root at the nodes, producing a fine, fibrous root system**. Roots are weakly connected to the stolons and are easily pulled from the ground.

FLOWERS AND FRUIT: Nimblewill flowers from August to October. The **seedheads are spike-like panicles** that are **produced both terminally and at axillary nodes. Panicles are slender**, 5–15 cm long, and flexible. Spikelets are 2 mm long, and the awns (2–5 mm long) are conspicuous. The seed is 1–1.4 mm long.

POSTSENESCENCE CHARACTERISTICS: Nimblewill turns brown in winter; mats of stolons persist and resprout the following spring.

HABITAT: A weed of turf, nurseries, and orchards, nimblewill thrives on moist, rich soil, often in the shade. It is found along shrub boarders, fences, and in uncultivated areas. In orchards, nimblewill is abundant where simazine has been used for several years. It rarely grows in conventionally tilled crops because it does not tolerate cultivation well.

DISTRIBUTION: Found from southern Maine, west to Minnesota and Nebraska, and south to Florida and Mexico.

SIMILAR SPECIES: **Bermudagrass** and **creeping bentgrass (*Agrostis stolonifera* L., AGSST)** both resemble nimblewill in growth habit. However, the foliage of creeping bentgrass is finer in texture, the ligule is larger, and there are no hairs present around the ligule. Bermudagrass has a ciliate (fringe of hairs) ligule.

J. Neal

Nimblewill habit

Nimblewill
collar region
Ciba-Geigy Corporation

J. Neal

Nimblewill stolon

Creeping bentgrass
collar region
Ciba-Geigy Corporation

R. Uva

Nimblewill seedling

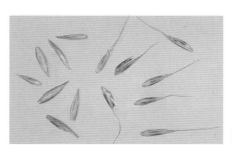

J. DiTomaso

Left, creeping bentgrass seeds (without awn), 2.5 mm; *right*, wirestem muhly seeds, 2.2 mm (not including awn)

Witchgrass (*Panicum capillare* L.) [PANCA]

Synonyms: old witch-grass, tickle-grass, witches-hair, tumble weed-grass, fool-hay

GENERAL DESCRIPTION: A tillering **summer annual**, erect to 80 cm tall, or decumbent, with **characteristically hairy blades and sheaths**.

PROPAGATION / PHENOLOGY: Reproduction is **by seed**; seeds germinate between late spring and midsummer.

SEEDLING: The first leaf blade is lanceolate to linear, about 3 times longer than wide and parallel to the soil surface. **Leaves are rolled in the bud, lack auricles, and the ligule is a fringe of hairs** (1–2 mm long). Subsequent leaf blades are 1.5–4 cm long by 4–6 mm wide. **The blade, sheath, and collar are very hairy.** Hairs are relatively stiff and at a 90° angle with the plant surface.

MATURE PLANT: **Leaves, hairs, and ligule are similar to those of seedlings. Blades** (10–25 cm long by 5–15 mm wide) **are hairy on both surfaces**, and the margins are rough. **Sheaths are densely hairy** and may be slightly purplish.

ROOTS AND UNDERGROUND STRUCTURES: **Root system is fibrous.** Tillers root at the base but not at the nodes of elongated shoots.

FLOWERS AND FRUIT: Flowering occurs from July through September. The **seedhead is a large, much-branched, open panicle** up to half the length of the entire plant (20–40 cm long). Spikelets are 2–4 mm long and produce 1 shiny, smooth green to dark brown or gray seed (1.5 mm long).

POSTSENESCENCE CHARACTERISTICS: Plants die at first frost, after which the large tillers persist well into the winter. Hairs of the sheaths are distinct well into winter. The panicle may break off and be dispersed by the wind.

HABITAT: Witchgrass is a common weed of agronomic, horticultural, and nursery crops. It is also found in landscapes, gardens, and roadsides, in sandy, dry soil as well as moist, fertile soil.

DISTRIBUTION: Common throughout the United States and southern Canada.

SIMILAR SPECIES: **Fall panicum** seedlings have densely hairy sheaths, but blades are hairy only on the lower surface. Mature fall panicum blades and sheaths are smooth on both surfaces.

Witchgrass, 5-tiller plant

Witchgrass leaf and sheath hairs

Witchgrass inflorescence

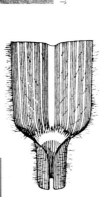

Witchgrass
collar region
Ciba-Geigy Corporation

Witchgrass seedling

Witchgrass seeds, 2.2 mm with
glumes, 1.4 mm without glumes

Fall panicum (*Panicum dichotomiflorum* Michx.) [PANDI]

Synonyms: smooth witchgrass, western witchgrass, sprouting crab-grass

GENERAL DESCRIPTION: A **summer annual** with an erect to sprawling or kneeling habit. It can form large loose tufts and usually grows from 50 cm to 1 m in height.

PROPAGATION / PHENOLOGY: Reproduction is **by seed**. Seedlings emerge in late spring to midsummer.

SEEDLING: The first leaf blade is lanceolate to linear, about 5 times longer than wide and opens parallel to the ground. **Leaves are rolled in the bud and lack auricles.** The **ligule is a fringe of hairs** approximately 1–2 mm long. Blades are 2–3.5 cm long and 5 mm wide. The **first few leaf blades are densely hairy only on the lower surface.** Also, **on the first few leaves, sheaths have dense 1 mm long hairs** and rough margins. **Collars are also densely hairy. Seedlings become less hairy with age and completely lack hairs at maturity.** Plants often have a purplish coloration.

MATURE PLANT: **Leaves are similar to those of seedlings,** and the **ligule is a fringe of hairs** 1–3 mm long. **Stems often have a waxy appearance,** and the swollen and irregular lower nodes give the stem a zigzag appearance. **Blades are smooth on both sides,** dull above and glossy beneath, about 10–50 cm long by 5–20 mm wide; **the midvein is conspicuously light green to white. Sheaths are smooth** (rarely hairy), purplish, and slightly compressed. Collars are continuous and broad.

ROOTS AND UNDERGROUND STRUCTURES: **Fibrous root system.** Stems root at the lower nodes.

FLOWERS AND FRUIT: Flowers are produced from July to October. The **seedhead is a large, freely branched, spreading panicle,** 10–40 cm long, which may appear purplish at maturity. Spikelets are 2.5–3.0 mm long, 2 mm wide, and straw-colored to purple-tinged. Spikelets produce 1 smooth, dull yellow to brown seed (1.5–2 mm long).

POSTSENESCENCE CHARACTERISTICS: Plants die with frost. Stems remain erect for only a short time into winter but persist on the soil surface through the winter and into spring. Remnants of the panicle can remain on the stems. In heavily infested areas, a mulch several inches thick can last until the following spring.

HABITAT: Fall panicum is a weed of cultivated agronomic, vegetable, and nursery crops but can also grow in turfgrass, landscapes, and noncrop areas.

DISTRIBUTION: Found throughout much of the United States.

SIMILAR SPECIES: **Witchgrass** is closely related to fall panicum but is very hairy throughout, even at the seedling stage. **Foxtails** also have a hairy ligule and can resemble fall panicum in the seedling stage; they can be distinguished by the location of hairs, which are on the lower surface of the fall panicum leaf blade but on the upper surface of foxtail leaf blades or absent altogether. Young foxtail seedlings can be distinguished from those of panicum by seed shape and shininess. Foxtail seeds are fat and dull; panicum seeds are slender and shiny. **Johnsongrass** has a distinctive white midvein and a panicle inflorescence similar to that of fall panicum; however, johnsongrass is a rhizomatous perennial with a membranous ligule that is sometimes fringed at the top.

Fall panicum seedling

R. Uva

J. Neal

Fall panicum collar region

Fall panicum
collar region
Ciba-Geigy Corporation

J. Neal

Fall panicum inflorescence

J. DiTomaso

Fall panicum seeds, 2.3 mm with
glumes, 2.0 mm without glumes

Wild-proso millet (*Panicum miliaceum* L.) [PANMI]

Synonyms: broomcorn millet, hog millet, panic millet

GENERAL DESCRIPTION: A **large tufted annual grass** (2 m tall) with erect stems branching from the base.

PROPAGATION / PHENOLOGY: Reproduction is **by seed. Seedheads shatter early in the season** and are often spread by harvest equipment.

SEEDLING: **Leaves are rolled in the bud, and auricles are absent. Ligules are 2–4 mm long, membranous at the base for about half their length, and fringed with hairs (ciliate) at the top. Blades and sheaths are densely covered with stiff hairs. The black seedcoat persists** under the surface of the soil on very young seedlings.

MATURE PLANT: **Leaves and ligule are similar to those of the seedling. Blades** are 10–30 cm long and 6–20 mm wide, rounded at the base, and have **long hairs on both surfaces. Sheaths** are open and **densely covered with stiff hairs**, especially on the lower leaves. Sheath margins are hairy, at least near the ligule.

ROOTS AND UNDERGROUND STRUCTURES: Fibrous root system.

FLOWERS AND FRUIT: Flowering occurs from July to September. The **seedhead is a pyramidal to cylindrical panicle, rather compact**, nodding or drooping to erect, 10–30 cm long. Spikelets are 4.5–5.3 mm long and produce a single shiny, smooth, yellow or olive-brown to black seed about 3 mm long.

POSTSENESCENCE CHARACTERISTICS: Stems, leaves, and inflorescence persist for a considerable time after frost. Inflorescence does not detach from plant. Plants can have a reddish coloration. Seeds remain attached to spikelets.

HABITAT: Domesticated forms of proso millet are used as forage in the United States and Europe. Although wild-proso millet is the same species as the domesticated forms, it is a weed of landscapes and of nursery, vegetable, and agronomic crops. It grows rapidly and tolerates sandy, dry soils and high temperatures.

DISTRIBUTION: Primarily found in the northern, southeastern, south-central, and western United States; also in Canada.

SIMILAR SPECIES: **Seedlings are large and resemble those of volunteer corn** (*Zea mays* L., ZEAMA) but have narrower leaves and are considerably hairier. **Domestic proso millet** has yellow or light brown seeds, whereas those of wild-proso millet are olive-brown to black. Although it also resembles **witchgrass**, wild-proso millet is considerably larger, especially the inflorescence and spikelets, and its inflorescence does not detach from the plant after senescence as does that of witchgrass.

Wild-proso millet habit

R. Hahn

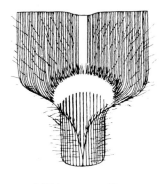

Wild-proso millet
collar region

Ciba-Geigy Corporation

R. Hahn

Collar region: *left*, witchgrass; *right*, wild-proso millet

R. Hahn

Left, witchgrass inflorescence; *right*, wild-proso millet inflorescence

J. DiTomaso

Left, cultivated proso millet seeds, 2.9 mm; *right*, wild-proso millet seeds, 2.9 mm

Dallisgrass (*Paspalum dilatatum* Poir.) [PASDI]

Synonym: caterpillar grass

GENERAL DESCRIPTION: A **coarse-textured perennial producing spreading clumps** and **short, thick rhizomes**. The center of the clump is often devoid of green leaves. It tolerates frequent mowing but can reach 0.5–1.5 m in height when undisturbed.

PROPAGATION / PHENOLOGY: Reproduction is **by seed**; seedlings emerge in the spring and early summer. Once established, **clumps expand by short rhizomes**.

SEEDLING: **Leaves are narrow and rolled in the bud. Ligule is tall and membranous** with a rounded or bluntly pointed tip. **Auricles are absent. Blades** of the first leaves may be softly hairy, but **most lack hairs** except for **long silky hairs at the collar**. Sheaths are flattened with a prominent midrib. **Those of the first leaves are softly hairy and persist through the growing season. Later leaves have smooth sheaths.**

MATURE PLANT: Robust plants, with prostrate or ascending leaves arising from tillers and short, shallow rhizomes. Most vegetative characteristics are similar to those of seedling plants. **Mature leaf blades are flat**, 10–30 cm long by 6–15 mm wide, and **lack hairs**, except for a **few long hairs at the collar. Leaf margins are finely hairy** and rough. **Sheaths lack hairs** (except for the few, older leaves), are **strongly compressed**, with a prominent midvein, and may be tinged red with age. The **collar is broad**, light green, smooth, often with long hairs at the edges. **Tillers are stout** and do not root at the nodes.

ROOTS AND UNDERGROUND STRUCTURES: Fibrous roots and **short, shallow rhizomes**.

FLOWERS AND FRUIT: Plants flower from midsummer to early fall. **Flowers and seeds are produced on a tall** (up to 1.5 m) **terminal stalk** (rachis) in a raceme that bears **3–5** (occasionally more) **spreading or loosely ascending spike-like branches** (5–10 cm long). The spikelets are ovate, 3–4 mm long and 2–2.5 mm wide, hairy, and crowded in 4 rows on the racemes. **Spikelets are covered with silky soft hairs.** Seeds are oval, shiny, yellow to brown (2.5–3 mm long).

POSTSENESCENCE CHARACTERISTICS: The foliage develops red to maroon pigmentation late in the season. Aboveground portions die back in winter, leaving clumps of straw-colored older leaves and tillers that persist into winter or, in the South, into spring.

HABITAT: A major turfgrass weed; also found in pastures, roadsides, and reduced-tillage crops. It is well adapted to a variety of soils but is most often found in moist sites.

DISTRIBUTION: Introduced from South America as a forage crop. Widely distributed in the southern and coastal mid-Atlantic states north to New Jersey and west to California.

SIMILAR SPECIES: Dallisgrass **seedlings strongly resemble large crabgrass**, with hairy leaves, rolled leaf buds, and membranous ligules; however, dallisgrass has rhizomes, and the leaves of more mature plants lack hairs, whereas large crabgrass leaves remain hairy. **Knotgrass (*Paspalum distichum* L., PASDI)** is a similarly coarse-textured perennial, but with a stoloniferous habit, shorter leaves, and fewer (2) racemes, on stalks arising from the leaf axils. **Fringeleaf paspalum (*Paspalum setaceum* Michx. var. *ciliatifolium* (Michx.) Vasey, PASCI)** is an uncommon perennial turf weed on Long Island, N.Y. Like knotgrass, it has fewer racemes on each stalk (1–3) than does dallisgrass and is easily recognized by the distinctive fringe of long (1–2 mm) hairs along the margins of the leaf blade.

Dallisgrass habit

Dallisgrass crown
Regina O. Hughes, USDA

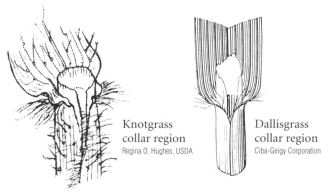

Knotgrass
collar region
Regina O. Hughes, USDA

Dallisgrass
collar region
Ciba-Geigy Corporation

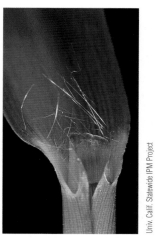

Dallisgrass membranous
ligule

Dallisgrass inflorescence

Left, fringeleaf paspalum seeds, 2.4
mm; *right*, dallisgrass seeds, 2.8 mm

Reed canarygrass (*Phalaris arundinacea* L.) [TYPAR]

Synonyms: lady-grass, spires, doggers, sword-grass, ladies'-laces, bride's-laces, London-lace

GENERAL DESCRIPTION: A **tall (1.5 m) aggressive, rhizomatous, colony-forming perennial** common in wet areas.

PROPAGATION / PHENOLOGY: Although plants produce **seeds**, encroachment is generally by **rhizomes** from ditch banks and other wet areas. Rhizomes can also spread when topsoil or sand is transported from riverbanks.

SEEDLING: Rarely encountered.

MATURE PLANT: **Leaves are rolled in the bud; auricles are absent.** The **ligule is membranous** (3–6 mm long) and rounded to flat-topped. **Stems appear bluish green** (glaucous). **Blades are flat** (10–35 cm long by 5–8 mm wide) and **rough along the margins** but **lack hairs. Sheaths are hairless and rounded. Collars are broad.**

ROOTS AND UNDERGROUND STRUCTURES: Fibrous root system associated with **thick creeping rhizomes.**

FLOWERS AND FRUIT: Flowers and seed are produced by August. **The seedhead is a dense, branched panicle** (7–25 cm long by 1–4 cm wide). The **distinctive pale straw-colored seedheads** extend well beyond the leaves. Although the seedheads are initially compact, the branches spread as they mature. Seeds are shiny, yellow to brown (3 mm long), with a hairy stalk attached to the base.

POSTSENESCENCE CHARACTERISTICS: Straw-colored stems remain erect well into the winter and produce a thick mulch that persists until the following spring.

HABITAT: Reed canarygrass is a weed of wet soils, primarily in roadsides and irrigation and drainage ditches. It does not survive under frequent close mowing or cultivation but may encroach from the edges of fields.

DISTRIBUTION: Found throughout the northern United States and Canada.

SIMILAR SPECIES: **Ribbon-grass (*Phalaris arundinacea* var. *picta*)** is a variety of reed canarygrass that is grown as an ornamental. It has distinctive green-and-white striped leaves. **Other reedgrasses, including common reed** and **giant reed**, can occasionally be confused with reed canarygrass, but both of those grasses are considerably taller (2–6 m tall) and have a larger, more open, inflorescence (15–60 cm long).

Reed canarygrass habit

J. Neal

R. Uva

Juvenile reed canarygrass

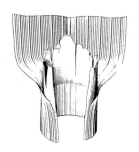

Reed canarygrass
collar region
Ciba-Geigy Corporation

J. Neal

Reed canarygrass ligule

J. Neal

Reed canarygrass inflorescence
and leafy shoot

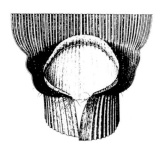

Giant reed
collar region
Ciba-Geigy Corporation

J. DiTomaso

Top, giant reed seed, 9.1
mm; *bottom*, reed canarygrass seeds, 3.2 mm

73

Timothy (*Phleum pratense* L.) [PHLPR]

Synonym: herd's grass

GENERAL DESCRIPTION: A **grayish green perennial forage grass** that produces a **swollen bulb-like base** and **forms large clumps as tall as 1 m**. The **distinctive flowering spike** produces a considerable amount of pollen and is **a common allergen**.

PROPAGATION / PHENOLOGY: Propagation is generally **by seed. Clumps enlarge by tillering** and **short rhizomes**.

SEEDLING: **Leaves are rolled in the bud**, and **auricles are absent. Ligule is membranous** (2–4 mm long) and **toothed at the corners** and at the apex. The **sheath is fused around the stem**, and the foliage lacks hairs.

MATURE PLANT: **Leaves, sheath, and ligules are similar to those of the seedling. Stems** are whitish and **swollen (bulb-like) at the base** and lack hairs. Leaves are flat and taper to a sharp point. Blades are 5–8 mm wide by 8–23 cm long, hairless, and have rough margins, especially toward the base. Sheaths are rounded.

ROOTS AND UNDERGROUND STRUCTURES: Fibrous root system predominates from **short rhizomes** and **occasionally short stolons**.

FLOWERS AND FRUIT: Flowers are produced from June through July in a **terminal spike-like panicle** (5–10 cm long by 5–8 mm wide). **Panicles are dense, cylindrical, stiff, and somewhat bristly.** Spikelets are flat, overlapping, and fringed with short hairs. Awns are 0.7–1.5 mm long.

POSTSENESCENCE CHARACTERISTICS: Plants persist through the winter. Dead, straw-colored flowering stems may persist, but for only a short time, and are recognized by the distinctive spike-like inflorescence.

HABITAT: Timothy is cultivated for hay but can occur as a weed of low-maintenance turfgrass, as well as nursery, orchard, agricultural, and forage crops. It also grows in roadsides and abandoned fields but generally requires nutrient-rich soil.

DISTRIBUTION: Has become naturalized throughout most of the United States and southern Canada.

SIMILAR SPECIES: The dense **cylindrical seedheads are similar to the foxtails**, but, unlike timothy, foxtails have hairy ligules and bristles subtending the spikelets. In early spring, **emerging shoots can resemble quackgrass or orchardgrass.** However, quackgrass has claw-like auricles; timothy does not. Orchardgrass is distinctly folded in the bud, whereas timothy is rolled in the bud.

Timothy habit

J. Neal

Timothy crown

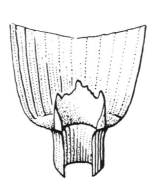

Timothy collar region
The Scotts Company

J. Neal

Timothy inflorescence

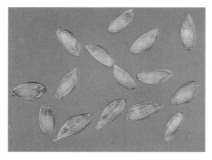

J. DiTomaso

Timothy seeds, 2 mm

Common reed (*Phragmites australis* (Cav.) Trin. *ex* Steud.) [PHRCO]

Synonyms: *Phragmites communis*, *Phragmites maximus*, common reedgrass, giant reed

GENERAL DESCRIPTION: A **very large perennial grass** with erect stems (2–4 m). It **spreads by rhizomes** to form large vegetative colonies in wet soils.

PROPAGATION / PHENOLOGY: Viable seeds are rarely produced, thus **reproduction is primarily by vegetative growth**. Populations often spread over long distances by rhizome fragments carried with soil or on equipment.

SEEDLING: **Viable seed seldom produced.**

MATURE PLANT: **Leaves are rolled in the bud; auricles are absent**, and the **ligule is a ring of silky hairs 1–2 mm long. Stems are hollow, round,** and thickest toward the base (0.5–1.5 cm). **Blades are flat, 20–60 cm long and 1–3 cm wide, conspicuously nerved above**, hairless or sparsely hairy below. **Margins are rough or sharp.** Sheaths are hairless except on the margins, which overlap.

ROOTS AND UNDERGROUND STRUCTURES: **Long, stout, scaly rhizomes.**

FLOWERS AND FRUIT: The inflorescence is a **conspicuous 15–40 cm long plume-like panicle** that is purple when young and turns light brown with age. Spikelets (1 cm long) are silky-hairy.

POSTSENESCENCE CHARACTERISTICS: Colonies of rigid stems can persist through the winter and continue to bear the conspicuous plume-like seedheads.

HABITAT: Common reed is found in roadside ditches, marshes, natural wetlands, and other wet areas. It tolerates salt and alkaline conditions and grows in stagnant or flowing water. Although rarely found in crops, it will survive in areas where the subsoil is very damp or where ditch banks are adjacent to agricultural fields.

DISTRIBUTION: Occurs throughout the United States and southern Canada.

SIMILAR SPECIES: Although **reed canarygrass** shares a similar habitat, it is considerably smaller than common reed and has a membranous ligule. **Giant reed (*Arundo donax* L., ABKDO)** is also commonly associated with wet habitats, but it has a hairy lemma and hairless spikelet stalk. In contrast, common reed has a hairy spikelet stalk and a hairless lemma. Common reed also has a brown (tawny) to purplish inflorescence, whereas the inflorescence of giant reed is whitish.

Common reed habit

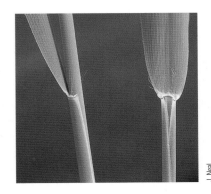

Common reed collar region

Common reed flowering shoot

Common reed
collar region
Ciba-Geigy Corporation

Common reed
shoot tip from
rhizome

Common reed seed, 9 mm
(to tip of awn)

Annual bluegrass (*Poa annua* L.) [POAAN]

Synonyms: annual meadowgrass, annual spear-grass, dwarf spear-grass, wintergrass

GENERAL DESCRIPTION: The **subspecies *Poa annua* ssp. *annua* is an upright, clump-forming, winter annual. *Poa annua* ssp. *reptans* is a prostrate, clump-forming perennial.** Both may grow to 30 cm in height, and both tolerate close mowing to <4 mm. Both are light green and are prolific seedhead producers.

PROPAGATION / PHENOLOGY: Reproduction is **by seed**; seeds germinate in late summer, early autumn, and spring. **Clumps enlarge by aggressive tillering.** Tillers of the perennial subspecies root at the base, forming dense patches. Seeds of the annual subspecies requires a warm after-ripening period before germination; perennial sub-species seeds have no dormancy and will germinate immediately if weather is conducive.

SEEDLING: The first leaf blade is linear and very narrow, about 30 times longer than wide, and opens perpendicular to the ground. **Leaves are light green, folded in the bud, lack auricles, and have a slightly pointed membranous ligule** (1–2 mm long). **Blades** are 2–5 cm long and 0.7–1.5 mm wide, hairless, **keeled, with a curved prow-shaped tip** and smooth margins. Blades can also be rippled or wrinkled. **Sheaths are compressed and hairless.** The collar is green and smooth.

MATURE PLANT: **Leaves and ligule are similar to those of the seedling. Blades** are 1–14 cm long by 1–3 mm wide, light green, smooth, and keeled, with **curved prow-shaped tips. Sheaths** are loose, **smooth, slightly compressed and keeled**. The collar is smooth and narrow.

ROOTS AND UNDERGROUND STRUCTURES: The **root system is fibrous and shallow.** Adventitious roots arise at the base of the tillers.

FLOWERS AND FRUIT: Plants flower from April through October. The **seedhead is an open greenish white pyramidal panicle** (2–7 cm long). Spikelets are about 4–6 mm long and produce 2–6 flowers.

POSTSENESCENCE CHARACTERISTICS: Hot, dry conditions cause annual bluegrass to become dormant or die. With the return of cool, moist conditions the perennial subspecies will resprout from the crown, and the annual subspecies will germinate from seed.

HABITAT: Annual bluegrass is a weed of turf (particularly golf greens), nursery crops, vegetable crops, landscapes, and other irrigated crops. It grows best in cool, moist conditions and rich soil but tolerates a variety of conditions including compacted soils. In golf greens, the perennial subspecies will often dominate the annual. Excess irrigation and fertilization will encourage growth.

DISTRIBUTION: Found throughout the United States and Canada.

SIMILAR SPECIES: **Canada bluegrass (*Poa compressa* L., POACO)** and **Kentucky bluegrass (*Poa pratensis* L., POAPR)** are both rhizomatous perennials and tend to be darker than annual bluegrass. Annual bluegrass may root at the nodes but is not rhizomatous.

Annual bluegrass habit

R. Uva

J. Neal

Annual bluegrass
collar region
Ciba-Geigy Corporation

Canada bluegrass
collar region
Ciba-Geigy Corporation

Kentucky bluegrass
collar region
Ciba-Geigy Corporation

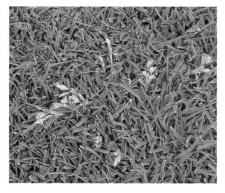

R. Uva

Annual bluegrass flower heads in
bentgrass

J. DiTomaso

Kentucky bluegrass (note
rhizomes)

Left to right: Kentucky bluegrass
seeds, 2.0 mm; Canada bluegrass
seeds, 2.4 mm; and annual
bluegrass seeds, 3.0 mm

79

Roughstalk bluegrass (*Poa trivialis* L.) [POATR]

Synonym: rough bluegrass

GENERAL DESCRIPTION: A **stoloniferous perennial** with erect, bending, or reclining stems (30 cm to 1 m tall). The leaves are often yellow-green, **turning brown to red during periods of drought.**

PROPAGATION / PHENOLOGY: Plants spread primarily by **stolons. Seeds** are a common contaminant of uncertified turfgrass seed and may emerge with adequate soil moisture and temperature.

SEEDLING: Seedlings are small and slow to establish. **Leaves are folded in the bud, with a large tapering membranous ligule** (4–6 mm long). **Scabrous hairs** are very small and **give the plant a rough feel**, accounting for the common name.

MATURE PLANT: **Leaves and ligule are similar to those of the seedling. Blades are flat, rough**, 3–20 cm long by 2–5 mm wide, with a **prow- or boat-shaped tip. Margins are rough. Sheaths are rough**, keeled, and compressed. The collar is broad and smooth.

ROOTS AND UNDERGROUND STRUCTURES: Fibrous roots and **stolons.**

FLOWERS AND FRUIT: Flowers are present mainly in May and June. The **seedhead is an open pyramidal panicle** 6–15 cm long, composed of whorled branches. Spikelets are flattened (3 mm long), with 2–3 flowers.

POSTSENESCENCE CHARACTERISTICS: Plants may go dormant in summer, but they remain green through the winter, although some winter tip burn is common. Under heat and drought stress, foliage has a maroon coloration.

HABITAT: Roughstalk bluegrass is primarily a weed of turfgrass but also grows in orchards, meadows, woods, roadsides, and waste areas. It flourishes in moist, shady locations and is sometimes used in turfgrass mixes for shady areas.

DISTRIBUTION: Found in the northern and southeastern United States, the Pacific Coast states, and southern Canada.

SIMILAR SPECIES: Roughstalk bluegrass can resemble other bluegrasses and some other turfgrass species, particularly **colonial bentgrass (*Agrostis tenuis* Sibth., AGSTE)** and **creeping bentgrass**. However, it is considerably larger than **annual bluegrass** and is lighter in color than **Kentucky bluegrass**. In addition, these latter bluegrass species lack stolons. Although the bentgrasses are stoloniferous, leaves are rolled in the bud, whereas leaves of bluegrasses are folded in the bud.

Roughstalk bluegrass habit

Roughstalk bluegrass
collar region

J. Neal

Colonial bentgrass
collar region

R. Uva

Roughstalk bluegrass stem

Creeping bentgrass
collar region

J. Neal

Roughstalk bluegrass
inflorescence

J. DiTomaso

Left to right: Kentucky bluegrass seeds,
2.0 mm; creeping bentgrass seeds, 1.5
mm; and roughstalk bluegrass seeds,
2.1 mm

Yellow foxtail (*Setaria glauca* (L.) Beauv.) [SETLU]

Synonyms: *Setaria lutescens*, summer-grass, golden foxtail, wild millet

GENERAL DESCRIPTION: A **clump-forming, erect summer annual** reaching 1 m in height, with characteristic bottle-brush or **"fox tail"–like seedheads**.

PROPAGATION / PHENOLOGY: Reproduction is **by seed**; seeds germinate from late spring through midsummer.

SEEDLING: The first leaf blade is linear, about 7 times longer than wide and opens parallel to the ground. **Leaves are rolled in the bud; auricles are absent, and the ligule is a fringe of hairs about 0.5 mm long.** Blades of young seedlings are 4.5–8 cm long and 3–5 mm wide, **smooth on the lower surfaces, with long wispy hairs on the basal portions of the upper surface.** The **margins are smooth or slightly rough**, and the blade is keeled in the lower portion. **Sheath is smooth and compressed.** The collar is green and smooth.

MATURE PLANT: **Ligule is a fringe of hairs about 1 mm long. Leaf blades** are 30 cm long by 4–10 mm wide, keeled, and have **long wispy hairs only on the upper surface at the base. Sheath is smooth, compressed, often reddish at the base**, and has a prominent midvein. The collar is narrow, light green or yellowish, and smooth.

ROOTS AND UNDERGROUND STRUCTURES: Root system is fibrous. Yellow foxtail does not root at the nodes, but tillers will produce roots at the base of the plant.

FLOWERS AND FRUIT: Blooms in mid to late summer. The **seedhead is a coarse bristly spike-like panicle**, 2–15 cm long and 1 cm wide. The mature seedhead is present from late summer through autumn. Spikelets are about 3 mm long, and each spikelet is subtended by 5 or more bristles. Bristles are about 10 mm long and yellowish at maturity. Seeds are 2–3 mm long, ridged, and yellow, with small dark markings.

POSTSENESCENCE CHARACTERISTICS: Yellow foxtail can be recognized by the yellowish bristly inflorescence that persists through early winter. Other foxtails also have persistent bristly inflorescences but turn brown after they senesce.

HABITAT: Yellow foxtail is a weed of most cultivated crops as well as turf, landscapes, and nurseries. It generally grows on nutrient-rich soil.

DISTRIBUTION: Yellow and green foxtail are important weeds worldwide. Giant foxtail is common in the eastern United States, excluding northern New England.

SIMILAR SPECIES: **Giant foxtail (*Setaria faberi* Herrm., SETFA)** and **green foxtail (*Setaria viridis* (L.) Beauv., SETVI)** closely resemble yellow foxtail in general characteristics—ligule, habitat, growth habit, and reproductive characteristics. **Giant foxtail** is the largest of the 3 species, and **its seedlings and mature plants have numerous short hairs on the upper surface of the blades and on the margins of the sheaths.** The green to purple, **nodding seedhead is also the largest of the 3. Green foxtail seedlings and mature plants have rough blades that lack hairs, and the sheaths have hairy margins.** The seedhead is larger and greener than that of yellow foxtail. Yellow foxtail seedlings can be confused with **fall panicum** but are easily recognized by the distinctive wispy hairs at the base of the blades. Fall panicum seedlings can be distinguished from foxtails by their hairy sheaths and their blades, which are hairy only on the lower surface.

Yellow foxtail habit

J. Neal

Yellow foxtail seedling

J. Neal

Yellow foxtail seedheads

J. DiTomaso

Green foxtail collar region
Ciba-Geigy Corporation

Yellow foxtail collar region
Ciba-Geigy Corporation

Giant foxtail collar region
Ciba-Geigy Corporation

Yellow foxtail, 5-tiller plant

J. Neal

Green foxtail seedhead
Ciba-Geigy Corporation

Yellow foxtail seedhead
Ciba-Geigy Corporation

Giant foxtail seedhead
Ciba-Geigy Corporation

J. DiTomaso

Left to right: green foxtail seeds, 2.4 mm; giant foxtail seeds, 2.5 mm; and yellow foxtail seeds, 3 mm

83

Shattercane (*Sorghum bicolor* (L.) Moench) [SORVU]

Synonyms: *Sorghum bicolor* var. *drummondii*, *Sorghum vulgare*, sorghum, black amber cane, wildcane, milo

GENERAL DESCRIPTION: A **summer annual with erect corn-like stems** that can reach 4 m in height. Stems usually grow individually but may form clumps. Shattercane is a very competitive weed in corn and sorghum and can hybridize with cultivated sorghum or johnsongrass.

PROPAGATION / PHENOLOGY: Flowers are produced from July to October. Reproduction is **by seed**; seeds germinate from midspring through early summer. The inflorescences shatter and spread their seeds earlier than do those of cultivated sorghum.

SEEDLING: **Leaves are rolled in the bud; auricles are absent, and the ligule is membranous at the base and fringed at the top.** The base of the blades is usually hairy on the upper and lower surfaces. **Hairs** can be **present or absent on sheaths**.

MATURE PLANT: **Ligule is about 5 mm long, membranous on the basal two-thirds and fringed on the top third. Stems are robust and purple-spotted. Blades** are flat, narrowing at each end, and are **30–60 cm long by 3–5 cm wide**. Leaves and sheaths are smooth or hairy, often hairy at the junction between the blade and the sheath (collar). **Tillers are produced at the crown.**

ROOTS AND UNDERGROUND STRUCTURES: **Fibrous root system**, often with adventitious roots arising from the nodes or tillers. Adventitious roots can act as prop roots as in corn.

FLOWERS AND FRUIT: The **seedhead is a large open panicle**, 15–50 cm long, and usually hairy along the main axis. Spikelets are in pairs. The lower one is fertile, awned (5–13 mm long), and large (4–6 mm long). The other is infertile, on a stalk (pedicel), and considerably smaller than the fertile spikelet. Seed is egg-shaped, rounded to flattened, shiny, and black to red at maturity.

POSTSENESCENCE CHARACTERISTICS: **Seedheads shatter before grain harvest** and do not persist. After harvest, stubble may remain in the field through the winter.

HABITAT: Shattercane grows primarily in cultivated areas and is a weed of agronomic crops, particularly sorghum and corn. It is less common in nursery and vegetable crops.

DISTRIBUTION: Most common in the northern, southeastern, south-central, and western United States.

SIMILAR SPECIES: **Johnsongrass** is closely related to shattercane and at certain stages of development may be difficult to distinguish; however, it is a perennial with large rhizomes and blades 1–2 cm wide, whereas shattercane does not produce rhizomes and has blades >3 cm wide. In addition, **seeds of shattercane are much larger and more rounded than those of johnsongrass and can be examined by carefully removing young seedlings from the soil**.

Shattercane
in corn

W. Curran

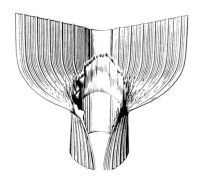

Shattercane
collar region
Ciba-Geigy Corporation

W. Curran

Shattercane inflorescence

W. Curran

Shattercane seedling

J. DiTomaso

Left, shattercane seeds, 5 mm; *right*,
cultivated sorghum seeds, 5 mm

85

Johnsongrass (*Sorghum halepense* (L.) Pers.) [SORHA]

Synonyms: *Holcus halepense*, means-grass, aleppo grass, grass sorghum, Egyptian millet

GENERAL DESCRIPTION: A **coarse-textured perennial** with stout unbranched stems and **thick aggressive rhizomes**. It can grow to 2 m in height and form large stands.

PROPAGATION / PHENOLOGY: Reproduction is **by seeds and rhizomes**. Rhizomes spread to form vegetative stands. When rhizomes are severed by cultivation, equipment can transport small pieces to other areas to form new colonies.

SEEDLING: The first leaf blade is only 8 times longer than wide and opens parallel to the ground. **Leaves are rolled in the bud; auricles are absent, and the ligule is membranous with shallow teeth across the top. Blades** are 4–18 cm long and 2–5 mm wide, **smooth on both surfaces** and margins, with a **prominent midvein** near the base of the blade. Sheaths are smooth, rounded to slightly compressed, green or with a maroon tinge. The collar is narrow and whitish.

MATURE PLANT: **Leaves are similar to those of seedlings.** The **ligule** (3–4 mm long) **is membranous** and **may be jagged across the top. Older ligules have a fringe of hairs on the top half, but are membranous at the base.** Blades are 15–50 cm long by 10–30 mm wide, smooth below and mostly smooth above, with some hairs present at the base of the blade near the ligule. The margins are rough, and the **blades are flat, with a thick prominent white midvein.** Sheath is smooth, pale green, reddish brown to maroon, compressed, often with hairy margins. The collar is broad, light green or white, and smooth.

ROOTS AND UNDERGROUND STRUCTURES: Fibrous root system is associated with **thick and aggressive rhizomes**. Rhizomes can be purplish and have scales at the nodes.

FLOWERS AND FRUIT: Flowers are present from June to July. The **seedhead is a large (15–50 cm long), open, coarse purplish panicle**. Spikelets are in pairs. The shorter, wider floret (4–5.5 mm long) produces a seed and has a 1–1.5 cm twisted awn that is easily detached. The seed is 3–5 mm long, oval, and dark reddish brown. The other infertile stalked spikelet is longer but narrower and lacks an awn.

POSTSENESCENCE CHARACTERISTICS: Aboveground portions are killed by frost. The stout stems and seedheads persist well into winter.

HABITAT: Johnsongrass is a weed of most cultivated, reduced-tillage, and perennial crops as well as roadsides, meadows, and waste areas. It prefers rich soil but will survive in nearly any soil type. It does not tolerate close mowing.

DISTRIBUTION: Introduced as a forage crop, johnsongrass has naturalized throughout the southern United States and the West Coast. It is spreading northward into New York, Massachusetts, Michigan, and other regions.

SIMILAR SPECIES: **Shattercane** is closely related to johnsongrass and at certain stages of development may be difficult to distinguish. But it is an annual and does not have large rhizomes. Shattercane also has leaf blades much wider (>3 cm) than those of johnsongrass (1–2 cm). In addition, **seeds of shattercane are much larger and more rounded than those of johnsongrass and can be examined by carefully removing young seedlings from the soil. Fall panicum** has similar foliage, particularly the white midvein on the left blade. However, it is an annual that is considerably smaller than johnsongrass and has a hairy ligule that is not membranous at the base.

Johnsongrass habit

Johnsongrass
seedling with
seedcoat
attached

Johnsongrass
collar region
Ciba-Geigy Corporation

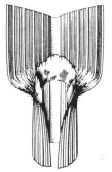

Johnsongrass rhizomes

Johnsongrass tillers

Left, johnsongrass seeds, 5.5 mm;
right, cultivated sorghum seeds,
5.0 mm

Carpetweed (*Mollugo verticillata* L.) [MOLVE]

Synonyms: Indian chickweed, whorled chickweed, devils-grip

GENERAL DESCRIPTION: A small, much-branched **prostrate annual forming circular mats** to 40 cm in diameter. Leaves are rounded, widest above the middle and narrowing to the base.

PROPAGATION / PHENOLOGY: Reproduction is **by seed**. Germination is generally later in the season than that of many other summer annuals, but growth is rapid.

SEEDLING: **Seedlings develop as small flattened basal rosettes.** Cotyledons are oblong, thick, smooth, 1.5–3.5 mm long and lack noticeable veins. Young **leaves are alternate, thickened, rounded above** and **narrowed to the base.** Petioles may have a few marginal hairs. Leaf surfaces are dull green, smooth, pale beneath, and pinkish brown toward the base.

MATURE PLANT: Stems are smooth and much-branched, forming **prostrate mats** along the soil surface. **Leaves are in whorls of 3–8 at each stem node.** Leaves are sessile, smooth, 1–3 cm long and <1 cm wide, rounded above and narrowed to the base (spatulate) or widest above the middle and tapering to the base (oblanceolate).

ROOTS AND UNDERGROUND STRUCTURES: Sparsely branched taproot.

FLOWERS AND FRUIT: Although they are occasionally present in June, flowers commonly bloom from July through September. Flowers, in clusters of 2–5 in the leaf axils, are small, 4–5 mm across, white or greenish white, with slender, 5–15 mm long stalks (pedicels). Fruit are small, thin-walled, 3-valved, egg-shaped capsules, 1.5–4 mm long. Seeds are small, 0.5 mm long, flattened, kidney-shaped, orange-red to orange-brown.

POSTSENESCENCE CHARACTERISTICS: None of note.

HABITAT: Carpetweed is a weed of most cultivated agronomic and horticultural crops and newly seeded or thin turfgrass. Abundant on damp, rich soil in tilled crops, it is also commonly found on dry, gravelly or sandy soils in waste areas.

DISTRIBUTION: Found throughout temperate North America. Common in the eastern United States, less common in the northern Great Plains.

SIMILAR SPECIES: Whorls of 3–8 leaves at the stem nodes and the profuse branching pattern easily distinguish carpetweed from other species. Prostrate weeds such as **common chickweed, mouseear chickweed**, and the **speedwells** have alternate or opposite leaves and do not have forked branching. The **bedstraws also have whorls of leaves** but can be distinguished by their **square stems**.

J. Neal

Carpetweed habit

J. Neal

Carpetweed flowering shoot

Carpetweed seeds, 0.5 mm

J. DiTomaso

Tumble pigweed (*Amaranthus albus* L.) [AMAAL]

Synonyms: tumble weed, tumbling pigweed, white pigweed

GENERAL DESCRIPTION: A **bushy-branched, rounded or globular annual**, 20 cm to 1 m in diameter. Senesced plants sever at the soil surface and scatter seeds by tumbling in the wind.

PROPAGATION / PHENOLOGY: Reproduction is **by seed**.

SEEDLING: Cotyledons are smooth, lanceolate, 3.5–8.5 mm long by 1–1.5 mm wide, green on the upper surface and magenta beneath. **Young leaves are ovate, dark green above, and tinged with magenta on the underside.** The **margins are entire** to wavy, and the **apex is notched**, with a temporary bristle in the notch (mucronate). **Expanding leaves** are sparsely hairy on the margins and veins of the underside. The hairs develop into rough projections as the leaves mature. **Stems are angled**, tinged magenta, with short rough hairs.

MATURE PLANT: **Stems are pale green to whitish**, usually smooth, much-branched, erect or prostrate at the base, with an ascending tip. **Leaves are alternate, pale green** on the upper surface and pale green to reddish-tinged on the underside. **Blades are ovate or spatulate** (2.5–8 cm long), with **wavy margins** and conspicuous venation. **Petioles are short** (1.3–3 cm long). **Leaves of the flowering branches are elliptic** to oblong or obovate.

ROOTS AND UNDERGROUND STRUCTURES: Well-developed **taproot**, relatively shallow, **usually not red**.

FLOWERS AND FRUIT: **Greenish flowers** are produced from July through August in **short, dense clusters in the leaf axils and not in terminal spikes** characteristic of many other *Amaranthus* species. Male (staminate) and female (pistillate) flowers are separate (monoecious). Petals are absent, but 3 uneven sepals are present in the pistillate flowers. The spiny bracts subtending the flowers are twice as long as the sepals. Fruit are thin-walled 1-seeded inflated structures (utricles), 1.3–1.7 mm long, opening around the middle by a cap-like lid. Seeds are glossy, black, round, small (0.7–1.5 mm in diameter), and convex on both sides.

POSTSENESCENCE CHARACTERISTICS: **At maturity, plants abscise just above the ground and are carried with the wind**, scattering seeds. Dead plants accumulate on the leeward side of fields along fences and hedges.

HABITAT: Tumble pigweed is a weed of agricultural and horticultural crops, including woody perennial crops such as those in nurseries, orchards, and vineyards. It also grows in ditch banks, waste areas, and roadsides.

DISTRIBUTION: A native of the arid regions of the Great Plains, now distributed throughout all but the northernmost areas of North America.

SIMILAR SPECIES: **See Table 8 for a comparison with other pigweeds. Prostrate pigweed** closely resembles tumble pigweed as a seedling, but it remains prostrate when mature. **Russian thistle (*Salsola iberica* Sennen & Pau, SASKR)** is also a "tumbleweed," but with much smaller leaves and a distinctly spiny foliage.

J. Neal

Tumble pigweed habit

J. Neal

Tumble pigweed stem, with flowers

J. Neal

Tumble pigweed seedling

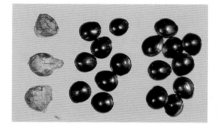

J. DiTomaso

Left to right: Russian thistle seeds, 1.6 mm; prostrate pigweed seeds, 1.3 mm; and tumble pigweed seeds, 1.4 mm

Prostrate pigweed (*Amaranthus blitoides* S. Wats.) [AMABL]

Synonyms: *Amaranthus graecizans* (an archaic synonym), spreading pigweed, mat amaranth

GENERAL DESCRIPTION: A **prostrate, mat-forming** and branching **summer annual** (15–60 cm wide) with erect or ascending tips.

PROPAGATION / PHENOLOGY: Reproduction is **by seed**.

SEEDLING: **Cotyledons are lanceolate to linear** (4–10 mm long by 0.75–1.5 mm wide), the lower surface magenta. **Young leaves** are obovate (**widest at the apex**), and the undersides are tinged magenta. **Margins** are somewhat rough, and the **apex is slightly notched**, with a bristle in the notch (mucronate). **Stems are smooth** and angled.

MATURE PLANT: **Stems are fleshy and pliable**, light green to reddish purple, and **smooth**. **Leaves** are numerous, often crowded at the branch tips, light green, **smooth**; they sometimes have lighter areas on the upper surface and a reddish coloration on the underside. Leaves are 1–2(–4) cm long, oblong to obovate or oval, but **broader at the notched tip** than at the petiole. Margins are entire and often membranous.

ROOTS AND UNDERGROUND STRUCTURES: **Taproot** with a secondary fibrous root system.

FLOWERS AND FRUIT: The small, green **flowers** are produced from June through August in small, **dense clusters only in the axils of the leaves** and **not on terminal spikes** characteristic of many other *Amaranthus* species. Male (staminate) and female (pistillate) flowers are separate (monoecious). Petals and sepals of the pistillate flower are alike (tepals) and number 4–5. Because the spiny bracts are the same length as the tepals, the inflorescence is only slightly bristly to the touch. Fruit are smooth inflated structures (utricles), 2–2.5 mm long, opening around the middle by a cap-like lid. Seeds are glossy, black, round, 1.5 mm in diameter, and convex on both sides.

POSTSENESCENCE CHARACTERISTICS: Prostrate stems have a web-like appearance after the leaves senesce.

HABITAT: Primarily a weed of arable land, prostrate pigweed is particularly abundant in vegetables grown on muck soils. It is also occasionally a weed in turf and can be found in roadsides and waste areas. It generally grows on coarse, sandy soils.

DISTRIBUTION: A native of western North America but has spread to become a common weed throughout the Northeast, except in the extreme northern states.

SIMILAR SPECIES: **See Table 8 for a comparison with other pigweeds. Prostrate spurge** is also prostrate, but it exudes a milky sap when cut and its leaves are smaller. **Common purslane** is prostrate but has succulent leaves and stems.

Prostrate pigweed habit

Prostrate pigweed seedling

Mature prostrate pigweed (note notched leaf tips)

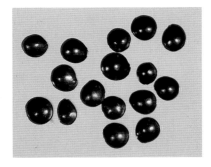

Prostrate pigweed seeds, 1.3 mm

93

Pigweeds:
Smooth pigweed (*Amaranthus hybridus* L.) [AMACH]
Powell amaranth (*Amaranthus powellii* S. Wats.) [AMAPO]
Redroot pigweed (*Amaranthus retroflexus* L.) [AMARE]

Synonyms: rough pigweed, amaranth pigweed, green amaranth, careless weed

GENERAL DESCRIPTION: **Redroot pigweed** is an erect freely branching **summer annual** (10 cm to as much as 2 m in height). The small flowers are enclosed by spiny bracts that give the terminal and axillary spikes a bristly appearance. Two very similar species—**Powell amaranth** or **green pigweed**, and **smooth pigweed**—often grow together with redroot pigweed in mixed populations in the Northeast (see Table 8 for comparison). Herbicide-resistant biotypes have been identified.

PROPAGATION / PHENOLOGY: Reproduction of all is **by seed**. Germination of all 3 species begins in midspring, with peak flushes occurring in late spring and summer. Flowering usually begins with decreasing day length in late June. Seeds are produced from late summer to fall, until severe frost.

SEEDLING:

Smooth pigweed: Very **similar to redroot pigweed** as a seedling. **Stems are more densely pubescent** and the **leaves are usually darker green and less wavy.**

Powell amaranth: **Leaves are shiny, entire (not undulate)**, and nearly or completely lack hairs. Blades are smaller and more pointed than are those of the other 2 species. **Lower stem is tinged red and nearly hairless.**

Redroot pigweed: Cotyledons are narrow and pointed (lanceolate), 10–12 mm long (4–5 times as long as wide), dull green to reddish on the upper surface and bright red beneath. **Stems are light green, hairy**, and often red at the base. **Young leaves are alternate, egg-shaped**, and sparsely hairy on the margin and veins. Hairs develop into tiny rough projections. The blade is green on the upper surface. The lower surface is red- or magenta-tinged, especially on the veins. **Margins are wavy** (undulate), and the apex is slightly notched, with a bristle in the notch. Petioles are purplish, with short stiff hairs.

MATURE PLANT:

Smooth pigweed: Stems are erect and slender. **Upper stem region is densely hairy**, and the hairs are short. **Leaves** are simple, alternate, **oval to egg-shaped**, green above, light green or magenta below.

Powell amaranth: **Stems** are usually erect and stout and **lack or nearly lack hairs throughout. Leaves** are simple, alternate, **diamond-shaped, more pointed than those of redroot or smooth pigweed.** Blades are shiny green above, with whitish veins on the lower surface.

Redroot pigweed: **Stems** are erect, stout; the lower part is thick and smooth, **the upper often branched and very hairy. Leaves** are simple, alternate, ovate or rhombic-ovate with **wavy margins. Blades are dull green above, hairy beneath** or at least along the veins. The veins on the lower surface are prominently white.

Smooth pigweed habit

Redroot pigweed seedling

Powell amaranth seedling

Redroot pigweed seedling (note hairy stem, reddish at base)

Pigweed stems, *left to right:* smooth pigweed, Powell amaranth, and redroot pigweed

95

ROOTS AND UNDERGROUND STRUCTURES: All have a shallow taproot, often pinkish or reddish.

FLOWERS AND FRUIT:

Smooth pigweed: There are 5 styles and tepals. Tepals are erect and pointed. Bracts are often equal to or only slightly exceed the flowers in length. The **utricle cap drops (dehisces)** as the seed matures. **The narrower, often lax, terminal spike, which is smaller and less bristly** than that of the other 2 species, accounts for the common name smooth pigweed.

Powell amaranth: There are 3–5 styles on the pistillate flowers and 3–5 tepals (petals and sepals), which look alike. Tepals are erect, tapering to an extended point (acuminate). The **utricle is indehiscent** and persists with the seed as it disperses.

Redroot pigweed: Small greenish flowers are produced in **dense, stiff, spike-like terminal panicles** (5–20 cm long and about 1.5 cm wide). Smaller inflorescences are in the axils of the lower leaves. Male and female flowers are separate (monoecious). The male flowers abscise soon after the pollen sheds. **Fruit** are thin-walled, 1-seeded utricles, 1.5–2 mm long, that **split open** by a cap-like lid around the middle. Seeds of all 3 species are glossy, black to dark brown, 1–1.2 mm long, ovate to elliptic, somewhat flattened, with a notch at the narrow end.

POSTSENESCENCE CHARACTERISTICS: Erect stems persist, bearing the brown inflorescences of dried bracts, flowers, and seeds. Naturally occurring intraspecifc hybrids are partially sterile and will remain green longer than seed-bearing plants.

HABITAT: All 3 species are weeds of horticultural and agronomic crops, landscapes and nursery crops, and rarely turf. They grow on a wide variety of soil types but thrive under sunny, fertile conditions.

DISTRIBUTION: All are native to North or Central America, or both, but have spread to become weedy throughout the United States and southern Canada. Powell amaranth has infested the northeastern United States and Canada only within the past 50 years.

SIMILAR SPECIES: **See Table 8 for a comparison with other pigweeds. Common lambsquarters**, at the **cotyledon stage**, is similar in habit and is often found growing with pigweeds. At the first true leaf stage, lambsquarters has opposite leaves, whereas pigweed leaves are alternate. In addition, lambsquarters has a granular leaf surface that pigweeds do not have. **Spiny amaranth (*Amaranthus spinosus* L., AMASP)** is a **summer annual** (0.5–1.5 m in height) with erect and freely branching stems bearing lax terminal spikes. The stem has a pair of **sharp spines** (5–10 mm long) at the base of most leaves. Stems are grooved and smooth, lacking hairs. Utricles are indehiscent. Spiny amaranth is abundant in the South, less common in the Northeast, extending north to Pennsylvania and New York.

J. Neal

Seedheads, *left to right:* smooth pigweed, redroot pigweed, and Powell amaranth

J. Neal

Spiny amaranth

R. Uva

Dead pigweed stems in early spring

J. DiTomaso

Left to right: spiny amaranth seeds, 0.7 mm; smooth pigweed seeds, 0.9 mm; Powell amaranth seeds, 1.0 mm; and redroot pigweed seeds, 1.0 mm

Poison-hemlock (*Conium maculatum* L.) [COIMA]

Synonyms: deadly hemlock, snake-weed, poison parsley, wode whistle, poison stinkweed

GENERAL DESCRIPTION: A **biennial** with a **basal rosette of leaves the first year** and an **erect branched stem (60 cm to 2 m in height) the second year. Flowers and foliage resemble carrot and parsley.** Plant parts have a disagreeable odor when crushed. All parts of the plant contain toxic alkaloids, including coniine, that cause **respiratory failure** in humans and other animals **when ingested.**

PROPAGATION / PHENOLOGY: Reproduction is **by seed.**

SEEDLING: Seedlings have a **parsnip-like odor** when crushed. Cotyledons are narrow, elongated-elliptic (30 cm long), with a long petiole (15 mm). The surface of the cotyledons is light green with prominent netted veins on the underside. The **first leaf is smooth** and **2 or 3 times deeply dissected; later leaves are 2 to 3 times pinnatifid.**

MATURE PLANT: A **basal rosette** is formed in the first year. **In the second year, plants produce erect stems** that are **hairless, purple-spotted, ridged**, and hollow between the nodes. **Leaves** are alternate, dark glossy green, **fern-like**, triangular, **20–40 cm long**, and 3–4 times pinnately compound. The **bases of the lower leaves form a sheath that encircles the stem.**

ROOTS AND UNDERGROUND STRUCTURES: Thick, white, often branched, **taproot,** 20–25 cm long, with a well-developed secondary fibrous root system.

FLOWERS AND FRUIT: Flowers are produced from June through August in flat to slightly convex umbrella-like clusters (compound umbels) about 4–6 cm wide. The 2 seeds are enclosed within the fruit (schizocarp). When the fruit is mature, the 2 halves separate. Each section is oval, 2–3.5 mm long, flattened on one side, with conspicuous pale brown wavy ribs.

POSTSENESCENCE CHARACTERISTICS: Dead flowering stem may persist well into winter. Fruit often remain attached for a considerable period of time after senescence.

HABITAT: Primarily a weed of pastures and landscapes, poison-hemlock is also found on borders of fields and in roadsides, ditch banks, and meadows. It thrives on rich, gravelly or loamy soils.

DISTRIBUTION: Distributed throughout the United States, including the western, northeastern, north-central states and adjacent areas of southern Canada. Poison-hemlock is not as common in parts of the northern Great Plains.

SIMILAR SPECIES: **Spotted waterhemlock (*Cicuta maculata* L., CIUMC) is a very poisonous perennial** found primarily in wet areas. It resembles wild carrot but has smooth and purple-spotted stems and leaves that are 2–3 times pinnately compound with considerably larger leaflets. Unlike wild carrot and poison-hemlock, waterhemlock has a cluster of fleshy taproots at the base. **Giant hogweed (*Heracleum mantegazzianum* Sommier & Levier)** is much larger than the other similar species (2–5 m tall) and has purple-blotched stems, leaves up to a meter long and 80 cm wide, and large white flower clusters. Its sap may cause **severe skin irritation**. Giant hogweed has become naturalized in central and western New York. **See Table 9 for a comparison with other weedy members of the carrot family.**

J. DiTomaso

Poison-hemlock stem

J. DiTomaso

Poison-hemlock mature foliage

J. DiTomaso

Poison-hemlock in flower

J. DiTomaso

Poison-hemlock seeds, 2.7 mm

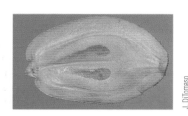
J. DiTomaso

Giant hogweed seed, 14 mm

Spotted waterhemlock
Regina O. Hughes, USDA

99

Wild carrot (*Daucus carota* L.) [DAUCA]

Synonyms: Queen Anne's lace, birds-nest, devils plague

GENERAL DESCRIPTION: A **biennial** forming a **basal rosette of leaves the first year** and **an erect flowering stalk** (1 m in height) **the following year**. The **foliage is fern-like** with a carrot-like odor.

PROPAGATION / PHENOLOGY: Reproduction is **by seed**. Germination occurs in the spring.

SEEDLING: Hypocotyls are pinkish brown. **Cotyledons are linear**, about 20 mm long by 1 mm wide, lack petioles, and taper at both the base and tip. **Young leaves form a basal rosette** (technically, are alternate), are smooth on the upper surface, grayish green, with short hairs on the veins of the lower surface and along the margins. **Leaves are 3-lobed; each lobe is deeply pinnately dissected**, with petioles longer than the blade. Seedlings resemble parsley and develop into basal rosettes.

MATURE PLANT: **In the second year, hollow and vertically ribbed hairy stems are produced from the rosette. Leaves are primarily basal**, with only a few sessile, alternate, reduced leaves on the stem. Leaves are triangular or oblong (up to 15 cm long), **twice pinnately compound** with narrow or lobed segments. Leaf margins are hairy.

ROOTS AND UNDERGROUND STRUCTURES: A stout **yellowish white taproot** with fibrous secondary roots.

FLOWERS AND FRUIT: Flowers are produced from July to September in the second year. Inflorescence is composed of numerous **white, lace-like flowers in a flat-topped compound umbel** (twice-branched). The lower branches of the umbel are subtended by deeply lobed leaf-like bracts. At maturity, flower clusters may close, resembling a bird's nest. Individual flowers are white, sometimes pinkish, with a single deep-purple flower in the center of the cluster. The 2 seeds are enclosed within the fruit (schizocarp). When the fruit matures, the 2 halves separate. Each section is 2–3 mm long, yellow to light grayish brown, flattened on one side, and ridged with barbed prickles that aid in dispersal. One plant can produce up to 4000 seeds.

POSTSENESCENCE CHARACTERISTICS: First-year basal rosettes remain green through the winter. After the second year, plants die, but stems persist, with remnants of the flower clusters and finely divided leaves remaining.

HABITAT: Wild carrot is a weed of low-maintenance turfgrass, pastures, landscapes, nursery crops, and other perennial crops. It is less common in cultivated agricultural crops, except under reduced-tillage practices. Wild carrot most commonly grows on well-drained to dry soils, particularly in old meadows and fallow fields.

DISTRIBUTION: Found throughout North America.

SIMILAR SPECIES: The **leaves and seedlings of mayweed chamomile** are similar to those of wild carrot, but mayweed plants produce erect, leafy flowering stems. **Seedlings of common yarrow** are easily confused with wild carrot. However, the leaves of common yarrow seedlings are not as wide and are more finely dissected, and the cotyledons are rounded, not linear. As a mature plant, common yarrow is a rhizomatous perennial with flowers typical of the aster family. **Poison-hemlock** can be distinguished from wild carrot by its smooth, purple-spotted, ridged stems. The stems of wild carrot are vertically ribbed, hairy, and lack the purple spotting. **(See Table 9 for a comparison with other weedy members of the carrot family.)**

A. Senesac

Wild carrot habit

J. DiTomaso

Wild carrot seedlings

J. Neal

Wild carrot rosette

J. DiTomaso

Left, spotted waterhemlock seeds, 3.0 mm; *right*, wild carrot seeds, 2.5 mm

Common milkweed (*Asclepias syriaca* L.) [ASCSY]

Synonyms: wild cotton, Virginia silk, silkweed, cotton-weed

GENERAL DESCRIPTION: A **perennial** with **stout, erect stems** (60 cm to 1.5 m in height). All parts of the plant exude a **milky sap** when broken.

PROPAGATION / PHENOLOGY: Reproduction is **by seeds and rhizomes**. In the spring, plants develop from buds either on the stem base or from rhizomes. Shoots emerge from April through May. **Cultivation can fragment and spread roots and rhizomes.** Seeds are dispersed by wind in late summer and fall.

SEEDLING: **Most milkweed plants emerge from overwintering root buds.** These are more robust than seedlings and lack cotyledons. Hypocotyls of seedlings are light green and smooth. Cotyledons are dull green, oval, rounded at the tips (1.2 cm long). **Young leaves** are **opposite**, dark green, waxy, **oblong, pointed at the apex**, with a **prominent white midvein** on the surface of the leaf. Seedlings do not flower during the first year of growth.

MATURE PLANT: **Stems** are **usually unbranched**, hollow, **erect**, covered with downy hairs, and exude a **milky sap**. Stems are green, becoming red later in the season. **Leaves are oblong-elliptic** to oval, 7–20 cm long, **opposite**, occasionally whorled, on short petioles (about 8 mm). **Blades** are green and smooth on the upper surface, with a prominent **white midvein**, and lighter green and downy hairy beneath. **Margins are entire**; pinnate veins do not reach the leaf margin.

ROOTS AND UNDERGROUND STRUCTURES: An extensive system of **thick, fleshy, white roots and rhizomes.**

FLOWERS AND FRUIT: Flowers are present from late June to early August. **Globe-like flower clusters (umbels)** develop at the end of stems and in the upper leaf axils. Individual flowers are **purplish pink to white, fragrant**, with 5 hooded petals above, 5 sepals below, and styles united into a disk. Each flower is on a long, slender stalk. **Fruit are large (8–13 cm long), teardrop-shaped pods**, grayish green, and hairy with soft spines. Each pod opens in early autumn and can contain over 200 seeds. **Seeds** are 6–10 mm long, brown, flattened, oval, with a winged margin and a **terminal tuft of long silky white hairs that facilitate wind dispersal**.

POSTSENESCENCE CHARACTERISTICS: The **characteristic pods** turn grayish brown and persist on dead stems throughout the winter. Pods are shiny yellow on the inside. Some seeds may remain within the pods for an extended period.

HABITAT: Common milkweed is frequently found in meadows and roadsides and is a weed of nursery crops and agricultural crops. It is a significant problem under no-till and reduced-tillage agricultural systems. Common milkweed prefers well-drained soil and does not tolerate frequent mowing or cultivation.

DISTRIBUTION: Found throughout the northeastern United States, south to Virginia and northern Georgia, and west to the Rocky Mountains.

SIMILAR SPECIES: **Hemp dogbane (*Apocynum cannabinum* L., APCCA)** is closely related to common miklweed. It is a large perennial with opposite leaves and **milky sap**, but its **leaves are smaller** than those of common milkweed, and its stem is much-branched in the upper third to half of the plant. In addition, the flowers are smaller, bell-shaped, and greenish white. The fruit are long, narrow, and curved (8–12 cm long by <4 mm wide).

Common milkweed habit

Juvenile common milkweed

Hemp dogbane leafy shoots
with seed pods

Common milkweed
fruit and seeds

Hemp dogbane habit

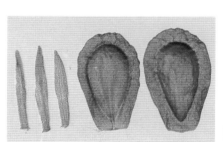

Left, hemp dogbane seeds, 6 mm;
right, common milkweed seeds, 9 mm

103

Black swallowwort (*Cynanchum nigrum* (L.) Pers.) [CYKNI]

Synonyms: *Vincetoxicum nigrum*, climbing milkweed

GENERAL DESCRIPTION: A **twining, vine-like perennial** with stems 1–2 m long. Climbing stems can envelop small trees and other desirable vegetation in natural areas.

PROPAGATION / PHENOLOGY: Reproduction is **by seed**. Vegetative propagation, suggested by dense infestations, is unconfirmed.

SEEDLING: Information unavailable.

MATURE PLANT: **Stems** are mostly unbranched, **twining**, and nearly smooth. **Leaves** are simple, **opposite, dark green**, petiolated, oblong to ovate (5–10 cm long), hairless, with entire margins. The **leaf tip gradually tapers to a point**, and the base of the leaf blade is rounded.

ROOTS AND UNDERGROUND STRUCTURES: Large root crown.

FLOWERS AND FRUIT: Flowers are produced from June through September. Clusters (cymose) of 6–10 flowers are located in the leaf axils on 0.5–1.5 cm long peduncles. **Flowers are purple-black** with a 5-lobed corolla. The **lobes are fleshy**, triangular, 1.5–3 mm long, with tiny (0.1–0.2 mm) hairs on the upper surface and a fleshy inconspicuous 5-lobed disk in the center (corona). The **fruit** grow in pairs. Each fruit is a smooth, **slender, elliptic, dark brown pod, 4–7 cm long. Seeds** are brown, flattened, 5–7 mm long, egg-shaped, with a wing margin and a **tuft of silky hairs** at one end, resembling common milkweed.

POSTSENESCENCE CHARACTERISTICS: Twining vine-like stems persist after death, bearing the papery pods. Pods are gray on the outside and yellow on the inside. Some seeds may remain inside.

HABITAT: Although primarily a wood land species, black swallowwort has become an invasive weed in recently cleared areas, conservation habitats, Christmas tree plantations, nursery crops, and other perennial crops such as alfalfa. It also grows in fields, pastures, and waste places and along fence rows, often in sunny areas and calcareous soils.

DISTRIBUTION: Found in the northeastern United States and Canada.

SIMILAR SPECIES: **White swallowwort (*Cynanchum vincetoxicum* (L.) Pers., CYKVI)** is very similar but is distinguished by the corolla lobes, which are greenish to yellowish white, or maroon to pinkish, lanceolate (2.5–4.5 mm long), and hairless.

J. Neal

Black swallowwort habit

R. Uva

Black swallowwort fruit

R. Uva

Black swallowwort flowers

J. DiTomaso

Left, white swallowwort seeds, 6.5 mm;
right, black swallowwort seeds, 6.0 mm

Common yarrow (*Achillea millefolium* L.) [ACHMI]

Synonyms: yarrow, milfoil, thousand-leaf, bloodwort

GENERAL DESCRIPTION: **Rhizomatous perennial** with pungent foliage, **finely cut leaves**, and heads of white flowers aggregated into flat-topped clusters at the ends of the stems. Although it can grow to 1 m in height, in mowed turf it forms dense patches.

PROPAGATION / PHENOLOGY: Reproduction is **by seeds and rhizomes**. Germination occurs in late April or early May. **Most infestations are due to creeping rhizomes,** which may be introduced with soil or plant material.

SEEDLING: Cotyledons are egg-shaped to oblong and approximately 3.5 mm long by 2 mm wide. **Seedlings initially form a basal rosette. Young leaves are finely dissected** (mostly twice) with sharply pointed lateral lobes or teeth. Surfaces have whitish appressed hairs and are aromatic when the foliage is crushed.

MATURE PLANT: Stems are mostly unbranched (sometimes forking above), with fine white hairs or nearly smooth surfaces. Plants usually grow together in clusters from a common rhizome. **Leaves are lanceolate and finely divided** (2–4 times pinnate), 3–15 cm long by 2.5 cm wide, with soft short hairs. Lower and basal leaves have petioles. Upper leaves are alternate and sessile, generally shorter than leaves on the lower stem.

ROOTS AND UNDERGROUND STRUCTURES: A **deep and extensive system of rhizomes** with fibrous roots enables common yarrow to survive long periods without water.

FLOWERS AND FRUIT: Flowers are produced beginning in June and extending throughout the summer. **Numerous white to sometimes pinkish composite flower heads are in flat-topped or occasionally rounded clusters** (compound corymbose) at the end of branches. Individual flower heads are 3–5 mm in diameter and are composed of 5, 3-toothed, mostly white or sometimes pinkish ray flowers (2–4 mm long) and 10–30 whitish cream to yellowish central disk flowers. Seeds are enclosed within the 1.5–3 mm long fruit (achene). Achenes are oblong and compressed, with fine longitudinal ribs and a winged margin.

POSTSENESCENCE CHARACTERISTICS: In the autumn and winter, the dead stems persist, bearing the flat-topped, much-branched flower clusters. Vegetative portions of the plant remain green through the winter.

HABITAT: Common yarrow is a weed of turfgrass, landscapes, nursery crops, and other perennial crops. It tolerates many soil types but is usually found on poor, dry, sandy soils, often where other plants grow poorly. It is also found in lawns, roadsides, and disturbed areas but is not common in cultivated fields.

DISTRIBUTION: Distributed throughout North America; common in the eastern states.

SIMILAR SPECIES: **Mayweed chamomile, corn chamomile, pineapple-weed**, and **wild carrot** have dissected leaves that may resemble those of common yarrow, but they are not as finely dissected as mature common yarrow leaves. In addition, those species do not have rhizomatous root systems. The youngest seedling leaves and cotyledons of common yarrow are relatively thick and can resemble **common groundsel**, but common groundsel is not as finely dissected. Some species and cultivars of *Achillea* are used as ornamentals.

Common
yarrow habit

J. Neal

Common yarrow
habit in turf

J. Neal

J. Neal

Common yarrow flowers

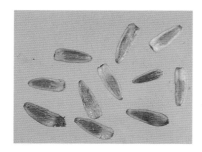

J. DiTomaso

Common yarrow seeds, 2.4 mm

Common ragweed (*Ambrosia artemisiifolia* L.) [AMBEL]

Synonyms: *Ambrosia elatior, Ambrosia media,* wild tansy, hog-weed, bitterweed, mayweed, hay-fever weed, blackweed, Roman wormweed, annual ragweed

GENERAL DESCRIPTION: An **erect, branching, summer annual** (30 cm to 2 m in height). Pollen from common ragweed is a primary cause of **hay fever**.

PROPAGATION / PHENOLOGY: Reproduction is **by seed**. Common ragweed emerges relatively early in the spring compared with other summer annual broadleaf weeds. Most germination occurs from May through June or when the soil is 10–27°C (50–80°F). High soil temperatures (30°C [86°F] and above) inhibit germination.

SEEDLING: Hypocotyls are spotted or entirely purple. **Cotyledons** are thick, **dark green, rounded above and narrowed to the base** (spatulate), 6–10 mm long, sometimes with purple spots along the margin. **Youngest leaves are opposite, becoming alternate** by the fourth node. The blades are hairy on the upper surface and margin and densely hairy on the underside. **Leaves are deeply cleft** on the margins, forming **rounded or slightly pointed lobes**.

MATURE PLANT: Stems are erect, branched, and have long (3 mm) rough hairs. **Leaves** are hairy to nearly smooth. **Blades** (4–10 cm long) are narrowly to broadly egg-shaped in outline and **once or generally twice compound (pinnatifid)**. Most of the **leaves are alternate; sometimes the lower leaves are opposite**. Petioles are conspicuous on lower leaves but sometimes inconspicuous on the upper leaves.

ROOTS AND UNDERGROUND STRUCTURES: Shallow fibrous root system.

FLOWERS AND FRUIT: Flowers are typically present from late summer to autumn (August–October). **Flowers produce large amounts of wind-dispersed pollen. Flower heads are small** (2–3 mm long), **green, and inconspicuous** in clusters on terminal branches. Male and female flowers are in separate heads (monoecious). The male flowers are in racemes at the top of the plant, and the female flowers are in the axils of the upper leaves and branches. A single seed is enclosed within each fruit (3–4 mm long). The fruit have several longitudinal ridges ending in short spines (resembling a crown) and can survive for up to 80 years in field soil.

POSTSENESCENCE CHARACTERISTICS: Stems persist throughout the winter with remnants of the inflorescence and finely dissected leaves still attached. Plant has a reddish to purplish coloration.

HABITAT: Common ragweed is a weed of most cultivated crops, landscapes, orchards, nurseries, roadsides, waste areas, and meadows. It grows in clay or sandy soil but prefers heavy moist soils. It does not tolerate frequent mowing and thus is rarely found in well-maintained turfgrass.

DISTRIBUTION: Found throughout North America; most common in the eastern and north-central states.

SIMILAR SPECIES: **Giant ragweed** is also a summer annual, but it is larger than common ragweed, growing to 2 m in height or occasionally taller. The leaves (20 cm long) have serrate margins and are palmately divided into 3 (sometimes 5) lobes.

Common ragweed habit

J. Neal

Mature common ragweed

L. Clark

J. DiTomaso

Common ragweed seedlings

J. DiTomaso

Common ragweed seeds, 4 mm

Giant ragweed (*Ambrosia trifida* L.) [AMBTR]

Synonyms: great ragweed, kinghead, crown-weed, wild hemp, horse-weed, bitterweed, tall ambrosia

GENERAL DESCRIPTION: An **erect summer annual** 1.5 m tall, but in fertile, moist soils can reach 4–6 m in height. Stems are unbranched to frequently branched and have **large distinctive 3-lobed (occasionally 5-lobed) leaves**. Pollen from giant ragweed can cause **hay fever**.

PROPAGATION / PHENOLOGY: Reproduction is **by seed**, with seedlings emerging mid to late spring. Seeds mature in mid-August.

SEEDLING: Cotyledons are round to oblong and thick, 1–1.5 cm wide by 2–4 cm long (3–4 times larger than common ragweed). **Young leaves are opposite** and have rough hairs. The **first pair of leaves is unlobed**, ovate to lanceolate, with large teeth to small lobes on the margin. **Subsequent leaves usually have 3 large lobes.**

MATURE PLANT: **Stems and leaves are rough and hairy.** Leaves are opposite (10–20 cm wide, 15 cm long) and **palmately lobed** (3-lobed, sometimes 5-lobed or simple). Lobes are ovate to lanceolate, and the margins are toothed. **Petioles are winged** on the margins. **Lower leaves are more deeply lobed; upper leaves** (subtending the inflorescence) **are often simple**.

ROOTS AND UNDERGROUND STRUCTURES: Roots are primarily fibrous, but a short taproot is also present.

FLOWERS AND FRUIT: Flowers are present from July through September. **Individual flowers are small, greenish, and inconspicuous.** Male flowers are in long (to 30 cm), narrow racemes at the ends of branches; female flowers are clustered at the base of the racemes and in the axils of the upper leaves. A single seed is enclosed within the large (6–12 mm long) fruit (achene). The brown or gray **achene is crown-shaped** with a long, pointed central beak surrounded by 5 shorter points.

POSTSENESCENCE CHARACTERISTICS: Erect woody stems persist well into winter. Persistent crown-shaped woody fruit indicate the presence of this species.

HABITAT: Giant ragweed is a weed of cultivated agronomic and horticultural crops. It is most commonly found in cultivated alluvial, fertile soils, as well as in drainage ditches, roadsides, and other disturbed sites.

DISTRIBUTION: Giant ragweed is less common than common ragweed. Nevertheless, it is found throughout much of the United States, particularly in the mid-Atlantic states, and the Ohio and Mississippi River valleys. It is not generally found in northern Maine, southern Florida, or on the West Coast.

SIMILAR SPECIES: Giant ragweed can be distinguished by the distinctive 3-lobed leaves. When a large number of leaves are unlobed, giant ragweed can appear similar to **common cocklebur** and **common sunflower**. However, the leaves of sunflowers and cocklebur are mostly alternate, whereas those of giant ragweed are opposite. The flowering heads and fruit of **common ragweed** are similar but smaller than those of giant ragweed. The leaves of common ragweed are usually twice divided and not 3–5 times lobed.

Giant ragweed
habit

J. Derr

W. Curran

Giant ragweed inflorescence

J. Neal

Giant ragweed flowering plant

J. DiTomaso

Giant ragweed seed, 10.5 mm

111

Mayweed chamomile (*Anthemis cotula* L.) [ANTCO]

Synonyms: dogfennel, stink-weed, dogs chamomile, dill-weed, stinking daisy, hogs fennel, fetid chamomile

GENERAL DESCRIPTION: A decumbent to erect freely branching **winter or summer annual** growing in large clumps from 10 to 60 cm tall. It has **finely divided foliage** that produces a **strong unpleasant odor** when crushed. The sap of this plant can cause **dermatitis** in humans.

PROPAGATION / PHENOLOGY: Reproduction is **by seed**. Germination is in late summer, early autumn, or early spring.

SEEDLING: The hypocotyl is green to maroon. Cotyledons are about 7–8 mm long, united at the base to form a transverse ridge across the shoot axis. Cotyledons do not have obvious petioles, and veins are not visible on the smooth surface. **The first true leaves are opposite**; the **subsequent leaves are alternate** but may be closely spaced, producing a **basal rosette. Blades** of the first leaves are **finely dissected** and thick. Leaf surfaces have short, somewhat glandular, hairs.

MATURE PLANT: **Elongating stems are highly branched**, erect to decumbent, and nearly smooth. Leaves are yellowish green, 1.5–6 cm long by 0.5–3 cm wide, alternate, and lack a petiole. **Leaves** are slightly pubescent and **finely 2–3 times pinnately divided**.

ROOTS AND UNDERGROUND STRUCTURES: Short thick **taproot** with secondary fibrous root system.

FLOWERS AND FRUIT: **Flower heads are white with yellow centers** and produced in terminal solitary heads on the ends of branches from June to October. Heads are 1.2–2.6 cm in diameter, on short flower-stalks. Bracts (phyllaries) taper to the apex. Flowers are of 2 types: **ray florets are white, 3-toothed**, 10–20 per head, each 1 cm long; **disk flowers are yellow** and numerous, **forming a cone in the center** of the flower head. The seed is enclosed within the fruit (achene), which is 1.2–1.8 mm long, rough with rounded bumps, light brown, roundish to nearly quadrangular with about 10 ribs. Achenes lack a pappus.

POSTSENESCENCE CHARACTERISTICS: Stems and remnants of leaves and flower heads can persist into the winter.

HABITAT: A weed of landscapes and nursery and agricultural crops, mayweed chamomile is generally found on rich, gravelly soil. It also grows in roadsides and meadows.

DISTRIBUTION: Widespread throughout North America.

SIMILAR SPECIES: **See Table 10 for a comparison with other finely dissected weeds in the aster family. Corn chamomile (*Anthemis arvensis* L., ANTAR)** is very similar to mayweed chamomile but **lacks the offensive odor** and acrid properties. **Pineapple-weed** is a summer or winter annual with similar foliage but emits the pleasant odor of pineapple when crushed. In addition, the flower head is composed of only greenish yellow disk flowers.

Mayweed chamomile flowers

Corn chamomile seedling

Corn chamomile basal rosette

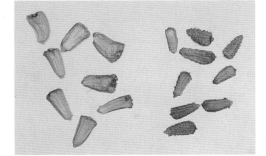

Left, corn chamomile seeds, 1.8 mm; *right*,
mayweed chamomile seeds, 1.6 mm (largest)

113

Common burdock (*Arctium minus* (Hill) Bernh.) [ARFMI]

Synonyms: *Lappa minor*, smaller burdock, clotbur, cockoo-button, cockle-button, lesser burdock

GENERAL DESCRIPTION: A **biennial**, producing a **large-leaved rosette in the first year** and **a tall (1.5 m) erect, much-branched stem in the second year**. Plants produce **spiny persistent burs**, from which the common name is derived.

PROPAGATION / PHENOLOGY: Reproduction is **by seed**.

SEEDLING: Cotyledons are obovate, with a waxy surface, about 2.5 cm long, on short stalks. **Young leaves are egg-shaped, truncated across the base**, coarse-veined, and downy on the undersurface. **Petioles** are flared and clasping at base to **form a tubular sheath**.

MATURE PLANT: Common burdock is a large **basal rosette the first year**, and a much-branched **erect plant the second year**. Stems are hollow, hairy, and grooved or angular. **Leaves are large** (50 cm by 40 cm), alternate, narrowly to broadly egg-shaped. The larger **basal leaves are heart-shaped** and broadest at the base, with toothed or wavy margins and hollow petioles. The **undersurface is light green and woolly**; the upper surface is darker green and smoother.

ROOTS AND UNDERGROUND STRUCTURES: **Large thick fleshy taproot**, as deep as 30 cm below the soil surface.

FLOWERS AND FRUIT: Flowers occur from July to October. Flower heads are 1.5–3 cm in diameter and develop from the leaf axils or raceme-like clusters at the end of branches. Bracts (phyllaries) are often covered with short cobweb-like hairs and are shorter than the **purple flowers**. The **outer bracts terminate in Velcro-like hooks** and are successively shorter from the flowers outward. The inner bracts are without hooks. All flowers are of the disk type. The seed is enclosed within the fruit (achene). Achenes are 4–7 mm long with a pappus of short chaffy bristles. The flower head dries to a **bur**, and the **hooked bracts** attach to animal fur or clothing to disperse the entire head.

POSTSENESCENCE CHARACTERISTICS: Dead erect stems are easily distinguished by the dictinctive branching pattern and the persistent hooked burs, which remain on the stems through the winter and into the following spring.

HABITAT: Common burdock is a weed of landscapes, and nursery and agricultural crops. It is also found on rich soil along fence rows and in roadsides, uncultivated areas, and waste areas.

DISTRIBUTION: Occurs throughout most of the United States.

SIMILAR SPECIES: The **flower head may resemble some thistles**, but thistles do not have the large leaves and hooked bracts of burdock. Young seedlings may superficially resemble **broadleaf dock** or **curly dock**, but the docks lack the downy coating on the undersurface of the leaves.

J. Neal

Common burdock habit

J. DiTomaso

Common burdock seedling

R. Uva

Common burdock mature foliage

J. Neal

Common burdock flower and hooks

J. DiTomaso

Common burdock seeds, 6 mm

Mugwort (*Artemisia vulgaris* L.) [ARTVU]

Synonyms: chrysanthemum weed, wormwood, felon herb

GENERAL DESCRIPTION: A **clump-forming rhizomatous perennial** with erect flowering stems (50 cm to 1.5 m tall). Tolerates mowing to 3.5 cm. **Foliage is aromatic.**

PROPAGATION / PHENOLOGY: Reproduction is usually vegetative **by rhizomes, rarely by seeds.** Rhizome fragments can be transported by cultivation or with infested balled and burlaped nursery stock, topsoil, or composted organic matter.

SEEDLING: **Seedlings are rarely encountered** because few viable seeds are produced in temperate North America. Cotyledons are egg-shaped (5 mm long) and lack petioles. Young leaves are opposite, bristly-hairy, with white, woolly hairs beneath. Leaves are egg-shaped to rounded, on long petioles. **Initial leaves are generally undivided with inconspicuous teeth,** whereas **older leaves are deeply lobed** and pointed.

MATURE PLANT: Unmowed stems are erect and branched in the upper ⅓ (flowering portion) and become woody with age. Stems are often red, brown, or purplish, almost hairless, and ridged or angular, but round in cross section. **Leaves** are simple, **alternate,** 5–10 cm long by 3–7 cm wide, with **large pinnatifid lobes.** Surfaces are green and smooth to slightly hairy above; the undersides are covered with white to gray woolly hairs. **Leaves emerging from rhizomes have shallower and broader lobes. Leaves on the mid and upper portion** of the plant have lobes that are **more linear** and more deeply pinnatifid than the lower leaves, and may lack petioles.

ROOTS AND UNDERGROUND STRUCTURES: Plants spread by **long stout rhizomes.**

FLOWERS AND FRUIT: **Flowers** are produced July to October in **inconspicuous composite heads** in leafy spike-like **clusters at the terminal ¼–⅓ of the stems.** Individual heads are **numerous,** 2.5–3 mm wide, on short flower-stalks. Flowers are greenish yellow and of the disk type. The seed is enclosed within the fruit (achene). Achenes are ridged, brown, oblong with a narrow base (1–2 mm long), and have minute bristles at the apex. Viable seeds are rarely produced, except in greenhouses.

POSTSENESCENCE CHARACTERISTICS: Dead, brown, woody stems persist well into winter, but seedheads will persist for only a short time.

HABITAT: A weed of turfgrass, nurseries, and landscapes. It is rarely encountered in field, grain, or vegetable crops but grows in waste places and roadsides. Its **persistent rhizomes make mugwort difficult to control in perennial crops.** It is also well adapted to mowing and cultivation and is relatively tolerant of most herbicides.

DISTRIBUTION: Found throughout the eastern United States. Most infestations have resulted from vegetative introduction in nursery stock, topsoil, or farm equipment.

SIMILAR SPECIES: The leaf shape and aroma of mugwort often lead to confusion with **garden chrysanthemums.** Mugwort can be distinguished by its leaves, which are white-woolly on the underside; garden chrysanthemum leaves may be only somewhat hairy. Young mugwort plants, 5–20 cm tall are easily confused with **common ragweed,** but leaf blades of common ragweed are more deeply dissected. Late autumn mugwort seedheads resemble the dense inflorescence of **horseweed,** but the species can easily be separated by differences in leaf shape.

Mugwort habit

J. Neal

Mugwort sprouts from rhizomes

J. Neal

Mugwort
Regina O. Hughes, USDA

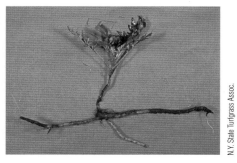

Mugwort rhizome

N.Y. State Turfgrass Assoc.

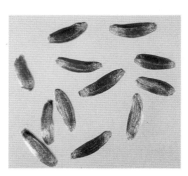

Mugwort seeds, 1.6 mm

J. DiTomaso

White heath aster (*Aster pilosus* Willd.) [ASTPI]

Synonyms: awl-aster, subulate-bracted aster

GENERAL DESCRIPTION: **A semiwoody, clump-forming perennial** with several branching erect stems (to 1.5 m high).

PROPAGATION / PHENOLOGY: Reproduction is **by seed.**

SEEDLING: Hypocotyls are short, green or purple. Cotyledons are green, smooth, lack evident veins, and are egg-shaped (0.5 cm long), with petioles almost as wide as the blade. Young leaves are alternate; both surfaces are smooth, the upper green, the lower grayish green. Margins are hairy throughout. The **first leaf is rounded** and <1 cm long, **subsequent leaves are more lanceolate**. Margins of young leaf blades and petioles are hairy.

MATURE PLANT: **Clumped erect stems are often woody at the base and branched in the upper portions**; they are usually hairy or sometimes smooth. Leaves are hairy. **Basal and lower leaves are lanceolate** to broadest above the middle (oblanceolate). Lower stem leaves and basal leaves **often do not persist** through the growing season. **Leaves on the midstem are linear** to lanceolate, lack distinct petioles, and are about 10 cm long by 1 cm wide, whereas the **uppermost leaves** on the branches near the flowers **are much reduced**, awl-shaped, bract-like, and numerous.

ROOTS AND UNDERGROUND STRUCTURES: White heath aster overwinters as a **woody crown of stems at or just below the soil surface**. Fibrous roots originate at the base of the stems.

FLOWERS AND FRUIT: **Small white flowers** are produced from late summer to autumn in numerous heads arranged **in a broadly branching panicle at the terminal end of stems**. Panicles can account for more than half the total height of the plant. Individual heads are about 1.5 cm in diameter, with **white (rarely pink or purplish) ray flowers** (16–35 per plant) and **yellow disk flowers**. Seeds are enclosed within the fruit (achene), which is 1 mm long, conical, light to dark brown, with bristles at the apex (4–5 mm long).

POSTSENESCENCE CHARACTERISTICS: Erect, leafless stems bearing the dried remains of the flower head and fruit persist through the winter.

HABITAT: White heath aster is a weed of pastures, open fields, roadsides, nursery crops, orchards, and less commonly of low-maintenance turfgrass and reduced-tillage crops. It grows on open sites in rather dry, often sandy soil.

DISTRIBUTION: Found from New England south to northwestern Florida and west to southeastern Minnesota, Nebraska, Kansas, and Louisiana.

SIMILAR SPECIES: **Many other species of asters** are similar in appearance and can also be weedy. **New England aster (*Aster novae-angliae* L., ASTNA)** has reddish purple ray flowers and larger clasping leaves. **Fleabanes (*Erigeron* spp.)** are closely related to the asters, with white (occasionally pinkish) ray flowers and central yellow disk flowers. However, they have more numerous (50+) and narrower ray flowers than the asters. In addition, fleabanes are annuals (occasionally biennials) that bloom in early summer (June) but may be found into September, whereas asters are perennials that bloom from late August through October. **Horseweed** is similar in habit but has much smaller flower heads (5 mm in diameter).

White heath aster habit

White heath aster, early spring growth from perennial crown

White heath aster flowering shoot

New England aster flowers

New England aster leafy shoot

New England aster seeds, 1.7 mm (not including pappus)

119

English daisy (*Bellis perennis* L.) [BELPE]

Synonyms: lawn daisy, European daisy

GENERAL DESCRIPTION: A **prostrate** spreading herbaceous **perennial** that **forms mats** of **basal rosettes** and **attractive daisy-like white flowers** on short scapes (5–15 cm long). Although English daisy was imported as a cultivated ornamental, it has since become a common weed of low-maintenance lawns.

PROPAGATION / PHENOLOGY: Plants spread from **wind-blown seeds** and vegetatively by **short, thick rhizomes.**

SEEDLING: Cotyledons are round and almost sessile. **Young basal leaves** are rounded to **ovate, narrowing to the petiole**, with short hairs.

MATURE PLANT: **Stems do not elongate.** The only stem-like structures present are the leafless flower-bearing scapes. Foliage may be nearly smooth to hairy. Elliptic, oval, or round **leaf blades** are 1–6 cm long by 0.4–2.5 cm wide and **abruptly narrow to the petiole.** Margins are usually **short-toothed** but may be entire.

ROOTS AND UNDERGROUND STRUCTURES: Fibrous roots are associated with **short rhizomes.** The root system is coarse and shallow.

FLOWERS AND FRUIT: Flowers are produced from early spring to mid-June and sometimes to November. **Flower heads are daisy-like** (2–3 cm in diameter), with **white or pinkish petals** (ray flowers) **and yellow central disk flowers. Solitary flower heads are on leafless stalks** (scapes) arising from the basal rosette. The seed is enclosed within a 1–2 mm long oblong achene, which is yellow-brown and marked with fine parallel lines.

POSTSENESCENCE CHARACTERISTICS: Plant is a perennial. Foliage persists well into winter but may decay by spring. New leaves emerge early in the spring.

HABITAT: English daisy is a weed of meadows, pastures, and low-maintenance turfgrass. It is usually found on heavy, moist, fertile soil.

DISTRIBUTION: Found throughout the northern United States and the Pacific Coast states.

SIMILAR SPECIES: **Rosettes resemble many asters**, but unlike aster, English daisy remains as a basal rosette. Habit and leaf shape are similar to **cudweeds**; however, English daisy leaves lack the whitish underside typical of cudweeds.

English daisy in turf

English daisy habit

English daisy rhizomes and roots

English daisy seeds, 1.2 mm

121

Devils beggarticks (*Bidens frondosa* L.) [BIDFR]

Synonyms: beggar ticks, stick-tights, devil's boot jack, bur-marigold, pitchfork-weed, tickseed sunflower

GENERAL DESCRIPTION: **Summer annual** with **erect** stems 20 cm to 1.5 m in height. Stem branches spread toward the top. Plants produce **dark brown, prickly fruit** that stick to skin, clothing, and animal fur, from which the common name is in part derived.

PROPAGATION / PHENOLOGY: Reproduction is **by seed**. Seeds germinate over an extended period of time, from midspring through late summer.

SEEDLING: **Cotyledons** (9–25 mm long by 3–5.5 mm wide) are **petiolated, spatulate-oblong** to ovate, smooth, and have prominent midveins. **Young leaves are opposite**, thin, deep green above, paler beneath, with **3 leaflets**, the central one larger than the other two; **margins are wavy** with irregular teeth and a few fine soft hairs.

MATURE PLANT: **Stems are smooth** to slightly hairy, somewhat 4-sided. **Leaves are opposite and compound**, with **3–5 leaflets** that are sparsely covered with short hairs. Petioles are 1–6 cm long. **Leaflets are lanceolate with toothed margins** (serrate); the terminal leaflets (and sometimes the others) are on slender stalks.

ROOTS AND UNDERGROUND STRUCTURES: Shallow much-branched **taproot** with a secondary fibrous root system.

FLOWERS AND FRUIT: Flowers (2.5 cm wide) are produced in heads from July to October. **Flowering heads are surrounded by 5–10 green bracts** (phyllaries), **which are longer than the orange-yellow ray flowers** (petals). Disk flowers in the center of the flower are brownish yellow. **Some heads may have only disk flowers.** The seed is enclosed within the fruit (achene), which is 6–12 mm long, dark brown to black, flat, and wedge-shaped. **Achenes have 2 barbed spines** that aid in dispersal on animal fur and clothing.

POSTSENESCENCE CHARACTERISTICS: Erect, smooth stems persist into early winter. Some seed will remain attached to the stems.

HABITAT: Devils beggarticks is primarily a weed of landscapes and nurseries but also grows in roadsides, pastures, and waste areas. It usually grows on moist to wet soil but is not limited to those areas.

DISTRIBUTION: Found throughout the United States and southern Canada but most common in the eastern and north-central states.

SIMILAR SPECIES: **Spanishneedles (*Bidens bipinnata* L., BIDBI) is similar but has leaves 2–3 times pinnately dissected. Nodding beggarticks (*Bidens cernua* L., BIDCE)** has simple and sessile leaves, nodding flowering heads, and ray flowers (petals) either absent or 1.5 cm long.

Devils beggarticks habit

Devils beggarticks stem and flowers

Mature devils beggarticks

Juvenile devils beggarticks

Nodding beggarticks habit

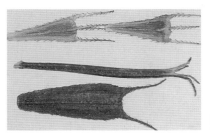

Top to bottom: nodding beggarticks seeds, 8.5 mm (to end of tip); spanish-needles seed, 13.5 mm (to end of tip); and devils beggarticks seed, 11.5 mm (to end of tip)

123

Musk thistle (*Carduus nutans* L.) [CRUNU]

Synonyms: plumeless thistle, nodding thistle

GENERAL DESCRIPTION: a **biennial** or occasionally a winter annual with erect stems (to 1.5 m in height) branching near the top of the plant. **Both leaves and stems are spiny**, the stems with spiny wings.

PROPAGATION / PHENOLOGY: Reproduction is **by seed**. After rosettes form, a period of cold temperature is required before they elongate.

SEEDLING: Seedlings develop into a **basal rosette**. Cotyledons are nearly sessile, oblong (7.5–15 mm long by 2.5–6 mm wide). Cotyledon veins are white and broad, and the tips of the blades are often square. The first 2 true leaves appear to be opposite; subsequent leaves are alternate but **form a rosette**. Leaves are oval to elliptic; a few hairs may be present on the upper surface and on the main veins beneath. Leaves are waxy and pale green. **Leaf margins** are **shallowly lobed** and are **irregularly prickly-toothed**.

MATURE PLANT: **Basal rosettes elongate in the second season. Stems are erect**, and leaves are alternate. **Leaves are deeply pinnately lobed** (25 cm long by 10 cm wide), elliptic to lanceolate, and **the margins are spine-tipped**. Long hairs are only along the main veins. **Leaf bases extend down the stem, creating spiny wings.** Leaves become gradually smaller up the stem.

ROOTS AND UNDERGROUND STRUCTURES: A **long thick fleshy taproot**, sometimes branched, can penetrate to 40 cm or more below the soil surface.

FLOWERS AND FRUIT: Flowering occurs from June through October. Flower heads often nod and are produced singly at the end of the branches. **Heads are 3–5 cm wide, with pink to purple or rarely white disk flowers.** The head consists of **many spine-tipped bracts** (phyllaries), the middle and outer bracts are wide (2–8 mm), long (9–27 mm), and flat. The seed is enclosed within the fruit, which is a 3.5–4 mm long achene. **Achenes** are oblong, straw-colored to brown at maturity, with a **hair-like white pappus** that aids in wind dispersal.

POSTSENESCENCE CHARACTERISTICS: Aboveground portions die with a hard frost. Plants remain intact for an extended period during the winter. They are easily distinguished by the persistent spiny nature.

HABITAT: Musk thistle is a weed of nursery crops, pastures, waste areas, roadsides, and ditch banks. It is often found on dry or gravelly soils.

DISTRIBUTION: Widely established throughout the United States and Canada.

SIMILAR SPECIES: **Bull thistle** has rough hairs on the upper surface of the leaf blade and thick whitish softer hairs below, whereas musk thistle leaves mostly lack hairs. In addition, the flower heads of bull thistle are constricted at the junction between the bracts and the flowers. Musk thistle, in contrast, in not constricted. On the upper surface of bull thistle seedlings, hairs are dense, white, and stiff, with projecting bases. Musk thistle seedlings also have hairs, but they are not on projecting bases. Although spiny, **Canada thistle** is smaller, is a rhizomatous perennial, and its leaves are not as deeply lobed.

R. Hahn

Musk thistle habit

R. Hahn

Musk thistle flower

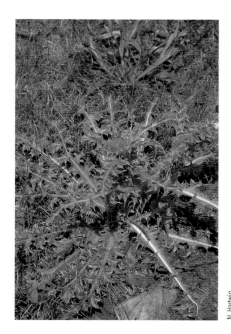

N. Hartwig

Musk thistle bolting rosette

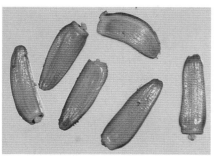

J. DiTomaso

Musk thistle seeds, 4 mm

Spotted knapweed (*Centaurea maculosa* Lam.) [CENMA]

Synonyms: *Centaurea stoebe*, star thistle

GENERAL DESCRIPTION: A **biennial or short-lived perennial** forming a basal rosette in the first year and growing to 1.5 m in height the following year.

PROPAGATION / PHENOLOGY: Reproduction is **by seed**.

SEEDLING: Cotyledons are about 25 mm long, narrow at the base, and rounded at the tip. **First leaves** are **rounded at the tip** and **taper to a short petiole. Subsequent leaves** become more slender and **lanceolate**, have **downy hairs**, and form a **basal rosette.**

MATURE PLANT: **In the first year, leaves are deeply lobed** (15 cm long) **and in a basal rosette. Stems elongate in the second year. Stems are erect** or ascending, **slender and wiry,** with several branches. **Stem surfaces are rough to slightly woolly-hairy. Leaves are gray-green,** alternate and **pinnately dissected** with many lobes. Surfaces may be rough with minute hairs; leaf margins have rough bristles. **Leaves near the flowers are smaller, narrow, and less lobed to unlobed.**

ROOTS AND UNDERGROUND STRUCTURES: **Stout taproot.**

FLOWERS AND FRUIT: Flowering occurs in mid to late summer. **Flower heads** (up to 200 per plant) are **solitary at the ends of main and axillary branches** and are 9–15 mm long by 8–15 mm wide. All **flowers are the disk type.** The marginal flowers are enlarged and **pink to purple (rarely white).** Bracts (phyllaries) are 10–13 mm long, with brown margins, **fringed black tips,** and a whitish fringe on each side. The seed is enclosed in the fruit (achene). Achenes are olive green to blackish brown, 2.5–4 mm long by 1.1–1.5 mm wide, and notched on one side of the base. Apex of the **achene** has a **short bristly pappus** that aids in dispersal by animal fur, wool, hairs, or feathers.

POSTSENESCENCE CHARACTERISTICS: Dead stems and heads persist over the winter. Dried bracts of flower heads form a cup, often containing a few fruit.

HABITAT: Spotted knapweed is an increasingly important weed of rangeland and pastures, generally on low-fertility, dry soils. It is also weed of low-maintenance turfgrass, roadsides, and, less commonly, landscapes, nurseries, and agricultural crops.

DISTRIBUTION: Spotted knapweed continues to spread and is now found throughout the northeastern and north-central states but is most common in the Rocky Mountain states and the Pacific Northwest.

SIMILAR SPECIES: **Cornflower or bachelor's buttons (*Centaurea cyanus* L., CENCY)** is a summer or winter annual. Its leaves are usually entire, sometimes toothed, but rarely lobed; when lobes are present, only the larger leaves are lobed.

Spotted knapweed habit

Spotted knapweed foliage and stem

Spotted knapweed rosette

Spotted knapweed flower

Left, cornflower seeds, 4.0 mm (not including pappus); *right*, spotted knapweed seeds, 3.7 mm (not including pappus)

127

Oxeye daisy (*Chrysanthemum leucanthemum* L.) [CHYLE]

Synonyms: *Leucanthemum leucanthemum, Leucanthemum vulgare*, white daisy, whiteweed, field daisy, marguerite, poorland flower

General Description: A **rhizomatous clump-forming perennial**. Erect stems (30–90 cm in height) emerge from a rosette of leaves and terminate in **attractive daisy-like flowers. Leaf shape varies with age and location on the plant.**

Propagation / Phenology: Reproduction is **by seeds and rhizomes.**

Seedling: Cotyledons are oval, narrowing into a short petiole. The bases of the petioles are united by a cup-shaped ridge across the axis of the stem. **Young leaves are smooth and mostly hairless** except in the unfolding bud leaves. The first 2 leaves are opposite, untoothed, and spatulate, with prominent petioles. **Subsequent leaves** are alternate but produce a **basal rosette** and have **distinctly rounded wavy lobes or teeth on the margin.**

Mature Plant: **Flowering stems develop from the rosettes. Stems are smooth,** hairless, **mostly unbranched** or only somewhat branched near the top. **All leaves are hairless**, smooth, alternate, and have **teeth or rounded lobes on the margins**. Lower and basal leaves are widest and rounded at the apex and taper to the base. They have shallow to deep rounded teeth or lobes. Petiolated leaves are 4–15 cm long. **Upper leaves are narrower than the basal leaves**, lanceolate, sessile, with less conspicuous rounded teeth than the basal leaves. **Leaves become gradually smaller up the stem.** In turfgrass, rosettes consist of mostly thick, leathery, basal-type leaves.

Roots and Underground Structures: Shallow fibrous roots and **short rhizomes**.

Flowers and Fruit: Flowers are present mainly from June through July and are produced in composite heads 3–5 cm in diameter, arranged singly at the ends of stems. The receptacle is flat and has many bracts (phyllaries) with brown margins. **Individual flowers of the head consist of 20–30 white ray flowers (10–15 mm long) surrounding numerous yellow disk flowers in the center.** The seed is enclosed within the fruit, which is a 1–2 mm long, narrow, **dark brown to black achene**, with white longitudinal ribs.

Postsenescence Characteristics: In late fall plants die back to the crown, although in milder climates some basal leaves may persist through winter.

Habitat: Oxeye daisy is not generally a problem on cultivated soil. It is found in turfgrass and nursery crops, primarily on low-fertility sites, but will tolerate a wide range of soil types. It is also found in meadows, roadsides, and waste areas.

Distribution: Occurs throughout much of the United States.

Similar Species: **English daisy** is also found in turfgrass, often growing in dense mats. It has flower heads similar to those of oxeye daisy, with white to pink marginal ray flowers and yellow central disk flowers. It can be distinguished by its leaves, which have smooth to only slightly toothed margins and usually reach no more than 10 cm in height. Flowers of English daisy are typically produced in early spring, whereas oxeye daisy flowers in June. **Mayweed chamomile and corn chamomile** have similar flowers and growth habit but have finely divided foliage.

Oxeye daisy habit

J. Neal

Oxeye daisy leaf shapes, *left to right:* basal to upper stem

J. Neal

J. Neal

Oxeye daisy rosette

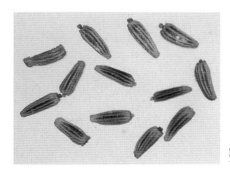

J. DiTomaso

Oxeye daisy seeds, 2 mm

129

Chicory (*Cichorium intybus* L.) [CICIN]

Synonyms: succory, blue sailors, blue daisy, coffee-weed, bunk

GENERAL DESCRIPTION: A **perennial** from a **basal rosette**. It has **dandelion-like leaves** but produces sparsely leaved, wiry, branching stems (30 cm to 1.7 m tall). Stems and leaves exude a **milky sap** when cut. The plant is sometimes grown as a vegetable crop, and the root has long been used as a substitute for coffee. Chicory occasionally causes **allergenic dermatitis** in humans.

PROPAGATION / PHENOLOGY: Reproduction is **by seed**.

SEEDLING: Cotyledons are oblong to egg-shaped, widest above the middle, with the apex abruptly indented and the base tapering into the petiole. **Young leaves are oblong** to egg-shaped, also **widest above the middle; margins are wavy or toothed**, with indentations or teeth widely spaced.

MATURE PLANT: Early in the season, chicory forms a **basal rosette very similar to that of dandelion**. The basal leaves may be absent later in the season during flowering. **Flowering stems are erect, round, hollow**, and smooth or with a few bristly hairs. Stems are usually much-branched near the top of the plant but are branched from the base in mowed areas. **Leaves are lanceolate, alternate**, and rough on the upper surface and on the lower surface of the lower leaves. **Leaf margins are coarsely toothed or pinnatifid.** Basal leaves, 8–25 cm long by 1–7 cm wide, are widest above the middle and strongly resemble the leaves of dandelion. The upper leaves are smaller, lanceolate, 3–7 cm long, with clasping leaf bases. Margins may be entire or have small irregular teeth.

ROOTS AND UNDERGROUND STRUCTURES: Dark brown, long, large, fleshy taproot.

FLOWERS AND FRUIT: **Bright blue (occasionally pink, purple, or white) flowers** are produced from late June into October and open primarily in the morning. Flower heads (4 cm in diameter) are produced in clusters of 1–3 on the upper flowering stems (racemes), either sessile or short-stalked in the axils of the much-reduced leaves. The bracts of the head (phyllaries) are in 2 series: an inner one of 8–10 longer bracts and an outer one of 5 shorter bracts. All flowers are ligulate (ray). The seed is enclosed in the fruit (achene), which is 2–3 mm long, wedge-shaped, widest at the apex, tapering to the base, and 4- or 5-angled, with a truncated apex. Minute bristle-like scaly pappus is present on the fruit.

POSTSENESCENCE CHARACTERISTICS: Dead stems persist through winter as branching, brown stalks bearing the remains of the flower heads. The bracts of the flower heads remain attached to the stem and occasionally contain achenes.

HABITAT: A weed of low-maintenance turfgrass, roadsides, meadows, pastures, and other uncultivated agricultural crops. It is most troublesome on calcareous soils but tolerates a wide range of conditions. It does not tolerate cultivation.

DISTRIBUTION: Found throughout the United States; most common in the northern and western states.

SIMILAR SPECIES: Chicory rosettes **strongly resemble dandelion**. But the toothed lobes of dandelion leaves are generally opposite each other and point back toward the rosette, whereas those of chicory are not always opposite and may point forward, perpendicular, or backward. Also, the basal leaves of chicory are rougher to the touch and have more-prominent coarse hairs. Mature dandelions are easily distinguished by the yellow flowers and leafless flower-stalks.

Chicory habit

J. Neal

R. Uva

Chicory rosette

R. Uva

Chicory seedlings

J. DiTomaso

Chicory flower

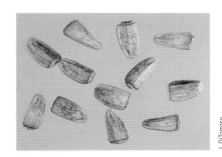

J. DiTomaso

Chicory seeds, 2.2 mm (largest)

131

Canada thistle (*Cirsium arvense* (L.) Scop.) [CIRAR]

Synonyms: *Carduus arvensis*, creeping thistle, small-flowered thistle, perennial thistle, green thistle

GENERAL DESCRIPTION: A spreading **rhizomatous perennial** (30 cm to 1.2 m in height). Leaves are conspicuously lobed with **spiny** margins.

PROPAGATION / PHENOLOGY: Reproduction is by **wind-blown seed and creeping rhizomes**. Rhizomes allow Canada thistle to form large colonies from a single plant. Seed germination takes place primarily in late spring or early autumn.

SEEDLING: Cotyledons are dull green, relatively thick, rounded-oval to oblong (1 cm long). **Young leaves are thick, egg-shaped** to lanceolate, and covered with **short bristly hairs. Margins are wavy-lobed with sharp spines**; the lobes develop into triangular indentations with age. Shoots emerging from rhizomes lack cotyledons. Newly emerging seedlings develop as a basal rosette but elongate later in the season.

MATURE PLANT: **Stems** are grooved, **erect**, smooth to slightly hairy, and branch at the apex. Upper surface of leaves is dark green and hairless, and lower surface is light green, with or without hairs. **Leaves are alternate, sessile**, oblong to lanceolate, irregularly lobed, with **spiny margins**. The **base of each leaf surrounds the stem**.

ROOTS AND UNDERGROUND STRUCTURES: An **extensive rhizome system** is present. Roots and rhizomes can extend more than a meter below the soil surface.

FLOWERS AND FRUIT: Flowers are present from June through August. Flower heads are numerous, arranged in clusters (corymbs) at the ends of the stems and from the upper leaf axils. Canada thistle is dioecious; fertile male and female flowers are produced on separate plants. The female flowers have a pappus of bristly hairs that is longer than the petals, whereas the pappus of male flowers is shorter than the petals. **Flower heads** (2–2.5 cm in diameter) **are composed of pink to purple, or rarely white disk flowers surrounded by spineless bracts**. The seed is enclosed in the fruit, which is a 2.5–4 mm long, flattened, brownish achene. Achenes are curved or straight, the apex abruptly cut off with a rounded bump in the center. The **pappus** is easily detached from the achene, but when present aids in wind dispersal.

POSTSENESCENCE CHARACTERISTICS: Aboveground portions die with a hard frost. The upright stem turns brown and may persist through the winter with prickly leaves and seedheads still attached.

HABITAT: Canada thistle is a weed of many crops but is most troublesome in perennial crops, rangeland, and areas where reduced tillage is practiced.

DISTRIBUTION: Found throughout the northern half of the United States and southern Canada.

SIMILAR SPECIES: Canada thistle is a rhizomatous perennial, whereas most **other thistle and thistle-like plants** are biennials. In addition, the flower heads of Canada thistle are generally spineless, but most other thistles and thistle-like weeds have spiny bracts (phyllaries). **Bull thistle** is often confused with Canada thistle but can be distinguished by its spiny winged stems and rough hairs on the upper leaf surface. Canada thistle has smooth stems and upper leaf surfaces.

Canada thistle habit

J. Neal

Canada thistle flowering stem

J. Neal

Young Canada thistle shoots from rhizomes

J. Neal

Canada thistle seedheads

J. DiTomaso

Canada thistle seeds (without pappus), 3 mm

Bull thistle (*Cirsium vulgare* (Savi) Tenore) [CIRVU]

Synonyms: *Carduus vulgare, Cirsium lanceolatum,* spear thistle

GENERAL DESCRIPTION: A **biennial** with **prominent spines**. The foliage is covered with coarse to **cobweb-like hairs**. A basal rosette is produced in the first year; erect and branching stems (50 cm to 1.5 m in height) develop in the second year.

PROPAGATION / PHENOLOGY: Reproduction is by wind-dispersed **seed only**.

SEEDLING: **Cotyledons** are 12–15 mm long, **egg-shaped**, and broadest at the apex. **Young leaves are oval** to oblong **with a fringe of spines**. The second true leaf is dull dark green with dense vertical whitish hairs on the upper surface. **Subsequent leaves are longer, more lanceolate, and have spine-tipped lobes. Young plants form a rosette.**

MATURE PLANT: In the spring and early summer, the overwintering rosettes of spiny leaves are present, but **by midsummer of the second year stems elongate. Stems are erect**, often branched, and **winged by the spiny bases of the leaves. Leaves** are alternate and have **stiff spines on the lobes** of the blade with coarse hairs on the upper surface and softer whitish hairs below. Leaves are lanceolate, with deep cuts or toothed margins. **Leaf bases continue** down the stem, **producing the winged-stem** appearance.

ROOTS AND UNDERGROUND STRUCTURES: Fleshy **taproot** formed in the first year, with a secondary fibrous root system.

FLOWERS AND FRUIT: Flowers are present from June to October and are produced in heads usually solitary at the end of branches. Heads are 3–4 cm long and 2–4 cm in diameter with **spine-tipped bracts (phyllaries) and numerous rose to reddish purple (rarely whitish) disk flowers**. The seed is enclosed within the fruit, which is a 3–4 mm long achene with a feathery pappus (20–30 mm long) that facilitates wind dispersal.

POSTSENESCENCE CHARACTERISTICS: Heads with spiny bracts and spiny leaf remnants persist on the dead stem during winter. The basal rosette of leaves in the first year remains green through the winter.

HABITAT: A weed of pastures, turfgrass, landscapes, nurseries, orchards, and reduced-tillage agronomic crops, bull thistle prefers a relatively rich, moist soil and is common in old fields and disturbed waste places.

DISTRIBUTION: Widespread throughout the United States and southern Canada.

SIMILAR SPECIES: **Canada thistle** is a rhizomatous perennial; its leaves are smooth above and smooth or hairy below. Bull thistle leaves are prickly hairy above and woolly below. Canada thistle lacks the basal rosette of leaves and usually occurs in clumps. Senesced bull thistle plants can be confused with **common burdock**, but the bracts of burdock are hooked not spiny-tipped.

Bull thistle habit

Bull thistle seedlings

Bull thistle rosette

Bull thistle flower

Bull thistle seeds, 3.5 mm (not including pappus)

135

Horseweed (*Conyza canadensis* (L.) Cronq.) [ERICA]

Synonyms: *Erigeron canadensis*, *Leption canadense*, marestail, fleabane, colt's-tail

GENERAL DESCRIPTION: A **winter or summer annual**. Seedlings develop into a **basal rosette**. Mature plants produce an **erect central stem** (30 cm to 2 m tall) with a terminal panicle of inconspicuous flowers.

PROPAGATION / PHENOLOGY: Reproduction is **by seed**; seeds germinate in late summer or spring. Late-summer germination results in overwintering rosettes.

SEEDLING: **Cotyledons are oval**, 2–3 mm long. **Young leaves are egg-shaped**, with **toothed margins**. The lower leaves are on prominent petioles; the upper ones are narrower and taper to the stalk. Seedling leaves form a **basal rosette** and are covered with spreading to ascending short hairs.

MATURE PLANT: **Stems** are erect, bristly **hairy**, with many small flowering branches in the upper portions. **Leaves** (10 cm long by 10 mm wide) **are hairy, alternate**, numerous, and **crowded along the stem. Blades are sessile, linear to elliptic**, broadest at the apex and tapering at the base. **Leaf margins** can be entire but are usually **toothed**. When growing as a winter annual, the basal rosette is produced in late summer. **After the stem elongates, the basal leaves deteriorate. Stem leaves** are lanceolate to linear, with **nearly entire margins**. Leaves become gradually smaller up the stem.

ROOTS AND UNDERGROUND STRUCTURES: **Short taproot** with secondary fibrous roots.

FLOWERS AND FRUIT: Flowers are present from July through October. Branches from the main stem produce **dense panicles consisting of numerous small (5 mm in diameter) flower heads.** Heads are subtended by 1–2 series of bracts (phyllaries). Ray flowers (25–50) are white or somewhat pinkish, disk flowers (7–12) are yellow. Seeds are enclosed within a 1 mm long achene. Achenes are broadest at the apex and taper to the base. **Pappus** consists of whitish bristles that facilitate **wind dispersal**.

POSTSENESCENCE CHARACTERISTICS: Plants turn brown before fruit dispersal. Dried, woody stems persist through winter. The main stem often breaks from the weight of the inflorescence. Many seedlings can be found close to the parent plant.

HABITAT: Primarily a weed of nursery crops, orchards, and other perennial crops; also common in waste areas and fallow fields and along fence rows. Less common in cultivated row crops, but reduced-tillage practices tend to increase its occurrence.

DISTRIBUTION: Common throughout North America.

SIMILAR SPECIES: **Annual fleabane (*Erigeron annuus* (L.) Pers., ERIAN)** is a summer annual or rarely a biennial with more prominent toothing on the leaves than horseweed. In addition, the flower heads are larger (about 1.3 cm in diameter), with showy white to rarely pinkish ray flowers. **Rough fleabane (*Erigeron strigosus* Muhl. *ex* Willd., ERIST)** has flowers similar to those of annual fleabane, but the lower leaves are more spatulate than horseweed leaves, and the leaf hairs are shorter and appressed. In the seedling rosette stage, horseweed can be distinguished from **shepherd's-purse** by the absence of branched (star-shaped) hairs characteristic of shepherd's-purse. **Virginia pepperweed seedling rosettes** have a strong odor when crushed, and leaf margins are more prominently toothed or lobed than those of horseweed.

Horseweed habit

Horseweed seedling

Horseweed rosette

Bolting horseweed

Annual fleabane flowers

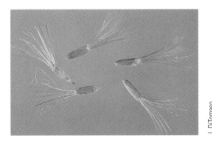

Horseweed seeds, 1.2 mm (not
including pappus)

137

Eclipta (*Eclipta prostrata* L.) [ECLAL]

Synonyms: *Eclipta alba*, yerba-de-tago, false daisy

GENERAL DESCRIPTION: A prostrate, ascending or erect **summer annual**. Plants commonly remain low, produce a mound, or grow to about 60 cm in height. **Stems are thick and succulent**, much branched, and root at the lower nodes. Foliage has stiff hairs appressed to the surface.

PROPAGATION / PHENOLOGY: Propagation is **by seed**; seeds germinate in late spring or early summer when soil temperatures are warm.

SEEDLING: Cotyledons (<1 cm long and 1.5–2 times as long as wide) are smooth, slightly thickened, and oval, tapering to a short petiole. **Young leaves are opposite**; the first 3–4 are hairy at the base of the upper surface and the underside. Subsequent leaves have short appressed hairs on both surfaces. **Leaves of young plants are ovate** to oblong, **becoming lanceolate** or elliptic **with age. Leaves have short teeth on the margins** that point toward the leaf apex. Blades are green; midveins are yellow-green on the upper surface and light green on the lower surface. Petioles are about one-fifth the length of the leaf. Stems branch at the base and become reddish with age.

MATURE PLANT: **Stems are freely branched**, 20–60 cm tall, green to reddish brown or purplish. **Lower nodes of stems often produce roots.** Stiff appressed hairs give leaves and stems a rough feel. **Leaves are sessile** (or with a short petiole), **opposite**, narrow to the base, **lanceolate** or lance-elliptic to lance-linear. **Margins have conspicuous widely spaced teeth.**

ROOTS AND UNDERGROUND STRUCTURES: Fibrous roots are associated with a **shallow taproot** or stem nodes.

FLOWERS AND FRUIT: **Flowers**, produced from August to October, are arranged in **small composite heads**, alone or in clusters of 2–3 on 0.5–4 cm long stalks at the end of stems or in leaf axils. Heads are 1.5–8 mm in diameter and composed of small whitish ray flowers (1–2 mm long) surrounding greenish to dusky white disk flowers. **Heads of ripening fruit are green and button-like.** The seed is enclosed within a 1.8–2.5 mm long **achene** that is 3- to 4-angled, **roughly triangular**, tapered to the base, and truncated at the apex. Some flower heads produce straw-colored seeds with a wrinkled or warty surface; others are dark gray to black, flattened, and smooth.

POSTSENESCENCE CHARACTERISTICS: None of significance.

HABITAT: Eclipta is a weed of cultivated agronomic and horticultural crops as well as irrigation and drainage ditches, banks, and riversides. It is often found in moist to wet places that dry out later in the season.

DISTRIBUTION: Found from New York and Massachusetts south to Florida and west to California; most common in the southern states.

SIMILAR SPECIES: Leaves are simple and opposite, resembling leaves of **nodding beggarticks**. However, leaf bases of the 2 opposite leaves in nodding beggarticks are often fused, whereas those of eclipta are separate. In addition, eclipta flowers are white, and nodding beggarticks has yellow flowers.

Eclipta habit

Eclipta seedlings

Eclipta flower and foliage

Eclipta seeds, 2.3 mm

139

Dogfennel (*Eupatorium capillifolium* (Lam.) Small) [EUPCP]

Synonyms: summer cedar, hogweed

GENERAL DESCRIPTION: A **short-lived perennial**, 50 cm to 2 m in height, with 1 to several stems from a thick woody base. Numerous small flower heads are produced from the upper stem branches. **Leaves are pinnately dissected into fine, linear segments.** Leaves and particularly flowers emit a **strong foul odor** when crushed.

PROPAGATION / PHENOLOGY: Reproduction is **by seed**.

SEEDLING: Cotyledons are petiolated, egg-shaped, and hairless. **Young leaves** are opposite; the first and sometimes the second pair of leaves **have 1–3 coarse teeth**, but **subsequent leaves are dissected. Blades are hairy.**

MATURE PLANT: **Stems are erect**, arising from the **woody base**, much-branched in the upper flowering portion, hairy, or sometimes smooth below, reddish purple at the base. Most leaves are alternate; some lower leaves may be opposite. **Leaves are once or twice pinnately dissected into fine linear segments** (2–10 cm long).

ROOTS AND UNDERGROUND STRUCTURES: Fibrous roots. Woody stem at ground level may resemble a taproot.

FLOWERS AND FRUIT: Flowers are produced in September and October. Flower heads are numerous, in much-branched panicles on the upper $1/3$–$1/4$ of the upright stem. **Individual heads are small**, 2–3 mm long, with 3–6 greenish white disk flowers on each head. The seed is enclosed within the fruit (achene), which is smooth, angled in cross section, gray to black, 1–1.6 mm long, and widest at the apex. The pappus consists of whitish bristles.

POSTSENESCENCE CHARACTERISTICS: Upright flowering stems persist through the winter and often into spring. In warmer climates, young plants may die back to the crown and resprout in the spring.

HABITAT: Dogfennel is a weed of nurseries, orchards, reduced-tillage crops, and landscapes. It also grows in roadsides and abandoned fields.

DISTRIBUTION: Found along the coastal plain from Massachusetts south, throughout the Southeast to Texas; most common from New Jersey southward.

SIMILAR SPECIES: Both **horseweed** and **mugwort** resemble dogfennel in habit and flowering characteristics. The mature leaves of mugwort are pinnatifid and may resemble dogfennel, but the leaf segments are not as narrow. Unlike dogfennel leaves, the leaves of mugwort are white-woolly beneath. Mugwort flowers are infertile and persist longer than dogfennel flowers. Horseweed leaves are lanceolate, not divided, as are mugwort and dogfennel leaves.

J. Derr

Dogfennel habit

J. Neal

Young dogfennel shoot

J. Neal

Dogfennel seedling

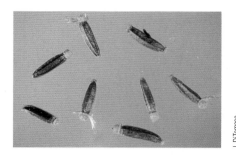

J. DiTomaso

Dogfennel seeds, 1 mm

141

Hairy galinsoga (*Galinsoga ciliata* (Raf.) Blake) [GASCI]

Synonyms: *Galinsoga quadriradiata*, common quickweed, shaggy soldier

GENERAL DESCRIPTION: **Summer annual** with erect, freely branching stems, 10–70 cm in height. **Leaves** are broadly **egg-shaped to triangular**, pointed at the apex and **coarsely toothed on the margins.**

PROPAGATION / PHENOLOGY: Reproduction is **by seed**; seeds germinate from early spring through midsummer. Peak emergence is in late spring or early summer, but seedlings can emerge between May and September, particularly in disturbed soils. Seeds apparently have **no dormancy** and can germinate soon after shedding, so there often are several generations per season.

SEEDLING: Hypocotyls are short, green, turning maroon with age. **Cotyledons** (1 cm long) are rounded to square, **abruptly tapered at the base, slightly indented at the apex**, and smooth on the margin and both surfaces. **Young leaves are opposite, egg-shaped to triangular**, pointed at the apex. **Blades have 3 prominent veins** and are lighter green on the lower surface. **Dense hairs cover the upper leaf surface, stems, and petioles.** Most hairs on the lower leaf surface are near the veins. **Margins are slightly toothed**, with hairs pointing toward the leaf apex.

MATURE PLANT: **Stems** are erect or spreading, much-branched, and **covered with somewhat coarse hairs. Leaves** (2.5–7 cm long by 1.5–5 cm wide) **are opposite**, petiolated, **broadly ovate to triangular**, and pointed at the apex. **Leaf margins are coarsely toothed and hairy.**

ROOTS AND UNDERGROUND STRUCTURES: Shallow fibrous root system.

FLOWERS AND FRUIT: Flowers are present from June to October. **Heads are numerous, <1 cm wide**, from terminal stems (in cymes) and leaf axils. **Heads are composed of 4–5 white, sometimes pink, 3-toothed, small (2–3 mm long) ray flowers and several yellow disk flowers.** The seed is enclosed in the fruit (achene). **Achenes** are 1.5 mm long, hairy, black, **4-sided**, widest at the apex, **tapered at the base**, with a **crown of chaffy scales (pappus).** A single plant can produce up to 7500 seeds. Seeds remain viable for only a few years under field conditions.

POSTSENESCENCE CHARACTERISTICS: Plants turn black at first frost; stems rot and do not persist through the winter.

HABITAT: Hairy galinsoga is **one of the most difficult-to-control weeds of vegetable crops.** It is also a weed of landscapes, gardens, ornamental beds, and nurseries. It is usually found on fertile soils.

DISTRIBUTION: Occurs throughout the world; most common in the eastern United States.

SIMILAR SPECIES: **Smallflower galinsoga (*Galinsoga parviflora* Cav., GASPA)** is similar, but the stems are smooth or only sparsely hairy, unlike the densely hairy stem of hairy galinsoga. The ray flowers of hairy galinsoga have a crown of chaffy scales (pappus), whereas a pappus is present only on the disk flowers of smallflower galinsoga. The achenes of the 2 species are nearly identical.

Mature hairy galinsoga

A. Senesac

Hairy galinsoga flowers

J. DiTomaso

Hairy galinsoga seedling

J. DiTomaso

J. DiTomaso

Hairy galinsoga seeds, 1.3 mm (not including pappus)

143

Purple cudweed (*Gnaphalium purpureum* L.) [GNAPU]

Synonyms: cudweed, chafe-weed, catfoot, rabbit tobacco, everlasting

GENERAL DESCRIPTION: A low-growing **summer or winter annual**, or frequently a biennial, forming a **rosette** of distinctly **white-woolly foliage. Erect woolly stems** may reach 40 cm in height.

PROPAGATION / PHENOLOGY: Reproduction is **by seed**; seeds germinate very soon after they are shed.

SEEDLING: Cotyledons are smooth, grayish green, sessile, rounded to oval, 1.5–2.5 mm long by 0.75–1 mm wide. Plants develop as **rosettes**, stems do not elongate in the seedling stage. **Young leaves are widest near the tip** and **taper to a broad petiole** (spatulate or oblanceolate) with a rounded or notched (mucronate) leaf tip. **Leaves** developing **in the bud are covered with a web of long silky hairs.** More mature leaf blades are mostly smooth above with woolly hairs beneath.

MATURE PLANT: **Rosette leaves** are as described above, up to 10 cm long and 2 cm wide. **Elongating stems**, arising from the rosette, do not usually branch and are generally **white-woolly. Leaves on the elongating stems** are alternate, **white-woolly**, sessile, and gradually reduced in size and width, becoming linear. Margins are wavy or entire.

ROOTS AND UNDERGROUND STRUCTURES: Taproot with a secondary fibrous root system.

FLOWERS AND FRUIT: Flowers bloom either from midspring to early summer or from August to September. **Flower clusters are formed at the ends of the erect stems.** Individual flowers are small, tannish white, and borne in the axils of reduced leaves. **Bracts are light brown, often pink or purple.** Each seed is enclosed in the **fruit (achene)**, attached to which is a **bristly pappus.** Achenes do not persist, as they shed soon after they ripen. The pappus bristles are united at the base and fall off in a ring.

POSTSENESCENCE CHARACTERISTICS: Dead stems do not persist, but plants may overwinter as a rosette.

HABITAT: Often found on sandy, dry soil, purple cudweed is a common weed of low-maintenance turf, including lawns, parks, and roadsides. Its presence is often an indicator of low fertility. It is less common in cultivated fields.

DISTRIBUTION: Found throughout the continental United States but most common in the South.

SIMILAR SPECIES: **Low cudweed (*Gnaphalium uliginosum* L., GNAUL)** is shorter (5–30 cm), much-branched, with smaller flower heads (2 mm long). **Clammy cudweed (*Gnaphalium viscosum* H.B.K., GNAMA)** is distinguished from purple cudweed by its decurrent leaf base, which clasps the stem at and below the node. **Fragrant cudweed (*Gnaphalium obtusifolium* L., GNAOB)** has similarly white-woolly foliage but is generally taller and more erect, with elliptic leaves and a strong tobacco-like fragrance. **Pussytoes (*Antennaria* spp.)** also have similar white-woolly foliage but are stoloniferous perennials with leafless stems arising from basal rosettes. They are also distinguished by their soft white flower heads that are aggregated into conspicuous tight clusters, giving the impression of a cat's toes.

Low cudweed habit

Purple cudweed seedlings

Pussytoes

Purple cudweed flowering spike

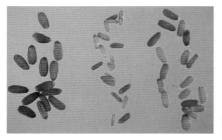

Left to right: clammy cudweed seeds, 0.7 mm; low cudweed seeds, 0.5 mm; and fragrant cudweed seeds, 0.7 mm

145

Jerusalem artichoke (*Helianthus tuberosus* L.) [HELTU]

Synonyms: girasole, earth-apple

GENERAL DESCRIPTION: A **tall (1–3 m) rhizomatous and tuberous perennial**. It is sometimes cultivated for its **edible tubers**, but once established is aggressive and difficult to control.

PROPAGATION / PHENOLOGY: Reproduction is **mainly by tubers** but also by seed. Tubers produced in the previous year begin to sprout in late spring. Tuber reserves are at their lowest in late June (60–70 days after initial shoot emergence). **Rhizome** production begins just before flowering. Tuber production begins in midsummer and reaches its peak in late summer to early autumn. The plant tubers can be spread by cultivation. **Dormant tubers are short-lived**; they do not survive for more than one or two seasons. Consequently, long-term control may be obtained by preventing new tuber formation for 2 years.

SEEDLING: **Cotyledons are oval**, twice as long as wide, and **united at the base**, forming a short tube. The **first leaves are opposite and elliptic**. Blades are dull green on the upper surface, pale on the underside, and covered with **short stiff hairs**.

MATURE PLANT: **Stems are coarse and stout** with rough hairs. **Leaves are simple,** ovate or **almost heart-shaped** to oblong-lanceolate, tapering to a narrow tip, 10–25 cm long by 4–12 cm wide. Leaf blades are **thick, rough on the upper surface**, with short **grayish hairs on the lower surface. Margins are coarsely toothed**, and petioles are **winged. Lower leaves are opposite**, but leaves on the **upper half** to two-thirds of the stem **are alternate**.

ROOTS AND UNDERGROUND STRUCTURES: **Short rhizomes bear tubers at their tips.** Tubers are irregularly oval, reddish on the outside, white inside, with knobs or bumps on the surface. Jerusalem artichoke is sometimes cultivated for the edible tubers. A single plant can produce over 200 tubers in a growing season.

FLOWERS AND FRUIT: **One to five flower heads** are produced at the terminal end of stems from August through October. Heads are about 5 cm in diameter with 10–20 **yellow ray flowers** (2–4 cm long) **surrounding the darker yellow disk flowers**. Each seed is enclosed within the fruit (achene), which is 4–8 mm long, oblong to wedge-shaped, and flattened.

POSTSENESCENCE CHARACTERISTICS: Aboveground plant parts die back after frost and do not persist. **Plant overwinters as a tuber.**

HABITAT: Jerusalem artichoke is a weed of nurseries, landscapes, orchards, and reduced-tillage agronomic crops, as well as roadsides and waste places. It is often found on rich, moist soil.

DISTRIBUTION: Jerusalem artichoke is continuing to spread in the eastern half of the United States and is increasing in many areas of the midwestern states and states adjacent to Canada. It is also found near the Pacific Coast.

SIMILAR SPECIES: **Common sunflower (*Helianthus annuus* L., HELAN)** is an annual with a fibrous root system. Unlike Jerusalem artichoke, it does not produce tubers.

Jerusalem artichoke habit

Left, Jerusalem artichoke; *right*, common burdock

Jerusalem artichoke flowers

Common sunflower habit

Common sunflower seedling

Left, common sunflower seeds, 5.5 mm (largest); *right*, Jerusalem artichoke seeds, 6.5 mm (largest)

147

Yellow hawkweed (*Hieracium pratense* Tausch) [HIECA]

Synonyms: *Hieracium caespitosum*, yellow king-devil, field hawkweed

GENERAL DESCRIPTION: A **prostrate stoloniferous and rhizomatous perennial** growing in patches or alone as a basal rosette. Leaves, stems, stolons, and flower-stalks are **conspicuously hairy. Bright yellow flowers** are on nearly leafless flower-stalks that reach 25–90 cm in height. Plants exude a **white sap** when broken.

PROPAGATION / PHENOLOGY: Reproduction is **by seeds, rhizomes, and stolons.** Seeds are dispersed by wind and have no specific dormancy requirements; they germinate soon after they are shed.

SEEDLING: Cotyledons are ovate to rounded (0.5–1 cm long), with short petioles and a small notch at the apex. **Young leaves are hairy,** egg-shaped to elliptic, tapering to very short petioles. Margins are entire and hairy. Leaves in the bud are folded from the base and conspicuously hairy on the inside surface.

MATURE PLANT: Mature plants produce a **rosette of conspicuously hairy leaves. Hairy stolons** root at the nodes and lead to the development of new rosettes. **Leaves are oblanceolate** or narrowly elliptic and **almost sessile. Blades** (5–25 cm long by 1–3 cm wide) are **covered with long hairs** above and below. The midvein is generally white and broadest toward the base. Margins are unlobed but may have a few inconspicuous teeth. Flower-stalks (scapes) have only 1–3 well-developed leaves near the base and are **covered with stiff, dark hairs.** Some hairs are tipped with glands; others are branched.

ROOTS AND UNDERGROUND STRUCTURES: Fibrous from rhizomes and stolons.

FLOWERS AND FRUIT: Flowers are produced 3–4 weeks after dandelion, primarily in June and early July, and sporadically throughout the summer. **Flower heads (5–30) resemble dandelion but are smaller** and are **produced in clusters of 2 or more** at the top of nearly leafless, 25–90 cm long, hairy, flower-stalks. **Unopened flower heads** are covered with **dense rows of black hairs.** Opened flower heads (2 cm in diameter) are made up entirely of **bright yellow ray flowers** with 5 teeth at the tip. The seed is enclosed in the fruit (achene). Achenes are 1.5–2 mm long, cylindrical, vertically ridged, dark brown or black, with a single row of small delicate bristles (pappus) 2–4 mm long.

POSTSENESCENCE CHARACTERISTICS: Foliage can persist throughout the winter.

HABITAT: Common in low-maintenance turfgrass, roadsides, abandoned fields, and meadows, yellow hawkweed does not generally persist in cultivated crops. It is often found on poor, dry, or gravelly soils that usually are low in fertility and acidic.

DISTRIBUTION: Found throughout the northeastern United States and southeastern Canada, west to Michigan, south to North Carolina, northern Georgia, and Tennessee.

SIMILAR SPECIES: **Orange hawkweed (*Hieracium aurantiacum* L., HIEAU)** has similar vegetative characteristics and is almost identical to yellow hawkweed, but the flowers are bright orange rather than yellow. **Common catsear (*Hypochoeris radicata* L., HRYRA)**, also known as false dandelion, has similar yellow flowers on tall, mostly leafless stems. The leaves of common catsear have irregular to rounded lobes on the margins, whereas those of the hawkweeds are not lobed. **All 3 species, as well as dandelion, exude a milky sap when injured.**

R. Uva

Yellow hawkweed (*foreground*), orange hawkweed (*background*)

R. Uva

Yellow hawkweed seedlings

A. Senesac

Yellow hawkweed rosette

R. Uva

Orange hawkweed flowers

R. Uva

Common catsear habit

J. DiTomaso

Left, common catsear seeds, 5.0 mm (shortest); *right*, yellow hawkweed seeds, 1.8 mm (not including pappus)

149

Prickly lettuce (*Lactuca serriola* L.) [LACSE]

Synonyms: *Lactuca scariola*, compass plant

GENERAL DESCRIPTION: A **summer or winter annual, or a biennial**, that produces erect stems (30 cm to 1.5 m in height) from a **basal rosette of leaves**. The leaf margin has fine prickles, and the midrib (lower leaf surface) is lined with **conspicuous prickles**. Leaves, roots, and stems exude a **milky juice** when injured.

PROPAGATION / PHENOLOGY: Reproduction is **by seed.**

SEEDLING: Cotyledons are rounded, tapering to the base, 7–8 mm long. Pale green leaves develop into a **basal rosette. Young leaves** are broadly club-shaped to egg-shaped, widest at the apex with **distinctly toothed or spiny**, wavy or slightly lobed margins. **Stiff prickles are present on prominent midrib of lower leaf surface.**

MATURE PLANT: **Flowering stems** are stiff, erect, prickly on the lower portions, and covered with a fine waxy coat. Stems are hollow, pale green to whitish, sometimes with reddish flecks. Usually 1 central stem arises from a basal rosette, branching only in the flowering portions. **Leaves are alternate** (5–25 cm long), oblong to lanceolate, stiff and coarse, unlobed or more often **lobed with rounded sinuses**. The **leaf bases clasp the stem with ear-like lobes**. The upper leaf surface is smooth; **prickles are present on the leaf margin and on the midrib of the lower surface**. Leaves often turn on edge and orient vertically toward the sun. Basal leaves are larger than upper leaves.

ROOTS AND UNDERGROUND STRUCTURES: Large taproot.

FLOWERS AND FRUIT: Flowers occur from July to September. Heads are 8–10 mm wide and grouped (13–27) in a pyramidal panicle. The heads are made up of **yellow ray flowers** (7–15), which fade to blue after senescence. The seed is enclosed in the fruit (achene), which is 3–4 mm long, 5–7 ribbed, and grayish yellow to brown. **A feathery pappus** is attached to a long stalk (4–5 mm).

POSTSENESCENCE CHARACTERISTICS: Plants may overwinter as rosettes in mild climates.

HABITAT: A weed of orchards, container-grown ornamentals, horticultural and agronomic crops, as well as roadsides and disturbed sites, prickly lettuce is most common in irrigated crops and on nutrient-rich soils.

DISTRIBUTION: Naturalized throughout much of the United States.

SIMILAR SPECIES: The **sowthistles** are similar to prickly lettuce but lack the prickles on the midrib of the lower leaves. **See Table 11 for a comparison with sowthistles.**

R. Uva

Prickly lettuce seedlings

J. DiTomaso

Prickly lettuce habit

J. DiTomaso

Prickly lettuce mature leaves
(note spines)

R. Uva

Prickly lettuce flowers

J. DiTomaso

Prickly lettuce seeds, 3 mm (not
including pappus)

151

Pineapple-weed (*Matricaria matricarioides* (Less.) C.L. Porter) [MATMT]

Synonyms: *Chamomilla suaveolens, Matricaria suaveolens, Matricaria discoidea,* rayless chamomile

GENERAL DESCRIPTION: A low-growing, bushy, branching **summer or winter annual,** reaching 5–40 cm in height with **finely divided pinnately compound leaves.** Crushed leaves have a **sweet odor** similar to pineapple.

PROPAGATION / PHENOLOGY: Reproduction is **by seed.** Seedlings emerge in late summer to early fall and again from early spring to early summer.

SEEDLING: **Cotyledons are bright green,** oblong and **narrow,** 3–12.5 mm long by 1 mm wide, slightly pointed to rounded at the apex and fused at the base. **Young leaves are fragrant, hairless,** shiny **bright green, thick and succulent**. The first pairs of leaves are opposite, linear, with the margins entire or with a few lobes. **Subsequent leaves** are alternate and **pinnately divided with linear lobes. Young plants form a dense rosette** (about 10 cm in diameter) of finely divided leaves.

MATURE PLANT: **Elongated stems** are smooth, hairless, erect or spreading, and branched. **Foliage has a sweet odor** similar to that of pineapple. **Leaves are hairless,** fleshy, **alternate,** 1–5 cm long, **1–3 times pinnately divided with short linear segments.**

ROOTS AND UNDERGROUND STRUCTURES: **Shallow taproot** with a secondary fibrous root system.

FLOWERS AND FRUIT: Flowers are produced from May through September. One to several flower heads are produced at the end of stems on short peduncles. **Heads** are 0.5–1 cm in diameter, **rounded to conical. All flowers are tubular (disk)** and **greenish yellow.** The seed is enclosed within the fruit (achene). Achenes (1–1.5 mm long) are oblong to obovate, 3–5 ribbed, warty at the apex, and yellow, light brown, or gray, often with 2 red stripes. **Pappus is absent** or an indistinct crown.

POSTSENESCENCE CHARACTERISTICS: Senesced plants do not persist, but rosettes remain green over the winter.

HABITAT: Pineapple-weed is a weed of low-maintenance turfgrass, landscapes, and nursery crops, as well as other perennial crops. It is frequently found in roadsides and waste areas but is not a significant problem in cultivated fields. It tolerates compacted soils and mowing, but a combination of frequent mowing and adequate fertilization and water will gradually eliminate pineapple-weed in turf.

DISTRIBUTION: Although native to the Pacific Coast, pineapple-weed is now distributed throughout the United States.

SIMILAR SPECIES: **See Table 10 for a comparison with other weedy members of the aster family that have finely dissected leaves.**

Pineapple-weed habit

J. Neal

Pineapple-weed rosette

J. Neal

J. DiTomaso

Pineapple-weed flowers

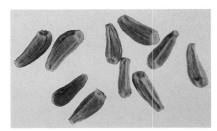

J. DiTomaso

Pineapple-weed seeds, 1.5 mm

153

Common groundsel (*Senecio vulgaris* L.) [SENVU]

Synonyms: groundsel, grimsel, simson, bird-seed, ragwort

GENERAL DESCRIPTION: A **branched, erect, winter or summer annual** (10–50 cm in height). Leaves are deeply lobed to dissected, irregularly toothed, and somewhat fleshy. Although **not as toxic as tansy ragwort (*Senecio jacobaea* L., SENJA)**, common **groundsel also contains pyrrolizidine alkaloids that cause liver damage in horses and cattle.** Small herbivores, such as sheep, rabbits, and goats are resistant to the toxic effect of *Senecio* spp.

PROPAGATION / PHENOLOGY: Reproduction is **by seed.** Germination begins in early spring and continues to late autumn. Three to four generations can be produced in one season.

SEEDLING: **Cotyledons are slender and club-shaped**, on elongated stalks 10 mm long. Stalks of the cotyledons and young leaves are grooved. **Young leaves** are dark green, egg-shaped to lanceolate, **shallowly toothed to pinnatifid**, sometimes deeply lobed (15–25 mm long). Leaf blades are smooth or softly hairy only on the midrib, with a narrow or winged petiole. Cotyledons and young leaves are often purplish on the lower leaf surface.

MATURE PLANT: **Erect stems** are usually **much-branched** and smooth, frequently rooting at the lower nodes. **Leaves are alternate**, sparsely hairy to smooth, with coarse and **irregular toothed to pinnatifid (deeply lobed) margins.** Lower leaf blades taper to the petiole; upper leaves are sessile.

ROOTS AND UNDERGROUND STRUCTURES: Root system is a small taproot with secondary fibrous roots. The taproot is not always evident.

FLOWERS AND FRUIT: Flowers can be present from April to October. **Flower heads** (1 cm in diameter) **are composed of several yellow disk flowers.** Bracts (phyllaries) subtending flower heads are often black tipped. Each seed is enclosed in the fruit (achene). Achenes are reddish brown to gray-brown, 2–4 mm long, vertically ridged, with short hairs along the margins. A pappus consisting of soft bristles that can easily become detached from the fruit aids in wind dispersal. **Opened flowers can develop fully mature seed after plants have been killed by cultivation or herbicides.**

POSTSENESCENCE CHARACTERISTICS: Plants die during extended hot, dry periods. Erect stems turn brown and persist for several months.

HABITAT: Common groundsel is a weed of container-grown and field nursery crops, vineyards, greenhouses, landscapes, and less often of agronomic crops. It is most commonly found on moist, nutrient-rich soil and is most troublesome in spring and autumn, when conditions are cool and wet. Common groundsel has biotypes resistant to triazine herbicides and is also somewhat tolerant of the dinitroaniline herbicides.

DISTRIBUTION: Found in the northern United States and Canada, south to Texas and California.

SIMILAR SPECIES: **Mugwort seedlings** are similar, but young leaves are bristly-hairy and have white, woolly hairs beneath. The lobes of the leaves of **seedling common ragweed** are much more deeply dissected than common groundsel or mugwort.

Common groundsel habit

J. Neal

Common groundsel seedlings

A. Senesac

J. Neal

Common groundsel flowers and seedhead

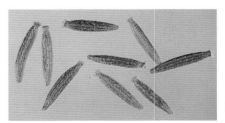

J. DiTomaso

Common groundsel seeds, 2.4 mm

Canada goldenrod (*Solidago canadensis* L.) [SOOCA]

Synonym: common goldenrod

GENERAL DESCRIPTION: **Tall, erect, leafy, rhizomatous perennial** (50 cm–1.5 m in height). A single rhizome can produce clusters of genetically identical plants.

PROPAGATION / PHENOLOGY: Reproduction is by **wind-dispersed seed and creeping rhizomes**, which form large patches or colonies. Shoots emerge from rhizomes in mid-April. Seedlings emerge in June or early July but do not produce flowers in their first year of growth. Rhizome production begins after the first year of seedling growth.

SEEDLING: Cotyledons are very small (about 5 mm), club-shaped, and elliptic. Young leaves are spatulate-rounded; the bases narrow into a short stalk. **Young leaves form a rosette.** Leaf margins are toothed.

MATURE PLANT: **Rosettes soon produce erect, slender, leafy, mostly unbranched stems.** The stems are generally smooth but have small, soft hairs at least above the middle. **Leaves** are alternate, sessile, **lanceolate** to lanceolate-elliptic (3–15 cm long by 0.5–2.2 cm wide), **tapering to the base and apex**, with mostly toothed margins. Blades are smooth above and hairy beneath, at least on the 3 main veins. Leaves become gradually smaller up the stem.

ROOTS AND UNDERGROUND STRUCTURES: Extensive fibrous root system is associated with long creeping **rhizomes**. Rhizomes are produced primarily from the base of aerial stems and are usually 5–12 cm long, frequently with a **reddish pigmentation**.

FLOWERS AND FRUIT: **Yellow flowers** are produced from August through October in composite heads arranged in backward-curving, **panicle-like clusters**. The branches of the inflorescence form a central axis with the flower heads arranged on only one side of the axis. Bracts are thin, pointed, yellowish with a green tip, about 2–4 mm long, and overlapping (imbricate). Individual flowers consist of 13 (10–17) **yellow ray flowers (1–1.5 mm long) surrounding 2–8 yellow disk flowers**. The seed is enclosed in the fruit (achene). A pappus of white hairs is attached to the achenes (1 mm long) to facilitate dispersal by wind.

POSTSENESCENCE CHARACTERISTICS: Erect stems remain somewhat rigid throughout the winter and are often in large clumps or patches. The remains of the branching flower head persist at the apex.

HABITAT: A weed of nursery crops, orchards, and other perennial crops; also found in roadsides, meadows, and ditches. Particularly troublesome in Christmas tree plantations. Canada goldenrod grows under a wide range of conditions but is typically found on moist, medium-textured or muck soils; it is less common on very wet or dry sites.

DISTRIBUTION: Found along the East Coast, west through the north-central states, and south to California, New Mexico, Texas, and Florida.

SIMILAR SPECIES: **Many other goldenrod species (*Solidago* spp.) are weedy.** They all produce yellow flowers in summer and are alternate, simple-leaved, rhizomatous perennials. Flower heads have both ray and disk flowers, with overlapping, variably lengthed bracts surrounding the ray flowers. The species differ in overall stature, width of the leaf blades, hairiness of leaves and stems, and shape of the flower cluster. Some taxonomists consider tall goldenrod (*Solidago altissima* L., SOOAL) to be the same species as Canada goldenrod. If positive identification is necessary, send a sample to your Cooperative Extension office or to the Extension taxonomist at your state's land grant college or university.

Goldenrod in flower

Young goldenrod shoots

Goldenrod rhizomes

Young shoots (from rhizomes) of two
Solidago species

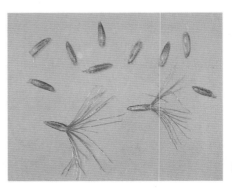

Canada goldenrod seeds, 1.2 mm (not
including pappus)

157

Perennial sowthistle (*Sonchus arvensis* L.) [SONAR]

Synonyms: field sow thistle, creeping sow thistle, gutweed, milk thistle, field milk thistle, corn sow-thistle, swine-thistle, tree sow-thistle, dindle

GENERAL DESCRIPTION: Perennial sowthistle **resembles annual sowthistle** with **prickly-toothed leaves** and erect stems (60–150 cm in height) but is a **rhizomatous perennial**. Flowers are similar to those of dandelion, although smaller, and the **sap is milky-white**.

PROPAGATION / PHENOLOGY: Plants reproduce **by seeds** and **spread by rhizomes**. In established stands, shoots emerge in late April. Seeds are mature by 10 days after flowering and germinate in mid to late May, after the soil has warmed. Most seedlings do not flower in the first year.

SEEDLING: Cotyledons are obovate (4–8 mm long by 1–4.5 mm wide) and sessile or on short stalks. **Young leaves** are alternate but form a **basal rosette. Blades are bluish green with a dull surface**; the lower leaf surface often has a powdery white or purplish bloom. Young expanding leaves may be pubescent but are smooth when fully expanded. **Margins are wavy and lobed** with backward-pointing **spiny teeth.**

MATURE PLANT: **Stems are bluish green** (glaucous), hollow, ridged, and **smooth**, branching only near the inflorescence. **Leaves** (5–30 cm long by 2–10 cm wide) are alternate and have **prickly-toothed margins**. The **margins** are often **deeply triangular-lobed** (occasionally entire). **Upper leaves** may be **smaller than lower leaves** and are often **unlobed** and **sessile**. The **lower leaves** have a **winged petiole**, and are **clasping at the base**, with rounded lobes (auricles).

ROOTS AND UNDERGROUND STRUCTURES: Thickened, spreading **rhizomes.**

FLOWERS AND FRUIT: Flowering begins in early July and extends through late summer. Flowers can resemble dandelion but are not solitary on leafless stalks. Flower heads (3–5 cm wide) consist entirely of ray flowers clustered at the end of branched stems. Flowers are **bright yellow to yellow-orange**. Each seed is enclosed within the fruit (achene). Achenes are 2.5–3.5 mm long, narrowly oval, with a wrinkled surface and 5 or more prominent ribs on each side. The **feathery**, white **pappus** aids in wind and water dispersal.

POSTSENESCENCE CHARACTERISTICS: Plants die back to the ground after first frost.

HABITAT: Perennial sowthistle is common in roadsides and waste areas but less common in landscapes. It prefers slightly alkaline or neutral, fine-textured, rich soils. It does not thrive on coarse sand.

DISTRIBUTION: Found throughout the northern United States and southern Canada, as far west as California.

SIMILAR SPECIES: **For a comparison with other sowthistles and prickly lettuce, see Table 11.**

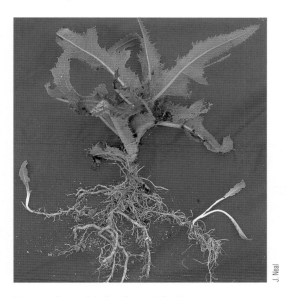
J. Neal

Perennial sowthistle plant with rhizomes

R. Uva

Perennial sowthistle sprouts from rhizome

R. Uva

Perennial sowthistle leaves and inflorescence

R. Uva

Perennial sowthistle mature stem and foliage

J. DiTomaso

Perennial sowthistle seeds, 2.5 mm (not including pappus)

Annual sowthistle (*Sonchus oleraceus* L.) [SONOL]

Synonyms: common sow-thistle, hares lettuce, colewort, milk thistle

GENERAL DESCRIPTION: An **unbranched annual** with smooth, erect stems (30 cm to 2 m in height). Leaves, stems, and roots exude a **white sap** when cut. Stems and foliage appear succulent and waxy whitish or bluish (glaucous). **Leaf margins are weakly prickly,** but **no other spines are present.**

PROPAGATION / PHENOLOGY: Reproduction is by wind-blown **seed**. Seeds germinate in mid to late spring but continue to emerge throughout the season in moist, cool sites.

SEEDLING: Cotyledons are smooth, circular to egg-shaped, 3–8 mm long by 1.5–4 mm wide, and petiolated. Cotyledons and young leaves have a **whitish powdery coating**. **The first few leaves** are alternate in a **basal rosette**, rounded to egg-shaped, with irregularly toothed margins. The blades taper abruptly to a winged petiole. **Subsequent young leaves are spatulate,** tapering more gradually to the base. **Leaves in the bud are surrounded by a tangled mesh of hairs,** but hairs are lacking in fully expanded leaves.

MATURE PLANT: **Leaves on elongated stems are alternate, smooth,** 6–30 cm long by 1–15 cm wide. **Blades vary in shape,** but are usually **pinnatifid, with a large triangular terminal lobe** and **about 3 pairs of lower lobes** that gradually become smaller toward the petiole. **Margins** are irregularly toothed and **only weakly prickly.** Lobes at the base of the petiole clasp the stem. Upper leaves are less divided and smaller than lower leaves.

ROOTS AND UNDERGROUND STRUCTURES: Short taproot.

FLOWERS AND FRUIT: Flowers are produced from July to October. Flower heads (1.2–2.5 cm in diameter), in clusters (corymbiform) at the end of the stems, are composed of **pale yellow ray flowers**. The seed is enclosed in the fruit (achene) and is 2–4 mm long, wrinkled, brown to olive, with 3–5 ribs on each surface. A long **white feathery pappus** aids in seed dispersal by wind.

POSTSENESCENCE CHARACTERISTICS: After frost, plants turn dark brown to black and persist for only a short time.

HABITAT: Annual sowthistle is a common weed of landscapes, nursery crops, orchards, grain fields, cultivated crops, and waste areas.

DISTRIBUTION: Found throughout the United States.

SIMILAR SPECIES: **For a comparison with another annual—spiny sowthistle (*Sonchus asper* (L.) Hill, SONAS)—as well as with perennial sowthistle and prickly lettuce, see Table 11.**

J. Neal

Annual sowthistle rosette

R. Uva

Annual sowthistle seedling

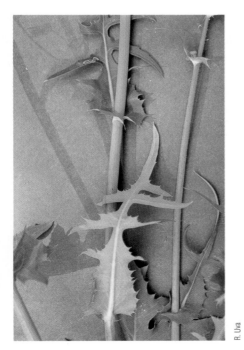

R. Uva

Annual sowthistle mature stems
and foliage

Spiny sowthistle habit

J. Neal

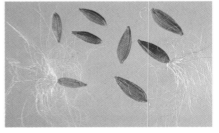

J. DiTomaso

Left, spiny sowthistle seeds, 3.0 mm
(largest); *right*, annual sowthistle seeds,
3.2 mm (not including pappus)

Dandelion (*Taraxacum officinale* Weber in Wiggers) [TAROF]

Synonyms: *Lentodon taraxacum*, lions-tooth, blow-ball, cankerwort

GENERAL DESCRIPTION: A **tap-rooted perennial** from a **basal rosette of leaves**. Yellow flowers are produced on leafless stalks.

PROPAGATION / PHENOLOGY: Reproduction is by **wind-blown seeds** and by new shoots that develop from broken segments of the taproot. Seeds germinate in the top 2 cm of soil. Seedlings emerge from late spring to early autumn, with most emerging in early summer (several weeks after seeds are shed).

SEEDLING: Cotyledons are yellow-green, smooth, and circular to oval to spatulate, with smooth margins. **Young leaves** lack hairs and are often grayish green on the lower surface; they are alternate but **form a basal rosette** and are **spatulate or oval with a long petiole. By the third true leaf,** the **margins are wavy** with irregular widely spaced teeth. **Older leaves** have a few appressed crinkled hairs on the upper and lower surfaces and widely spaced **teeth that point toward the leaf base.**

MATURE PLANT: Leaves, flower-stalks, and the taproot exude a **milky juice** when cut. Vegetative stems form a **basal rosette of leaves** and do not elongate. The only noticeable stems are those bearing flower heads. Leaves generally lack hairs but are sometimes sparsely hairy, especially on the midrib and undersurface. Leaves are oblong to spatulate (7.5–25 cm long). The **margins are deeply lobed to pinnatifid; the lobes point toward the base.** The terminal lobe is usually the largest, with the segments becoming smaller and more deeply divided toward the base. Margins may be variably cleft or entire (primarily on seedlings).

ROOTS AND UNDERGROUND STRUCTURES: A thick, long, **fleshy taproot** that may be branched.

FLOWERS AND FRUIT: Flowers are produced from May to June, with a second bloom in autumn (when the day length is less than 12 hours). Flowers do not require pollination to develop viable seed (apomixis). **Bright yellow flower heads**, consisting entirely of ray flowers, are 3–5 cm in diameter, solitary, at the ends of leafless, hollow flower-stalks (5–50 cm long). Bracts are in 2 rows; the outer row is bent backward, and the inner row is erect and linear. Each seed is enclosed in the fruit (achene). Achenes are yellow-brown (3–5 mm long), with a **feathery pappus attached to a long stalk** (8–10 mm). Collectively, the fruit form a conspicuous, **globe-like, grayish white seedhead**. Seeds are dispersed by wind.

POSTSENESCENCE CHARACTERISTICS: Rosettes remain green throughout the year.

HABITAT: Dandelion is a weed of turfgrass, orchards, nursery crops, alfalfa, and other perennial crops. It tolerates many soil types and cultural practices but does not tolerate cultivation.

DISTRIBUTION: Widespread throughout North America.

SIMILAR SPECIES: **Chicory** rosettes strongly resemble those of dandelion. Toothed lobes of dandelion leaves, however, are generally opposite each other and point toward the rosette; those of chicory are not always opposite and point forward or backward. In addition, the basal leaves of chicory are rougher, with more prominent coarse hairs, and the flowering stems are branched and leafy, with several bright blue flower heads. Chicory branches persist even after senescence. **Common catsear** has yellow flowers on tall, mostly leafless stems. But, unlike the pointed and pinnate lobes of dandelion leaves, its leaves have irregular to rounded lobes. **All 3 species exude a milky sap when cut.**

J. Neal

Dandelion habit

R. Uva

Dandelion seedlings

Common catsear (or false
dandelion) habit

J. Neal

A. Senesac

Dandelion seedheads

J. DiTomaso

Dandelion seed, 4.5 mm (to top of seed)

Western salsify (*Tragopogon dubius* Scop.) [TRODM]

Synonyms: yellow goat's beard, yellow salsify, western goat's-beard

GENERAL DESCRIPTION: An unbranched (or, rarely, branched) erect **biennial** or occasionally an annual (30 cm to 1 m in height). The **foliage is grass-like**, and the **seedhead resembles that of a very large dandelion**. Leaves, stems, and taproot exude a **milky sap** when damaged.

PROPAGATION / PHENOLOGY: Reproduction is by **wind-dispersed seed**; seeds germinate in early summer or autumn. **Seeds remain viable in soil for only 2 years or less.**

SEEDLING: **Cotyledons** are linear and **grass-like** (13 cm long by 2 mm wide). **Young leaves** form a **basal rosette** and are **long and narrow**, usually with a few long, soft, fine, **cobwebby hairs. Blades** are keeled, with **parallel veins**.

MATURE PLANT: The **basal rosette** formed in the first year **produces an erect stem the following year. Stems are smooth, round, somewhat fleshy**, and thickest at the base. Leaves are also fleshy and smooth, sometimes with a few hairs in the leaf axils. **Leaves are long, linear, and grass-like** (30 cm by 2 mm), tapering uniformly from the base to the apex. The **leaf base is clasping**, enclosing the stem.

ROOTS AND UNDERGROUND STRUCTURES: **Branched fleshy taproot with milky sap.**

FLOWERS AND FRUIT: **Yellow flowers** are produced in early summer, June or July. Flower heads (2–4 cm in diameter) are produced singly at the end of stems. Flowers open from morning to midday and are oriented toward the sun. The **bracts** (phyllaries, 2.5–4 cm long) **surpass the flowers in length** and continue to elongate (4–7 cm long) as fruit matures. All flowers are yellow and ligulate (ray). The **stalk below the flower head (peduncle) is enlarged and hollow.** The seed is enclosed in the 12–17 mm long fruit (achene). The **spherical fruiting head** is similar to dandelion but is considerably larger (7–10 cm in diameter). The pappus aids in wind dispersal, which can scatter the fruit more than 250 m.

POSTSENESCENCE CHARACTERISTICS: After seed dispersal, a dead central stalk can persist for a short time. Biennial plants persist as a basal rosette through the winter.

HABITAT: Primarily a weed of nursery crops and other perennial horticultural crops, western salsify is found on relatively dry open sites, along roads and railroad tracks, and in disturbed soils. It is less commonly found in cultivated row crops.

DISTRIBUTION: Occurs throughout most of the United States but most common in the West and sporadic in the East; increasing in importance as a weed in the Northeast.

SIMILAR SPECIES: **Meadow salsify (*Tragopogon pratensis* L., TROPR)** has recurved, abruptly tapering, slender leaves, often with curled or wrinkled margins and leaf tips. The western salsify stem is hollow and gradually tapered from flower to stem; the meadow salsify stalk (peduncle) below the flower head is abruptly narrowed and not hollow. Both species exude a milky sap when damaged. Seedlings of western salsify and meadow salsify are often mistaken for grasses, but they lack ligules and distinct sheaths.

Western salsify habit

A. Senesac

Western salsify seedling

R. Uva

Western salsify rosette

R. Uva

Western salsify seedhead

J. Neal

Western salsify taproots

A. Senesac

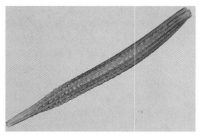

Meadow salsify seed, 14 mm

J. DiTomaso

Common cocklebur (*Xanthium strumarium* L.) [XANST]

Synonym: clotbur

GENERAL DESCRIPTION: An erect (20 to 1.7 m), branched, **summer annual** with **distinctive prickly burs** in late summer and fall. Stems are brown- to purple-spotted and leaves are triangular with a sandpaper texture. *Xanthium* spp. cause **liver damage in pigs**, and probably dogs, when ingested at 0.75 to 3% body weight. The toxin, carboxyatractyloside, is limited to the seedlings and seeds. The spiny coats of mature burs can also cause mechanical injury or obstruction of the intestine in livestock.

PROPAGATION / PHENOLOGY: Reproduction is **by seed**; seeds germinate from early spring through summer. **Seeds can germinate as deep as 15 cm below the soil surface.**

SEEDLING: Hypocotyls are stout and purple toward the base. Spiny burs remain underground at the base of the hypocotyl. **Cotyledons** are thick, fleshy, lanceolate, tapered at both ends, and **very large** (5 cm long by 1 cm wide). The upper surface of the cotyledons is dark green, the lower light green. The **first pair of leaves are opposite, subsequent leaves are alternate**. Leaf surfaces are rough with short stiff hairs. **Young leaves are triangular**, with 3 prominent main veins. Leaf **margins have sharp teeth. Stems are green, with purple to brown spots**, and are covered with stiff ascending hairs.

MATURE PLANT: **Stems** are branched, rough, and **hairy with dark spots** and longitudinal ridges. **Leaves are alternate, long-petiolated**, and **similar to those of seedlings but much larger, up to 15 cm long**. Leaf blades occasionally have 3–5 shallow lobes and are often heart-shaped at the base.

ROOTS AND UNDERGROUND STRUCTURES: **Stout taproot**, somewhat woody in texture.

FLOWERS AND FRUIT: Blooms from July to September. Male and female flowers, produced in the axils of the upper leaves, occur on separate heads of the same plant. The male flowers are rounded, abscising soon after pollen is shed; female flowers are enclosed within the bur. At maturity, the **burs** are **elliptic to egg-shaped**, 1–3.5 cm long, **hard, woody, and covered with hooked prickles. Two long beaks project from the tip of the bur**. The prickles help facilitate dispersal, and burs are buoyant in water. **Each bur contains 2 fruit (achenes)**, each with 1 seed. The lower seed can germinate soon after dehiscence, but the upper seed remains dormant for 1 to several years.

POSTSENESCENCE CHARACTERISTICS: Stems, bearing burs, persist into winter.

HABITAT: Primarily a weed of cultivated and reduced-tillage crops; also found in uncultivated fields, nursery crops, waste areas, and sandy beaches.

DISTRIBUTION: Found throughout the United States and other temperate areas of the world. Particularly troublesome in the southern states and in Mexico.

SIMILAR SPECIES: **Spiny cocklebur (*Xanthium spinosum* L., XANSP)** has narrower leaves and 3-parted yellow spines at the leaf bases. Its burs lack the 2 beaks present on common cocklebur. **Common burdock** has similar foliage and hooked spines on burlike fruit, but its leaves and overall size are much larger. Also, unlike cocklebur, it has numerous seeds in each fruit and the hooked spines are easily separated from the flowering head. **Jimsonweed** seedlings may resemble common cocklebur, but the stems and leaves are smooth, unlike the rough hairy leaves of common cocklebur. Jimsonweed also has a single midvein, entire or lobed margins, and a foul odor.

Common cocklebur habit

Spots on stems of
common cocklebur

Common cocklebur seedling

Spiny cocklebur foliage, spines,
and fruit

Fruiting shoot of common cocklebur

Common cocklebur bur, 30 mm long

167

Yellow rocket (*Barbarea vulgaris* R. Br.) [BARVU]

Synonyms: winter cress, St. Barbaras cress, bitter cress, rocket cress

GENERAL DESCRIPTION: A **winter annual, biennial**, or seldom a perennial, with numerous stems branching from a **basal rosette of deep-green glossy foliage**. It can grow from 30 to 90 cm in height and tolerates mowing.

PROPAGATION / PHENOLOGY: Reproduction is **by seed**, which are produced from May through June and germinate in cool, moist soil in the spring or fall. Seeds may persist in the soil for several years, and each plant may produce 1000 to 10,000 seeds, which germinate to a depth of 1 cm in the soil.

SEEDLING: **Cotyledons are egg-shaped** to round **on long stalks**, and the apex is slightly notched. **Young leaves are rounded**, some with a **heart-shaped base. Margins** are entire or wavy and **become distinctly toothed with age**. Seedlings develop into **basal rosettes** of alternate leaves that remain throughout the first year.

MATURE PLANT: **Flowering stems are produced in the second year.** Stems are smooth, angular or ridged, erect, simple or branching near the top. Leaves are fairly thick and deep-green. Leaves forming the dense basal rosette are smooth and glossy, thick, 5–20 cm long, often persisting through the winter. **Basal and lower stem leaves are lobed**, with 1–5 small, **oppositely arranged lateral lobes and a larger terminal lobe**. The terminal lobe has a distinctive heart-shaped base. Lobes are rounded with wavy toothed margins. **Stem leaves** are alternate and **become progressively shorter**; the uppermost leaves are about 2.5 cm long, with **fewer and smaller lateral lobes** than the lower leaves.

ROOTS AND UNDERGROUND STRUCTURES: Taproot with secondary fibrous roots.

FLOWERS AND FRUIT: **Bright yellow flowers appear in early spring (late April to June)**, and sporadically throughout the summer, on spike-like racemes that form pyramidal clusters at the ends of branches. Flowers have 4 yellow petals, 4 sepals, and 6 stamens (2 stamens are shorter than the other 4). Long fruit (siliques) are produced on 3–6 mm long stalks (pedicels). **Siliques** are about 2.5 cm long by 2.4 mm in diameter, beaked at the tip, quadrangular, splitting into 2 valves at maturity. Each valve contains seeds arranged in rows along a central membranous septum. Seeds are 1–1.5 mm long, broadly oval to oblong, notched at one end, light yellow to brown or gray, and somewhat square.

POSTSENESCENCE CHARACTERISTICS: In unmowed areas, the fruiting stalk remains through summer. After the fruit disperse, the central septum of the silique may persist as a thin silvery membrane with a beak at the tip. Plants survive as perennials in mild summers with adequate moisture but die after fruiting in midsummer under drier conditions.

HABITAT: A weed of turfgrass, nurseries, and agricultural crops; also found in roadsides and pastures. It is most common on nutrient-rich sandy and loamy soils.

DISTRIBUTION: Found throughout much of the United States but most common in the eastern and central regions.

SIMILAR SPECIES: **The heart-shaped base of the terminal lobe separates yellow rocket from other members of the mustard family.** The **seedling** can be confused with **shepherd's-purse** and **pepperweeds** (***Lepidium* spp.**). The deeper green and glossy foliage and the much rounder terminal lobe distinguish it from those species. Yellow rocket blooms earlier (late April to June) than **wild mustard** and **wild radish**.

Yellow rocket habit

A. Senesac

J. Neal

Yellow rocket seedling

J. DiTomaso

Yellow rocket seed stalk

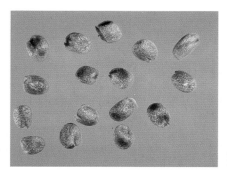

J. DiTomaso

Yellow rocket seeds, 1.2 mm

169

Wild mustard (*Brassica kaber* (DC.) L.C. Wheeler) [SINAR]

Synonyms: *Brassica arvensis, Sinapis arvensis,* charlock, field mustard, field kale, kedlock, common mustard

General Description: A **winter or sometimes summer annual**. Flowering stems are erect (20–80 cm tall). At least 2 distinctly **different forms exist: one with prickly hairy stems, one with smooth stems**. Otherwise the characteristics are similar.

Propagation / Phenology: Reproduction is **by seed**; seeds germinate in late summer, early fall, or spring. **Seeds persist in the soil for many years** and germinate to a depth of 2 cm in the soil. Approximately 1200 seeds can be produced by each plant.

Seedling: **Cotyledons are kidney-shaped** or heart-shaped (5 mm long by 8 mm wide) with a **distinct indentation at the cotyledon tip** and a prominent petiole. **Young leaves** are elliptically **oblong with wavy-toothed margins** and occasionally wrinkled surfaces. Hairs are present on the leaves and stems. Plants initially develop into a **basal rosette**.

Mature Plant: **Flowering stems are erect**, usually branched toward the top with **stiff hairs on the lower portions. Leaves are alternate, roughly hairy**, egg-shaped, broadest at the apex and tapering to the base, 5–20 cm long by 2.5–10 cm wide. **Lower leaves** have relatively long petioles and **deep, jagged, irregularly lobed blades. Upper leaves become progressively smaller**; they are lanceolate, not pinnately lobed, and slightly toothed; petioles are absent or short.

Roots and Underground Structures: Slender taproot with fibrous secondary root system.

Flowers and Fruit: Flowers are produced from May to August at the ends of branches in dense clusters of racemes that elongate with fruit maturation. Flowers are about 1.5 cm wide. The 4 **yellow petals** are 8–12 mm long and clawed. **Fruit capsules (siliques)** are 2.5–4.5 cm long by 2–3 mm wide on 5–7 mm long flower-stalks (pedicels). Siliques are rounded in cross section, with a **flattened quadrangular conical beak** about half as long as the pod. Seeds are smooth, round, about 1.5 mm in diameter, black or dark purplish brown.

Postsenescence Characteristics: Upright fruiting stems persist for several months bearing remnants of the siliques.

Habitat: Wild mustard is a common weed of nursery, horticultural, and agricultural crops, particularly small grains and fall-seeded forage crops. It is also frequently found in fields, pastures, waste areas, and disturbed sites.

Distribution: Widespread throughout the United States.

Similar Species: **Wild radish** has stiffer hairs on the leaves than wild mustard. In addition, the leaves of wild radish have more and deeper lobes. The hypocotyl and root of wild radish have a distinctive hot radish flavor when chewed. Wild radish is found predominantly on the coastal plains of the Northeast; wild mustard is found mainly on upland soils. Other similar species of mustard occur less commonly as weeds throughout the Northeast: **birdsrape mustard (*Brassica rapa* L., BRSRA), black mustard (*Brassica nigra* (L.) W.J.D. Koch, BRSNI), Indian mustard (*Brassica juncea* (L.) Czern. & Coss., BRSJU), and white mustard (*Brassica hirta* Moench, SINAL)**.

J. Neal

Wild mustard habit, in alfalfa

R. Uva

Wild mustard seedling

J. Neal

Wild mustard rosette

J. Neal

Wild mustard flowering shoots

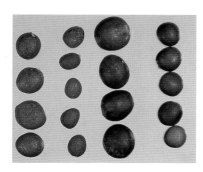

J. DiTomaso

Left to right: Indian mustard seeds, 1.5 mm; black mustard seeds, 1.3 mm; birdsrape mustard seeds, 2.0 mm; and wild mustard seeds, 1.3 mm

Shepherd's-purse (*Capsella bursa-pastoris* (L.) Medicus) [CAPBP]

Synonyms: shepherds-bag, pepper plant, case weed, pick-purse

GENERAL DESCRIPTION: A **winter annual** producing a **prostrate basal rosette**. The flowering stems are mostly unbranched, reaching 10–60 cm in height, producing **characteristic heart-shaped seed pods**.

PROPAGATION / PHENOLOGY: Reproduction is **by seed**; seeds germinate in late summer, early autumn, or early spring.

SEEDLING: Hypocotyl is often tinted purple. Cotyledons are egg-shaped to rounded and narrowed to the base. Young leaves are slightly hairy on the upper surface with unbranched and branched (star-shaped) hairs. The **young rosettes have variable leaf margins**. The **first leaves are rounded**, becoming elongated with age, **with untoothed or slightly toothed margins**, but no distinctive lobing. The **older leaves are deeply toothed or lobed** with triangular segments, the largest segment at the apex. Leaves are dark green to silvery gray and occasionally are tinged with purple. **Leaves become more lobed and tapered as seedlings mature.**

MATURE PLANT: **Flowering stems** are produced in the same year as germination or in the following year. Stems are **erect, slender**, covered with gray hairs, and are usually unbranched or sparsely branched. Leaves are smooth or hairy, variously toothed or lobed, and alternate. The **lower leaves** are 5–10 cm long, oblong, tapering to the base, **deeply toothed** or lobed, and **arranged in a rosette**.

ROOTS AND UNDERGROUND STRUCTURES: Slender, often branched, taproot with secondary fibrous roots.

FLOWERS AND FRUIT: **Flowers** are produced in racemes on elongating stems and are present from **spring to early summer and sporadically in late autumn**. Individual flowers are relatively small and inconspicuous. Both white petals (2–4 mm long) and green sepals are in fours. The **fruit is a triangular to heart-shaped, 2-parted, flattened pod**, 4–8 mm long, and nearly as wide (silicle). Seeds are about 1 mm long, oblong, grooved and yellowish to red or brown. Each plant can produce thousands of long-lived seeds.

POSTSENESCENCE CHARACTERISTICS: Plants die soon after fruiting in late spring or early summer. Dead flower clusters of triangular or heart-shaped pods may persist.

HABITAT: A worldwide weed of cultivated crops, including nursery, agronomic, and vegetable crops, shepherd's-purse is also common in disturbed soils and waste areas.

DISTRIBUTION: Very common throughout North America.

SIMILAR SPECIES: **Virginia pepperweed** is similar in appearance; however, the fruit of Virginia pepperweed are flat and round not triangular to heart-shaped. Leaves of pepperweed seedlings are less tapered at the base than are shepherd's-purse leaves. In addition, pepperweed leaves have a distinctive tangy peppery taste.

Shepherd's-purse habit

L. Clark

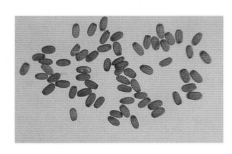

Shepherd's-purse seedlings

R. Uva

Shepherd's-purse basal rosette

R. Uva

Shepherd's-purse seeds, 0.8 mm

J. DiTomaso

173

Hairy bittercress (*Cardamine hirsuta* L.) [CARHI]

Synonym: hoary bittercress

GENERAL DESCRIPTION: A **winter or summer annual**, or occasionally a biennial. Fruiting stems arise from a prominent **basal rosette of pinnate leaves**. Stems are ascending (30 cm in height), branching mainly at the base.

PROPAGATION / PHENOLOGY: Reproduction is **by seed; several generations may be produced in a growing season**. Seeds germinate in moist, cool soils throughout the growing season.

SEEDLING: Cotyledons are rounded, about 3 mm long, on long petioles. The **first 2 true leaves are heart-shaped** to kidney-shaped. **Subsequent leaves have 2–4 pairs of alternately arranged leaflets, the terminal one the largest.** The leaf surface is often hairy. Plants develop as **basal rosettes**.

MATURE PLANT: **Flowering stems** are **smooth**, ascending to more often **erect**, angled, usually branched at the base **with few leaves. Basal leaves may or may not be hairy** on the upper surface and are more numerous than the smaller stem leaves. **Leaves are pinnate**, with **1–3 pairs of alternate**, round to kidney-shaped **leaflets**. Margins are shallowly toothed or with a few lobes. Petioles are prominent and hairy. **Upper leaves** are infrequent, **smaller than the basal leaves**, and usually hairy on the upper surface.

ROOTS AND UNDERGROUND STRUCTURES: Yellow, slender, much-branched taproot.

FLOWERS AND FRUIT: Flowers are present over an extended period of time when cool, moist conditions prevail but are most prolific in mid to late spring. **Flowers**, arranged **in dense racemes at the ends of stems, are small**, 2–3 mm in diameter, with 4 white petals, 4 sepals, and 4 or sometimes 6 stamens. **Fruit is a flattened capsule**, 1.5–2.5 cm long and much narrower (silique), often ascending past the adjacent flowers. The 2 valves of the silique coil as they mature. **Siliques are explosively dehiscent**, propelling seeds over 3 m from the plant. Seeds are 0.8–1 mm long, elliptic to square and flattened, yellowish brown.

POSTSENESCENCE CHARACTERISTICS: In mild climate, plants may overwinter as rosettes. Otherwise, no distinct postsenescence characteristics.

HABITAT: Hairy bittercress is a weed of nurseries, landscapes, turf, and greenhouses, particularly container crops. It grows on moist, sandy or organic soils in waste places and cultivated areas.

DISTRIBUTION: Most common in the northern and southeastern United States.

SIMILAR SPECIES: **Smallflowered bittercress (*Cardamine parviflora* L., CARPA)** has 4–10 stem leaves and no basal leaves at maturity. Hairy bittercress has 2–5 leaves on the elongated stem and persistent basal leaves. **Lesser-seeded bittercress (*Cardamine oligosperma* Torrey & A. Gray)** is a new introduction to the Northeast. It is similar to hairy bittercress, but has rounder and more numerous leaflets.

Hairy bittercress plant

J. Neal

R. Uva

Hairy bittercress seedling

A. Senesac

Lesser-seeded bittercress rosettes

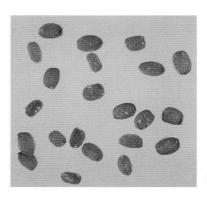

J. DiTomaso

Hairy bittercress seeds, 1 mm

Field pepperweed (*Lepidium campestre* (L.) R. Br.) [LEPCA]

Synonyms: field-cress, field peppercress, field pepperwort, field pepper-grass, downy pepper-grass

GENERAL DESCRIPTION: A **winter annual** forming a **basal rosette of finely toothed leaves**. Rosettes overwinter and produce erect branched flowering stems (20–60 cm tall) in early to midspring of the following year.

PROPAGATION / PHENOLOGY: Reproduction is **by seed**; seeds **germinate in late summer or early autumn**, less commonly in early spring, to a depth of 2 cm in the soil. Each plant can produce between 200 and 600 seeds.

SEEDLING: Cotyledons lack hairs, are petiolated, 12–15 mm long, club-shaped to oval. **Young leaves** are alternate (but **form a basal rosette**), rounded to ovate, on long petioles; the blades taper at the base and are rounded at the apex, with **wavy-toothed to deeply cut margins**.

MATURE PLANT: **Lower stem leaves and basal leaves** are oblong, lanceolate, **rounded at the tips and tapering to the base. Margins are lobed, toothed, or entire. Upper stem leaves** are alternate, 2–4 cm long, **sessile, arrowhead-shaped, and clasping at the base.** Margins are entire to partially toothed. Both leaves and stems are densely covered with short hairs.

ROOTS AND UNDERGROUND STRUCTURES: Taproot with secondary fibrous root system.

FLOWERS AND FRUIT: Flowering occurs primarily in May or June and sporadically until September. **Flowers are in dense racemes** to 15 cm long on 4–8 mm stalks (pedicels). **Petals (4) are small**, 2–2.5 mm long, white or greenish. Six stamens are present. The **fruit (silicle)** is broadly ovate, 5–6 mm long by 4 mm wide, oblong to **egg-shaped with wing-like structures** at the apex. Fruit collectively give the flower cluster a **bottle-brush appearance**. The seed is 2–2.5 mm long, oval, and brown.

POSTSENESCENCE CHARACTERISTICS: Dead stems and dried fruit persist throughout the summer.

HABITAT: A weed of orchards, nurseries, and reduced-tillage agricultural crops, field pepperweed is also found on disturbed sites and waste places.

DISTRIBUTION: Distributed throughout North America; particularly abundant in the northeastern and north-central United States.

SIMILAR SPECIES: **Virginia pepperweed** is similar in appearance; however the foliage and stem are nearly smooth, and the upper stem leaves taper to the base and do not clasp the stem, as do those of field pepperweed. The fruit of Virginia pepperweed are flat and round; those of field pepperweed are oblong to oval with a wing-like structure at the apex.

Field pepperweed habit

Field pepperweed seedlings

Field pepperweed bolting rosette

Field pepperweed seedhead

Left, Virginia pepperweed seeds, 2.0 mm; *right*, field pepperweed seeds, 2.5 mm

Virginia pepperweed (*Lepidium virginicum* L.) [LEPVI]

Synonyms: poor-man's pepper, pepper-grass, Virginian peppercress

GENERAL DESCRIPTION: A **winter or summer annual**, occasionally a biennial forming a **basal rosette of deeply lobed leaves** and an erect highly branched stem, 10–50 cm in height. Through much of the growing season the upper portion of the plant produces numerous small white flowers and dried seed capsules. Collectively, **the fruit capsules give the ends of stems a bottle-brush appearance.** Young leaves and mature capsules have a **peppery taste.**

PROPAGATION / PHENOLOGY: Reproduction is **by seed**; seeds germinate **in late summer or early fall.** Some germination can also occur in early spring.

SEEDLING: Cotyledons lack hairs, have a peppery taste, and are unequally oval, 7–10 mm long by 2–3 mm wide with long petioles. The first 2 leaves are opposite; subsequent leaves are alternate in a **basal rosette. Young leaves are oval, have long petioles and toothed margins,** and are hairy on the upper surface, the veins of the lower surface and the margins. **Fully expanded leaves are smooth and develop irregular lobes extending to the midrib.** The terminal lobe is large and ovate; the lateral lobes become smaller toward the petiole.

MATURE PLANT: **Erect, branched stems** develop in early spring after overwintering. Stems are covered with tiny hairs. **Basal and lower leaves lack hairs** and are obovate to oblanceolate, pinnately lobed with toothed margins. **Basal leaves do not persist on mature plants. Leaves in upper portions are lanceolate to linear, sessile,** and smaller than the basal leaves. Upper stem leaves are pointed at the apex and narrowed to the base, with toothed or entire margins.

ROOTS AND UNDERGROUND STRUCTURES: Slender taproot with secondary fibrous roots.

FLOWERS AND FRUIT: **Flowers** are produced from May through early summer and sporadically until autumn on numerous, **dense, terminal racemes** at the top of the plant. Flower arrangement gives the plant a bushy appearance. Individual flowers are small (0.7–1 mm long), with 4 white or greenish petals and 2 (rarely 4) stamens. **Fruit (silicle)** is rounded, 2.5–4 mm wide, flattened, **slightly winged and shallowly notched at the apex,** with a short style that does not exceed the notch. Seeds are light brown, oval (1.5 mm long), with one side straight and the other rounded and winged. Seed pods have a peppery taste.

POSTSENESCENCE CHARACTERISTICS: Dead, light brown or tan stems persist through summer. Mature seed are retained on dead stalks throughout the summer and can be dispersed from broken stems blown in the wind. Plants overwinter as rosettes.

HABITAT: A weed of agronomic, vegetable, orchard, nursery, and other perennial horticultural crops; also found in landscapes, roadsides, and waste areas, often on dry soil in full sun.

DISTRIBUTION: Occurs throughout much of the United States.

SIMILAR SPECIES: **Field pepperweed** is densely covered with short hairs, and the leaves on the stem are sessile with clasping bases. The seedlings tend to be somewhat larger than those of Virginia pepperweed, and the fruit are ovate, 5–6 mm long by 4 mm wide, with a more prominent wing at the apex. **Rosettes of horseweed** are very similar from fall through spring but lack the peppery taste and are not as deeply dissected as pepperweed.

J. Neal

Virginia pepperweed late-season habit

A. Senesac

Virginia pepperweed rosette

J. Neal

Virginia pepperweed flowering shoot

J. DiTomaso

Left, Virginia pepperweed seeds, 2.0 mm; *right*, field pepperweed seeds, 2.5 mm

179

Wild radish (*Raphanus raphanistrum* L.) [RAPRA]

Synonyms: jointed charlock, white charlock, jointed radish, wild kale, wild turnip, cadlock; sometimes incorrectly called wild mustard

GENERAL DESCRIPTION: A **winter or summer annual**, or rarely a biennial. **Erect, branched flowering stems**, 30–80 cm tall, develop from a **basal rosette**. Leaves taper toward the base and are elliptic and pinnatifid with a large terminal lobe. Leaf surfaces are covered with bent, coarse, bristly hairs.

PROPAGATION / PHENOLOGY: Reproduction is **by seed**; seeds germinate in late summer, autumn, or early spring.

SEEDLING: Hypocotyls are purple. **Cotyledons are petiolated, heart- or kidney-shaped**, with a **deeply indented apex** and an abruptly tapered base. Young leaves have appressed hairs and are rough to the touch. The **margins are irregular, wavy, and pinnatifid**, with the rounded and slightly pointed terminal lobe the largest. **Leaf bases are deeply cut**, producing 1 or 2 independent lobes. Petioles are relatively long.

MATURE PLANT: **Erect, branching flowering stems develop from overwintering basal rosettes. Stems have stiff hairs**, especially on the lower parts, that are parallel to angled lines on the surface. **Leaves are alternate, with toothed margins and coarse hairs. Lower leaves** are long-petiolated, elliptic, 20 cm long by 5 cm wide, **tapered toward the base, and pinnately lobed with a large terminal lobe. Upper leaves** are lanceolate, entire to toothed, sessile, and smaller than the lower leaves.

ROOTS AND UNDERGROUND STRUCTURES: Stout **taproot** with a **radish taste and odor.**

FLOWERS AND FRUIT: Flowers are 1–1.5 cm in diameter in long terminal racemes that bloom from June to September. **Petals (4) are light to pale yellow, fading to white with age**, and have purple veins. Sepals have stiff erect hairs. Flower-stalks (pedicels) are ascending, 5–20 mm long. **Pod-like fruit (siliques) are constricted between the seeds**, resembling beads on a string. Each fruit (2–4 cm long) has prominent ribs with a 1–3 cm long beak at the tip. Fruit lower on the flowering stem may be smaller and seedless. At maturity, **the segments break into fragments**, each containing 1–2 seeds. The seeds do not generally become detached from the fruit. Seeds are 2–3 mm long by 1.5–2 mm wide, egg-shaped, grooved in a net-like pattern, and have light brown to black flecks. Each plant produces about 160 seeds.

POSTSENESCENCE CHARACTERISTICS: Fruit pods persist on erect stems through the summer and into autumn. Plants may overwinter as rosettes.

HABITAT: A weed of cultivated nursery, horticultural, and agricultural crops, wild radish is also commonly found in fall-seeded forage crops, waste places, and disturbed sites. It thrives on nutrient-rich sandy and loamy soils.

DISTRIBUTION: Found throughout the United States, especially in the Pacific Northwest and the northeastern and north-central states.

SIMILAR SPECIES: **Wild mustard** has smoother leaves in contrast to the rough hairs on the leaves of wild radish. The leaves of wild radish contain more lobed divisions than those of wild mustard. Hypocotyls and roots of wild radish have a distinctive hot mustard taste. At maturity, the fruit of wild radish break into fragments containing 1–2 seeds each; the fruit of wild mustard open lengthwise along a suture. Wild radish is found predominantly on the coastal plains of the Northeast, whereas wild mustard is mainly distributed on upland soils.

Wild radish seedling

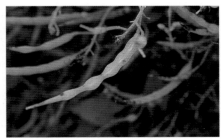
Wild radish fruit

Wild radish rosette

Wild radish in flower

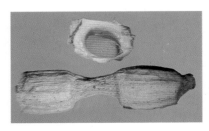
Wild radish seed, 2.5 mm, and seed pod

181

Marsh yellowcress (*Rorippa islandica* (Oeder) Borbas) [RORIS]

Synonyms: *Nasturtium palustre, Radicula palustris, Rorippa palustris,* marsh cress, yellow water cress, common yellow-cress

GENERAL DESCRIPTION: An **annual, biennial, or rarely a short-lived perennial**, initially forming a **basal rosette of deeply lobed leaves** then producing ascending to **erect flowering stems** (30–80 cm tall). Larger plants are commonly much branched.

PROPAGATION / PHENOLOGY: Reproduction is **by seed, produced 2 or 3 times per year**, and by new **adventitious shoots initiated from the crown or the roots.**

SEEDLING: Cotyledons are petiolated, elliptic to round, 1–2 cm long. **Young leaves are petiolated, egg-shaped** to elliptic or heart-shaped, **with wavy margins.** More **mature leaves are deeply lobed, pinnatifid.** Plants form a **basal rosette.**

MATURE PLANT: **Elongating stems are erect, rarely ascending or prostrate,** unbranched or branched, angular, smooth or somewhat hairy below and smoother above. **Leaves are alternate,** petiolated (occasionally sessile above), and **pinnatifid with 3–7 irregularly toothed lateral lobes and a larger terminal lobe.** The bases of the petioles of stem leaves are sometimes auriculate (with lobe-like appendages). Upper leaves may be pinnatifid to deeply toothed to entire.

ROOTS AND UNDERGROUND STRUCTURES: Slender, pale yellow taproot with secondary fibrous roots.

FLOWERS AND FRUIT: Flowers are produced from June to September in unbranched racemes on the terminal end of stems or in the upper leaf axils. The flowers are 2–3 mm in diameter. **Petals (4) are pale yellow,** 1–2.5 mm long, with 6 stamens. The fruit (silique) is cylindrical to spherical, slightly curved upward, 4–14 mm long by 1–3 mm wide, and consists of 2 valves containing several seeds each. Seeds are egg-shaped, yellow-brown, slightly flattened and notched, and about 0.6 mm long.

POSTSENESCENCE CHARACTERISTICS: Overwinters as a rosette of finely lobed leaves.

HABITAT: Marsh yellowcress has become an increasingly important weed of small fruit, vegetable, and nursery crops. It is commonly found on heavy, wet, nutrient-rich soil in poorly drained fields, meadows, pastures, and wet ditch banks but tolerates a range of soil types and conditions. Infestations usually start in wet areas and spread outward.

DISTRIBUTION: Found throughout the United States; most common in the eastern and north-central states.

SIMILAR SPECIES: **Yellow fieldcress (*Rorippa sylvestris* (L.) Bess., RORSY)** is a **perennial** that spreads by **rhizomes** and can form large patches. Its leaves are more finely cut than those of marsh yellowcress. Yellow fieldcress is spreading and becoming increasingly important in the Northeast.

Marsh yellowcress habit

A. Senesac

A. Senesac

Juvenile marsh yellowcress

Marsh yellowcress rosettes

A. Senesac

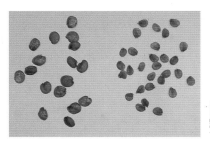

J. DiTomaso

Left, yellow fieldcress seeds, 0.7 mm; *right*, marsh yellowcress seeds, 0.4 mm

R. Uva

Yellow fieldcress foliage, flowers, and fruit

Hedge mustard (*Sisymbrium officinale* (L.) Scop.) [SSYOF]

Synonyms: *Chamaeplium officinale, Erysimum officinale*, hedge weed

GENERAL DESCRIPTION: A **winter or summer annual**, or rarely a biennial, that produces a rosette in the first season. Flowering stems are erect (30 cm to 1 m tall) with spreading branches.

PROPAGATION / PHENOLOGY: Reproduction is **by seed**; seeds germinate in late summer to early spring.

SEEDLING: Cotyledons are petiolated, elliptic-oblong to club-shaped. **Young leaves** are circular to egg-shaped, with **wavy toothed margins and petioles. Leaves become deeply lobed to narrowly pinnatifid with age. Surfaces are bristly.**

MATURE PLANT: **Flowering stems are erect, bristly-hairy**, rounded, with spreading branches. **Leaves are alternate, pinnately lobed or divided, with wide irregular wavy-toothed segments.** Both leaf surfaces are **bristly-hairy**. The leaf apex is the largest, most distinctly toothed segment. **Lower rosette leaves are deeply pinnatifid**, with oblong to egg-shaped segments and a rounded terminal segment. **Upper leaves are mostly sessile, oblong to lanceolate**; the terminal lobe is narrow, and the margins are toothed or entire.

ROOTS AND UNDERGROUND STRUCTURES: Slender branched taproot.

FLOWERS AND FRUIT: Flowers are produced from June through September in clusters at the ends of elongated stems. Flowers are 3–6 mm in diameter, have 4 sepals, 4 **yellow petals** (3–4 mm long), and 6 stamens. Flower cluster expands as flowers mature. The **fruit** is an elongated, **awl-shaped**, 1–2 cm long by 1–1.5 mm wide **capsule (silique)** that is **tightly appressed to the stem**. Siliques separate into 2 valves containing 10–20 seeds each. Seeds are egg-shaped to triangular (1–1.5 mm long), light or dark brown to reddish yellow. Each plant can produce about 2700 seeds.

POSTSENESCENCE CHARACTERISTICS: Tightly appressed fruit or remnants of the fruit remain attached to the dead stems.

HABITAT: Hedge mustard is a weed of nursery, horticultural, and agricultural crops. It grows on dry, nutrient-rich loamy, sandy to stony soils, primarily in cultivated areas and disturbed sites.

DISTRIBUTION: Found throughout most of the United States.

SIMILAR SPECIES: **Tumble mustard (*Sisymbrium altissimum* L., SSYAL)** is a less hairy winter or summer annual with more deeply and finely dissected skeleton-like foliage. Its fruit are longer and narrower, almost thread-like, and are not usually appressed to the stem as are those of hedge mustard. Tumble mustard plants are brittle late in the season; they become detached from the roots and distribute seeds by tumbling in the wind.

Tumble mustard rosette

R. Uva

Tumble mustard seedlings

J. DiTomaso

Tumble mustard habit

Univ. Calif. Statewide IPM Project

Tumble mustard mature stems and foliage

J. DiTomaso

J. DiTomaso

Left, tumble mustard seeds, 0.9 mm; *right*, hedge mustard seeds, 1.3 mm

Field pennycress (*Thlaspi arvense* L.) [THLAR]

Synonyms: fan-weed, penny-cress, French-weed, stink-weed, bastard-cress

GENERAL DESCRIPTION: A **winter or summer annual** that initially produces a **rosette** of leaves then an **erect flowering stem** (10–60 cm tall). Stems and foliage are smooth and emit an unpleasant odor when bruised. **Fruit are distinctively round to elliptic, winged pods.**

PROPAGATION / PHENOLOGY: Reproduction is **by seed**; seeds germinate in late summer, autumn, or early spring from as deep as 1 cm in cool, moist soil.

SEEDLING: Cotyledons are bluish green, oval to elliptic-oblong, about 6–8 mm long by 5–6 mm wide, on 5–7 mm long petioles. The tips of the cotyledons curve downward. **Young leaves** are smooth, **round to oval, with distinct petioles. Subsequent leaves** are also petiolated and are **ovate-lanceolate**, with a **wavy, slightly toothed margin.** Young plants produce a **basal rosette** of leaves. Fall-germinating plants will overwinter in this stage.

MATURE PLANT: Basal leaves are light green, hairless, narrowly egg-shaped, with entire or toothed margins and 1.3–5 cm long petioles. **Basal leaves do not persist at maturity. Flower-producing stems are erect, unbranched** or branched above, and smooth. Upper leaves are oblong to lanceolate, with smooth surfaces and toothed or entire margins. **Stem leaves are sessile, with projecting lobes (auricles) where the leaf clasps the stem.**

ROOTS AND UNDERGROUND STRUCTURES: Slender taproot with secondary fibrous roots.

FLOWERS AND FRUIT: Flowers bloom from April through June and are 4–6 mm in diameter, in dense racemes at the end of the stems. **Petals (4) are white**, 3–4 mm long, and about twice as long as the 4 sepals. Six stamens are present. **Racemes elongate with age.** The **distinctive fruit (silicles)** are flat, circular to elliptic, about 1.3 cm in diameter, and distinctly **winged around the margins, with a 2–3 mm notch at the apex.** Silicles separate into 2 valves, each containing 2–8 seeds. Seeds are dark brown, 1.5–2.3 mm long and flattened, with 10–14 concentric granular ridges on each side. A single plant produces about 900 seeds.

POSTSENESCENCE CHARACTERISTICS: The upright stems and fruit clusters may persist. In late summer, the capsules remain as silvery membranes with flat wings and a notch at the apex.

HABITAT: A weed of nursery, horticultural, and agricultural crops, field pennycress is usually found on nutrient-rich soil in cultivated areas.

DISTRIBUTION: Occurs throughout the United States; most common in the northwestern states.

SIMILAR SPECIES: **Thoroughwort pennycress (*Thlaspi perfoliatum* L., THLPE)** is similar, but the lobes (auricles) at the base of the stem leaves are rounded; those of field pennycress are pointed. Thoroughwort pennycress has shorter fruit (4–7 mm long), with notches that are mostly wider than deep, whereas field pennycress has notches that are deeper than wide.

Field pennycress habit

J. Neal

Field pennycress seedlings

A. Senesac

Field pennycress flowering shoot

Univ. Calif. Statewide IPM Project

Field pennycress flowers
and fruit

J. DiTomaso

Left, thoroughwort pennycress
seeds, 1.1 mm; *right*, field
pennycress seeds, 1.6 mm

J. Neal

Common Venus' looking-glass (*Triodanis perfoliata* (L.) Nieuwl.) [TJDPE]

Synonyms: *Specularia perfoliata*, round-leaved triodanis, clasping bellwort

GENERAL DESCRIPTION: A **winter or summer annual**, or occasionally a perennial. The main stem is **erect** ($\leq$0.5 m in height). Unbranched side shoots arise from the base of the plant and may run perpendicular to the primary shoot. Plants can appear prostrate if the main stem dies. Cut stems exude a milky sap.

PROPAGATION / PHENOLOGY: Reproduction is **by seed**; seeds germinate primarily in the spring.

SEEDLING: **First leaves are opposite**, ovate, with a petiole about as long as the leaf blade. **Subsequent leaves become alternate and sessile** (or nearly so) with age.

MATURE PLANT: **Stems are erect, sparsely branched**, and hairy or rough on the lower portions. **Leaves** are alternate, 0.5–3 cm long by 6–25 mm wide, rounded to egg-shaped, palmately veined, with **heart-shaped bases that clasp the stem**. Margins are usually toothed.

ROOTS AND UNDERGROUND STRUCTURES: Fibrous root system.

FLOWERS AND FRUIT: Sessile **flowers** (2 cm wide), present in May and June, are produced in **clusters of 1–3 in the leaf axils.** Flowers in the lower leaf axils are self-pollinating and remain closed (cleistogamous), producing seed without opening. The sepals (4–5) are fused. Base of the **petals** (5) are fused into a 2–4 mm long **deep purple to pale lavender tube**. Five stamens surround a 3-parted pistil. The **fruit is a vase-like oblong capsule**, opening by 3 small elongated pores at or slightly below the middle. Seeds are 0.4–0.6 mm long, egg-shaped, dark reddish brown, smooth, and glossy.

POSTSENESCENCE CHARACTERISTICS: Upright stems with the characteristic seed pods persist only a short time in late summer.

HABITAT: Common Venus' looking-glass is a weed of low-maintenance turfgrass and landscapes. It is often found on nutrient-poor, dry, sandy or gravelly soil and on disturbed sites with plants that offer little competition.

DISTRIBUTION: Distributed throughout most of the continental United States.

SIMILAR SPECIES: **Small Venus' looking-glass (*Triodanis biflora* (R. & P.) Greene, TJDBI)** has narrower leaves, less pronounced venation, and only 1 flower per node (all flowers open); otherwise, small and common Venus' looking-glass are similar. The alternate, sessile stem leaves of **corn speedwell** resemble those of common Venus' looking-glass, but the leaves on the base of corn speedwell (nonflowering parts) are opposite and distinctly hairy, with short (1–3 mm) petioles.

J. Neal

Common Venus' looking-glass habit

J. Neal

Venus' looking-glass seedling

A. Senesac

Common Venus' looking-glass flowers

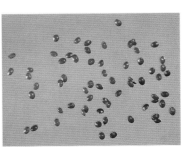

J. DiTomaso

Common Venus' looking-glass
seeds, 0.4 mm

189

Corn cockle (*Agrostemma githago* L.) [AGOGI]

Synonyms: *Lychnis githago*, purple cockle, corn rose, corn campion, crown-of-the-field, corn mullein, old maids pink

GENERAL DESCRIPTION: A **winter annual** with **erect stems** (30–60 cm tall, sometimes to 1 m), branching mostly in the upper half. Leaves are opposite, long and narrow, with gray hairs. Seeds contain the glucoside githagin, which is a saponin that causes gastrointestinal irritation when ingested. **Grain contaminated with corn cockle seed may be detrimental to livestock and poultry.**

PROPAGATION / PHENOLOGY: Reproduction is **by seed; seeds germinate in autumn**.

SEEDLING: Cotyledons are relatively large (15–30 mm long by 5–10 mm wide), often unequal in size, dull green, and somewhat waxy. Cotyledon blades are thick; the apex is rounded, and the base gradually narrows into a short petiole. Petioles of the 2 cotyledons are joined by a ridge across the hypocotyl. **Young leaves are opposite**; surfaces are dull green and **densely covered with long, soft appressed hairs. Blades are lanceolate** and taper to the petiole and to a sharp point at the apex.

MATURE PLANT: **Stems are swollen at the nodes**, branching in the upper parts, and covered with silky hairs. **Leaves** are opposite, **linear to lanceolate**, 8–12 cm long by 5–10 mm wide, with entire margins and appressed **gray hairs. Petioles are joined by a ridge across the node.**

ROOTS AND UNDERGROUND STRUCTURES: Shallow taproot.

FLOWERS AND FRUIT: **Red to purplish red flowers** are most abundant from May to July but are also present later in the summer. Flowers (2–4 cm in diameter) are solitary on long stalks at the end of branches. The 5 sepals are longer than the petals and are fused into a 12–18 mm long tube with 10 prominent ribs. There are 10 stamens and 5 petals (not fused); each petal is 2–3 cm long. The fruit is an oval, 10-ribbed capsule, 14–22 mm long by 10–15 mm wide. Seeds are 2–4 mm in diameter, triangular, kidney-shaped to round, black or brown with pointed projections (tubercles) on the surface. **Seeds are poisonous** and have a **short viability in the soil.**

POSTSENESCENCE CHARACTERISTICS: Dead stems can persist, with the distinct long fused sepal attached. Young plants overwinter as sparsely leafed basal rosettes.

HABITAT: A common weed of winter grain crops, other agricultural crops, and nurseries, corn cockle prefers slightly acid to neutral, nutrient-rich soils.

DISTRIBUTION: Widely distributed throughout the United States but most common in the southeastern states.

SIMILAR SPECIES: **White campion** (also commonly known as white cockle) is a biennial or short-lived perennial that vegetatively resembles corn cockle but has white flowers and shorter, broader leaves. White campion can produce new plants from fragmented segments of the root.

R. Uva

Corn cockle flowering habit

A. Senesac

Corn cockle flower and buds

A. Senesac

Corn cockle stem and foilage

J. DiTomaso

Corn cockle seeds, 3.1 mm

Mouseear chickweed (*Cerastium vulgatum* L.) [CERVU]

Synonyms: large mouseear chickweed, mouse-ear

GENERAL DESCRIPTION: A **perennial with prominently hairy prostrate stems** (15–50 cm long) **and leaves**. Stems root at the nodes to form dense mats, especially in turfgrass. In unmowed areas, plants form mounds with ascending branches to 30 cm tall.

PROPAGATION / PHENOLOGY: Reproduction is **by seed**. Seedlings emerge in late summer, fall, or early spring. In cool moist or irrigated areas, emergence can continue throughout the summer.

SEEDLING: **Cotyledons are rounded** to ovate, 2–7 mm long by 0.5–2 mm wide, generally lacking hairs on the blade but with a few prominent hairs at the base of the stalk. **Young leaves are opposite, spatulate**, dull green, **with prominent hairs** (0.5–1 mm long) on the upper surface and on the veins below. **Stems have 2 rows of dense hairs** and **root at the nodes** when in contact with the soil.

MATURE PLANT: **Stems are similar to those of the seedling. Distinctly hairy leaves** are opposite, sessile, dark green above, elliptic or spatulate to oval or oblanceolate, 1–3 mm wide by 2–12 mm long. **Margins are entire.**

ROOTS AND UNDERGROUND STRUCTURES: Fibrous root system.

FLOWERS AND FRUIT: Flowers are produced from May through October in clusters at the end of stems. **Petals (5) are white**, about 6 mm long, and **deeply lobed or notched at the tip (possibly giving the appearance of 10 petals)**. Fruit are cylindrical capsules, 8–10 mm long by 2–3 mm wide, and produce many seeds. Seeds are triangular or angular (up to 1 mm long), flattened, notched on the margin, reddish to chestnut brown with rounded bumps.

POSTSENESCENCE CHARACTERISTICS: Plant may die during hot, dry conditions but generally remains green through the winter.

HABITAT: Mouseear chickweed is primarily a weed of turfgrass and other mowed areas, but it is also found in many crops, as well as in landscapes and nurseries. It can survive in shaded areas.

DISTRIBUTION: Found throughout most of the United States and southern Canada.

SIMILAR SPECIES: **Common chickweed** is a winter annual resembling mouseear chickweed in growth habit; however, it does not have hairy leaf blades and does not root at the nodes. **Thymeleaf speedwell (*Veronica serpyllifolia* L., VERSE)** has a similar leaf shape and growth habit but also lacks hairs on the leaves and stem. Two other members of the genus *Cerastium* are also weedy. **Sticky chickweed (*Cerastium glomeratum* Thuill., CERGL = *Cerastium viscosum*)** is an annual with glandular sticky hairs. **Field chickweed (*Cerastium arvense* L., CERAR)** has petals 2–3 times longer than the sepals, whereas the petals of mouseear chickweed are nearly the same length as the sepals. In addition, the leaves of field chickweed are more linear, and the hairs are shorter than those on mouseear chickweed.

Flowering mouseear chickweed in turf

Young mouseear chickweed seedlings

Older mouseear chickweed seedling

Thymeleaf speedwell habit

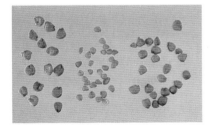

Left to right: field chickweed seeds, 0.7 mm; sticky chickweed seeds, 0.4 mm; and mouseear chickweed seeds, 0.6 mm

193

Birdseye pearlwort (*Sagina procumbens* L.) [SAIPR]

Synonyms: procumbent pearlwort, birdseye

GENERAL DESCRIPTION: A **small stoloniferous perennial forming dense turf-like mats** with erect stems. Under close mowing, such as golf course greens, birdseye pearlwort will have few leaves and resembles moss or mowed grass.

PROPAGATION / PHENOLOGY: Propagates **primarily by seeds**, but also **spreads by stolons** or can be transported by stolon fragments, which root at the nodes. **Tiny seeds are dispersed when capsules are shaken by wind or rain.** A short after-ripening period (2–4 weeks) is necessary for germination. Seedlings emerge in cool, moist soil in early spring to fall.

SEEDLING: Seedlings develop as **small tufted rosettes. Cotyledons are awl- or needle-shaped**, circular in cross section, <1 mm wide and only a few millimeters long. **Young leaves are similar** in shape but somewhat longer (up to 1 cm).

MATURE PLANT: Stems are smooth and slender. They root at the nodes. **Leaves are opposite**, simple, smooth, mostly hairless, **linear to awl-shaped** (1.5 cm long by 1 mm wide), and sharply pointed at the apex. **Leaves may appear whorled when short shoot clusters are congested** in the leaf axils.

ROOTS AND UNDERGROUND STRUCTURES: Shallow fibrous root system associated with stolons.

FLOWERS AND FRUIT: Flowers appear from May through frost and are produced singly on relatively long and erect pedicels (0.3–2 cm). The pedicels extend beyond the foliage arising from the ends of the stems and the leaf axils. Flowers nod with age, but pedicels become erect again in fruit. **Flowers are inconspicuous**, with 4 green sepals (2–2.5 mm long) and 4 white unlobed petals (occasionally absent) slightly shorter than the sepals. The **fruit** is a **many-seeded**, 2–3.5 mm long, persistent **capsule. Seeds are tiny** (0.2–0.3 mm long) and dark brown.

POSTSENESCENCE CHARACTERISTICS: In mild winters, plants persist but will become discolored by hard frost.

HABITAT: Sometimes cultivated as an ornamental in rock gardens or between paving stones, birdseye pearlwort has escaped to become an aggressive weed of turfgrass, particularly golf course greens and tees, and container nurseries. It is commonly found in rocky areas and paved footpaths, especially in the crevices of brick walks. It prefers moist soil and cool climates.

DISTRIBUTION: Found throughout the United States and southern Canada but most common in cooler regions.

SIMILAR SPECIES: The small erect capsules and the prostrate mat-forming growth habit are sometimes mistaken for the spore capsules and low habit of many **mosses**. Birdseye pearlwort can also be confused with weedy members of the pink family. **Knawel** can be distinguished by its flowers, which lack petals and are sessile in the leaf axils. **Corn spurry (*Spergula arvensis* L., SPRAR)** is an annual with similar but longer (1–3 cm) linear awl-shaped leaves. Its flowers are on terminal branches and have 5 conspicuous white petals. **Red sandspurry (*Spergularia rubra* (L.) J. & C. Presl, SPBRU)** is an annual or short-lived perennial with narrow leaves up to 2.5 cm long and conspicuous chaffy stipules. It grows prostrate to ascending and produces pinkish red flowers in loose terminal cymes.

Birdseye pearlwort habit

R. Uva

R. Uva

Birdseye pearlwort seedlings

Birdseye pearlwort flowers

R. Uva

A. Senesac

Red sandspurry habit

J. DiTomaso

Left, red sandspurry seeds, 0.5 mm;
right, birdseye pearlwort seeds, 0.3 mm

Knawel (*Scleranthus annuus* L.) [SCRAN]

Synonyms: German knot-grass, annual knawel

GENERAL DESCRIPTION: A **winter or summer annual**, low-growing to prostrate (reaching only 10 cm in height) and branching. Its **grass-like appearance** enables it to become established in turfgrass without notice. In dry open areas it forms **low mats or sprawling clumps**.

PROPAGATION / PHENOLOGY: Reproduction is **by seed**; seeds germinate primarily in early spring but also in late summer or autumn.

SEEDLING: Hypocotyls are light green and smooth. **Cotyledons** are smooth, **sessile, linear**, <1 cm long and about 1 mm wide. **Young leaves are sessile, opposite**, linear, bristle-tipped at the apex, and have short hairs along the basal portion of the margin. **Opposite leaves are connected at the base by a translucent membrane** surrounding the node. Lateral branches do not develop until late in the seedling stage.

MATURE PLANT: **Stems are branched and spreading. Leaves are linear**, 5–25 mm long, <1 mm wide, **sharply pointed at the tip**. Leaves are opposite and joined at the node by a translucent membrane, although leaves may appear to be whorled when new shoots are expanding from leaf axils.

ROOTS AND UNDERGROUND STRUCTURES: Small taproot with a secondary fibrous root system.

FLOWERS AND FRUIT: Flowers appear from May to October on sessile or short stalks (pedicels) in clusters from the leaf axils. Flowers are small, green, and spiny to the touch. The fruit, a small, thin-walled, 1-seeded inflated utricle, is enclosed by the 5-toothed, persistent sepal tube (3–4 mm long). Sepal tube and fruit become light brown at maturity.

POSTSENESCENCE CHARACTERISTICS: On dry sites, dead plants can remain throughout the summer, but they do not persist in moist areas.

HABITAT: Knawel is primarily a weed of low-maintenance turfgrass and nursery crops. It is most commonly found on dry, sandy soils.

DISTRIBUTION: Occurs throughout the eastern half of the United States.

SIMILAR SPECIES: Knawel can be distinguished from other similar members of the pink family by its flowers, which lack petals and are sessile in the leaf axils. **Corn spurry** is also an annual with similar but slightly longer (1–3 cm) linear awl-shaped leaves. Its flowers have 5 white petals and are on terminal branches. **Red sandspurry** is an annual or short-lived perennial with very similar leaves; however, it grows prostrate to ascending and produces pinkish red flowers in loose terminal cymes. **Birdseye pearlwort** is a summer or winter annual that grows as a moss-like mat with awl-shaped leaves approximately 1.5 cm in length. Its flower-stalks are erect and bear small white flowers and persistent seed capsules.

J. Neal

Knawel habit

R. Uva

Knawel seedling

R. Uva

Knawel stems and foliage

Knawel flowering shoot

J. Neal

Corn spurry seedlings

J. DiTomaso

Left, corn spurry seeds, 1.3 mm; *right,* knawel seeds, 3.5 mm (including calyx)

White campion (*Silene alba* (Mill.) E.H.L. Krause) [MELAL]

Synonyms: *Lychnis alba, Melandrium album, Silene latifolia*, white cockle

GENERAL DESCRIPTION: A **winter or summer annual, biennial, or short-lived perennial** initally forming a **basal rosette, subsequently producing a thick, erect** (30 cm to 1 m tall), **branched, leafy stem** with hairy or downy foliage and **white inflated (balloon-like) flowers**. The stems may become almost woody with age. Seedlings and mature flowering plants are commonly found together in spring and early summer.

PROPAGATION / PHENOLOGY: Reproduction is primarily **by seed** but cultivation can fragment plants and spread **adventitious buds on root and stem segments**. Seedlings emerge in mid to late spring and again in late summer.

SEEDLING: Cotyledons are sessile, narrowly oval to egg-shaped (1.5 cm long by 5–7 mm wide), pointed at the apex and tapering to the base. The surface is slightly granular. **Young leaves are opposite**, lanceolate to ovate, **dull green, soft-hairy**, with some gland-tipped hairs. Leaf blades gradually taper down the long petiole margin. Margins are fringed with hairs. **Young plants produce a rosette.**

MATURE PLANT: **Winter annual and biennial plants overwinter as basal rosettes. Basal leaves wither when erect stems reach maturity** in summer. **Stems are covered with short hairs**, some glandular on the upper stem. Nodes are swollen. **Leaves are hairy, opposite**, entire, lanceolate to ovate to broadly elliptic (3–10 cm long and 1–4 cm wide). Lower leaves taper into long petioles; upper leaves are sessile. Margins are softly hairy.

ROOTS AND UNDERGROUND STRUCTURES: Taproot and **thick lateral roots**.

FLOWERS AND FRUIT: Flowers are produced from May to fall in clusters (or solitary) on long stalks. Plants are dioecious (male and female flowers on separate plants). Male and female flowers have **white (occasionally pink) petals** (2–4 cm long) notched at the tip. The **female flowers have fused inflated sepals** (calyx), 2–3 cm long, with 20 veins. The sepals of the male flowers are also fused, but they are more slender and have only 10 veins. Flowers open in the evening and have a sweet scent. **Fruits are cone-shaped capsules** opening at the top **with 10 teeth**. As each fruit forms, the surrounding calyx continues to inflate. Seeds are brown to gray, rounded to kidney-shaped (1–1.4 mm in diameter), and flattened on one side, with blunt bumps.

POSTSENESCENCE CHARACTERISTICS: The **calyx disintegrates, leaving the shiny, smooth, light brown capsule**. Winter annuals and biennials survive as basal rosettes.

HABITAT: A weed of grains and legume forage crops, other field and vegetable crops, nurseries, waste places, and roadsides. Common in full sun and on rich, well-drained soils.

DISTRIBUTION: Found throughout much of North America, particularly in the eastern and north-central United States and southern Canada.

SIMILAR SPECIES: **Nightflowering catchfly (*Silene noctiflora* L., MELNO)**, a summer annual, has dense, coarse hairs below, sticky hairs above, pink to yellowish flowers, and seed capsules with 6 teeth at the top. **Sleepy catchfly (*Silene antirrhina* L., SILAN)** has few hairs, except for glandular hairs near the stem nodes, and does not have an inflated calyx. **Bladder campion (*Silene vulgaris* (Moench) Garcke, SILVU)** lacks hairs and is a robust perennial with creeping rhizomes. Young rosettes of white campion **may resemble some asters**, but aster stem leaves are alternate, not opposite.

White campion habit and seed pods

White campion seedling

White campion perennial root and shoot

White campion flowers

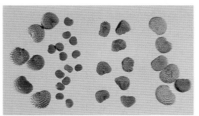

Left to right: bladder campion seeds, 1.3 mm; sleepy catchfly seeds, 0.6 mm; nightflowering catchfly seeds, 1.0 mm; and white campion seeds, 1.3 mm

Little starwort (*Stellaria graminea* L.) [STEGR]

Synonyms: grass-leaved stichwort, grassy starwort

GENERAL DESCRIPTION: A slender **perennial**, nearly prostrate or ascending (10–50 cm tall), with **angular or square stems** and small white flowers.

PROPAGATION / PHENOLOGY: Reproduction is **by seed**, but plants are **not prolific seed producers** and **seedlings are rarely encountered**. Once established, plants can spread vegetatively when fragmented **stems root at the nodes**. Seeds germinate in the fall or spring in cool, moist soils.

SEEDLING: Cotyledons are slender, egg-shaped, petiolated, and pointed at the apex. Young leaves are similar to cotyledons, narrowly egg-shaped and pointed at the apex.

MATURE PLANT: **Stems** are smooth and hairless, **angular to square**, branched, and light green. They **root at the nodes. Leaves are opposite, sessile**, simple, somewhat succulent, linear or **narrowly lanceolate** (1.5–2.5 cm long by 4–7 mm wide). Plants lack hairs, except for a few marginal hairs near the leaf base.

ROOTS AND UNDERGROUND STRUCTURES: Shallow fibrous root system.

FLOWERS AND FRUIT: **Small white flowers** are produced for a only short time between May and July. Numerous flowers are produced in spreading clusters (cymes) at the ends of stems and in the leaf axils. Each flower is on a long slender stalk (pedicel). There are **usually 5 (sometimes 4) petals (5 mm long), which are cleft almost to the base, appearing to be 10 (or 8) petals**. Fruit are egg-shaped capsules (5 mm long). Seeds are 0.8–1.2 mm long, brownish, circular to broadly egg-shaped, with small rough irregular ridges on the surface.

POSTSENESCENCE CHARACTERISTICS: None of significance.

HABITAT: Primarily a weed of turfgrass, meadows, and roadsides, little starwort is commonly found in moist to damp areas, often on sandy soils. It is rarely encountered in cultivated crops.

DISTRIBUTION: Common in the northeastern United States and southeastern Canada, especially the Maritime provinces.

SIMILAR SPECIES: **Common chickweed** is a winter annual with similar leaves and **nearly identical flowers**, but the leaves are petiolated and broadly elliptic to egg-shaped. Those of little starwort are linear to lanceolate and sessile. In addition, stems of common chickweed are round with 1 or 2 rows of hairs, whereas little starwort stems are angled or square and lack hairs. **Corn spurry** is similar in habit but has needle-like leaves in whorls around the stem.

Mature little starwort plant and flower

Little starwort stem

Little starwort flowers

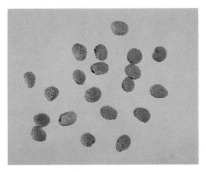

Little starwort seeds, 0.9 mm

R. Uva

R. Uva

R. Uva

J. DiTomaso

Common chickweed (*Stellaria media* (L.) Vill.) [STEME]

Synonyms: *Alsine media*, starwort, starweed, bindweed, winterweed, satin flower, tongue-grass

GENERAL DESCRIPTION: A **winter annual** that **can become perennialized in cool, moist areas.** Common chickweed forms prostrate, dense patches in turfgrass, but it can reach 40 cm in height in other areas.

PROPAGATION / PHENOLOGY: Reproduction is **by seed**; seeds usually germinate in early spring and late summer. In shady moist areas, germination can occur throughout the summer. **One or two generations can be produced each year.**

SEEDLING: Cotyledons are slender (1 cm long by 3 mm wide), ovate, with a hairy stalk as long as the blade. **Young leaves are opposite**, rounded to **egg-shaped, pointed at the apex**, with petioles about half the length of the blade. Young plants are erect and begin to branch at the base after 5 leaf pairs have developed.

MATURE PLANT: Stems are prostrate, branching, and smooth, except for 1 or 2 rows of hairs; the upper portions are erect or ascending. Stems and leaves are **light green. Leaves are opposite, broadly elliptic to egg-shaped**, 1–3 cm long, and **pointed at the apex**. Hairy petioles are present on most leaves, but petioles are lacking on some upper leaves.

ROOTS AND UNDERGROUND STRUCTURES: The **root system is fibrous and shallow**, the foliage is easily detached from the roots when pulled.

FLOWERS AND FRUIT: Flowering occurs from early spring to autumn, particularly on protected sites and in mild climates. The flowers are small (3–6 mm wide) and consist of 5 sepals (5 mm long) and **5 white petals**. The petals are shorter than the sepals and are **deeply lobed, giving the appearance of 10 petals**. The fruit is a 1-celled, oval capsule containing numerous seeds. Seeds are flattened, circular with a marginal notch, 1.0–1.3 mm in diameter, light brown to reddish brown, with minute bumps on the surface.

POSTSENESCENCE CHARACTERISTICS: Usually senescing in lawns and other sunny areas by midsummer. Dead plant parts do not persist.

HABITAT: A common weed of turfgrass, landscapes, golf course greens, nursery crops, and irrigated horticultural and agronomic crops, common chickweed tolerates close and frequent mowing. It thrives on moist, shady sites with nutrient-rich soils but is not limited to those areas.

DISTRIBUTION: Widely distributed throughout the world and common in all regions of the United States.

SIMILAR SPECIES: **Mouseear chickweed** is a perennial that resembles common chickweed in growth habit; however, its leaves are oblong and densely covered with hairs. **Thymeleaf speedwell** is found in similar habitats and has a similar growth habit, color, leaf shape, and arrangement (opposite leaves). It is distinguished by the **leaf tips**, which are rounded to notched, compared with the pointed leaf tips of common chickweed. The appearance and habit of **thymeleaf sandwort (*Arenaria serpyllifolia* L., ARISE)** are similar to common chickweed. However, the leaves of thymeleaf sandwort are somewhat smaller, the foliage is sparsely hairy, the hairs are stiff, and the flower petals are entire (appearing as 5), not deeply lobed (appearing as 10) as are common chickweed and mouseear chickweed petals.

Juvenile common chickweed

A. Senesac

Common chickweed seedlings

J. Neal

R. Uva

Mature common chickweed

J. Neal

Thymeleaf sandwort leafy shoot

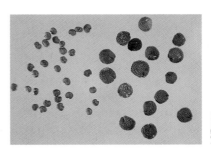

J. DiTomaso

Common chickweed foliage and flowers

J. DiTomaso

Left, thymeleaf sandwort seeds, 0.6 mm; *right*, common chickweed seeds, 1.2 mm

Common lambsquarters (*Chenopodium album* L.) [CHEAL]

Synonyms: lamb's quarters, pigweed, white goosefoot, fat-hen, mealweed, frost-blite, bacon-weed

GENERAL DESCRIPTION: An **erect summer annual** (to 1 m in height) with a **gray-mealy coating**, particularly on the surfaces of younger leaves.

PROPAGATION / PHENOLOGY: Reproduction is **by seed**; seedlings emerge in spring or early summer.

SEEDLING: Hypocotyls are green or tinged with maroon, smooth and fragile. **Cotyledons are narrowly elliptic**, about 12–15 mm long, dull green on the upper surface with maroon on the underside, becoming green with age. **Young leaves have a gray-mealy coating, especially on the leaf undersides and the emerging leaves. The first pair of leaves are opposite; all other leaves are alternate.** Margins on very young leaves are entire or have a few teeth. **Stems** of young seedlings are covered with **mealy-white granules**.

MATURE PLANT: **Stems are erect, branching**, hairless, vertically ridged, often with maroon stripes. **Leaves** are petiolated, rhombic–egg-shaped to lanceolate, **alternate**, 3–10 cm long, and **irregularly toothed**. Some blades have a white-mealy coating, but this is usually restricted to the younger leaves. Lower leaves are 2.5–7.5 cm long, almost always irregularly toothed. Upper leaves are sometimes linear, lack petioles, and may have entire margins.

ROOTS AND UNDERGROUND STRUCTURES: Short and branched taproot.

FLOWERS AND FRUIT: Flowers are produced from June to September on spikes grouped into a **panicle arising from the ends of stems and the leaf axils. Individual flowers are inconspicuous**, sessile, small, green, and aggregated into dense small clusters. The fruit is a utricle with a thin papery covering over a single seed. **Seeds** are of 2 types; the most common **can persist for years in the soil** and are round, black, 1–2 mm in diameter. A second, less common type, is brown, slightly larger, oval, and more flattened. It does not undergo an extended dormancy period. **A single plant can produce thousands of seeds**, which generally germinate at a depth of 0.5–3 cm below the soil surface.

POSTSENESCENCE CHARACTERISTICS: Erect woody stems and seedheads persist through the winter. Dead stems and remnants of the inflorescence are often red to purple.

HABITAT: A common weed of most agricultural and horticultural crops, particularly cultivated crops and gardens, common lambsquarters also grows in landscapes, waste places, and disturbed sites, on both acidic and alkaline soils.

DISTRIBUTION: Common throughout the United States.

SIMILAR SPECIES: **Other *Chenopodium* species** may be weedy, but none are as common as common lambsquarters. The distinctive rhombic to egg-shaped to lanceolate leaves and gray-mealy coating distinguish common lambsquarters from other weed species.

Common lambsquarters habit

J. Neal

L. Clark

Common lambsquarters seedlings

R. Uva

Common lambsquarters mature foliage

Common lambsquarters inflorescence

J. DiTomaso

J. DiTomaso

Common lambsquarters seeds, 1 mm

Kochia (*Kochia scoparia* (L.) Schrad.) [KCHSC]

Synonyms: belevedere, mock cypress, summer-cypress, Mexican fireweed, red belevedere, belevedere-cypress

GENERAL DESCRIPTION: An **erect, profusely bushy branched annual** with **fine-textured foliage** (30 cm to 1.5 m tall). Plants are **blue-green to gray-green** but take on a reddish or **purplish coloration later in the season**.

PROPAGATION / PHENOLOGY: Reproduction is **by seed**; seedlings emerge in the spring.

SEEDLING: Cotyledons are narrow (4.5 mm long by 1.25 mm wide), elliptic to oblong, sessile, thick, dull green above, often magenta on the underside, narrow and covered with soft fine hairs. **Young leaves are grayish** with **dense soft hairs**, linear to narrowly elliptic or oblanceolate and pointed at the apex. Blades are sometimes magenta-tinged beneath; leaves lack defined petioles. Young plants initially develop into a **basal rosette**. Elongated stems are hairy and may be reddish.

MATURE PLANT: **Stems are erect**, much-branched, round, **often red-tinged**, usually with soft hairs above. **Leaves** are simple, **sessile, alternate, linear** to lanceolate (2.5–5 cm long), and hairy to almost smooth, with entire, hairy margins.

ROOTS AND UNDERGROUND STRUCTURES: Taproot with branched fibrous root system.

FLOWERS AND FRUIT: **Small, green, inconspicuous flowers** are produced from July to September in small spikes (5–10 mm long) in the upper leaf axils and in terminal panicles. Spikes are subtended by leafy hairy bracts (3–10 mm long). **Fruit** are small **bladder-like utricles**. Seeds are about 1.8 mm long, irregularly shaped, brown with yellow markings, and grooved on each side.

POSTSENESCENCE CHARACTERISTICS: Dried plant material persists into the winter. Bracts subtending flowers are generally evident.

HABITAT: Kochia is a drought-tolerant weed of dry-land grain crops, rangeland, pastures, and waste areas.

DISTRIBUTION: Introduced as an ornamental for its bright red autumn color but has escaped to become naturalized throughout most of the northern half of the United States and western and southwestern rangelands. Significance as a weed is increasing in the Northeast, as far south as Maryland.

SIMILAR SPECIES: The inflorescence is similar to that of the closely related to **common lambsquarters**. It can also resemble **mugwort** in appearance and habitat. However, the leaves of kochia are narrow, whereas those of both common lambsquarters and mugwort are toothed or lobed and considerably wider than kochia leaves.

W. Curran

Kochia habit

Univ. Calif. Statewide IPM Project

Kochia stem and flowering branch

Univ. Calif. Statewide IPM Project

Kochia vegetative and flowering stems

J. DiTomaso

Kochia seeds, 1.8 mm

207

Hedge bindweed (*Calystegia sepium* (L.) R. Br.) [CAGSE]

Synonyms: *Convolvulus sepium*, wild morningglory, devil's-vine, great bindweed

GENERAL DESCRIPTION: A **rhizomatous perennial** with long (3 m) climbing or trailing **viny stems, distinctive triangular leaves**, and **white morningglory-like flowers**.

PROPAGATION / PHENOLOGY: Reproduction is **by seeds and rhizomes**. Rhizome pieces are spread by cultivation, on farm implements, and in the topsoil. Shoots from rhizomes emerge in early spring. Seedlings emerge in spring and early summer.

SEEDLING: Cotyledons are smooth, long-petiolated, almost square, with prominent indentations at the apex, heart-shaped bases, and entire margins. **Young leaves are triangular, heart-shaped, or sharply lobed at the base** (hastate) and on relatively long petioles. No cotyledons are present when plants emerge from rhizomes.

MATURE PLANT: **Stems** are smooth or hairy and **trail along the ground or climb on vegetation and other objects.** Leaves are alternate, **triangular-oblong**, 5–10 cm long, smooth, **with a pointed tip and prominent, angular, heart-shaped bases. Lobes point away from the petiole at the base.**

ROOTS AND UNDERGROUND STRUCTURES: Extensive but relatively shallow (to 30 cm) root system with an extensive, deep system of branched, fleshy **rhizomes**.

FLOWERS AND FRUIT: **Flowers**, from July through August, are **solitary in leaf axils** on prominently long flower-stalks (5–15 cm). **Two large (1–2 cm) leafy bracts** conceal the 5 overlapping sepals at the base of the flower. **Petals are usually white, sometimes pink, and are fused into a funnel-shaped tube**, 3–6 cm long. The fruit is an egg-shaped to rounded capsule (8 mm in diameter) containing 2–4 seeds. Capsules are usually covered by the 2 subtending bracts. Seeds are large (4–5 mm long), dull gray to brown or black, with 1 rounded side and 2 flattened sides.

POSTSENESCENCE CHARACTERISTICS: Smooth, round, capsules persist, surrounded with dried bracts. Dead stems remain twined around vegetation or other objects.

HABITAT: A weed of landscapes, nurseries, and row crops; also common on fences and hedges. It thrives in rich, moist lowland areas.

DISTRIBUTION: Native to the eastern United States, hedge bindweed has spread throughout the United States.

SIMILAR SPECIES: **Field bindweed** leaves are smaller than hedge bindweed leaves and have a rounded, rather than a pointed, apex. The leaf bases of field bindweed are pointed or rounded with outwardly divergent lobes. Hedge bindweed leaf bases are cut squarely (truncate). Flowers of field bindweed are smaller (1.2–2.5 cm long) than those of hedge bindweed. Hedge bindweed may also be distinguished from field bindweed by large bracts beneath and concealing the sepals. **Wild buckwheat** is a vining annual that has small inconspicuous flowers in axillary or terminal clusters and a sheath around the stem just above the base of the leaf (ocrea). Wild buckwheat has similar leaves, but it can be distinguished from the other 2 species because the lobes at the base of the leaf point in toward the petiole. **For a detailed comparison with field bindweed and wild buckwheat, see Table 12.** Both bindweeds are sometimes mistaken for **morningglory**, but the morningglories encountered in the northeastern United States are seed-propagated annuals that have broader, heart-shaped leaves and rounded basal lobes. Bindweed leaves have angular basal lobes.

J. DiTomaso

Hedge bindweed foliage and flower

R. Uva

Hedge bindweed sprouts from rhizomes

J. DiTomaso

Hedge bindweed flowers (note leafy bracts)

J. DiTomaso

Left, field bindweed seeds, 3.8 mm; *right*, hedge bindweed seeds, 5.0 mm

Field bindweed (*Convolvulus arvensis* L.) [CONAR]

Synonyms: small bindweed, bindweed, morningglory, creeping jenny

GENERAL DESCRIPTION: A **rhizomatous perennial** with slender climbing or trailing **viny stems** (to 2 m long), **arrowhead-shaped leaves**, and white to pink **morningglory-like flowers**.

PROPAGATION / PHENOLOGY: Reproduction is **by seeds and rhizomes**. Rhizome pieces are spread by cultivation, on farm implements, and in the topsoil. Shoots from rhizomes emerge in early spring. Seedlings emerge in spring and early summer.

SEEDLING: Cotyledons are smooth, dark green, relatively large, long-petioled, square to kidney-shaped, usually with a slight indentation at the apex. The margins of the cotyledon are entire, and the venation is whitish. **Young leaves are bell-shaped** (1.5–3.5 cm long), **lobed at the base (hastate)**, and on petioles. No cotyledons are present when young plants emerge from established rhizomes.

MATURE PLANT: **Stems** are smooth to slightly hairy and **trail along the ground or climb on vegetation and other objects.** Leaves are alternate, very **similar to seedling** leaves, 4–6 cm long. **Lobes point away from the petiole at the base.**

ROOTS AND UNDERGROUND STRUCTURES: **Extensive and deep** (6 m or more) **rhizome system**.

FLOWERS AND FRUIT: Flowers, from June through September, are solitary or 2-flowered (occasionally to 5) in the leaf axils. The flower-stalks are shorter than the leaves. **Two small (3 mm long) leafy bracts are at the base of the flower. Petals are usually white, sometimes pink, and fused into a funnel-shaped tube**, 1.2–2.5 cm long. The fruit is an egg-shaped to rounded capsule with 4 seeds. Seeds are large (3–4 mm long), rough, dull gray to brown or black with 1 rounded side and 2 flattened sides.

POSTSENESCENCE CHARACTERISTICS: Dead stems remain twined around vegetation or other objects.

HABITAT: Field bindweed is a weed of most agronomic and horticultural crops, as well as landscapes and turf. It is also commonly found growing on fences, hedges, and in fence row thickets.

DISTRIBUTION: One of the most troublesome weeds throughout North America and the world.

SIMILAR SPECIES: **Hedge bindweed** has larger leaves than field bindweed, and they have a pointed, rather than a rounded, apex. The **leaf bases** of field bindweed are pointed or rounded with outwardly divergent lobes (hastate). Hedge bindweed leaf bases are cut squarely (truncate). Flowers of hedge bindweed are larger (3–6 cm long) than those of field bindweed. Hedge bindweed may also be distinguished from field bindweed by large bracts beneath and concealing the sepals. **Wild buckwheat** is a vining annual with similar leaves, but it can be distinguished from the other 2 species because the lobes at the base of the leaf point toward the petiole. It also has small inconspicuous flowers in axillary and terminal clusters and a sheath around the stem just above the base of the leaf (ocrea). **For a detailed comparison of the bindweeds and wild buckwheat, see Table 12.** Both bindweeds are sometimes mistaken for **morningglory**, but the morningglories encountered in the northeastern United States are seed-propagated annuals that have broader, heart-shaped leaves and rounded basal lobes. Bindweed leaves have angular basal lobes.

Field bindweed foliage and flower

Field bindweed seedlings

Field bindweed from rhizome

Left, field bindweed seeds, 3.8 mm; *right*, hedge bindweed seeds, 5.0 mm

Dodder (*Cuscuta* spp.)

GENERAL DESCRIPTION: A **parasitic annual vine** lacking chlorophyll and distinct leaves. **Thread-like stems twine on other plants** and **are yellow, orange, or red**.

PROPAGATION / PHENOLOGY: Reproduction is **by seed**. Seeds are **long-lived in the soil**, germinating in the spring and early summer.

SEEDLING: Seedlings develop a small temporary root system to support 4–10 cm long thread-like stalks that attach to the host plant. After attachment, the root system no longer functions.

MATURE PLANT: **Stems are yellowish or reddish to orange-brown**, twining counterclockwise and **enveloping other vegetation** to form dense branching masses. **Leaves are reduced to inconspicuous scales**.

ROOTS AND UNDERGROUND STRUCTURES: **Roots are modified to penetrate the host plant** and extract nutrients and carbohydrates.

FLOWERS AND FRUIT: **Flowers are small, white** or sometimes pink, and numerous **in compact clusters**. The fruit is a small (about 3 mm) rounded capsule usually with 4 tiny orange seeds (1–1.5 mm in diameter).

POSTSENESCENCE CHARACTERISTICS: Plants die at first frost. Dead, matted stems do not persist through the winter.

HABITAT: A weed of landscapes, nursery crops, and agricultural crops, dodder survives only if the appropriate host is present. Common hosts include alfalfa, clover, and other legumes, as well as many bedding plants, chrysanthemums, azaleas, and cranberries.

DISTRIBUTION: **Many different species of dodder** are found throughout the United States.

SIMILAR SPECIES: The orange-red stems easily distinguish this genus.

J. Derr

Dodder in cantaloupe

J. Neal

Dodder flowering stem

J. DiTomaso

Commercial alfalfa seeds (larger) contaminated with dodder seeds (smaller; 1.3 mm)

Morningglories:
Ivyleaf morningglory (*Ipomoea hederacea* (L.) Jacq.) [IPOHE]
Pitted morningglory (*Ipomoea lacunosa* L.) [IPOLA]
Tall morningglory (*Ipomoea purpurea* (L.) Roth) [PHBPU]

Synonyms: *Ipomoea barbigera, Ipomoea hirsutula, Pharbitis barbigera, Pharbitis hederacea*

GENERAL DESCRIPTION: **Summer annual** weeds with long climbing or trailing **viny** stems, **heart-shaped to 3-lobed leaves** and **attractive funnel-shaped flowers**. Morningglories are very competitive and generally difficult to control in most crops.

PROPAGATION / PHENOLOGY: Reproduction is **by seed**; seeds germinate in early summer.

SEEDLING: Seedlings of all are similar in many aspects but can be identified by the shape of the cotyledons and first few leaves. Hypocotyls of all are maroon at the base, green near the apex, and grooved with the extension of the cotyledon stalk margin.

Ivyleaf morningglory: Cotyledons are butterfly-shaped, deeply notched at the apex, notched at the base, but rather squarish in outline compared with some other morningglories. The upper surfaces of the cotyledons are green, with translucent glands. The **first leaf is unlobed. Subsequent leaves are ivy-shaped** (3 main lobes), with both surfaces covered with **erect hairs** swollen at the base. Petioles and stems are densely hairy.

Pitted morningglory: Cotyledons are similar to those of the other species but **more deeply notched at the tip**; the **angle of the notch is greater**, and the lobes are more slender and pointed. First and subsequent **leaves are heart-shaped, taper to a more pointed tip** than those of the other species, and **lack hairs** (or are nearly hairless).

Tall morningglory: Cotyledons and first leaf are nearly identical to those of ivyleaf morningglory. Subsequent **leaves are heart-shaped and hairy. Hairs are appressed** (lie flat).

MATURE PLANT: **Vining stems** are branched, twining around other plants or spreading on the ground.

Ivyleaf morningglory: Leaves are alternate, **deeply 3-lobed** (rarely 5-lobed or entire), ivy-like, with rounded sinuses and a heart-shaped base (5–12 cm long). Erect hairs are on stems, petioles, and leaves.

Pitted morningglory: Similar to tall morningglory, but leaves are generally smaller, **leaf tips are tapered** to a more slender and **pointed tip**, and **foliage is hairless** or nearly so.

Tall morningglory: Leaves are alternate, **heart-shaped**, and densely covered with **appressed hairs** (lying on the surface).

ROOTS AND UNDERGROUND STRUCTURES: Coarsely branched root system.

FLOWERS AND FRUIT: Flowers are present from July to September and are produced on stalks shorter than or equaling the petioles (1–3 flowers at the leaf axil).

Ivyleaf morningglory habit

A. Senesac

Tall morningglory seedling

J. Neal

Ivyleaf morningglory seedling

J. Derr

Ivyleaf morningglory: Sepals are long (15–25 mm), abruptly tapering to a long, linear recurved tip. The basal portions of the flower are densely hairy. **Petals are purple to pale blue or white** (2.5–4.5 cm long) and **fused into a funnel**. Fruit are spherical capsules containing 4–6 seeds separating into 2–4 portions at maturity. Bristly sepals remain around the capsule. Seeds are 5–6 mm long, minutely hairy, dark brown to black, wedge-shaped with 1 rounded and 2 flattened sides.

Pitted mornningglory: Flowers are smaller (1.5–2 cm long) than those of the other mornningglories and **white; seeds are smooth** but otherwise similar.

Tall morningglory: Flowers are similar in color and shape to those of ivyleaf morningglory, but they are larger (4.5–7 cm long) with **shorter sepals** (10–15 mm long). Seeds are similar.

POSTSENESCENCE CHARACTERISTICS: Plants die with the first frost. Vines and fruit will persist into winter.

HABITAT: Weeds of most agronomic, horticultural, and nursery crops, as well as landscapes, fence rows, and noncrop areas, morningglories prefer rich, moist soil but are adapted to a wide range of conditions.

DISTRIBUTION: Common in the southern and central United States; less common in the cooler regions of the Northeast but found as far north as New York and Pennsylvania.

SIMILAR SPECIES: **Several species of *Ipomoea*** can extend into the southern region of the northeastern United States. **Bigroot morningglory (*Ipomoea pandurata* (L.) G.F.W. Meyer, IPOPA)** is a tuber-producing perennial with unlobed or slightly 3-lobed leaves, funnel-shaped white flowers (5–8 cm long) with red centers, and seeds fringed with soft hairs. **A variety of ivyleaf morningglory with unlobed leaves** is sometimes distinguished as *Ipomoea hederacea* **var.** *integriuscula* **Gray, IPOHG**. Both this variety and bigroot morningglory are more abundant in the southern United States than in the northern states.

W. Curran

Tall morningglory flowers

J. Neal

Pitted morningglory seedling

Seeds of pitted morningglory, 4.0 mm (*top left*);
red morningglory, 3.5 mm (*top right*);
tall morningglory, 4.0 mm (*bottom left*); and
ivyleaf morningglory, 5.0 mm (*bottom right*)

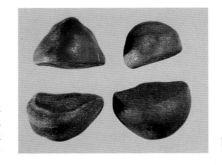

J. DiTomaso

Burcucumber (*Sicyos angulatus* L.) [SIYAN]

Synonyms: one-seeded bur cucumber, star cucumber, nimble kate

GENERAL DESCRIPTION: A **summer annual vine** with branching **stems (>3 m long) that climb by tendrils. Fruit resemble small cucumbers**, but are covered with burs.

PROPAGATION / PHENOLOGY: Reproduction is **by seed**; seeds germinate in midspring through early summer.

SEEDLING: Hypocotyls are covered with short downward-pointing hairs. **Cotyledon** blades are **thick, rounded** to elliptic, often with dense short spreading hairs on both surfaces. The stalks of the cotyledons are flat on the upper surface. **Young leaves** are alternate, **hairy**, usually with **5 angles or pointed lobes** and a **toothed margin**. Petioles are short and rounded, with downward-pointing hairs.

MATURE PLANT: **Stems are sticky-hairy**, especially at the nodes, longitudinally ridged, and **climb by branched tendrils. Leaves** are alternate, 6–20 cm long and 6–20 cm wide, **sticky-hairy**, rounded to heart-shaped, with **3–5 shallow angled lobes**, a sharp apex, and toothed margins.

ROOTS AND UNDERGROUND STRUCTURES: Roots are fibrous.

FLOWERS AND FRUIT: Flowers are produced from July to September. Male and female flowers are separate (monoecious) in the leaf axils. Flowers are greenish white, with 5 sepals and 5 petals. **Fruit are oval or elliptic**, 1–2 cm long, nearly as wide, **pointed at the apex**, in clusters of 3–20. The **surface of the fruit is covered with long stiff bristles** and shorter hairs. Each fruit produces 1 seed. Seeds are about 1–1.5 cm long, oval, flattened, bumpy, light brown to black, with 2 whitish swellings at the base.

POSTSENESCENCE CHARACTERISTICS: Plants die at first frost. Stems and fruit persist for only a short time.

HABITAT: Burcucumber is a weed of cultivated row crops and vegetables. It is also found in fence rows, thickets, and waste places, generally on damp, rich soils. Burcucumber is a major problem in mechanically harvested vegetables, because the viny stems interfere with harvesting procedures.

DISTRIBUTION: Found throughout the eastern United States, as far south as Florida, and west to Minnesota and Arizona.

SIMILAR SPECIES: Although less commonly encountered, **wild cucumber (*Echinocystis lobata* (Michx.) T. & G., ECNLO)** is similar in leaf shape and vining habit and the fruit has weak prickles. **See Table 13 for a comparison of burcucumber and wild cucumber.**

W. Curran

Burcucumber habit

R. Ritter

Burcucumber seedling

R. Ritter

Flowering burcucumber (fruit in background)

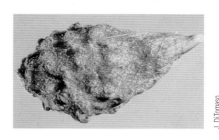

J. DiTomaso

Burcumber seed, 15 mm

J. Neal

Wild cucumber foliage and flowers

J. DiTomaso

Wild cucumber seed, 17 mm

Common teasel (*Dipsacus fullonum* L.) [DIWSI]

Synonyms: *Dipsacus sylvestris*, wild teasel, card teasel, venus-cup, card thistle, gypsy-combs

GENERAL DESCRIPTION: A **large biennial** (0.5–2 m in height), easily recognized by its **prominent spiny flower heads that persist throughout the year**. Dried flower heads are often used in dried plant arrangements.

PROPAGATION / PHENOLOGY: Reproduction is **by seed**; seeds germinate in late summer and fall and **overwinter as basal rosettes**.

SEEDLING: Plants develop as **basal rosettes**. Cotyledons are smooth and oval to round, with short stalks. **Young leaves** are oval to egg-shaped, with toothed margins; **surfaces have a wrinkled appearance**.

MATURE PLANT: Basal leaves are widest above the middle, tapering to the base, with rounded teeth along the margin. **Basal leaves generally die early in the second season when the erect stem and flowers are produced. Stems** are angled, marked with fine parallel lines, and **covered with many short downward-turning prickles**, especially toward the top of the plant. **Leaves are opposite**, 20–60 cm long, and **prickly on the underside** on the midrib. **Upper leaves are lanceolate and sessile**, with their bases fused around the stem. Margins on the upper leaves are mostly untoothed.

ROOTS AND UNDERGROUND STRUCTURES: Shallow taproot with fibrous secondary root system.

FLOWERS AND FRUIT: Flowers are present from July to September in the second year of growth. **Flower heads are cylindrical to egg-shaped**, 3–10 cm long, **with large spine-like bristly bracts** curving up around the head, the longer ones surpassing the head in length. Heads are **covered with straight spines**. Individual flowers are 10–15 mm long and bloom in a spiral arrangement around the head. The white petals are tubular, with short (1 mm) **pale purple lobes, giving the head a purple thistle-like appearance**. Flower clusters are on long prickly stalks (peduncles). Each seed is enclosed within the fruit (achene). Achenes are 3–4 mm long, 4-angled, and grayish brown with parallel ridges.

POSTSENESCENCE CHARACTERISTICS: The woody erect stems and **characteristic dead flower heads persist** throughout the winter. Dead flower heads are spiny, egg-shaped, and have bracts that curve up and around the head from underneath. Dead stems are spiny.

HABITAT: A common weed of roadsides and low-maintenance turfgrass, meadows, and waste areas, common teasel is rarely a problem in cultivated crops. It is often found on damp, rich soils.

DISTRIBUTION: Found throughout most of the United States except for the northern Great Plains. Most common in the Northeast, including New York, Pennsylvania, and New Jersey; less common in New England. Also common in the Pacific Coast states.

SIMILAR SPECIES: **Cutleaf teasel (*Dipsacus laciniatus* L., DIWLA)** can be distinguished by its pinnatifid upper leaves. Common teasel can be mistaken for a **thistle** owing to the similar shape and color of the flower head and the presence of prickles on the stem. Unlike thistle leaves, however, common teasel leaves are wrinkled and have spineless margins.

Common teasel habit

Common teasel rosettes

Common teasel inflorescence

Left, cutleaf teasel seeds, 4.0 mm; *right*, common teasel seeds, 3.5 mm

J. Neal

R. Uva

R. Uva

J. DiTomaso

221

Virginia copperleaf (*Acalypha virginica* L.) [ACCVI]

Synonyms: three-seeded mercury, wax balls, copper-leaf, mercury-weed

GENERAL DESCRIPTION: A **summer annual** with **erect, branched stems** (10–60 cm tall). **Foliage develops a distinct copper pigmentation**, particularly when growing in sunny locations.

PROPAGATION / PHENOLOGY: Reproduction is **by seed**; seeds germinate in late spring.

SEEDLING: **Cotyledons are round, notched** at the apex, smooth, and on short petioles. **First leaves are opposite; subsequent leaves are alternate.** Leaves are narrow to widely ovate, glossy, and sparsely hairy, with rounded teeth on the margin.

MATURE PLANT: Stems are hairy to sparsely hairy. **Leaves are similar to those of the seedling**, but are narrowly to **broadly lanceolate** (2–8 cm long) and petioled (1–4 cm long). Lower leaves are opposite and glossy green, upper leaves are alternate. **Younger leaves have a copper coloration.** In many areas, leaves soon become damaged by insect feeding.

ROOTS AND UNDERGROUND STRUCTURES: Shallow taproot with a secondary fibrous root system.

FLOWERS AND FRUIT: **Flowers** are produced from June through October. Male and female flowers are produced separately on the same plant (monoecious). Both flower types are **greenish, inconspicuous**, and produced **in clusters in the leaf axils** on the upper portions of the stem. Female flowers are surrounded by **conspicuous, deeply 9–15 lobed bracts**. Bract persists, sheathing the **3-chambered seed pod** (1 seed per chamber). Seeds are egg-shaped, 1.4–1.8 mm long, dull reddish brown or gray with reddish brown spots.

POSTSENESCENCE CHARACTERISTICS: After frost, upright woody stems persist for a short time. Otherwise, no distinctive winter characteristics.

HABITAT: Virginia copperleaf is a weed of nursery crops, landscapes, roadsides, fields, stream banks, and waste areas. It can also be found in cultivated, agronomic, and horticultural crops under a wide variety of soil types and moisture conditions, ranging from dry to wet.

DISTRIBUTION: Occurs throughout much of the eastern two-thirds of the United States from Maine south to Florida, west to South Dakota and Texas.

SIMILAR SPECIES: The leaves of **rhombic copperleaf (*Acalypha rhomboidea* Raf., ACCRH**) are lanceolate to ovate or rhombic (diamond-shaped), and the petioles are usually more than half as long as the blades. The female flowers of rhombic copperleaf are surrounded by bracts that are 5–9 lobed; those of Virginia copperleaf are 9–15 lobed. **Galinsoga** seedlings can look similar to Virginia copperleaf, but the cotyledons of galinsoga are not notched at the apex. Mature leaves of galinsoga are opposite; those of copperleaf are alternate.

Virginia copperleaf habit

Virginia copperleaf seedling

Virginia copperleaf mature foliage

Virginia copperleaf flowering shoot
(note leafy bracts)

Virginia copperleaf seeds, 1.5 mm

223

Leafy spurge (*Euphorbia esula* L.) [EPHES]

Synonyms: *Tithymalus esula*, Faitour's grass

GENERAL DESCRIPTION: A **colony-forming perennial** with **erect, tough woody stems** (30–70 cm tall). All parts of the plant exude a **milky sap** when injured. Although palatable to sheep and goats, leafy spurge is **mildly toxic to cattle,** who will avoid foraging in areas contaminated with only 10% of the weed.

PROPAGATION / PHENOLOGY: Reproduction is **by seeds, buds of lateral roots**, and **buds that develop on root segments** fragmented by cultivation. Shoots emerge from crowns and root buds in early spring. Seeds germinate in early spring.

SEEDLING: **Cotyledons** are smooth (13–19 mm long by 2–4 mm wide), linear to oblong, often with a **powdery grayish or whitish coating** (glaucous). The first few leaves are opposite; subsequent leaves are alternate. **Young leaves are thin, narrowly elliptic,** entire, **bluish green,** smooth, and hairless.

MATURE PLANT: **Stems are smooth, yellowish green, unbranched** or branched above. **Leaves are sessile,** alternate, **linear to lanceolate** (3–8 cm long by 4–8 mm wide), usually wider above the middle (oblanceolate), and **spirally arranged on the stem,** making them appear whorled. The margins are entire but slightly wavy. Leaves associated with the inflorescence are much shorter, broader, and heart- to kidney-shaped.

ROOTS AND UNDERGROUND STRUCTURES: New shoot buds are produced from **vertical and horizontal fleshy roots**. Developing **crowns** remain attached to the parent plant by lateral roots. Many **pinkish scaly buds** form on the crowns and roots just below the soil surface. Extensive root and crown systems contain large nutrient reserves that enable the plant to survive mechanical weed control efforts.

FLOWERS AND FRUIT: Both male and female flowers are clustered into a cup-like structure (cyathium). The cyathium is small and inconspicuous but surrounded by **conspicuous greenish yellow bracts** (1–1.3 cm long). Flower clusters are produced from June through August on axillary shoots and on **flat-topped umbellate inflorescences** at the end of branched stems (7–15 branches). The **fruit** is a 3–3.5 mm long, 3-celled capsule (1 seed per cell) that can **explode at maturity, projecting seeds 5 m**. Seeds are about 2–3 mm long, oval to elliptic, grayish, with red markings and a dark line on one side.

POSTSENESCENCE CHARACTERISTICS: Neither leaves nor fruit persist on unbranched stems. However, stiff erect stems persist throughout the winter and often into the following spring. Pink buds (1 cm long) are evident on the root crown just below the soil surface throughout the year.

HABITAT: A weed of rangeland, pastures, roadsides, uncultivated perennial crops, and reduced-tillage crops, leafy spurge is less common in traditionally cultivated crops.

DISTRIBUTION: Found throughout much of the northern United States; less common in the Northeast than in other northern states. A major rangeland weed from Idaho to Minnesota, south to Colorado and Nebraska.

SIMILAR SPECIES: **Cypress spurge (*Euphorbia cyparissias* L., EPHCY)** is similar in both appearance and habit, but it is shorter (15–30 cm tall) and has narrower leaves (1–3 cm long by 1–3 mm wide) congested on side branches. In spring, emerging shoots of leafy spurge may resemble **yellow toadflax,** but yellow toadflax does not exude a milky latex when cut.

Leafy spurge habit

Leafy spurge flowers

Cypress spurge vegetative shoots

Left, cypress spurge seeds, 2.0 mm; *right*, leafy spurge seeds, 2.4 mm

225

Spotted spurge (*Euphorbia maculata* L.) [EPHMA]

Synonyms: *Chamaesyce maculata*, *Euphorbia supina*, prostrate spurge

GENERAL DESCRIPTION: A **prostrate** to ascending, branching, **mat-forming summer annual** (40 cm in diameter). Stems and foliage exude a **milky sap** when injured.

PROPAGATION / PHENOLOGY: Reproduction is **by seed**; seeds germinate from early to late summer. Spotted spurge **does not root at the nodes. Seeds are produced when emerging plants are only a couple of weeks old.**

SEEDLING: Hypocotyls are short, pink, and smooth. Cotyledons are oval, green on the upper surface, maroon below, and have short purple petioles. **Young leaves are opposite**, hairy, **green, often with a maroon blotch** on the upper surface. The lower surface is maroon with a powdery coating. Leaf bases are unequal, and the petioles are reddish. Stems are pinkish and densely hairy.

MATURE PLANT: **Stems and leaves are similar to those of the seedling. Leaves are opposite, oblong** or somewhat egg-shaped or linear (5–15 mm long and less than half as wide, widest below the middle), on short petioles subtended by lanceolate stipules. Leaf margins may be toothed toward the apex.

ROOTS AND UNDERGROUND STRUCTURES: Shallow taproot with secondary fibrous roots.

FLOWERS AND FRUIT: **Flowers** are present from July to September **in the axils of the upper leaves**. Flowers appear to be single but are composed of several male and 1 female flower aggregated into a small cluster (cyathium) and surrounded by a cup-like structure (involucre). The **fruit is a 3-lobed**, 3-seeded **capsule**, 1.5 mm long, with stiff hairs on the surface. Seeds (1 per cell) are about 1 mm long, 4-angled, oblong or egg-shaped, grayish brown to reddish brown, with transverse ridges. Seeds become mucilaginous and sticky when wet, facilitating dispersal.

POSTSENESCENCE CHARACTERISTICS: Stems persist for only a short time after frost.

HABITAT: Spotted spurge is a common summer weed of landscapes, turfgrass, and nursery crops. It is also found in cultivated fields, gardens, brick walks, and waste areas. It survives on dry or sandy, low-nutrient soil and on compacted or disturbed sites and thrives in container-grown nursery crops.

DISTRIBUTION: Throughout the East and Midwest, and on the Pacific Coast.

SIMILAR SPECIES: **Prostrate spurge (*Euphorbia humistrata* Engelm. *ex* Gray, EPHHT) is difficult to distinguish from spotted spurge. Some taxonomists consider the 2 to be the same species**, and spotted spurge is often referred to as prostrate spurge. But, unlike spotted spurge, **prostrate spurge has pale green leaves and often roots at the lower nodes.** The leaves of prostrate spurge are egg-shaped, widest at the apex (obovate) to oblong, 5–15 mm long and more than half as wide. The involucre (cup-like whorls of bracts) of prostrate spurge is cleft on one side for at least half its length; that of spotted spurge is cleft on one side for ¼–⅓ of its length. Unlike spotted and prostrate spurge, the stems of **nodding spurge (*Euphorbia nutans* Lag., EPHNU)** are **ascending or almost erect**. Also, leaves of nodding spurge are usually larger than those of the other 2 species (1–3.5 cm long). **Prostrate knotweed** is found in similar habitats and resembles spotted spurge in growth habit and leaf shape, but unlike all three spurges, it does not exude a milky sap when injured.

J. Neal

Spurge habit: *left*, spotted spurge; *right*, nodding spurge

A. Senesac

Prostrate spurge flowers

J. Derr

Prostrate spurge

R. Uva

Prostrate spurge seedlings

J. DiTomaso

Left, nodding spurge seeds, 1.1 mm; *right*, spotted spurge seeds, 0.8 mm

Birdsfoot trefoil (*Lotus corniculatus* L.) [LOTCO]

Synonyms: bloom-fell, cat's-clover, crow-toes, ground honeysuckle, sheep-foot, hop o'my thumb, devil's-claw

GENERAL DESCRIPTION: A **low to prostrate mat-forming perennial** resembling **clover**, but with 2 leaf-like stipules at the base of the petiole. Stems are about 60 cm long and can become woody with age.

PROPAGATION / PHENOLOGY: Reproduction is **by seeds** and also by **stolons and rhizomes** that spread to form large colonies. Most aboveground growth occurs in early spring. Rhizome growth and new shoot development occur in the fall. Seed germination is primarily in the spring, occasionally in the fall.

SEEDLING: Minute cotyledons emerge in midspring, but seedlings are rarely seen.

MATURE PLANT: Stems are square at the top, round at the base, with or without hairs. **Leaves** are alternate, nearly sessile, **compound with 3 terminal leaflets** (trifoliolate) and 2 leaf-like stipules at the base of the petiole. **Leaflets** are oval to **oblanceolate**, pointed at the apex, 5–20 mm long, 2–9 mm wide. The margins are usually entire but can be minutely serrate.

ROOTS AND UNDERGROUND STRUCTURES: Well-developed **rhizomes and stolons** and a coarse secondary root system.

FLOWERS AND FRUIT: **Flowers** are produced in late June through the fall in **branched clusters** (umbels with 2–6 flowers) at the end of a 3–10 cm long stalk arising from the upper leaf axils. Flowers **resemble those of pea** and are 1.3 cm long, **bright yellow** (sometimes coppery or brick red), often with fine red lines. **Fruit are 2.5 cm long pods arranged in the form of a bird's foot**, accounting for its common name. Seeds are irregularly rounded to somewhat flattened (1–1.3 mm long), shiny, brownish to black and frequently speckled.

POSTSENESCENCE CHARACTERISTICS: Plants die back to the ground at first frost. Dead stems become brittle and do not persist long into winter.

HABITAT: Birdsfoot trefoil is **often seeded for soil stabilization or as a forage crop** but can easily escape into roadsides and waste areas. It can become a persistent weed in turfgrass and meadows and tolerates a wide variety of soil types (e.g., gravelly areas) and moisture regimes, including drought. Its presence is often indicative of low-fertility, drought-prone soils.

DISTRIBUTION: Found throughout the United States; common in the Northeast and southern Canada.

SIMILAR SPECIES: **See Table 14 for a comparison of weedy trifoliolate legumes and oxalis.** Birdsfoot trefoil resembles **black medic** and **some clovers**; however, birdsfoot trefoil has entire or very nearly entire leaflets, whereas black medic and clovers have more conspicuously toothed leaflets. The center leaflet of black medic is on a short stalk (petiolate); the clovers and birdsfoot trefoil have a sessile terminal leaflet. Black medic also has yellow flowers, but they are smaller and more numerous than birdsfoot trefoil flowers. Among the weedy clovers, only **hop clover (*Trifolium aureum* Pollich, TRFAU)** and **large hop clover (*Trifolium campestre* Schreb., TRFCA)** have yellow flowers, but the flowers are numerous in rounded heads.

J. Neal

Birdsfoot trefoil habit

R. Uva

Birdsfoot trefoil mature leaf

J. Neal

Birdsfoot trefoil flowers and fruit

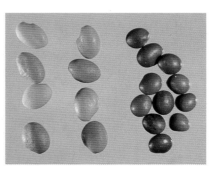

J. DiTomaso

Left to right: white sweetclover (*Melilotus alba*) seeds, 2.0 mm; yellow sweetclover (*M. officinalis*) seeds, 2.0 mm; and birdsfoot trefoil seeds, 1.2 mm

229

Black medic (*Medicago lupulina* L.) [MEDLU]

Synonyms: trefoil, black clover, none-such, hop medic, hop clover

GENERAL DESCRIPTION: A low-growing to **prostrate summer annual**, or less commonly a winter annual or biennial, with stems 10–60 cm long.

PROPAGATION / PHENOLOGY: Reproduction is **by seed**; seeds germinate in early autumn or spring.

SEEDLING: **Cotyledons** are dull green above, pale on the underside, and oblong (4–9 mm long). Young leaves have a few short hairs. **The first leaf is simple; subsequent leaves are palmately compound with 3 leaflets.** Petioles are long and hairy, with stipules at the base. In early stages of growth, numerous leaves arise from the base, but stems elongate and begin to trail with age.

MATURE PLANT: Stems are hairy, somewhat square and much-branched at the base; they do not root at the nodes. **Leaves** are alternate, **compound with 3 wedge- to egg-shaped leaflets**, widest near the apex, with a small projecting tip (mucronate). **Leaflet margins are toothed.** The **center leaflet has a longer stalk (2–4 mm long petiolule) than the lateral leaflets**. Toothed stipules are present at the base of the petiole. The lower leaves have longer petioles than the upper leaves.

ROOTS AND UNDERGROUND STRUCTURES: Shallow **taproot** with secondary coarsely branched roots. Small nodules are attached to the roots.

FLOWERS AND FRUIT: Flowers are present from May to September. The inflorescence is composed of **10–50 flowers in a spherical to short-cylindrical clover-like cluster**. Individual flowers are 4–5 mm long, with 5-cleft sepals that persist during fruit formation and 5 **yellow** irregularly shaped petals resembling those of a tiny pea flower. Flowers have 10 stamens, 9 fused and 1 separate. The **fruit** is a recurved, kidney-shaped, **black**, hairy, **1-seeded pod**, 2–3 mm long. Seeds are 1.5–2 mm long, oval to kidney-shaped, and yellow-green to brown.

POSTSENESCENCE CHARACTERISTICS: Prostrate stems turn dark brown to black and persist for several months, with black seed pods remaining attached.

HABITAT: Primarily a weed of turfgrass, particularly in nutrient-poor and drought-prone soils, black medic is also found on disturbed soils and waste areas.

DISTRIBUTION: Occurs throughout the United States.

SIMILAR SPECIES: **See Table 14 for a comparison of weedy trifoliolate legumes and oxalis. Hop clover** and **large hop clover** have similar habits, foliage, and yellow flowers, but the leaves and flowers are larger than those of black medic. Also, the flower petals of hop clovers turn brown and remain attached, whereas the petals of black medic drop off, revealing a cluster of pods that turn black at maturity. The **woodsorrels** also have 3 leaflets on each leaf; however, the individual leaflets are prominently indented at the apex and appear heart-shaped. **Birdsfoot trefoil** also has trifoliolate leaves with entire (not toothed) or nearly entire margins; black medic leaflet margins are toothed.

J. Neal

Black medic habit

R. Uva

Black medic seedling

R. Uva

Hop clover

R. Uva

Black medic leaves, flowers, and fruit

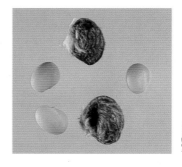

J. DiTomaso

Black medic seed pods, 2.3 mm, and seeds, 1.5 mm

Kudzu (*Pueraria lobata* (Willd.) Ohwi) [PUELO]

Synonym: *Pueraria thunbergiana*

GENERAL DESCRIPTION: An **aggressive, climbing or trailing, herbaceous to semi-woody perennial vine** with **large trifoliolate leaves** (3 leaflets). **Vines can grow 10–30 m in a growing season** (up to 30 cm a day) but die back to the ground in fall. If not managed, kudzu can rapidly overgrow all other vegetation, including trees.

PROPAGATION / PHENOLOGY: Reproduction is **by seeds** and **spreading roots** that **develop adventitious shoots.** Seedlings and adventitious shoots emerge in spring.

SEEDLING: Little information is available on seedling characteristics. **Young vines are covered with tan to bronze hairs. Leaves** are alternate and compound, with **3 leaflets.** The lateral leaflets are on short (≤1 cm) stalks; the center leaflet is on a longer stalk (1.5–2 cm). Leaflets are broadly ovate and hairy, with 1–3 lobes. The 2 lateral leaflets are often lobed on one side, whereas the center leaflet has lobes on both sides (much like an ivy leaf).

MATURE PLANT: Vegetative characteristics are **similar to juvenile growth, except larger** (leaflets up to 18 cm long and 12 cm wide). **Hairs deteriorate on mature vines**, and **stems become woody with age.**

ROOTS AND UNDERGROUND STRUCTURES: **Extensive fleshy root system** with **large mealy tuberous roots.** Adventitious shoots are produced from the roots and tuberous roots.

FLOWERS AND FRUIT: Plants flower in late July through early September. Plants may not flower in more northern limits of its range. **Reddish purple flowers** are produced in **axillary, 10–20 cm long racemes** (resembling a small wisteria flower cluster). Legume-like flowers are **fragrant**; each is 2–2.5 cm long. Flattened hairy **fruiting pods** mature in late summer or early fall. Pods (4–5 cm long) produce numerous kidney-shaped seeds, about 3–4 cm long. Seeds are retained within the pod.

POSTSENESCENCE CHARACTERISTICS: Very susceptible to frost. Aboveground portions die back to the ground in the fall, leaving tan or straw-colored vines.

HABITAT: Kudzu is a weed of forests, rights-of-way, roadsides, abandoned fields, fence rows, and noncrop areas. It thrives on many soil types, including nutrient-deficient, sandy, clayey, or loamy soils. It does not tolerate cultivation or repeated mowing but may encroach into managed areas from adjacent infestations.

DISTRIBUTION: Introduced as a forage and soil conservation plant from Japan. Escaped cultivation and is now common throughout the southeastern United States, west to Texas, and in the mid-Atlantic states. Can occasionally be found as far north as the southern portions of New York.

SIMILAR SPECIES: None of note.

J. Neal

Kudzu habit, on hillside

Kudzu leaf (3 leaflets per leaf)

J. Neal

A. Senesac

Kudzu young inflorescence

J. DiTomaso

Kudzu seeds, 3.5 mm

Rabbitfoot clover (*Trifolium arvense* L.) [TRFAR]

Synonyms: stone clover, old-field clover, hare's-foot clover

GENERAL DESCRIPTION: A **winter or summer annual** with erect (10–40 cm tall), freely branching, **densely hairy stems and leaves**. Rabbitfoot clover can tolerate mowing. The **grayish hairy flower heads** resemble a rabbit's foot.

PROPAGATION / PHENOLOGY: Reproduction is **by seed**.

SEEDLING: Cotyledons are round to oval, on short stalks. **First leaves are simple** (lacking leaflets), semicircular to kidney-shaped, and petiolated. **Subsequent leaves are trifoliolate** (3 leaflets), **densely hairy**, on 1–3 cm long petioles. As seedlings, leaves form a **basal rosette** or mound.

MATURE PLANT: **Stems are erect**, much-branched, **soft-hairy**, often reddish. **Leaves are alternate, trifoliolate, with 3 narrow oblong (strap-like) leaflets** (1–2.5 cm long). **Leaflets have soft hairs** on the upper and lower surfaces and smooth margins, except for small teeth at the apex. Petioles are usually shorter than the leaflets, and stipules are longer than the petioles.

ROOTS AND UNDERGROUND STRUCTURES: Taproot (5–20 cm long) with a secondary fibrous root system.

FLOWERS AND FRUIT: **Flowers** are produced from July to September **in dense, grayish, hairy, egg-shaped to cylindrical (1–3 cm long) clusters**. Flower heads are attached to a relatively short (1.5–2.5 cm) stalk (peduncle). Individual flowers are pale pink to whitish and are enveloped by 5 bristly sepals (3–5 mm long) covered with silky hairs. Flowers are hidden within the hairy sepals. The fruit is a 1-seeded pod. Seeds are 1 mm long, yellow to brown and oval.

POSTSENESCENCE CHARACTERISTICS: Dried stems and leaves are hairy, and seedheads persist on plant.

HABITAT: Rabbitfoot clover is a weed of low-maintenance turfgrass and is most often found on low-nutrient, dry, sandy or rocky soil.

DISTRIBUTION: Occurs throughout much of the United States; most common on the eastern coastal plain. Restricted to dry, sandy locations inland.

SIMILAR SPECIES: **See Table 14 for a comparison of weedy trifoliolate legumes and oxalis.** Rabbitfoot clover can **superficially resemble prostrate spurge** but does not exude a milky latex when cut. Other weedy clovers have rounded rather than cylindrical flower heads: **white clover, strawberry clover, alsike, hop clover**, and **red clover**. White, strawberry, and alsike clover are perennials with petioles much longer than the leaflets; petioles of rabbitfoot clover are shorter than the leaflets. Hop clover has yellow flowers, and red clover is a perennial with red flowers.

A. Senesac

Rabbitfoot clover habit

R. Uva

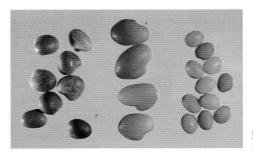
J. DiTomaso

Left to right: alsike seeds, 1.1 mm; red clover seeds, 1.9 mm; and rabbitfoot clover seeds, 0.8 mm

Rabbitfoot clover flowering stem

White clover (*Trifolium repens* L.) [TRFRE]

Synonyms: Dutch clover, honeysuckle clover, white trefoil, purplewort

GENERAL DESCRIPTION: A mat-forming **perennial** with **low creeping branched stems** that root at the nodes, trifoliolate leaves, and white flowers.

PROPAGATION / PHENOLOGY: Reproduction is **by seeds** and **stolons. Seedcoats are very hard, ensuring extended dormancy.** Seeds germinate under cool, moist conditions in spring, early summer, or early fall. Stolons can spread at a rate of 18 cm per year. Clones can persist indefinitely even though few plant parts survive more than a year.

SEEDLING: Cotyledons are smooth and spatulate (6–7 mm long), with blades tapering into the petiole. The **first leaf is simple** (no leaflets), rounded to broadly oval, truncated at the base. **Subsequent leaves are trifoliolate** (3 leaflets), alternate, smooth, grayish green on the lower surface, green on the upper surface, usually with a light green splotch near the base of each leaflet. Leaflet margins have small teeth; apexes are very slightly indented. Petioles have 2 small membrane-like stipules at the base.

MATURE PLANT: **Stems are prostrate and rooting at the nodes**, smooth or only sparsely hairy. **Leaflets resemble those of the seedling**, broadly elliptic to egg-shaped (1–3.5 cm long) and widest at the apex. The apex is rounded, with an indentation at the tip. **Petioles are long** (3–8 cm) and perpendicularly upright from the prostrate stems. Two stipules are appressed to the petiole to form a pale tubular clasping sheath.

ROOTS AND UNDERGROUND STRUCTURES: Plants spread by creeping aboveground stems (stolons) that root at the nodes.

FLOWERS AND FRUIT: **Flowers** are produced throughout the summer in **rounded heads** (1.5–2 cm wide) at the end of long (to 7 cm) flower-stalks (peduncles) that arise from the leaf axils. **Heads are an aggregate** of 20–40 individual flowers, each 8–10 mm long, **white or sometimes pinkish**, with minute greenish veins. Individual flowers are on 6-mm stalks (pedicels). Flowers turn brown and persist while the fruiting pods (legumes) develop. Fruit are 4–5 mm long, 3–6 seeded. Seeds are about 1 mm long, yellow to brown, kidney-shaped, or irregularly rounded, somewhat flattened.

POSTSENESCENCE CHARACTERISTICS: Foliage may discolor and decompose over the winter, but stolons persist and produce new shoots in early spring.

HABITAT: White clover is a weed of turfgrass, landscapes, orchards, and nursery crops. Because it tolerates close mowing, it is a common weed of high-maintenance turfgrass. It grows on many soil types, especially clays, and tolerates a wide range of soil acidity.

DISTRIBUTION: Found throughout most of North America.

SIMILAR SPECIES: **See Table 14 for a comparison of weedy trifoliolate legumes and oxalis.** Strawberry clover (***Trifolium fragiferum* L., TRFFR**) is less frequently a turfgrass weed but is almost identical to white clover. It can be distinguished by its rosy flowers, which appear swollen when mature, and by the lack of a whitish band typically present on the leaflets of white clover. **Alsike (*Trifolium hybridum* L., TRFHY**) and **red clover (*Trifolium pratense* L., TRFPR**) are similar but have more upright, clump-forming growth habits and generally larger, more elongated leaflets than white clover. Alsike has similar flower color, white to tinged pink, but red clover flowers are distinctly pink to red. Unlike white clover, **black medic** and **hop clovers** have a stalked central leaflet and yellow flowers. The **woodsorrels** are also trifoliolate, but a prominent indentation at the apex of the individual leaflets produces heart-shaped leaflets.

White clover habit

Cotyledons and first leaves of white clover

Red clover habit

Left to right: strawberry clover, white clover, alsike, and red clover

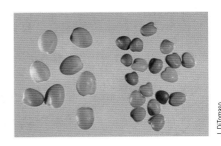
Left, strawberry clover seeds, 1.5 mm; *right,* white clover seeds, 1.0 mm (red clover seeds are shown on p. 219)

Vetches (*Vicia* spp.)

GENERAL DESCRIPTION: The weedy vetches are trailing, **vine-like herbaceous annuals** or perennials that form sprawling mats or envelop other plants. **Leaves are alternate, pinnately compound**, with a terminal leaflet modified into a **twining tendril**.

PROPAGATION / PHENOLOGY: Life cycles and season of emergence vary with species. All propagate by seed.

SEEDLING: Cotyledons remain within the seedcoat below the soil surface. **First leaves lack tendrils** and **have 1–2 (sometimes more) pairs of elliptic or linear leaflets.**

MATURE PLANTS: **Older leaves develop tendrils and have many leaflet pairs.** Stem bases can become somewhat woody with age.

ROOTS AND UNDERGROUND STRUCTURES: Branched fibrous root system.

FLOWERS AND FRUIT: Flowers and fruiting pods differ in number per cluster and in color.

SPECIES DESCRIPTIONS:

Bird vetch (*Vicia cracca* L., VICCR): Perennial with **spreading rhizomes** and **trailing or climbing stems** (1–2 m long). **Leaflets are linear** to narrowly oblong, pointed at the tip (1–3 cm long), **5–11 pairs per leaf.** Flowers (July to August) are **bluish purple** (occasionally white), 8–13 mm long, **20–50 flowered** on 1-sided long-stalked racemes. **Pods are light brown** at maturity, **flat**, 2–3 cm long. Found throughout the northern United States and southern Canada.

Narrowleaf vetch (*Vicia sativa* L. ssp. *nigra* (L.) Ehrh., VICAN) (also known as *Vicia angustifolia* L.): A **summer or winter annual** with erect to ascending or climbing stems (1 m long). **Leaflets are linear** to narrowly elliptic, 1.5–3.0 cm long, **3–5 pairs per leaf.** Flowers (July to August) are **blue or violet** (occasionally white), 1–1.8 cm long, in pairs arising from the upper leaf axils. **Pods** are 4 cm long, **dark brown** to blackish at maturity. Found throughout the United States and southern Canada. **Common vetch (*Vicia sativa* L., VICSA) is similar** to narrowleaf vetch but has larger flowers (1.8–3 cm long) and light brown pods at maturity.

Sparrow vetch (*Vicia tetrasperma* (L.) Schreb., VICTE) (also known as four-seed vetch): A **fine-textured climbing annual** with long stems (30–60 cm), prostrate at the base and ascending at the tip. **Leaflets are linear-oblong** to narrowly elliptic (1–2 cm long), **2–5 pairs per leaf.** Seedlings emerge mostly in early spring and fall, some in summer. **Flowers** (June to September) are **light purple** to white, 3–7 mm long, 1–6 flowers (usually in pairs) on 1–3 cm stalks (peduncles) from the upper leaf axils. **Pods are smooth** and 4-seeded. Found throughout the eastern and southeastern United States; also in northern California.

Hairy vetch (*Vicia villosa* Roth, VICVI): A summer or winter annual, or biennial, with **hairy stems** (1 m long). **Leaflets are narrowly oblong** to linear-lanceolate, 1–2.5 cm long, **5–10 pairs per leaf.** Flowers (June to August) are **reddish purple** to violet, 1.5–1.8 cm long, **10–14(–30) flowers** on a long-stalked 1-sided raceme. Fruit

Bird vetch flowering shoot

R. Uva

J. Neal

Common vetch foliage and flower

J. Neal

Immature sparrow vetch habit

are 2–3 cm long pods. Found throughout the northern United States and southern Canada, as far west as California.

POSTSENESCENCE CHARACTERISTICS: Mat of dead brown stems and occasionally leaves remains entangled around other plants.

HABITAT: All species are weeds of waste places, roadsides, meadows, pastures, and perennial horticultural crops, including landscapes. Hairy vetch and narrowleaf vetch are common weeds in fall-sown winter annual cereals. Vetches are often found on, but are not limited to, sandy or gravelly soils. Some species are used as cover crops.

DISTRIBUTION: Varies with species.

SIMILAR SPECIES: **Trailing crownvetch (*Coronilla varia* L., CZRVA)** is a perennial similar in appearance; however, its leaves lack the terminal tendril, and its flowers are arranged in an umbel. Trailing crownvetch is often planted as a cover along highways and on embankments.

J. Neal

Sparrow vetch foliage, flowers, and fruit

Sparrow vetch seedling

J. Neal

J. DiTomaso

Left, hairy vetch seed, 4.0 mm;
center top, sparrow vetch seeds, 1.8 mm;
center bottom, common vetch seed, 4.0 mm;
right, bird vetch seeds, 2.1 mm

Redstem filaree (*Erodium cicutarium* (L.) L'Hér. *ex* Ait.) [EROCI]

Synonyms: filaree, common storksbill, heronsbill, alfilaria, pin-weed, pin-grass

GENERAL DESCRIPTION: A **winter annual or biennial** that overwinters as a **prostrate basal rosette**. Stems elongate the following spring and can reach 10–50 cm in height. **Leaves and stems are often reddish.**

PROPAGATION / PHENOLOGY: Reproduction is **by seed**; seeds germinate in late summer, early autumn, or spring.

SEEDLING: **Cotyledons are deeply 3–4 lobed**, the center lobe the largest. **Young leaves** are alternate or opposite and also **deeply lobed or cut**. Stems and leaves are bristly hairy. **Young plants develop into rosettes the first year.**

MATURE PLANT: **Stems** are low, hairy, sparsely leaved, and **develop from a prostrate basal rosette. Basal leaves** are petiolated, **hairy, compound (3–9 leaflets)**, 3–20 cm long by 0.5–5 cm wide, dark green (with some red coloration), and lanceolate. **Leaflets are deeply cut**, nearly to the midvein. **Stem leaves are reduced** but also **compound and deeply cut**, sessile, 1–2.5 cm long. Stipules are present.

ROOTS AND UNDERGROUND STRUCTURES: Coarsely branched shallow taproot with secondary fibrous root system.

FLOWERS AND FRUIT: Flowers are produced primarily from April to June but occasionally throughout the summer. **Flowers are in umbel-like clusters of 2–8**, each on a 1–2 cm stalk (pedicel). The flower clusters are attached to a long leafless stalk (peduncle) arising from the stem leaf axils. The sepals (5) are 5–7 mm long and bristle-tipped. The **petals (5) are pink to purple**, 5–8 mm long. Each flower (1–1.3 cm wide) produces a **beak-like fruit** that separates into 5 sections (mericarps) when mature. Each section consists of a **seed and a spirally twisted hairy tail** (style) that coils under dry conditions and uncoils when moist. Seeds are cylindrical, about 5 mm long, hairy, light brown to orangish. Each plant can produce up to 600 seeds.

POSTSENESCENCE CHARACTERISTICS: Leafless stems with characteristic fruit persist for only a short time.

HABITAT: Redstem filaree is a weed of many perennial crops including nursery crops, orchards, and Christmas trees. It can also be a problem in turfgrass and landscapes. It is usually found on dry, sandy soil.

DISTRIBUTION: Established throughout the United States.

SIMILAR SPECIES: **Whitestem filaree (*Erodium moschatum* (L.) L'Hér. *ex* Ait., EROMO)** has much broader, longer compound leaves (up to 30 cm) and leaflets much less deeply cut than redstem filaree. Whitestem filaree stems are whitish and larger (60 cm tall). The flowers and seedheads of **Carolina geranium** resemble redstem filaree, but its leaves are rounded and palmately veined. In addition, the fruit beaks of Carolina geranium are outwardly coiled at maturity, whereas redstem filaree beaks are tightly twisted.

Redstem filaree rosette

Redstem filaree seedlings

Redstem filaree flowers and fruit

Redstem filaree stem with foliage, flowers, and fruit

Top, redstem filaree seeds, 5.5 mm (seed without stalk); *bottom*, whitestem filaree seeds, 5.9 mm (not including stalk)

243

Carolina geranium (*Geranium carolinianum* L.) [GERCA]

Synonyms: wild geranium, Carolina crane's-bill, crane's-bill

GENERAL DESCRIPTION: **Usually a biennial**, sometimes a winter or summer annual. Leaves initially form a branching **basal rosette**, the stems subsequently elongate, freely branch, and reach a height of 10–80 cm.

PROPAGATION / PHENOLOGY: Reproduction is **by seed**; seeds germinate in late summer, early autumn, or spring.

SEEDLING: Seedlings develop into a **basal rosette** of leaves. Hypocotyls are brownish pink, with short downward-pointing hairs. Cotyledons are broadly kidney-shaped to square-oval; the apex is indented (emarginate) and has a small point (mucronate). Cotyledons are heart-shaped at the base, green above, and pink below with short hairs on both surfaces. **Young leaves** are alternate, **palmately veined**, with brownish pink petioles that are covered with downward-pointing hairs. **Two stipules** are present **at the base of the petiole**. The leaf blades are green on the upper surface, often tinged pink below, and have short hairs on both surfaces. The **margins of the blade are deeply toothed or lobed.**

MATURE PLANT: **Elongated stems are erect**, branching near the base. Stems are densely hairy and greenish pink to red. **Leaves** are hairy on both surfaces, rounded to kidney-shaped, and **deeply palmately divided into usually 5 segments. Each segment is also lobed or coarsely toothed.** Leaves are 2.5–7 cm wide, on long petioles subtended by stipules. Leaves are usually alternate near the base and opposite above. Leaves and stems are reddish in sunny, low-fertility, or dry sites.

ROOTS AND UNDERGROUND STRUCTURES: Fibrous roots with a shallow taproot.

FLOWERS AND FRUIT: Flowers are present from May to August. Two or more flowers are clustered at the tip of stems and branches arising from the upper leaf axils. Sepals (5) are awl-shaped and awn-tipped, about equal in length to the 5 (1 cm long) **whitish pink to purple petals. Fruit are produced at the base of long styles, giving the entire structure the appearance of a crane's bill.** At maturity, the fruit splits into 5 curled sections (mericarps), each bearing 1 seed. Seeds are 1.5–2 mm long, oval to oblong, light to dark brown, with a conspicuous network of veins.

POSTSENESCENCE CHARACTERISTICS: Plants overwinter as rosettes. Plant parts do not persist after fruiting.

HABITAT: Carolina geranium is a weed of turfgrass, landscapes, orchards, and nursery crops. Also found in wooded areas, fields, and roadsides, it generally grows on dry, sandy, and nutrient-poor soils.

DISTRIBUTION: Found throughout the United States; most troublesome in the southern and western states.

SIMILAR SPECIES: **Dovefoot geranium (*Geranium molle* L., GERMO)**, also known as cranesbill, and **smallflower geranium (*Geranium pusillum* L., GERPU)**, also known as smallflower cranesbill, are biennials with rounded leaves not as deeply divided as those of Carolina geranium. They can also be distinguished from Carolina geranium because their sepals are not awn-tipped, the flowers are red-violet, and the seeds are smooth. The ovaries of Carolina geranium and smallflower geranium are hairy; the ovaries of dovefoot geranium are wrinkled and lack hairs.

Carolina geranium habit

Carolina geranium foliage, flowers, and fruit

Smallflower geranium rosette

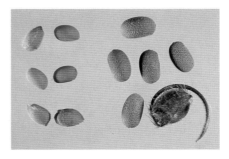

Left, dovefoot geranium seeds, 1.3 mm; *right,* Carolina geranium seeds, 2.0 mm

Ground ivy (*Glechoma hederacea* L.) [GLEHE]

Synonyms: *Nepeta hederacea*, gill-over-the-ground, creeping Charlie, cats-foot, field balm

GENERAL DESCRIPTION: A **perennial** with long (20–75 cm), **creeping, square stems that root at the nodes** and form dense prostrate patches. The foliage emits a strong **mint-like odor** when bruised, uprooted, or mowed.

PROPAGATION / PHENOLOGY: Reproduction is primarily by **creeping stems** that root at the node and **less commonly by seeds**. Infestations occur primarily by encroachment of vegetative fragments from adjacent areas.

SEEDLING: Cotyledons are short-oblong to broadly spatulate, curving abruptly into a long stalk. **Young leaves are opposite**, shiny on the upper surface, smooth to minutely hairy, **kidney-shaped to rounded** or heart-shaped (1–4 cm in diameter), with **broad rounded teeth** on the margin. Seedlings are rarely encountered.

MATURE PLANT: **Stems are lax, square**, mostly smooth or with backwardly directed, short, stiff hairs. **Stems trail along the ground, rooting at the nodes. Leaves are similar to those of the seeding** and are on long horizontal petioles (3–5 cm). Blades are prominently palmately veined.

ROOTS AND UNDERGROUND STRUCTURES: Fibrous roots are produced at the base of the plant and from nodes on trailing stems. **Rhizomes are also present.**

FLOWERS AND FRUIT: **Flowers** are produced as early as April to June on stems that are shorter and more ascending than the long and trailing vegetative stems. Flowers are 1–2 cm long on short flower-stalks arranged **in clusters of 2–3 in the upper leaf axils**. Sepals are fused into a hairy **5-lobed tube. Petals are tubular, purplish blue, and 2-lipped**, the upper lip 2-cleft, the lower lip 3-lobed. Fruit are egg-shaped nutlets (<1 mm long), smooth, elliptic, brown, flat on 2 sides and round on the third side.

POSTSENESCENCE CHARACTERISTICS: Plants remain green throughout the winter.

HABITAT: Ground ivy is a common weed of turfgrass and landscapes as well as perennial fruit crops. It is most commonly found in damp shady areas but can tolerate full sunlight.

DISTRIBUTION: Most common throughout the northeastern and north-central United States but also found in the southern states.

SIMILAR SPECIES: Ground ivy can look similar to **slender speedwell** when leaf size is reduced, as occurs under stress or with close mowing. But it has square stems, unlike the round stems of slender speedwell. Although **henbit** can sometimes resemble ground ivy, its stems do not creep along the ground or root at the nodes. The leaf shape of ground ivy leads to confusion with **common mallow**, but common mallow has alternate leaves, pointed teeth, and rounded stems.

J. Neal

Ground ivy encroaching from turfgrass into landscape bed

Ground ivy flowering stem

J. Neal

Ground ivy seeds and pod

J. Neal

Henbit (*Lamium amplexicaule* L.) [LAMAM]

Synonyms: dead nettle, blind nettle, bee nettle

GENERAL DESCRIPTION: A **winter annual** branching at the base (10–40 cm tall).

PROPAGATION / PHENOLOGY: Reproduction is **by seed**; seedlings emerge from moist, cool soil in early spring and fall. Self-pollinated flowers may produce seeds without opening (cleistogamy).

SEEDLING: Hypocotyls initially are green but become purple with age. Cotyledons are round to oblong on hairy petioles. The base of the cotyledon blade is notched where it meets the petiole. **Young leaves** have petioles and are **opposite**, with **soft hairs** on the dark green upper surface and along the veins of the lower surface. The **upper surface is prominently veined and crinkled**. Leaf blades have **2–4 large rounded teeth on each side**. **Stems are square**, green to purple, with basally pointing hairs.

MATURE PLANT: **Mature stems** are square, green to purple, nearly hairless, prostrate or curved at the base, with an **erect or ascending tip.** Leaves (1.5–2 cm long) are **palmately veined. Lower leaves are petiolated**, rounded to heart-shaped, with rounded teeth. **Upper leaves are sessile, deeply lobed, encircling the stem at the base.** In the flowering portions, stem internodes are shorter and leaves can look whorled.

ROOTS AND UNDERGROUND STRUCTURES: Fibrous root system. Stems root where the lower nodes contact the soil surface.

FLOWERS AND FRUIT: **Showy pink to purple flowers** are produced in April but may appear sporadically from March to November. **Flowers are in whorls in the axils of the sessile upper leaves.** Sepals are united into a tube with 5 teeth; petals are pink to purple, united into a 2-lipped tube, 1–1.5 cm long. Fruit (nutlets) are egg-shaped to oblong, 3-angled, brown with white spots, and 1.5–2 mm long. Four nutlets, each with 1 seed, are enclosed within the persistent sepals. Each plant can produce 200 seeds.

POSTSENESCENCE CHARACTERISTICS: Henbit and other members of the mint family have persistent square stems and fused, persistent sepals (in whorls at the nodes) that often contain the seeds. Henbit may overwinter as a seedling.

HABITAT: More common in warm-season than cool-season turf; also found in landscapes, orchards, gardens, nurseries, winter grain crops, and other winter annual crops. Thrives in early spring and fall on cool, rich, fertile soils.

DISTRIBUTION: Found throughout the United States; most common in eastern North America and on the West Coast.

SIMILAR SPECIES: **Purple deadnettle**, also known as red deadnettle (*Lamium purpureum* L., LAMPU), is a winter annual that flowers in early spring. The upper leaves and square stems are conspicuously red. The leaves are more triangular and less deeply lobed than those of henbit and differ also in that the upper leaves are petiolated and crowded at the end of the branches. Purple deadnettle flowers are also lighter purple than henbit flowers. **Spotted deadnettle (*Lamium maculatum* L., LAMMA)** is a perennial ground cover with white markings on its leaves and square stems. It has escaped cultivation to become a weed in some areas. **Persian speedwell** can resemble henbit, especially as a young seedling or in dense stands. Leaves of Persian speedwell seedlings are similar to henbit leaves but are more triangular, and the stems are round.

R. Uva

Henbit habit

J. DiTomaso

Henbit seedling

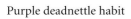

Purple deadnettle habit

R. Uva

J. Neal

Left, henbit; *right*, purple deadnettle

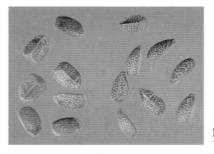

J. DiTomaso

Left, purple deadnettle seeds, 1.9 mm; *right*, henbit seeds, 1.8 mm

Healall (*Prunella vulgaris* L.) [PRUVU]

Synonyms: *Brunella vulgaris*, self-heal, carpenters-weed

GENERAL DESCRIPTION: A branched **prostrate stoloniferous perennial** that spreads to form dense patches but can grow erect to 5–60 cm tall in unmowed areas.

PROPAGATION / PHENOLOGY: Reproduction is **by seeds** and **creeping stems that root** at the nodes.

SEEDLING: Cotyledons are ovate, widest toward the base, notched at the apex, with lobed margins pointing toward the hypocotyl. **Young leaves are egg-shaped, pointed** at the apex, with entire or round-toothed (crenate) margins. Young plants branch at the base; adventitious roots are produced at the nodes.

MATURE PLANT: **Stems are square**, hairy when young, becoming smooth with age. **Leaves are opposite**, ovate (2–9 cm long by 0.7–4 cm wide), and have petioles. Leaf blades are sparsely hairy to smooth, broadest at the base, and taper to a rounded tip. The margins are obscurely round-toothed or untoothed. **Lower leaves are wider** and more rounded at the base than the upper leaves. **Upper leaves may be sessile.** Drought, low fertility, and mowing reduce leaf size and internode length. Shade and infrequent mowing result in larger leaves, longer petioles, and larger internodes.

ROOTS AND UNDERGROUND STRUCTURES: **Creeping stems root freely at the nodes**, producing a shallow but aggressive fibrous root system.

FLOWERS AND FRUIT: **Flowers** are present from June to September **in dense spikes at the end of ascending stems**. Sepals are green or purple, 7–10 mm long, and fused into a toothed tube. **Petals** are also **fused into a tube, pale violet to deep purple** (rarely pink or white), 1–2 cm long, and 2-lipped. Flowers are sessile and subtended by large, hairy, green to purple bracts. Fruit are slightly flattened nutlets (4 per flower) about 1.5 mm long. Each pear-shaped, brown nutlet encloses 1 seed.

POSTSENESCENCE CHARACTERISTICS: Plants remain green and persist year-round. Flower spikes, bracts, sepals, and nutlets remain for an extended period.

HABITAT: Primarily a weed of turfgrass, healall is found on shady, moist or sandy, drought-prone areas. It frequently grows in recently cleared woodland areas, where it prefers shady, moist sites. It is rarely a problem in crops because it does not tolerate cultivation or intense crop management.

DISTRIBUTION: Found throughout the United States; common in the northeastern United States and southern Canada.

SIMILAR SPECIES: **Creeping thyme** is similar in habit but has smaller leaves and flowers. **Purple deadnettle** (also called red deadnettle) is a winter annual flowering in early spring. Upper leaves and stems are conspicuously red, and leaves are triangular and crowded at the end of the branches. The upper leaves of **henbit** encircle the stem, whereas those of healall are petiolated.

Healall habit in turfgrass

Healall cotyledons and first leaf pair

Healall flowering stem

Healall seeds, 1.7 mm

Creeping thyme (*Thymus serpyllum* L.) [THYSE]

Synonyms: wild thyme, hillwort, penny mountain, lemon thyme, mother of thyme

GENERAL DESCRIPTION: A **mat-forming stoloniferous perennial** with diffusely branched, **square stems**. Usually prostrate but can grow to 20 cm in height.

PROPAGATION / PHENOLOGY: Reproduction is by **seeds or creeping stems** that can spread or become fragmented to infest adjacent areas.

SEEDLING: Seedlings are not commonly encountered.

MATURE PLANT: **Stems are prostrate, slightly 4-angled**, and finely hairy; they **root at the nodes** and become somewhat woody at the base with age. **Leaves are opposite**, elliptic to oblong-oval (≤1 cm long), with short petioles. Margins are entire, and leaf surfaces are smooth (lacking hairs) with glandular dots.

ROOTS AND UNDERGROUND STRUCTURES: Roots form at the nodes where the stems contact the soil surface.

FLOWERS AND FRUIT: **Flowers** are present from June through the summer in **terminal spike-like clusters** (1–4 cm long) or crowded axillary whorls on upright (to 10 cm) hairy flowering stems. Sepals are tubular, 3–4 mm long, tinged with purple, slightly 2-lipped, with awl-shaped teeth and marginal hairs. **Petals are tubular, lavender, 2-lipped**, 4–6 mm long, with 4 unequally lengthed stamens on each flower. Fruit (nutlets) are elliptic with a minute white point at the base. Each flower has 4 nutlets, and each nutlet (0.5–1 mm long) encloses a single seed.

POSTSENESCENCE CHARACTERISTICS: Foliage remains green throughout the year.

HABITAT: Creeping thyme is a weed of low-maintenance turfgrass. It is most common on dry, stony, or high pH soils and is rarely encountered in crops or high-maintenance turfgrass.

DISTRIBUTION: Found from New England through New York and south to West Virginia and South Carolina.

SIMILAR SPECIES: **Resembles a miniature version of healall** in habit, leaf shape, and flowering structure. Leaves are smaller and less ovate than those of healall. Also similar to many of the herbal thymes.

R. Uva

Creeping thyme habit

R. Uva

Creeping thyme in flower

R. Uva

Creeping thyme flower head

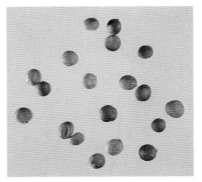

J. DiTomaso

Creeping thyme seeds, 0.7 mm

Purple loosestrife (*Lythrum salicaria* L.) [LYTSA]

Synonyms: purple lythrum, bouquet-violet

GENERAL DESCRIPTION: A much-branched (as many as 30–50 branches), **erect** (1–2 m tall), **perennial** that forms a **large tough root crown** with age. **Large colonies develop near moist or marshy sites** and are particularly conspicuous when **showy purple-magenta flowers** bloom from July through September.

PROPAGATION / PHENOLOGY: Reproduction is **by seeds and thick, fleshy roots that produce adventitious shoots.** Plants can produce seed in their first growing season. Seeds germinate in late spring or early summer. After mowing, **stem fragments can root** to produce new plants.

SEEDLING: Seedlings are very small and resemble the adult plants. Young plants also develop from root buds or the root crown. Leaves are lanceolate and opposite. Shoots emerging from the roots or crown lack cotyledons.

MATURE PLANT: **Stems are square, sometimes 6-sided.** Stems and leaves either lack hairs or more often have short upward-pointing hairs. **Leaves are sessile,** lanceolate to linear, 3–10 cm long, **opposite or in whorls of 3.** Larger leaves are heart-shaped at the base.

ROOTS AND UNDERGROUND STRUCTURES: **Thick, fleshy roots** and a fibrous root system are produced. Forms a **large woody crown** with age.

FLOWERS AND FRUIT: **Purple-magenta flowers** are produced from July to September in **conspicuous 10–40 cm long terminal spikes.** Fused sepals form a tube surrounding the ovary. Petals (5–7) and stamens (10–14) are attached to the top of the fused sepals. Numerous small reddish brown seeds (1 mm long) are contained within the capsules. A single plant can produce more than 2 million seeds a year.

POSTSENESCENCE CHARACTERISTICS: Foliage turns red at the end of the season. Dead brown stalks persist through winter, with capsules arranged in spire-shaped spikes.

HABITAT: Purple loosestrife was introduced from Europe and has become widely distributed in wet or marshy sites. It is **a major weed of wetlands and natural areas,** where it displaces native vegetation and wildlife. It is also a weed of roadsides, canals, ditches, spring-flooded pastures, and cranberry bogs. Although purple loosestrife is **classified as a noxious weed in many states,** it continues to be sold in the nursery and landscape trade.

DISTRIBUTION: Common in the temperate regions of North America, including southern Canada and the northern and northeastern United States to Virginia and Missouri; also in scattered areas along the Pacific Coast.

SIMILAR SPECIES: **Few plants are mistaken for purple loosestrife. Early in the season, northern willowherb (*Epilobium ciliatum* Raf.) and hairy willowweed (*Epilobium hirsutum* L., EPIHI)** may resemble purple loosestrife seedlings or root sprouts, but both of those plants are annuals and much smaller than purple loosestrife. Northern willowherb may be distinguished by its round stems and smaller, fewer pink flowers, which only have 4 petals. Hairy willowweed is similar to northern willowherb but has long spreading hairs. The willowherbs are common weeds of container- and field-grown nursery crops.

Purple loosestrife habit in cranberries

R. Uva

Purple loosestrife
young shoot

J. Neal

Northern willowherb habit

J. Neal

Purple loosestrife
flowering stem

J. DiTomaso

Hairy willowweed flowers

J. Neal

Purple loosestrife seeds, 0.9 mm

J. DiTomaso

255

Velvetleaf (*Abutilon theophrasti* Medicus) [ABUTH]

Synonyms: pie marker, buttonweed, Indian mallow, butter print, velvet weed, butter-weed, Indian hemp, cotton-weed, wild cotton

GENERAL DESCRIPTION: An **erect** (1–1.5 m tall) **summer annual**, usually with unbranched stems. Heart-shaped **leaves and stems are covered with soft hairs, velvety to the touch.**

PROPAGATION / PHENOLOGY: Reproduction is by seed, which can germinate from several inches below the soil surface. Seedlings emerge in mid to late May.

SEEDLING: Hypocotyls are stout, green or maroon at the base, and covered with short hairs. **Cotyledons are heart-shaped**, sometimes tinted with maroon. The cotyledon margins and both surfaces are **covered with short hairs. Young leaves are heart-shaped, densely hairy on both surfaces (velvety)**, and **bluntly toothed along the margin**. Leaves are alternate, angled downward over the seedling, with the apexes pointing to the ground. **Stems are hairy.** Leaves and stems emit an **unpleasant odor** when crushed.

MATURE PLANT: **Stems are erect**, mostly **unbranched**, and covered with short **velvety** branched **hairs. Leaves are heart-shaped**, gradually and concavely tapering to a sharp point (acuminate), 10–15 cm long and nearly as wide, **soft-hairy**, with toothed margins. Petioles are about equal in length to the blades. Leaves are alternate and palmately veined.

ROOTS AND UNDERGROUND STRUCTURES: Fibrous root system with a shallow **taproot**.

FLOWERS AND FRUIT: Plants flower from July or August into the autumn. Flowers (1.5–2.5 cm wide) are produced on short stalks (pedicels) in the upper leaf axils and consist of 5 fused sepals, **5 yellow petals**, and numerous stamens fused into a tube. The **fruit is a circular cup-shaped disk of 9–15 carpels** (schizocarp), **each with a beak on the margin** of the disk. Each carpel contains 3–9 seeds and splits along a central suture. Seeds are about 3 mm long, grayish brown to black, flattened, and notched. **Seeds** have small star-shaped hairs on the surface and **can remain viable in the soil for up to 50 years.**

POSTSENESCENCE CHARACTERISTICS: The **stems persist** throughout the winter, **bearing the characteristic disk of beaked fruit.** Fruit turn black, and each section falls off individually throughout the autumn and winter.

HABITAT: Velvetleaf is considered to be one of the most important weeds of corn production in the United States. It is common in nursery, horticultural, and agronomic crops, particularly in areas of continuous corn production or in other crops where triazine herbicides are commonly used. Is also grows in roadsides and gardens. Velvetleaf thrives on nutrient-rich cultivated soils.

DISTRIBUTION: Common throughout the United States.

SIMILAR SPECIES: **Common mallow seedlings** have cotyledons that are also heart-shaped, but they lack hairs. At maturity, the leaves of common mallow are roundish not heart-shaped.

Velvetleaf habit

J. Neal

J. DiTomaso

Velvetleaf seedlings

J. Neal

Velvetleaf flower and fruit

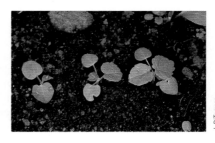

J. DiTomaso

Velvetleaf seeds, 3 mm

Venice mallow (*Hibiscus trionum* L.) [HIBTR]

Synonyms: flower-of-an-hour, bladder ketmia, modesty, shoo-fly

GENERAL DESCRIPTION: A **summer annual** with **3- or sometimes 5-lobed or deeply cut leaves**, each with rounded teeth or lobes on the margins. Stems are usually branched at the base, spreading to erect (20–50 cm tall).

PROPAGATION / PHENOLOGY: Reproduction is **by seed**; seedlings may emerge throughout the summer, particularly after cultivation. **Seeds persist in the soil**, remaining dormant for long periods.

SEEDLING: Hypocotyls are stout and hairy. **Cotyledon blades** are yellow-green, thick, **rounded or heart-shaped**. Cotyledon petioles are hairy and longer than the blades. **Young leaves are alternate.** The **first 2 leaves are toothed and irregular in shape; subsequent leaves are deeply 3-lobed.** Leaf blades are densely hairy below and sparsely hairy above.

MATURE PLANT: Stems are hairy, branching near the base to form a tuft. **Leaves are alternate**, about 7.5 cm long and wide, and **deeply 3-lobed or sometimes 5-lobed; each lobe has coarse rounded teeth or small lobes.** Leaves are oblong to egg-shaped, larger toward the apex, on long petioles subtended by 2 stipules. Leaves are reduced near the top of the plant.

ROOTS AND UNDERGROUND STRUCTURES: Fibrous root system with a **shallow taproot**.

FLOWERS AND FRUIT: **Flowers** are present from July to September, **opening only for a few hours a day in the morning**. Flowers are subtended by several linear bracts and are produced singly or in groups of 2 or 3 in the upper leaf axils. Sepals (5) are pale green with dark green veins and are fused into an inflated membranous bladder. **Petals (5) are 1.5–4 cm long, pale yellow to white with purple bases.** Stamens are united into a column; the filaments are dark purple, and the anthers are yellow-orange. The fruit (capsule) contains 30 seeds and is enclosed within the expanded bladder. Seeds are about 2 mm long, kidney-shaped to triangular, rough, and grayish black. Seeds have small star-shaped hairs on the surface.

POSTSENESCENCE CHARACTERISTICS: Plant parts do not persist after frost. The distinctive seedheads remain attached for only a short time.

HABITAT: Venice mallow is a weed of nursery, horticultural, and agronomic crops. Most common in cultivated areas, it tolerates drought and gravelly, sometimes alkaline, soils.

DISTRIBUTION: Initially introduced from southern Europe as an ornamental but has escaped to become a common weed in the eastern half of the United States, particularly in the southeastern and midwestern states.

SIMILAR SPECIES: **Musk mallow (*Malva moschata* L., MALMO)** has similar foliage, but its leaves are 5–7 parted, whereas those of Venice mallow are usually 3-parted. In addition, the basal leaves of musk mallow are rounded and lobed; those of Venice mallow are dissected. Musk mallow flowers are rose-colored or white with pink veins.

Venice mallow seedling

J. Neal

Young Venice mallow

J. Neal

J. DiTomaso

Venice mallow flower, fruit, and mature leaves

J. DiTomaso

Venice mallow seeds, 2.1 mm

259

Common mallow (*Malva neglecta* Wallr.) [MALNE]

Synonyms: cheese-weed, cheeses, cheese mallow, dwarf mallow, running mallow, malice, round dock, button weed, round-leaved mallow, low mallow

GENERAL DESCRIPTION: A **winter or summer annual, or biennial**, growing erect (10–30 cm tall) or, more often, **prostrate to decumbent.**

PROPAGATION / PHENOLOGY: Reproduction is **by seed**, which may emerge continuously between spring and early autumn. **Fragmented stems can produce adventitious roots** from the nodes under moist conditions.

SEEDLING: Hypocotyls are green to white, with short soft hairs. **Cotyledons are smooth, heart-shaped, with 3 main veins,** 5–7 mm long by 3–4 mm wide, on relatively long and grooved stalks that are hairy on the ridges. Plants initially develop as **basal rosettes. Young leaves** are alternate, somewhat crinkled, and hairy on both surfaces. **Blades are circular, shallowly lobed, and toothed.** Petioles are grooved, hairy, 2–3 times longer than the width of the blade.

MATURE PLANT: Stems branch and elongate at the soil surface. The **base of each stem lies close to the soil surface**, with the **tip turned upward** (decumbent). **Leaves are alternate**, on narrow petioles (5–20 cm long), **palmately veined, circular to kidney-shaped** (2–6 cm wide), with **toothed margins** and 5–9 lobes. Short hairs are present on both leaf surfaces and on the margins and stem.

ROOTS AND UNDERGROUND STRUCTURES: Short to deep, straight taproot with coarsely branched secondary root system.

FLOWERS AND FRUIT: **Flowers** are present from May throughout the summer and into October, either singly or in clusters arising from the leaf axils. Petals (5) are 0.6–1.3 cm long, 2 times as long as the sepals, **white or whitish lavender, often tinged with purple.** Flowers are on long stalks (1–4 cm) and produce **fruit that resemble a button or a wheel of cheese.** Fruit consist of 12–15 wedge-shaped, 1-seeded segments arranged in a flattened round disk (schizocarp). Seeds are reddish brown to black, flattened, circular with a marginal notch (1.5 mm in diameter).

POSTSENESCENCE CHARACTERISTICS: Green stems persist well into winter. Plants can occasionally sprout from the crown the following spring.

HABITAT: Common mallow is a weed of low-maintenance turfgrass, landscapes, and nursery crops. It is less common in agronomic crops.

DISTRIBUTION: Widespread throughout North America.

SIMILAR SPECIES: Few species are confused with common mallow. The **leaves of ground ivy** are similar but opposite, with rounded teeth. Ground ivy also emits a mint-like odor and has square stems. **Musk mallow** is related to common mallow but has much more deeply dissected 5–7 parted leaves.

Common mallow habit

A. Senesac

Common mallow
seedlings

R. Uva

J. DiTomaso

Common mallow fruit

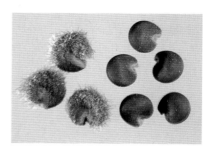

J. DiTomaso

Left, musk mallow seeds, 2.0 mm;
right, common mallow seeds, 1.6 mm

Prickly sida (*Sida spinosa* L.) [SIDSP]

Synonyms: false mallow, Indian mallow, spiny sida, thistle mallow

GENERAL DESCRIPTION: An **erect, branched, summer annual** (20–50 cm tall). **Spiny projections on the stem nodes** account for the common and scientific names.

PROPAGATION / PHENOLOGY: Reproduction is **by seed**; seeds may germinate over an extended period from spring through midsummer.

SEEDLING: Cotyledons are rounded to heart-shaped (6.5–14 mm long by 5–8 mm wide), with a shallow indentation or notch at the apex. The hypocotyl and the margins of the leaves and cotyledons are densely covered with short, gland-tipped hairs. Young leaves are alternate. **Initial leaves are rounded to egg-shaped; subsequent leaves develop a pointed tip.** Blades are thin, soft, hairy, with prominent veins beneath. Petioles of young leaves are rounded, at least one-third as long as the blade, and bear short gland-tipped hairs. Stipules are present at the base of the third and subsequent leaves.

MATURE PLANT: **Stems are much-branched** and **softly hairy, with small spines** at the leaf nodes. Hairs are branched (star-shaped). **Leaves are alternate, softly hairy**, 2–5 cm long, and oval or oblong to lanceolate. Margins are round- to sharp-toothed. Petioles are 1–3 cm long, with **linear stipules** (5–8 mm long) at the base.

ROOTS AND UNDERGROUND STRUCTURES: Slender branching **taproot**.

FLOWERS AND FRUIT: **Flowers** are produced from June to September **alone or in clusters** on 2–12 mm flower-stalks arising **from the leaf axils**. Flowers are **pale yellow**, with 5 petals, 4–6 mm long. Stamens are united over half their length to form a column. The **fruit** (schizocarp) is a ring of five 1-seeded segments (mericarps), 1.8–3 mm long, with 2 sharp spines at the apex. The **seed** usually **remains enclosed within the mericarp**, but is flattened on 2 sides and rounded on the other (2–2.5 mm long).

POSTSENESCENCE CHARACTERISTICS: Woody erect stems with spines in the axils may persist into early winter.

HABITAT: A weed of most cultivated, agronomic, and horticultural crops, prickly sida is also found in landscapes, fields, pastures, gardens, and waste places.

DISTRIBUTION: Found throughout the eastern United States extending north to Massachusetts and Michigan, and west to Nebraska; most common in the southeastern states.

SIMILAR SPECIES: Very young **seedlings may resemble velvetleaf**, but they lack the velvety foliar hairs. Foliage is also similar to **Virginia copperleaf** but can be distinguished by the coloration and spines at the stem nodes.

Prickly sida habit

J. Neal

R. Uva

Prickly sida seedlings

J. Neal

Prickly sida spines (at node)

J. Derr

Prickly sida in flower

J. DiTomaso

Prickly sida seeds, 2.2 mm, and mericarps

Cutleaf eveningprimrose (*Oenothera laciniata* Hill) [OEOLA]

Synonyms: *Oenothera sinuata, Raimannia laciniata*

GENERAL DESCRIPTION: A **biennial, winter or rarely a summer annual, branching from a basal rosette.** Elongating stems can sprawl close to the ground or grow erect to 10–80 cm in height.

PROPAGATION / PHENOLOGY: Reproduction is **by seed**; seeds germinate in warm, moist soil from early summer through early fall.

SEEDLING: Cotyledon blades are oval, gradually tapering to a stalk, or occasionally kidney-shaped on a flattened petiole. **Leaves form a basal rosette.** The upper surface of young leaves is covered by short hairs; the lower surface is smooth. **Blades are oblong with distinct white midveins** on the upper surface. **Subsequent leaves develop deeply cut teeth** or regular lobes. Purple to reddish coloration may be present on and around the petiole. Seedling overwinters as a basal rosette.

MATURE PLANT: **Stems** are hairy, often reddish, **prostrate to ascending** from the base with an erect tip. Leaves are green, sparsely hairy to smooth above. Blades are long (3–8 cm) and narrow, oblanceolate, oblong, or lanceolate. **Margins are wavy, coarsely toothed, irregularly lobed, or pinnatifid.** Leaves are alternate and petiolated. Upper stem leaves are sessile and smaller than lower leaves.

ROOTS AND UNDERGROUND STRUCTURES: Taproot.

FLOWERS AND FRUIT: **Flowers** bloom from May through October and are **sessile in the upper leaf axils.** Flowers are **usually yellow** but **occasionally reddish brown.** Petals are 5–25 mm long, attached at the base of the fused sepals. Sepals form a 1.5–3.5 cm long narrow tube. The tips of the sepals (6–12 mm long) are reflexed downward. The **fruit** is a 2–4 cm long, 3–4 mm wide, 4–lobed, **cylindrical and often curved capsule.** Seeds are angular (1 mm long), pale brown, conspicuously pitted, and arranged in rows within the capsule.

POSTSENESCENCE CHARACTERISTICS: Stems and hairy capsules persist for a short time into late fall.

HABITAT: Cutleaf eveningprimrose is a weed of nurseries, Christmas tree plantations, orchards, landscapes, and low-maintenance turfgrass; it is less common in agronomic row crops. It is also found in pastures, waste areas, and roadsides, frequently growing on dry, usually sandy soil.

DISTRIBUTION: Native to the southern and eastern United States. Exists as a weed from Maine, throughout the Southeast, and west to New Mexico and California.

SIMILAR SPECIES: **Common eveningprimrose (*Oenothera biennis* L., OEOBI)** is similar while **in the rosette stage** but has an **erect growth habit** and **entire (unlobed) leaf margins.** Common eveningprimrose stems and seed capsules are woody and often persist through the winter. Capsules of common eveningprimrose are thickest near the bottom, whereas capsules of cutleaf eveningprimrose are linear throughout.

Cutleaf
eveningprimrose
habit

J. Neal

J. Neal

Cutleaf eveningprimrose rosette,
branching from the base

J. Neal

Common eveningprimrose seedling

R. Uva

Common eveningprimrose rosette

R. Uva

Common
eveningprimrose
flowering shoot

J. DiTomaso

Left, common eveningprimrose
seeds, 1.4 mm; *right*, cutleaf
eveningprimrose seeds, 1.1 mm

Yellow woodsorrel (*Oxalis stricta* L.) [OXAST]

Synonyms: *Oxalis dillenii, Oxalis europaea, Xanthoxalis cymosa, Xanthoxalis stricta*, sour-grass

GENERAL DESCRIPTION: A **clover-like** erect **perennial** that **can act as a summer annual** in cooler climates. Plants grow from as low as 3 cm to as high as 50 cm.

PROPAGATION / PHENOLOGY: Reproduction is **primarily by seeds**, but plants can also **spread by rhizomes.** Seeds germinate shortly after dispersal, when conditions allow.

SEEDLING: **Cotyledons** are smooth, **rounded** to oblong, <0.5 cm long, often tinged pink on the underside, on short stalks. **Young leaves are trifoliolate** (3 leaflets) and alternate, **with heart-shaped leaflets.** The upper surface of leaflets is smooth; margins and veins of the lower surface are sparsely hairy. Petioles are hairy, long, pinkish brown toward the base.

MATURE PLANT: **Stems** are green to purple, hairy, **usually erect**, and mostly unbranched or with several **branches from the base. Leaves** are alternate and **long-petioled**; they consist of **3 heart-shaped leaflets**, 1–2 cm wide, which often fold up at midday and night. Leaf surfaces are smooth, and the margins are fringed with hairs.

ROOTS AND UNDERGROUND STRUCTURES: **Long, slender, succulent, white to pink rhizomes** with a secondary fibrous root system.

FLOWERS AND FRUIT: **Flowers** are produced from May to September, year-round in greenhouses, **in clusters that arise from long stalks at the leaf axils.** Flowers are 7–11 mm wide with 5 sepals and 5 **yellow petals**, 4–9 mm long. Stamens are in 2 groups of 5, one group short and the other long. **Fruit** are 5-ridged, **cylindrical, pointed, erect, hairy capsules**, 1–1.5 cm long. **Seeds** are brown to maroon, oval, 1–1.5 mm long, and flattened with a transversely ridged surface and a **sticky coating. Seeds disperse from capsules by explosively ejecting as far as 4 m.**

POSTSENESCENCE CHARACTERISTICS: Plants die back to the ground in cold climates, often leaving branched yellow stems.

HABITAT: A weed of turfgrass, container-nursery stock, and greenhouse crops, as well as landscapes, yellow woodsorrel is also found on disturbed sites, in roadsides, and on the edge of woodlands. It thrives on nutrient-rich, moist soil but tolerates a wide range of soil types and site conditions, from moist and shady to sunny and drought-prone.

DISTRIBUTION: Distributed throughout the world.

SIMILAR SPECIES: **Creeping woodsorrel (*Oxalis corniculata* L., OXACO)** is more prostrate, frequently roots at the nodes, and often has more purplish leaves than yellow woodsorrel. However, **leaf color is variable in both species and cannot be used as a diagnostic characteristic.** Creeping woodsorrel lacks the underground rhizomes of yellow woodsorrel but **spreads by aboveground stolons.** It is a more common weed problem in and around greenhouses and container crops than yellow woodsorrel. The woodsorrels can be distinguished from trifoliolate legumes, such as **clovers and black medic**, by the absence of stipules at the base of the petiole and by heart-shaped leaflets. **See Table 14 for a comparison with weedy trifoliolate legumes.**

J. Neal

Creeping woodsorrel habit

J. Neal

Creeping woodsorrel seedling

J. Neal

Mature yellow woodsorrel with rhizome

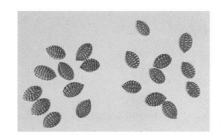

J. DiTomaso

Left, creeping woodsorrel seeds, 1.2 mm; *right*, yellow woodsorrel seeds, 1.2 mm

Common pokeweed (*Phytolacca americana* L.) [PHTAM]

Synonyms: *Phytolacca decandra*, pokeberry, Virginia poke, scoke, pigeonberry, garget, inkberry, red ink plant, coakum, American cancer, cancer jalap

GENERAL DESCRIPTION: **A large**, branched, **herbaceous perennial** (0.9–3 m tall) **resembling a small tree. Fresh leaves and roots** are particularly **toxic**, and leaves must be cooked properly to avoid poisoning. The primary toxicant is the triterpene saponin phytolaccin, which causes gastrointestinal irritation. **Berries can also be poisonous.** Poisoning rarely results in fatalities in humans; however, deaths have been reported in pigs and cattle.

PROPAGATION / PHENOLOGY: Reproduction is **by seed**. Seedlings may emerge from midspring through early summer.

SEEDLING: Hypocotyls are tender, succulent, and swollen at the base, often tinged with purple. Cotyledons are egg-shaped (25 mm long by 12 mm wide) and pointed at the apex. Cotyledons and young **leaves are pale green, often tinted reddish on the underside and the petioles.** Young leaves are alternate, smooth, egg-shaped to rounded, and pointed at the apex. The reddish coloration of the petioles continues down the stem. **Shoots emerging from established plants** in spring **are similar to seedlings, but are more robust,** lack cotyledons, **and are in compact clusters.**

MATURE PLANT: **Mature plants are tree-like. Stems are smooth, erect**, and branched above, **usually reddish. Leaves are alternate,** petiolated, **egg-shaped** to lanceolate-oblong (9–30 cm long by 3–11 cm wide), and decrease in size toward the top of the plant. Margins are entire or slightly wavy.

ROOTS AND UNDERGROUND STRUCTURES: **Large fleshy taproot**, 30 cm long by 10 cm thick in older plants. Taproot is white inside.

FLOWERS AND FRUIT: **Flowers** are present from July to the autumn on long (10–20 cm), narrow, **nodding to erect, reddish-stemmed racemes** at the end of the upper branches. Individual flowers are small, 6 mm wide, and have 5 white (or greenish white to pink) rounded, petal-like sepals. **Fruit are conspicuous berries, green when immature, turning purple to dark purple-black at maturity.** Berries produce a profuse amount of red juice. Fruit are rounded, slightly flattened, about 1 cm in diameter, and contain 10 seeds each. Seeds are small, glossy black, round and flattened, 3 mm in diameter.

POSTSENESCENCE CHARACTERISTICS: Dead, brown to black stems persist throughout the winter. Stems turn pale tan and decay early the following spring.

HABITAT: Common pokeweed is a weed of landscapes and nursery crops, but it also is found where seeds are dropped by birds: around fields and in roadsides and fence rows. It thrives in deep rich gravelly soils.

DISTRIBUTION: Most common in the eastern, southern, and southeastern United States but also occurs as far west as California.

SIMILAR SPECIES: Shoots from the taproot may resemble **Japanese knotweed** or **some hardwood seedlings such as common cottonwood**; however, the leaves of Japanese knotweed are subtended by a membranous sheath (ocrea), and the stems of hardwood species are woody.

A. Senesac

Common pokeweed habit

J. Neal

Common pokeweed seedling

A. Senesac

Common pokeweed shoots from perennial root stock

J. Neal

Common pokeweed foliage and fruit

J. DiTomaso

Common pokeweed seeds, 3 mm

Buckhorn plantain (*Plantago lanceolata* L.) [PLALA]

Synonyms: English plantain, narrow-leaved plantain, rib-grass, ribwort, black-jacks

GENERAL DESCRIPTION: A **narrow-leaved, parallel-veined perennial** forming **a basal rosette** or a clump of several rosettes.

PROPAGATION / PHENOLOGY: Reproduction is **by seeds** and by new shoots produced at the base of the plant. Buckhorn plantain often flowers in the first year of growth and is a prolific seed producer. Most seedlings emerge in spring or early autumn. Seeds may germinate in darkness and can become established even in tall, dense vegetation.

SEEDLING: **Cotyledons are grass-like** (linear), smooth, narrow (>5 times as long as wide), with a furrow on the upper surface. The first leaves are hairy only on the margins; subsequent leaves are sparsely hairy and have cobwebby hairs near the base. **Leaves are lanceolate** (>5 times as long as wide), **parallel-veined**, and widened at the base, where they clasp the short stem forming the **basal rosette**.

MATURE PLANT: **Leaves remain in a basal rosette.** Well-established plants may produce a clump of several rosettes from the same crown. **Leaves are lanceolate** to elliptic, widest above the middle, often twisting or curled, 5–25 cm long by 1–2.5 cm wide, with 3–5 **prominent parallel veins on the blade**. Margins can be entire or slightly toothed. Blades are usually smooth, but **can have long silky hairs at the base**. Leaves are somewhat erect, except in turfgrass, where they tend to be more prostrate. **Overwintering leaves are wider than those produced in the summer.**

ROOTS AND UNDERGROUND STRUCTURES: Fibrous roots are produced from a **thick** tough, short, **taproot-like woody underground stem** (caudex).

FLOWERS AND FRUIT: **Flowers and seedheads** are present from June through September **on the ends of leafless, unbranched, ridged stalks in dense cylindrical, cone-like spikes or heads**. Individual flowers of the heads are inconspicuous. Fruit are 2-seeded, 3–4 mm long, capsules opening transversely by a lid. Seeds are 1.5–3.5 mm long, brownish, shiny, with an indentation on one side. Seeds become sticky when wet, aiding in animal dispersal.

POSTSENESCENCE CHARACTERISTICS: Plants overwinter as basal rosettes. Flower-stalks and cylindrical, cone-like spikes can persist for an extended period.

HABITAT: Buckhorn plantain is a weed of turfgrass, landscapes, orchards, nursery crops, and other perennial crops. It is common on drier sites and on neutral to basic soils. Although buckhorn plantain often grows on compacted soils, it does not survive in areas that are routinely trampled. It tolerates close mowing.

DISTRIBUTION: Widespread throughout the United States and Canada.

SIMILAR SPECIES: **Bracted plantain (*Plantago aristata* Michx., PLAAR)** is vegetatively similar, but has narrower, hairier leaves that lack the deep ribs common to buckhorn plantain. In addition, **the flower spikes have conspicuous hairy bracts** up to 2 cm in length. Bracted plantain is most commonly found on sandy, drought-prone sites.

Buckhorn plantain habit

Bracted plantain (note bracts on inflorescence)

Buckhorn plantain seedlings

Bracted plantain seeds, 2.3 mm

Buckhorn plantain rosette

Buckhorn plantain seeds, 2.8 mm (largest)

271

Broadleaf plantain (*Plantago major* L.) [PLAMA]

Synonyms: *Plantago asiatica*, dooryard plantain, common plantain

GENERAL DESCRIPTION: **Broadleaf plantain** and the closely related species **blackseed plantain (*Plantago rugelii* Dcne., PLARU) are rosette-forming perennial weeds** of high- or low-maintenance turf. Both have **broad oval leaves** with somewhat **parallel venation**. For a short period in summer plants produce **leafless, unbranched, flowering stems** (scapes) (5–30 cm long) with small, inconspicuous flowers.

PROPAGATION / PHENOLOGY: Reproduction is **by seed**, which germinate in late spring through midsummer and sporadically in the early fall.

SEEDLING: Seedlings develop as **basal rosettes. Cotyledons are 3-veined, spatulate,** 0.7–1.75 cm long by 0.5–1 mm wide, united at the base, and temporarily covered with a powdery coating. **Young leaves** are pale green, with **3–5 prominent veins.** Leaves are **oval to elliptic**, abruptly narrowing to a well-defined petiole that encircles the rosette and curves upward. The leaf surface often has scattered hairs on short, rounded, blunt projections. Blade margins become wavy on older leaves.

MATURE PLANT: **Leaves** are smooth or inconspicuously hairy, **elliptic to oval,** 4–18 cm long by 1.5–11 cm wide, **abruptly narrowing to a well-defined petiole.** Prominent veins run parallel with the margins, which are entire, often wavy, rarely toothed. Leaf surfaces are often waxy and blue-green. Petioles are sometimes reddish at the base.

ROOTS AND UNDERGROUND STRUCTURES: **Short taproot** with fibrous roots.

FLOWERS AND FRUIT: Small, inconspicuous **flowers** are produced from June through September on 5–30 cm **long leafless flower-stalks** (scapes) arising from the rosette. Petals are whitish, about 1 mm long. **Bracts** surrounding the flowers are **broad, ovate, blunt,** 2–4 mm long, with a sharp-pointed keel. **Seeds** are produced in an **oval, 2-celled, 3–5 mm long capsule, opening by a lid around the middle.** Each capsule contains 6–30 light to dark brown, glossy seeds, 1–1.5 mm long.

POSTSENESCENCE CHARACTERISTICS: Overwintering rosettes remain green where winters are mild, but die back to the crown in colder climates. Fruiting stalks turn dark brown or black and persist for an extended period.

HABITAT: Broadleaf and blackseed plantain are primarily turfgrass weeds; they are also weedy in nurseries, landscapes, orchards, and reduced-tillage crops. Although they grow in roadsides and waste areas, they prefer nutrient-rich, moist soils. Both tolerate close mowing, heavily compacted soils, wet soils, and dry sites.

DISTRIBUTION: Broadleaf plantain is found throughout the United States and southern Canada. Blackseed plantain is generally restricted to the eastern United States.

SIMILAR SPECIES: **Blackseed plantain, very similar** to broadleaf plantain, can be distinguished by its **cylindrical, 4–6 mm long, 4–10 seeded capsules that split below the middle,** and its **lanceolate,** gradually tapering, **slender-tipped bracts.** Blackseed plantain **leaves tend to be lighter green, less waxy,** more tapered at the tip, and are **more red to purple at the base of the petiole.** Petioles also tend to be narrower. **See Table 15 for a detailed comparison of broadleaf and blackseed plantain. Bracted** and **buckhorn plantain** have narrower leaves than blackseed or broadleaf plantain.

Broadleaf plantain
habit

J. Neal

R. Uva

Left, broadleaf plantain; *right*, blackseed plantain

J. Neal

Broadleaf plantain with flower heads
and seedheads

J. Neal

Broadleaf plantain seedling

J. DiTomaso

Left, blackseed plantain seed capsule, 6.0
mm, and seeds, 2.0 mm; *right*, broadleaf
plantain seed capsule, 4.9 mm, and seeds,
1.0 mm

273

Prostrate knotweed (*Polygonum aviculare* L.) [POLAV]

Synonyms: knot-grass, door-weed, mat-grass, pink-weed, bird-grass, stone-grass, way-grass goose-grass

GENERAL DESCRIPTION: A **summer annual** with **prostrate** to ascending, branching stems, 10–60 cm long, rarely over 10–20 cm tall.

PROPAGATION / PHENOLOGY: Reproduction is **by seed**. Prostrate knotweed is **one of the first summer annual weeds to emerge in the spring** (up to a month before crabgrass) but can also emerge throughout the spring and summer. Seedlings develop slowly, becoming more noticeable in midsummer.

SEEDLING: Hypocotyls are brownish red and smooth. Both cotyledons and young leaves have a waxy whitish coating. **Cotyledons are very narrow** (10–15 mm long by 1–2 mm wide), almost grass-like. **Young leaves** are alternate, elliptic to lanceolate, and **dull blue-green**. Emerging leaves are rolled, with the upper sides facing outward. **A whitish brown membranous sheath (ocrea) surrounds the stem at the base of the leaf.**

MATURE PLANT: Plants form a tough, prostrate, wiry mat. Stems are slender, branched, longitudinally ridged, and swollen at the nodes. **Leaves are alternate**, lanceolate or **elliptic** to oblong (1–3 cm long by 1–8 mm wide), narrowed at the base and pointed at the apex. Petioles are very short, with a **conspicuous ocrea sheathing the stem at the leaf base**.

ROOTS AND UNDERGROUND STRUCTURES: **Thin taproot.**

FLOWERS AND FRUIT: **Flowers** are produced from June through November in groups of **1–5 in axillary clusters** on short flower-stalks slightly longer than the membranous, tubular sheaths. **Flowers are small and inconspicuous**; the sepals (2–3 mm long) are white to green with pinkish margins. Petals are absent. The seed is enclosed in the fruit (achene). Achenes are 2–3 mm long, 3-angled, teardrop-shaped, and dark reddish brown to black. **Fruit mature before the sepals fall off** but have a complex dormancy.

POSTSENESCENCE CHARACTERISTICS: **Clusters or mats of dead wire-like stems** remain through the winter around walkways and in lawns. Remnants of the cylindrical membranous sheath (ocrea) may persist at the nodes.

HABITAT: Prostrate knotweed is a weed of turfgrass, nursery crops, landscapes, and occasionally agricultural crops. In turfgrass, it is most often found on **hard compacted soil or areas damaged** in spring or summer by traffic or trampling, including paths and walkways, areas where road salt accumulates, and athletic fields. Prostrate knotweed is not particularly competitive; it usually survives in stressed areas where other species do not grow well or are damaged.

DISTRIBUTION: Found throughout the United States and southern Canada.

SIMILAR SPECIES: *Polygonum aviculare* is divided into various groups by some taxonomists. In the Northeast, these include *Polygonum arenastrum* Boreau. and *Polygonum monspeliense* Pers. *Polygonum arenastrum* is a prostrate weed of compacted sites, such as walkways. Its leaves are equal in size, whereas the leaves of *Polygonum monspeliense* become progressively smaller toward the apex. The latter species grows prostrate to somewhat ascending and is weedy in cultivated sites. **Prostrate spurge** and **spotted spurge** resemble the prostrate *Polygonum* species in habit, habitats, and leaf shape, but spurges exude a milky sap when injured; knotweed does not.

Prostrate knotweed habit

J. Neal

J. Neal

Prostrate knotweed seedlings in early spring

J. DiTomaso

Prostrate knotweed mature shoot
(note ocreae at nodes)

J. DiTomaso

Prostrate knotweed seeds, 2 mm

275

Wild buckwheat (*Polygonum convolvulus* L.) [POLCO]

Synonyms: *Fallopia convolvulus*, black bindweed, knot bindweed, bear-bind, ivy bindweed, climbing bindweed, climbing buckwheat, corn-bind

GENERAL DESCRIPTION: A fast-growing **annual vine** that can trail along the ground or twine around other plants, shading and strangling them or interfering with mechanical harvesting. **Heart-shaped leaves** and growth habit strongly resemble field or hedge bindweed.

PROPAGATION / PHENOLOGY: Reproduction is **by seed**. Most germination occurs from mid-May through June.

SEEDLING: **Cotyledons are oblong-oval**, about 20 mm long and 3 mm wide, and rounded at the apex, with a **granular waxy surface. Young leaves are alternate, bluish green** on the upper surface, and reddish on the lower surface and stem. **Leaf blades are heart-shaped, pointed at the apex**, with entire to minutely toothed margins. Petioles on older leaves have discrete rough projections on the upper surface at the base of the midrib. A **membranous cylindrical sheath (ocrea)** surrounds the stem at the base of each leaf. On emerging leaves, margins are rolled under the blade.

MATURE PLANT: Stems and leaves lack hairs. Vining stems are branched at the base, and internodes are long. **Leaves are alternate, triangular to heart-shaped** (2–6 cm long), with the **basal lobes pointing inward toward the petiole. Upper leaves are more lanceolate.** The blade tapers toward the apex, and the margins are entire. An **ocrea** encircles the stem at the base of the petiole.

ROOTS AND UNDERGROUND STRUCTURES: Fibrous root system.

FLOWERS AND FRUIT: **Flowers** are produced from July through October. Individual flowers are inconspicuous, greenish white, about 4 mm long, and **clustered in irregularly spaced groups (3–6) on 2–6 cm long elongated racemes originating from the leaf axils.** The seed is enclosed in the fruit (achene). **Achenes are 3-angled,** dull black (3–4 mm long), and enclosed in the remains of the green, **flattened and winged sepals.**

POSTSENESCENCE CHARACTERISTICS: Dead woody vines can persist through the winter, particularly where they cover other plants.

HABITAT: Wild buckwheat is a weed of landscapes, orchards, and nursery, vegetable, and agronomic crops, especially grain crops. It usually grows in cultivated areas, but is also found in roadsides and waste areas. It is well adapted to a wide range of climates and soil types.

DISTRIBUTION: Found throughout the United States and southern Canada.

SIMILAR SPECIES: **For a detailed comparison with field and hedge bindweed, see Table 12.**

Wild buckwheat habit

J. Neal

Wild buckwheat seedling

J. Neal

J. Neal

Wild buckwheat cotyledons

J. DiTomaso

Wild buckwheat seedhead

J. DiTomaso

Wild buckwheat seeds, 3 mm

Japanese knotweed (*Polygonum cuspidatum* Sieb. & Zucc.) [POLCU]

Synonyms: *Pleuropterus zuccarinii*, Japanese bamboo

GENERAL DESCRIPTION: A **fast-growing, aggressive, rhizomatous perennial** reaching **2 m in height**, often appearing to be a woody shrub. Often **forms dense clumps** in which little or no other vegetation survives. Both manual and chemical control are difficult. Young, newly emerged shoots are edible.

PROPAGATION / PHENOLOGY: Spreads **primarily by rhizomes** but **produces viable seeds**. The shoots are stout and easily emerge through heavy mulch or, on occasion, asphalt.

SEEDLING: Seedlings rarely encountered. Young reddish shoots emerge from rhizomes in early spring.

MATURE PLANT: **Stems** are hollow and jointed, **bamboo-like**, and stout. Leaf base and branching points are sheathed with elongated stipules forming an **ocrea**. The **leaves** are alternate, **broadly egg-shaped**, 7.5–15 cm long.

ROOTS AND UNDERGROUND STRUCTURES: **Thick rhizomes.**

FLOWERS AND FRUIT: **Small white flowers** are produced **in elongated** (10–13 cm long) **erect clusters (panicles)** arising from the leaf axils. Flowers bloom in **late summer**. A single seed is enclosed within the 3-winged calyx. Seeds are triangular (3 mm) and dark brown.

POSTSENESCENCE CHARACTERISTICS: Plants are very susceptible to frost. Dead, hollow, bronze-colored stems persist through the winter. The fruit remain on the stems for only a short time after senescence.

HABITAT: Introduced to North America from Japan as an ornamental, Japanese knotweed has escaped cultivation and become a weed of landscapes, sodded storm drains, and riverbanks. It also grows in roadsides, waste areas, and untended gardens. It thrives on moist, well-drained, nutrient-rich soil, particularly on shaded banks.

DISTRIBUTION: Found throughout the Northeast, west to California, and south to Maryland.

SIMILAR SPECIES: Stems can resemble **bamboo** (*Bambusa* spp.), but leaves are clearly not grass-like.

Japanese knotweed habit

J. Neal

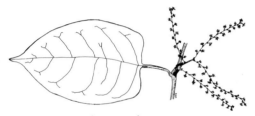

Japanese knotweed
R. Uva

J. Neal

Japanese knotweed flowering shoot

R. Uva

Japanese knotweed shoots from rhizomes

J. DiTomaso

Japanese knotweed seeds, 3 mm, and
seed capsule

279

Pennsylvania smartweed (*Polygonum pensylvanicum* L.) [POLPY]

Synonyms: *Persicaria pensylvanica*, swamp persicary, glandular persicary, purple head, pinkweed, hearts-ease

GENERAL DESCRIPTION: An erect or **ascending much-branched summer annual** (30 cm to 1.2 m in height).

PROPAGATION / PHENOLOGY: Reproduction is **by seed**; seeds germinate in the spring or early summer.

SEEDLING: Hypocotyls are smooth, pink at the base. Cotyledons are elliptic-oblong to lanceolate, smooth on the upper and lower surfaces, with gland-tipped hairs on the margins. **Young leaves are alternate, lanceolate to elliptic**, tinged purple on both surfaces, hairy on the upper surface and margins, smooth on the lower surface. A **conspicuous membranous sheath (ocrea)** surrounds the stem at the base of the leaves. **Stems are smooth, reddish purple**, with swollen and angled nodes.

MATURE PLANT: **Stems** are branched, green or reddish, **swollen and jointed at the nodes**, smooth or often with appressed stiff hairs. Upper parts of the stems have stalked glands. An **ocrea** is present at the base of the petiole. **Leaves** are alternate, lanceolate to elliptic or egg-shaped (5–15 cm long and up to 3 cm wide), smooth or with sparse hairs. The center of both surfaces of the leaf is **sometimes marked with a purple blotch**. The blotch is more prevalent in other, closely related species.

ROOTS AND UNDERGROUND STRUCTURES: Fibrous roots from a shallow taproot.

FLOWERS AND FRUIT: **Bright pink to white flowers** bloom from July to October. **Individual flowers are small and organized into dense spike-like clusters** on glandular hairy stalks. The seed is enclosed in the fruit (achene). Achenes are glossy black, smooth, circular to oval (2.5–3.5 mm wide), flattened and pointed at the apex.

POSTSENESCENCE CHARACTERISTICS: Foliage turns brown to reddish with first frost. Stems are angled at the swollen nodes. Ocrea remains, but plants do not persist through the winter.

HABITAT: A weed of horticultural, agronomic, and nursery crops, as well as landscapes, Pennsylvania smartweed is rarely a problem in turfgrass. It tolerates a range of soil types and conditions, including sandy and nutrient-rich soils and particularly moist areas.

DISTRIBUTION: Distributed throughout the United States.

SIMILAR SPECIES: **Ladysthumb (*Polygonum persicaria* L., POLPE)** and *Polygonum caespitosum* Blume (no approved common name) **each have a distinctly fringed ocrea, whereas that of Pennsylvania smartweed can be torn or ragged but is never fringed.** The fringes on the *Polygonum caespitosum* ocrea are long—as long as the membranous ocrea, whereas those on ladysthumb are short, less than half the length of the membranous ocrea. **Ladysthumb** and *Polygonum caespitosum* **generally have a darkly pigmented mark on the leaf blade that is usually lacking on Pennsylvania smartweed.**

Ladysthumb habit

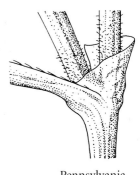

Pennsylvania
smartweed ocrea
Ciba-Geigy Corporation

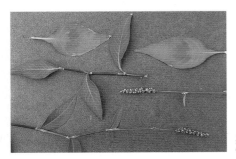

Smartweed (*Polygonum caespitosum*)
seedlings

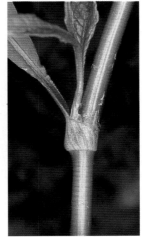

Pennsylvania smartweed
leafy shoot (note ocrea)

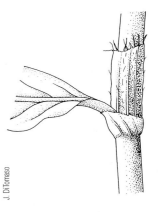

Ladysthumb ocrea
Ciba-Geigy Corporation

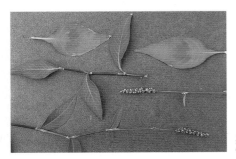

Smartweed (*Polygonum caespitosum*)
mature foliage and flowering shoots

Left, ladysthumb seeds, 2.3 mm;
right, Pennsylvania smartweed
seeds, 3.0 mm

281

Mile-a-minute (*Polygonum perfoliatum* L.) [POLPE]

Synonyms: *Persicaria perfoliata*, *Tracaulon perfoliatum*, minute weed, mile-a-minute vine, giant climbing tear-thumb

GENERAL DESCRIPTION: A **spiny summer annual vine** growing to 7 m in length. Stems can become woody with age. It can climb over shrubs, small trees, and structures, forming dense mats. Its **stems, petioles, and major leaf-veins have 1–2 mm long reflexed prickles.**

PROPAGATION / PHENOLOGY: Reproduction is **by seed.** Seedlings are established by late April and grow rapidly between May and August.

SEEDLING: No information available.

MATURE PLANT: **Stems** are branched, green vines, red-brown toward the base, with **reflexed prickles (1–2 mm long). Leaves are alternate,** smooth, **waxy,** light green or often reddish when young, **triangular to somewhat heart-shaped at the base, pointed at the apex** (3–8 cm long and as wide at the base). Leaf margins are rough. **Petioles have recurved spines** and are slightly longer than the blade. **A prominent leaf-like sheath (ocrea)** encircles the stem at the base of the petiole. The upper branches may have ocreae without developed leaves.

ROOTS AND UNDERGROUND STRUCTURES: Shallow fibrous root system.

FLOWERS AND FRUIT: **Flowers** are produced as early as June, but typically from late July through August, at the end of branches or in the leaf axils **in spike-like racemes,** 1–2 cm long. **Individual flowers are inconspicuous,** greenish white to yellow, rarely pink, 3–5 mm long. The **fruit** (achene) is enclosed within a **berry-like (4–6 mm in diameter) structure consisting of swollen metallic-blue floral parts (perianth).** The outer coating dries and wrinkles with age. Achenes are round, black, and shiny (3 mm long), ripening late in the season (mid-September into November).

POSTSENESCENCE CHARACTERISTICS: Fruit and prickles may remain after the vine is dead.

HABITAT: Mile-a-minute is a weed of landscapes, nursery crops, and orchards, as well as clear-cut timberlands, roadsides, drainage ditches, and rights-of-way. It grows on moist, well-drained soil, and although it tolerates shady areas, it thrives in full sunlight.

DISTRIBUTION: Has recently become well established in Pennsylvania, Maryland, and West Virginia and is continuing to spread into Delaware, New Jersey, and Virginia.

SIMILAR SPECIES: **Wild buckwheat** is a summer annual vine lacking reflexed prickles. In addition, it has heart-shaped, not triangular, leaves. **Most other similar vines also lack the prickles.**

Mile-a-minute habit

Mile-a-minute leafy shoot

Mile-a-minute "prickles"

Mile-a-minute fruit

Mile-a-minute seeds, 3 mm

283

Red sorrel (*Rumex acetosella* L.) [RUMAA]

Synonyms: sheep sorrel, sour-grass, Indian cane, field sorrel, horse sorrel, sour weed, red-top sorrel, cow sorrel, red-weed, mountain sorrel

GENERAL DESCRIPTION: A **rhizomatous perennial** (to 45 cm tall) **with primarily basal, arrowhead-shaped leaves** and a sparsely leaved flowering stem. Plants accumulate high concentrations of soluble oxalates, which give them a **sour taste** and **occasionally cause fatalities in livestock, particularly sheep.**

PROPAGATION / PHENOLOGY: Reproduction is **by seeds and rhizomes**. Rhizome buds sprout in early spring and produce basal rosettes.

SEEDLING: Cotyledons are dull green, smooth, slightly thickened, and oblong (10 mm long). Stalks of the cotyledon are flattened on the upper surface and united basally to form a short membranous tube (**ocrea**). **Seedlings produce a rosette of foliage** in which **leaf shapes change with age. Young leaves are egg-shaped**, smooth, and slightly thickened; the margins are entire, and the bases taper into the petiole. Both **surfaces of the leaves are covered with waxy granules. The characteristic basal lobes develop on the third, fourth, or fifth leaf.** Petioles are grooved on the upper surface and expand basally into a white membranous **ocrea. Shoots emerging from rhizomes are more robust** than seedlings.

MATURE PLANT: **Leaves** are thick, petiolated, smooth, 2.5–7.5 cm long, dull green, and **arrowhead-shaped with 2 narrow and spreading basal lobes.** A papery or membranous sheath (**ocrea**) surrounds the stem just above the point of leaf attachment. Most leaves develop from the **basal rosette; stem leaves are fewer and alternate.** Upper leaves on the stem are linear, sometimes without basal lobes. **Flowering stems** (1 to several) are **slender, erect**, branched toward the top, 4-sided, **vertically ridged**, and usually maroon, especially toward the base. In spring, leaves are narrow and thin; in autumn, leaves are broader and fleshy.

ROOTS AND UNDERGROUND STRUCTURES: Extensive but shallow root system consists of a **yellow taproot** and numerous **slender rhizomes.**

FLOWERS AND FRUIT: **Flowers** are produced from May to September in **branched terminal clusters (panicles)**. Male and female flowers are produced on separate plants (dioecious). **Male flowers are yellowish green; female flowers are reddish brown.** The panicles appear reddish when mature. The **seed is enclosed** within a **triangular achene**, 1–1.5 mm long, reddish brown, and usually surrounded by rough persistent flower parts.

POSTSENESCENCE CHARACTERISTICS: Foliage often turns yellowish in late autumn, but plants typically are green throughout the year.

HABITAT: Red sorrel is a weed of turfgrass, landscapes, and nursery crops. It is often found on, but not limited to, acid soils and areas with poor drainage, low nitrogen, and little competition from other species.

DISTRIBUTION: Distributed throughout the United States and southern Canada.

SIMILAR SPECIES: The unique leaf shape and sour taste can distinguish it from other weed species.

Red sorrel habit

Red sorrel seedlings

Red sorrel rosette from rhizome

Red sorrel mature leaves

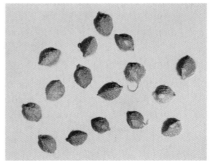

Red sorrel seeds, 1.2 mm

Curly dock (*Rumex crispus* L.) [RUMCR]

Synonyms: *Rumex elongatus*, sour dock, yellow dock, narrow-leaved dock

GENERAL DESCRIPTION: A **taprooted perennial** developing a **basal rosette of wavy-margined leaves** and a sparsely leaved flowering stem reaching 1 m in height. **At maturity, fruit and flowering stems are conspicuously reddish brown.**

PROPAGATION / PHENOLOGY: Reproduction is **by seed**; seeds germinate in cool, moist soil from late spring through early fall as conditions permit. Perennial plants emerge from the taproot in midspring, producing a robust rosette.

SEEDLING: Hypocotyls are green, tinged maroon at the base. Cotyledons are hairless, dull green, granular-coated, and spatulate to long-oval, with petioles that are connected by a ridge across the shoot axis. **Young leaves** are in a **basal rosette**, smooth, **egg-shaped**, with **red spots** on the upper surface. **Older leaves** have slightly **wavy margins**. A papery membranous sheath (ocrea) surrounds the stem at the base of the petiole (difficult to see in rosettes). Emerging leaf margins are rolled underneath the blade.

MATURE PLANT: Emerging perennials produce a robust **basal rosette of 15–30 cm long leaves with wavy margins**. Leaves are shiny, progressively becoming more reddish purple through the season. **Lower leaves are longer** and **more rounded** than the stem leaves. **Elongating flowering stems** are smooth, **ridged**, often reddish, branched toward the top with enlarged nodes. **Stem leaves are alternate, subtended by an ocrea**, and **reduced** in both number and size compared with basal leaves.

ROOTS AND UNDERGROUND STRUCTURES: Large thick, somewhat branched **taproot**.

FLOWERS AND FRUIT: Flowers primarily in June but also throughout the summer. **Flowers are in clusters** (15–60 cm long) on narrowly spaced branches **on the upper portions of the elongating stem**. Flowers consist of greenish sepals that become **reddish brown at maturity**. The seed is enclosed within the fruit (achene). The calyx develops into a **papery or corky 3-winged triangular structure that surrounds the achene**. Achenes (about 2 mm long) are **triangular, glossy**, and reddish brown at maturity. Corky structures on the outside of the calyx allow the fruit to float on water, thus facilitating dispersal.

POSTSENESCENCE CHARACTERISTICS: Erect, brown, ridged **flower-stalks persist** through winter, bearing the **distinctive reddish brown**, 3-winged fruit.

HABITAT: Curly dock is a weed of low-maintenance turfgrass, orchards, nursery crops, landscapes, roadsides, meadows, pastures, and forage crops, but usually not cultivated row crops. It also grows along drainage ditches and in waste areas. Curly dock thrives on nutrient-rich, heavy, damp soils but does not tolerate cultivation.

DISTRIBUTION: Found throughout the United States and southern Canada.

SIMILAR SPECIES: The leaves of **broadleaf dock (*Rumex obtusifolius* L., RUMOB)** have **heart-shaped lobes at the base** and are **wider and less wavy than those of curly dock**. The calyx lobes that develop into the wings of the fruit have toothed margins in broadleaf dock but are entire in curly dock. Both species have ocreae.

R. Uva

Dock rosettes: *left*, broadleaf; *right*, curly

J. DiTomaso

Broadleaf dock seedlings

J. Neal

Curly dock flowering shoot

J. Neal

Broadleaf dock leaf shapes, *right to left:* basal to flower stalk

J. DiTomaso

Left, curly dock seeds (achenes), 1.8 mm (without papery bracts); *right*, broadleaf dock seeds (achenes), 2.0 mm (without papery bracts)

287

Common purslane (*Portulaca oleracea* L.) [POROL]

Synonyms: pusley, pursley, wild portulaca

GENERAL DESCRIPTION: A **summer annual** with a **prostrate mat-forming habit** (30 cm or more in diameter) and **thick, succulent stems and leaves**.

PROPAGATION / PHENOLOGY: Reproduction is **by seeds** and by fragmented stem segments that root at the nodes. Seeds germinate from late May or early June through August, when soil-surface temperatures are high, 30°C (86°F).

SEEDLING: Young seedlings are erect but soon become prostrate. Hypocotyls are maroon, succulent, erect to ascending (about 16 mm long). **Cotyledons** are oblong (10 mm long), somewhat **club-shaped and succulent**, green or maroon on the top surface and maroon on the lower surface. **Young leaves are opposite** or nearly opposite; **blades** are smooth, green on the upper surface, maroon-tinged or maroon on the lower surface, **oblong, broadest and rounded at the apex**, tapering toward the base (7 mm long by 4 mm wide). Petioles are short (< 2 mm) or absent. **Stems are succulent**, green in the younger portions, maroon in the older portions.

MATURE PLANT: **Stems are much-branched, purplish red** or green, smooth, completely **prostrate** or turned up at the ends. **Leaves are opposite or alternate**, 1–3 cm long, **thick and fleshy**, with smooth untoothed margins. **Blades are wedge-shaped, rounded at the apex, and narrowed to the base** (spatulate). **Petioles are absent**; stipules may be present, but if so, are reduced to soft bristles.

ROOTS AND UNDERGROUND STRUCTURES: A thick taproot with many fibrous secondary roots.

FLOWERS AND FRUIT: **Flowers** appear from July through September, only 4–6 weeks after seedlings emerge. Flowers are 5–10 mm wide, alone in the leaf axils or **clustered at the end of stems**. The **yellow petals** (5) are slightly shorter than the sepals and open only when it is sunny. The fruit is an oval, 4–8 mm long, many-seeded capsule opening by splitting transversely around the middle. Seeds are black, flattened, rounded to kidney-shaped, 1 mm or less in diameter, with rounded bumps on the surface.

POSTSENESCENCE CHARACTERISTICS: Leaves decay quickly after frost, leaving the prostrate branched stems. Stems persist for only a short time and are generally decomposed by spring.

HABITAT: A weed of landscapes, thin or newly seeded turfgrass, and nursery, vegetable, fruit, and agronomic crops, common purslane is found in most cultivated crops, home gardens, and annual flower beds. It is also a weed of crevices between bricks and in cracked cement. Common purslane thrives on nutrient-rich, sandy soils but tolerates poor, compacted soils and drought. It prefers areas of high light and warm growing conditions.

DISTRIBUTION: Widespread throughout the world.

SIMILAR SPECIES: Prostrate habit may lead to confusion with the **spurges** or with **prostrate knotweed**. Spurges, however, exude a milky latex when stems and leaves are injured. Prostrate knotweed is not succulent and has small papery sheaths (ocreae) around the leaf bases. Seedlings of prostrate knotweed generally emerge earlier in the spring than those of common purslane or spurge.

Common purslane habit

Common purslane seedlings

Common purslane flower

Common purslane seed pods

Common purslane seeds, 1 mm

Scarlet pimpernel (*Anagallis arvensis* L.) [ANGAR]

Synonyms: poor man's weather-glass, red chickweed, poison chickweed, shepherds clock, eye-bright

GENERAL DESCRIPTION: A **prostrate or ascending** to erect, **low-growing**, branching, **annual** with a delicate appearance. Scarlet pimpernel tolerates mowing and is usually <15 cm tall (occasionally to 30 cm).

PROPAGATION / PHENOLOGY: Reproduction is **by seed**. Seedlings may emerge over an extended period of time.

SEEDLING: Seedlings are dark green and shiny. **Cotyledons** are smooth, **triangular to diamond-shaped** (0.75–3 mm wide by 1–6 mm long), broadest at the base, with a dull point at the apex, with tiny glandular hairs. **Young leaves are opposite, triangular** to almost rounded or heart-shaped. **Petioles are very short or absent. Leaf surfaces** are **smooth** or have glandular hairs; the **lower surfaces have small, purple spots**.

MATURE PLANT: **Stems are 4-angled or square**, smooth, and branched from the base, ascending upward. **Leaves are similar to seedling leaves**, although more egg-shaped to elliptic (2 cm long) and **occasionally in whorls of 3**.

ROOTS AND UNDERGROUND STRUCTURES: Shallow fibrous root system.

FLOWERS AND FRUIT: Flowers are present mainly from June to August. **Small bell-shaped flowers** are produced singly in the leaf axils on relatively long, nodding stalks. Petals (5) are **salmon to brick-red** (rarely white), ovate with a fringe of tiny glandular hairs on the margin. Sepals (5) are green and awl-shaped. The fruit is a smooth, rounded, 1-celled, many-seeded capsule; the top half comes off like a lid at maturity. Seeds are about 1.3 mm long, 3-angled, elliptic, dull brown or black.

POSTSENESCENCE CHARACTERISTICS: None of note.

HABITAT: Primarily a weed of turfgrass and landscapes, scarlet pimpernel is also found in roadsides and waste areas. It is less common in cultivated crops.

DISTRIBUTION: Introduced from Europe; now distributed throughout the United States, particularly in sandy soils. Most troublesome in the mid-Atlantic states and on the Pacific Coast.

SIMILAR SPECIES: **Common chickweed** is similar in leaf shape and habit; however, chickweed has round stems, whereas scarlet pimpernel stems are 4-angled or square. The 2 species also differ in flower and leaf color. The flowers of chickweed are white with 5 deeply lobed petals (giving the appearance of 10), and leaves do not have purplish dots on the underside, as do scarlet pimpernel leaves.

Scarlet pimpernel habit

Scarlet pimpernel stem and leaves (note square stem and spots on underside of leaves)

Scarlet pimpernel flower

Scarlet pimpernel seeds, 1 mm

Moneywort (*Lysimachia nummularia* L.) [LYSNU]

Synonyms: creeping loosestrife, yellow myrtle, creeping Jenny, creeping Charlie, herb twopence, two-penny grass

GENERAL DESCRIPTION: An introduced ornamental; still sold in the nursery industry as a **creeping perennial ground cover**. Forms mats of prostrate branched stems (15–50 cm long).

PROPAGATION / PHENOLOGY: Reproduction is **primarily by creeping and rooting stems**. Although **viable seeds are produced**, they are not considered to be a major means of plant dispersal.

SEEDLING: No information available.

MATURE PLANT: Foliage lacks hairs but has smooth glandular dots on the surface. **Leaves are opposite, square to round**, 1–3 cm long, with a **pointed tip**. Petioles are short.

ROOTS AND UNDERGROUND STRUCTURES: **Stems root at the nodes**, producing a shallow fibrous root system.

FLOWERS AND FRUIT: **Bright yellow flowers** (2–3 cm in diameter) are produced **individually on stalks (pedicels) in the leaf axils**. Petals (5) are 10–15 mm long and lobed. The fruit is a 1-celled spherical capsule that splits vertically when mature. Seeds are about 1 mm long, elliptic, 3-angled, dark brown to black, with a rough surface produced by scaly ridges.

POSTSENESCENCE CHARACTERISTICS: Plants are not conspicuous during the winter.

HABITAT: Although primarily a weed of turfgrass and landscapes, moneywort is also found in gardens, ditches, and low fields. It prefers moist, shady sites and seldom survives under excessively dry conditions.

DISTRIBUTION: Escaped cultivation and has become naturalized throughout the northeastern United States, north to Newfoundland and Ontario, south to Georgia, and west to Missouri and Kansas.

SIMILAR SPECIES: Moneywort can be distinguished from **thymeleaf speedwell** by its leaves. Thymeleaf speedwell leaves are often slightly notched at the tip, whereas those of moneywort are rounded to pointed. Individual leaves may also resemble a robust specimen of **common chickweed**; however, common chickweed is an annual with white flowers, and moneywort is a perennial with yellow flowers. Also, the leaves of common chickweed taper to a point; moneywort leaf tips are rounded or squarish with a pointed end.

J. Neal

Moneywort habit

R. Uva

Moneywort flowers and foliage

Moneywort flower buds

R. Uva

Bulbous buttercup (*Ranunculus bulbosus* L.) [RANBU]

Synonyms: bulbous crowfoot, yellow weed, blister flower, gowan

GENERAL DESCRIPTION: A **tufted perennial** forming a **basal rosette of 3-parted leaves** arising from a thickened **bulb-like (corm) base**. Flowering stems are usually erect (20–60 cm tall) but are low to prostrate in turfgrass. Buttercup can be **poisonous to livestock** but is usually not palatable. Dried plants in hay are not toxic because the toxic compounds volatilize during drying.

PROPAGATION / PHENOLOGY: Plants **overwinter as corms** but **reproduction is by seed**.

SEEDLING: Cotyledons are elliptic, rounded at the apex, with relatively long petioles that sheathe the stem at the base. **Young leaves** are hairy and **3-lobed** on relatively **long petioles**. Young **plants form a tuft**.

MATURE PLANT: The **basal and lower stem leaves** are on **long hairy petioles** and are **3-parted** with rounded to ovate, **deeply cleft and lobed divisions**. The **middle lobe is on a stalk; the 2 lateral lobes are sessile on the petiole**. In the late spring, plants produce sparsely leaved, **erect flowering stems**. Stems are hairy at the base and sometimes hairy above. Stem leaves are alternate and similar to the basal leaves. **Upper leaves are sessile, less divided, and smaller** than the lower leaves.

ROOTS AND UNDERGROUND STRUCTURES: The stem is thickened at, and just below, the soil surface into a **bulb-like base (corm)** with fibrous roots below.

FLOWERS AND FRUIT: Flowers (1.5–3 cm wide) appear from April to July and are solitary at the ends of long, furrowed stalks. **Bright shiny yellow petals** (5–7) are broadly rounded at the apex and have wedge-shaped bases. Sepals (5) are green and curve back toward the stem (reflexed). Both stamen and pistils are numerous. Each seed is enclosed within the fruit (achene), and numerous achenes are produced in rounded heads. Individual fruit are flattened (2.5–3.5 mm long), with short curved beaks and distinct margins.

POSTSENESCENCE CHARACTERISTICS: Foliage dies back to the corm. No distinctive winter characteristics.

HABITAT: A common weed of turfgrass, landscapes, and pastures, bulbous buttercup is rarely weedy in traditionally cultivated crops.

DISTRIBUTION: Common in the northeastern, southeastern, and western United States and in Canada.

SIMILAR SPECIES: **Tall buttercup (*Ranunculus acris* L., RANAC)** is similar in habit, but the leaves are not as deeply lobed and the central lobe is not on a long stalk, the sepals are not curved back (reflexed) toward the flower-stalk, and it does not have a bulb-like base. **Creeping buttercup (*Ranunculus repens* L., RANRE)** is similar but lacks the bulb-like base, and it spreads by stolons that creep and root at the nodes. The middle lobe also has a long-stalked base, but the 3 lobes are not as deeply toothed as those of either tall or bulbous buttercup. In addition, the flowers are twice as large as those of the other 2 species, and the sepals are not reflexed as in bulbous buttercup.

Bulbous buttercup habit

Bulbous buttercup seedling
with cotyledons

Young bulbous buttercup

Bulbous buttercup leaf

Creeping buttercup foliage, stolon,
and root

Left to right: creeping buttercup seeds, 3.0
mm; tall buttercup seeds, 3.0 mm; and
bulbous buttercup seeds, 3.5 mm (largest)

Wild strawberry (*Fragaria virginiana* Duchesne.) [FRAVI]

Synonym: thick-leaved wild strawberry

GENERAL DESCRIPTION: A low-trailing **perennial spreading by creeping stolons** and forming dense patches. Usually 7.5–15 cm in height; tolerates mowing to <5 cm. Wild strawberry is **similar to cultivated strawberry** but has smaller leaves, much smaller fruit, and a stronger stoloniferous habit.

PROPAGATION / PHENOLOGY: Reproduction is **by seeds and stolons**. Although seedlings are rarely noticed, seed dispersal by animals and birds is an important means of spread. Once established, plants spread by stolons, forming large patches.

SEEDLING: Because seedlings are rarely noticed, little information is available. Seedlings are slow to establish. They produce a rosette of small, trifoliolate (3 leaflets) leaves, which resemble those of mature plants but are smaller.

MATURE PLANT: **Basal leaves arise from a crown or from long creeping stolons**. **Leaves** are **trifoliolate**, nearly smooth to long-silky beneath, and on **long** (up to 15 cm), **hairy petioles**. Leaflets are dark green to blue-green, thick and firm, 2.5–3.8 cm long, with **toothed margins** on the upper ⅔–¾ of the leaf.

ROOTS AND UNDERGROUND STRUCTURES: Shallow fibrous root system from crowns and stolon nodes.

FLOWERS AND FRUIT: Flowers (2 cm wide) are produced from April to June and have **white petals (5)** with many yellow stamens and pistils. Sepals (5) alternate with bracts. Flowers are oriented **in loose clusters** (corymbiform) on stalks (peduncles); most stalks are shorter than the leaves. The receptacle of the flower enlarges into a **small red strawberry** (1–1.5 cm thick) with many small seed-like fruit (achenes) in shallow pits on the surface. Achenes are brown, oval, and curved at the tip (1–1.5 mm long). Fruit mature in early summer.

POSTSENESCENCE CHARACTERISTICS: Plants remain green throughout the winter.

HABITAT: Primarily a weed of low-maintenance turfgrass and landscapes, wild strawberry is also found in meadows, fields, and on the edges and in the clearings of woods. It thrives on gravelly, well-drained soils.

DISTRIBUTION: Found throughout much of the United States and Canada.

SIMILAR SPECIES: **Indian mock-strawberry (*Duchesnea indica* (Andr.) Focke, DUCIN)** is a low-trailing perennial usually found in moist shady locations. Its leaves are also trifoliolate but have roundish teeth (crenate), whereas wild strawberry leaves have sharp-pointed teeth. The flowers of Indian mock-strawberry are yellow; those of wild strawberry are white. **Oldfield cinquefoil** has a similar low-trailing habit, but it has 5 leaflets rather than 3. **Rough cinquefoil** produces a crown of trifoliolate leaves that are hairy on both surfaces; wild strawberry leaflets are mostly smooth or hairy only on the underside. Rough cinquefoil produces yellow flowers on erect stems.

J. Neal

Wild strawberry habit

R. Uva

Wild strawberry stolon and leaves

M. Pritts

Wild strawberry fruit

J. Neal

Indian mock-strawberry flower, fruit, and leaves

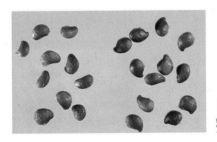

J. DiTomaso

Left, Indian mock-strawberry seeds, 1.0 mm; *right*, wild strawberry seeds, 1.2 mm

Oldfield cinquefoil (*Potentilla simplex* Michx.) [PTLSI]

Synonym: old-field five-fingers

GENERAL DESCRIPTION: A low-growing **perennial** with **prostrate wiry** tough **stoloniferous stems** radiating from a **small crown** and **palmately compound leaves** with **3 to (more commonly) 5 leaflets**. Often found on poor soils. Valued for its **attractive yellow flowers**, selections are sold in nurseries.

PROPAGATION / PHENOLOGY: Reproduction is **by stolons and seeds**.

SEEDLING: Seedlings develop into **small crowns**. Cotyledons are egg-shaped, widest at the apex, 1.5 mm long by 3 mm wide. The **first leaves** are simple, alternate, and egg-shaped, with **a few tooth-like lobes**, petioles that clasp the stem, and a dull surface. **Subsequent leaves have stipules** and are compound with **3 leaflets**. The **lateral leaflets may be cleft nearly to the petiole**, giving the appearance of 5 leaflets.

MATURE PLANT: Stems and basal leaves grow from a **small rosette**. Early in the season, **stems elongate, but then arch to the ground and root at the tips**. Stems are hairy to almost smooth, slender, tough and wiry. Hairs on stems and petioles are appressed. Leaves are alternate; the blades are glossy, dark green on the upper surface and hairy to sometimes white-woolly beneath. **Leaves are palmately compound with 5 leaflets** and have stipules at the base of the petiole. **Leaflets** are narrow, elliptic or egg-shaped, widest at the top, tapering to the base (obovate); **margins are toothed**.

ROOTS AND UNDERGROUND STRUCTURES: **Long stolons** are important in spread. **Short rhizomes** (to 8 cm) are also present. Coarse fibrous roots are associated with both.

FLOWERS AND FRUIT: **Bright yellow flowers** (10–15 mm wide) bloom from May through June and are produced singly on long slender pedicels in the leaf axils. Petals (5) are bright yellow, and stamen and pistils are numerous. Each seed is enclosed in the fruit (achene). Achenes are smooth, yellowish brown, 1.2 mm long, on hairy receptacles.

POSTSENESCENCE CHARACTERISTICS: Foliage generally dies back to the crown and stolons in winter but may persist in mild climates.

HABITAT: A weed of low-maintenance turfgrass and landscapes. It is also found in meadows, and dry woods and fields, generally on acidic, nutrient-poor, dry, sandy soils.

DISTRIBUTION: From Newfoundland to Minnesota, south to Alabama and Texas.

SIMILAR SPECIES: **Indian mock-strawberry** and **wild strawberry** are similar in habit but have 3 leaflets, and wild strawberry has white flowers. **Common cinquefoil (*Potentilla canadensis* L.)** is a prostrate rhizome- and stolon-producing perennial **very similar** to oldfield cinquefoil. But the rhizomes are shorter (0.5–2 cm long), hairs on the stem and petiole are spreading, not appressed, and stipules on basal leaves are oblong-lanceolate and flat; those of oldfield cinquefoil are linear-lanceolate and rolled. **The following weedy cinquefoils** have yellow flowers but **are not stoloniferous** and do not root at the nodes. Reproduction in these species is by seed only. **Silvery cinquefoil (*Potentilla argentea* L., PTLAG)** has erect to almost prostrate stems, 5–7 leaflets, with a dense mat of **silvery-white hairs** on the undersides, and yellow flowers 7 mm to 1.0 cm wide. **Rough cinquefoil (*Potentilla norvegica* L., PTLNO)** has erect branched stems, **3 leaflets**, which are hairy and green on both sides, and small yellow flowers, 0.7–1.0 cm wide. **Sulfur cinquefoil (*Potentilla recta* L., PTLRC)** has erect unbranched stems, **5–9 leaflets**, 1.5–2.5 cm wide yellow flowers, and long hairs on the stems and leaves.

R. Uva

Oldfield cinquefoil habit

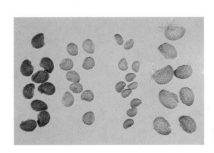

R. Uva

Sulfur cinquefoil mature leaf and flowering shoot

J. Neal

Rough cinquefoil habit

R. Uva

Silvery cinquefoil flowering shoot

Rough cinquefoil flowering shoots

R. Uva

J. DiTomaso

Left to right: sulfur cinquefoil seeds, 1.0 mm; rough cinquefoil seeds, 0.9 mm; silvery cinquefoil seeds, 0.6 mm; and oldfield cinquefoil seeds, 1.2 mm

Virginia buttonweed (*Diodia virginiana* L.) [DIQVI]

Synonyms: *Diodia hirsuta*, *Diodia tetragona*, buttonweed

GENERAL DESCRIPTION: A **prostrate** to ascending, spreading **perennial** that tolerates close mowing but can grow 20–80 cm tall if undisturbed. The light to dark green **foliage is often yellow-mottled by a virus**. Stems are thick and stout, often tinged red.

PROPAGATION / PHENOLOGY: Reproduction is by **seeds and adventitious sprouts from fleshy roots**. Once introduced, plants spread by root sprouts and **prostrate stems** that **root at the nodes**.

SEEDLING: Cotyledons are elliptic, rounded at the apex, thickened, green on the upper surface and light green underneath. **Young leaves are opposite, elliptic**, with **short hairs** on the margin; they **lack petioles** and are **connected across the stem by a membrane with 1–3 bristly, linear stipules** (3–5 mm long). **Stems are covered with gland-tipped hairs.**

MATURE PLANT: **Vegetative characteristics are similar to those of the seedling. Stems** are generally **prostrate, rooting at the lower nodes**, sometimes hairy on the angles, and frequently tinged red. **Leaves are opposite, elliptic** to oblong-lanceolate, 3–6 cm (rarely to 10 cm) long and 1–2 cm wide, with rough margins. Petioles are absent. **The center stipule is often thickened and thorn-like.**

ROOTS AND UNDERGROUND STRUCTURES: A coarse, branched **fleshy root system** giving rise to **adventitious shoots. Underground flowers** are also produced.

FLOWERS AND FRUIT: **Flowers** are produced from June through August, both aboveground in the leaf axils and belowground. Little is known about the belowground flowers. Aboveground flowers are **white, sometimes tinged pink**, about 1 cm wide by 7–11 mm long, and sessile, 1 or (rarely) 2 in the leaf axils. Two sepals are linear to lance-shaped, 4–6 mm long. **Petals (4) are star-shaped**, united into a tube at the base (salverform). **Sepals and petals are hairy.** The **fruit** is an oval to elliptic (5–9 mm long), **8-ribbed**, hairy (occasionally smooth), **leathery capsule** that floats in water. Each capsule contains 2 indehiscent seeds.

POSTSENESCENCE CHARACTERISTICS: Aboveground portions die back to the ground in the winter.

HABITAT: Although Virginia buttonweed is a major weed of turf in the southeastern United States, it does not tolerate cultivation and thus is rarely encountered in conventionally tilled crops. It is difficult to control with currently available technologies. It is found on sandy soils as well as moist areas.

DISTRIBUTION: Primarily a weed in the coastal southeastern United States west to Texas but has been identified as far north as southern New Jersey and southern Illinois.

SIMILAR SPECIES: **Poorjoe (*Diodia teres* Walt., DIQTE)** is a summer annual with a similar leaf shape, stem, and flower, but leaves are narrower and flowers have 4 sepals. **Florida pusley (*Richardia scabra* L., RCHSC)** is also a summer annual vegetatively resembling Virginia buttonweed; however, the leaves and stems are densely hairy and the flowers are 6-parted not 4-parted.

Virginia
buttonweed
(without virus),
habit in turfgrass

J. Neal

Virginia buttonweed shoot
(note bracts at nodes)

J. Neal

J. Neal

Virginia buttonweed flower and fruit

J. DiTomaso

Virginia buttonweed seed capsules,
6.5 mm (largest)

Catchweed bedstraw (*Galium aparine* L.) [GALAP]

Synonyms: cleavers, bedstraw, catchweed, goose-grass, scratch-grass, grip-grass

GENERAL DESCRIPTION: A **semiprostrate or mat-forming summer or winter annual**, often attached to or climbing over other vegetation. **Stems, leaves, and fruit have short, prickly hairs.**

PROPAGATION / PHENOLOGY: Reproduction is **by seed**, which germinate in cool, moist soil over an extended season, from very early to late spring and late summer to early autumn.

SEEDLING: Hypocotyls are stout, greenish or purple, and smooth. **Cotyledons are egg-shaped** (8–15 mm long by 6–9 mm wide), **on prominent petioles**, notched at the apex, green on the upper surface, and maroon on the lower surface. The upper cotyledon surface and margins have rough, short, ascending hairs. **Young leaves are produced in whorls of 4 or more**; the upper surfaces, margins, petioles, and lower midvein have **short stiff sharp hairs**.

MATURE PLANT: **Stems are square** (20 cm to 1.5 m long), **with recurved prickles** on **the 4 ridges and leaves.** Prickles allow foliage to cling to other plants. Upper leaf surfaces are hairy; lower surfaces have short spiny hairs along the midrib. **Leaves are sessile, in whorls of 6–8 at the nodes.** Blades are narrow, oval to lanceolate (3–8 cm long by 4–10 mm wide), pointed at the apex, rough on the margins.

ROOTS AND UNDERGROUND STRUCTURES: Branched shallow fibrous roots.

FLOWERS AND FRUIT: **Flowers** are produced from late May to mid-June **on stalked clusters in the axils of the leaf whorls.** Flowers are 2 mm in diameter and consist of 4 white petals and 4 stamens. **Fruit (schizocarps)** are composed of **2 rounded segments**, 1 seed per segment, that separate at maturity. Fruit are rounded (2–3 mm in diameter), brownish at maturity, and **generally are covered with curved hooks** but occasionally are smooth. Seeds are dispersed by animals or float on water.

POSTSENESCENCE CHARACTERISTICS: Dead stems turn dark brown or gray and often have remnants of the spiny fruit. Stems become brittle and persist for only a short time.

HABITAT: Primarily a weed of small grains, landscapes, nursery crops, and high-cut turfgrass, catchweed bedstraw is also found in meadows, along fence rows, on recently cleared land, near woodlands and thickets, and in shaded mulched beds. It thrives in moist areas, usually in the shade, and prefers nutrient-rich, high-organic soils.

DISTRIBUTION: Widespread throughout North America.

SIMILAR SPECIES: **Smooth bedstraw (*Galium mollugo* L., GALMO) is a perennial that spreads by rhizomes and stolons.** Unlike catchweed bedstraw, it has **smooth or nearly smooth stems and fruit** and **smaller whorled leaves** (1–3 cm long by 2–4 mm wide). The leaves are rough only on the margins. Smooth bedstraw is a weed of low-maintenance turfgrass, small grains, nursery crops, landscapes, and roadsides. **Carpetweed** also has 3–8 whorled leaves and a prostrate growth habit, but carpetweed does not have square stems and is much more branched than the bedstraws.

J. Neal

Catchweed bedstraw habit

J. Neal

Catchweed bedstraw
seedling with cotyledons

J. Neal

Catchweed bedstraw
flowers and fruit

J. DiTomaso

Catchweed bedstraw
mature stem and foliage

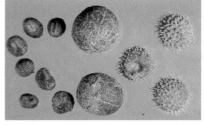

R. Uva

Smooth bedstraw habit

J. DiTomaso

Left, smooth bedstraw seeds, 1.2 mm;
right, catchweed bedstraw seeds, 3.0
mm (nonhairy variety) and 2.0 mm
(hairy variety)

Yellow toadflax (*Linaria vulgaris* Mill.) [LINVU]

Synonyms: butter-and-eggs, ramsted, flaxweed, wild snapdragon, eggs-and-bacon, Jacobs-ladder

GENERAL DESCRIPTION: A **colony-forming perennial with creeping roots. Stems** are mostly **unbranched** (30–90 cm tall), with many long, **narrow, gray-green leaves,** and terminate in a cluster of **attractive yellow flowers.**

PROPAGATION / PHENOLOGY: Reproduction is **by seeds** and **creeping roots** that produce adventitious shoots, forming clumps or colonies of plants. Creeping roots are spread by cultivation, in topsoil, and with infested nursery stock.

SEEDLING: Cotyledons are diamond-shaped to lanceolate; the apex is rounded at the tip. **First true leaves are smooth, egg-shaped, but subsequent leaves** are longer and **lanceolate to linear.** Margins of young leaves are rolled inward. Leaves are covered with white spots.

MATURE PLANT: **Stems are erect, smooth, mostly unbranched, pale green,** and very leafy. **Leaves are alternate,** pale green to **gray-green,** sessile, **linear** (2–6 cm long by 2–4 mm wide), and narrowed at the base, with entire margins. Leaves are numerous, often so closely spaced on the stem they appear to be whorled. Some of the lowermost leaves may be opposite or whorled, but these do not persist.

ROOTS AND UNDERGROUND STRUCTURES: **Creeping roots** (resembling rhizomes) and a secondary fibrous root system.

FLOWERS AND FRUIT: **Yellow snapdragon-like flowers** are produced from June through early autumn **in compact clusters (racemes) at the end of stems.** Flowers are 2–3.5 cm long and consist of 5 sepals and 5 petals fused to form 2 yellow lips with an orange throat on the lower lip and an elongated spur at the base. Fruit are round to egg-shaped, 2-celled capsules containing many seeds. Capsules open by 2–3 pores located below the apex. Seeds are 1.5–2 mm in diameter, dark brown or black, circular, flattened, and winged.

POSTSENESCENCE CHARACTERISTICS: Dead plants bearing the 2-celled toothed capsules persist for a considerable time. Dead branches, when present, twist and curve around each other.

HABITAT: Yellow toadflax is a weed of low-maintenance turfgrass, landscapes, orchards, nursery crops, and other perennial crops, but it is not common in cultivated crops. It often grows in areas with dry, gravelly or sandy soils, such as roadsides and waste areas.

DISTRIBUTION: Found throughout much of North America; most common in the eastern states and on the Pacific Coast.

SIMILAR SPECIES: **Oldfield toadflax (*Linaria canadensis* (L.) Dumont, LINCA)** is a biennial or winter or summer annual with very slender, smooth, erect stems (10–75 cm tall) and short trailing prostrate stems produced in rosette-like clusters at the base of the plant. Leaves are linear; flowers are blue to purple, rarely white. Spring shoots may resemble some **narrow-leaved goldenrods.**

Yellow toadflax habit

J. Derr

Yellow toadflax rhizomes

R. Uva

Yellow toadflax flowering
shoot

J. Neal

Left, oldfield toadflax seeds, 0.4 mm;
right, yellow toadflax seeds, 1.6 mm

J. DiTomaso

Common mullein (*Verbascum thapsus* L.) [VESTH]

Synonyms: velvet dock, big taper, candle-wick, flannel-leaf, woolly mullein

GENERAL DESCRIPTION: A **biennial** forming a **large (20–60 cm in diameter) basal rosette** the first year and an erect, usually unbranched, stem (to 1.8 m tall) in the second year. The **entire plant is densely hairy** and has a grayish green appearance.

PROPAGATION / PHENOLOGY: Reproduction is **by seed**, which germinate in late summer or early autumn or spring.

SEEDLING: **Fuzzy,** slightly serrated **oval leaves form a basal rosette** (20–60 cm in diameter).

MATURE PLANT: **Leaves of the basal rosette are densely hairy,** oblong or lanceolate, widest at the apex, about 30 cm long, tapering to a short petiole. **Densely hairy, erect,** stout, and usually unbranched **stems** elongate in the second year. **Leaves** on the upright stem are **alternate, woolly-hairy,** with entire or bluntly toothed margins. Upper leaves are sessile, narrower, and more pointed at the apex than the basal leaves. Leaves are reduced in size progressively up the stem.

ROOTS AND UNDERGROUND STRUCTURES: Thick, fleshy **taproot** with shallow secondary fibrous root system.

FLOWERS AND FRUIT: **Flowers,** present from June through September, are **sessile on 1 or 2 terminal cylindrical spikes** (20–50 cm long by 3 cm wide). Individual flowers are 2.5 cm in diameter and have **fused yellow petals** (rarely white) with 5 lobes. Sepals are 5-lobed and woolly. There are 5 stamens; the upper 3 are shorter than the lower 2. The fruit is a 2-celled, many-seeded, rounded capsule (6 mm in diameter). Seeds (0.8 mm long) have wavy ridges alternating with deep grooves, resembling corn cobs.

POSTSENESCENCE CHARACTERISTICS: Basal rosettes remain light green over winter. After flowering, plants die, leaving the remains of the tall stem and capsules. Dead stems can persist for more than a year.

HABITAT: Common mullein is a weed of landscapes, perennial crops, and roadsides, and less commonly of cultivated nursery and agricultural crops. It is often found where the soil is dry and gravelly or stony.

DISTRIBUTION: Widespread throughout the United States and southern Canada.

SIMILAR SPECIES: Owing to its distinctively hairy leaves, few species could be confused with common mullein. A **related species, moth mullein (*Verbascum blattaria* L., VESBL),** lacks hairs on the leaves and has a toothed margin. The rosette leaves are sessile, whereas common mullein leaves are on short petioles. Flowers of moth mullein are yellow to white with soft purple hairs on the stamens. Although moth mullein may reach 1.5 m in height, it has slender stems, smaller leaves, and lacks the robust appearance of common mullein.

Common mullein rosette in turfgrass

Common mullein
immature flowering
shoot

Common mullein bolting rosette

Common
mullein
flowers

Moth mullein mature stem, flowering shoot,
and rosette

Left, moth mullein seeds, 0.8;
right, common mullein seeds, 0.7 mm

307

Corn speedwell (*Veronica arvensis* L.) [VERAR]

Synonyms: rock speedwell, wall speedwell

GENERAL DESCRIPTION: A **winter annual** with **ascending branched stems** (5–15 cm, occasionally to 35 cm, in height) **radiating from the base** of the plant.

PROPAGATION / PHENOLOGY: Reproduction is **by seed**; seeds germinate in late summer, fall, or early spring, sometimes throughout the growing season in cool, moist areas.

SEEDLING: Seedlings branch at the base, forming a **dense mat**. Cotyledons are about 2 mm wide, triangular to 4-angled, with rounded apexes. **Leaves** are **opposite**, sparsely **hairy, egg-shaped**, on short petioles. Margins have **rounded teeth.**

MATURE PLANT: **Stems branch and radiate from the base** of the plant. **Lower leaves** on nonflowering parts of the plant are **opposite, petioled** (1–3 mm long), hairy, egg-shaped or (less commonly) round (6–15 mm long), with 5–12 broad to narrow **rounded teeth on the margin. Upper leaves** on flowering stems are **alternate, sessile**, and narrow or oblong. They are much **smaller than lower leaves** and have **fewer teeth**, which occur only near the leaf base.

ROOTS AND UNDERGROUND STRUCTURES: Fibrous, shallow root system.

FLOWERS AND FRUIT: Flowering peaks in late spring but may continue through August. **Flowers** are borne **solitary in the leaf axils, crowded on the upper 2/3 of the flowering stem**, which becomes elongated with age. **Flowers are small**, 2–4 mm in diameter, **pale blue to white**, and borne on stalks (pedicels) <1 mm long. The **fruit is a heart-shaped hairy pod**, deeply notched at the apex, with a minute, <1 mm long style at the apex. Each pod contains 14–20 tiny yellow seeds (0.7 mm long).

POSTSENESCENCE CHARACTERISTICS: Erect stems turn dark brown to dark gray and can persist through summer, but brittle stems do not persist in heavily trampled areas.

HABITAT: A weed of lawns, landscapes, nursery crops, and winter grains; also found in gardens and open waste areas. Not as common in cultivated fields, where fall or spring cultivation provides effective control. Although adapted to a wide range of conditions, it usually grows in dry, sandy or rocky soils and shaded lawns and woods.

DISTRIBUTION: Abundant throughout much of North America; a common lawn and landscape weed in the northeastern and upper midwestern states.

SIMILAR SPECIES: **See Table 16 for a comparison of *Veronica* species. Persian speedwell (*Veronica persica* Poir., VERPE)** is a winter annual with a similar leaf shape but long, slender flower-stalks. The stalks of corn speedwell flowers are <1 mm long. The leaves of Persian speedwell are generally larger, less hairy, and more deeply lobed than those of corn speedwell. Also, Persian speedwell leaves retain their basic shape and size on vegetative and flowering stems, whereas leaves on the flowering stem of corn speedwell become reduced upward. **Ivyleaf speedwell (*Veronica hederifolia* L., VERHE)** is also a winter annual with a similar habit but has distinctive **3-lobed, ivy-like leaves. Field speedwell (*Veronica agrestis* L., VERAG)** and **wayside speedwell (*Veronica polita* Fries, VERPO)** are similar but are summer annuals and are less common than corn speedwell. Their larger leaves are petiolated, even on the flowering stem. **Purslane speedwell (*Veronica peregrina* L., VERPG)** has a growth habit similar to corn speedwell's, but its **leaves are hairless.**

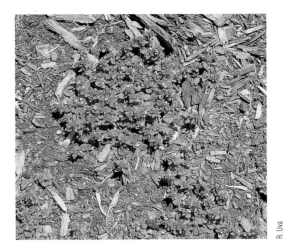

R. Uva

Corn speedwell habit

J. Neal

Corn speedwell seedling

D. Loparco

Corn speedwell flowering shoots: *left*, leaves alternate on upper stem; *right*, leaves opposite on lower stem

R. Uva

Persian speedwell habit

J. Neal

Purslane speedwell seedling

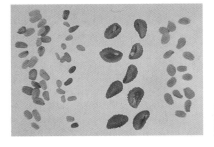

J. DiTomaso

Left to right: Persian speedwell seeds, 0.7 mm; purslane speedwell seeds, 0.5 mm; field speedwell seeds, 1.5 mm; and corn speedwell seeds, 0.7 mm

Slender speedwell (*Veronica filiformis* Sm.) [VERFI]

Synonyms: creeping speedwell, creeping veronica, Whetzel weed

GENERAL DESCRIPTION: A **prostrate, creeping perennial** with **slender stolons, small round leaves with scalloped leaf margins,** and **attractive light blue flowers in the spring**. Slender speedwell may form dense mats, particularly in turfgrass. The stems grow up to 50 cm long and root at the nodes.

PROPAGATION / PHENOLOGY: Reproduction is **predominantly vegetative in North America**. Creeping and fragmented stems can root at the nodes. Even 1 cm long stem fragments with a single node can produce adventitious roots and continue to grow. Plants are generally spread by mowers, in lawn clippings, yard compost, or landscape plant material.

SEEDLING: **In North America, this species apparently does not produce viable seed.**

MATURE PLANT: **Stems** are relatively **slender and delicate, rooting at the nodes** and becoming densely intertwined. **Leaves** are small, 8–12 mm wide, **rounded to kidney-shaped**, and sparsely hairy. Lower leaves are **opposite; those on the flowering stems are alternate**. Petioles are short (2 mm long). Leaf **margins** have **rounded teeth**.

ROOTS AND UNDERGROUND STRUCTURES: Creeping stems root at the nodes, forming a shallow fibrous root system.

FLOWERS AND FRUIT: **Attractive light blue flowers** (8 mm in diameter) are produced from May to early summer singly in the leaf axils on long (up to 2.5 cm), slender flower-stalks. Flowering among a population is usually synchronized over a 2-week period, producing an attractive floral display. The fused (4-lobed) petals are light blue with darker blue stripes. Only 2 stamens are present, and the style is 2–3 mm long. In North America, this species does not produce seed, but **in Europe the seeds are produced in heart-shaped pods**. All plants in North America are suspected to have originated from a single self-incompatible parent. When present, empty pods are heart-shaped, 3 mm long and about as wide, hairy, and broadly notched.

POSTSENESCENCE CHARACTERISTICS: Plants remain green through winter, although many leaves senesce. Stems become defoliated in hot, dry weather, but stolons survive and reestablish when weather permits.

HABITAT: A weed of turfgrass and adjoining landscapes, slender speedwell is found only in lawns, gardens, parks, and golf courses. It does not tolerate cultivation and, thus, is rarely found in cultivated fields. It tolerates a wide variety of soil types and conditions but thrives in cool, moist, shaded turf, on nutrient-rich soils.

DISTRIBUTION: Introduced into the northeastern United States as an ornamental in the 1920s; has spread via introductions to the north-central states and the Pacific Northwest.

SIMILAR SPECIES: See Table 16 for a comparison of *Veronica* species. Similar to **corn speedwell, Persian speedwell, field speedwell,** and **germander speedwell (*Veronica chamaedrys* L., VERCH)**, except that slender speedwell leaves are more rounded and have rounded teeth. The other species have leaves that are longer than wide and have pointed teeth or lobes on the margins. **Ground ivy** may look similar to slender speedwell when closely mowed or when growing under stressful conditions that markedly reduce the leaf size, but its square stems easily distinguish it from slender speedwell, which has round stems.

Slender speedwell habit

N.Y. State Turfgrass Assoc.

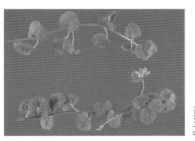

D. Loparco

Slender speedwell vegetative and flowering stems, with opposite and alternate leaves, respectively

R. Uva

Germander speedwell habit in turfgrass

D. Loparco

Germander speedwell flowering and vegetative stems

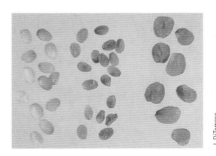

J. DiTomaso

Left to right: common speedwell seeds, 1.0 mm; thymeleaf speedwell seeds, 0.8 mm; and germander speedwell seeds, 1.3 mm

Jimsonweed (*Datura stramonium* L.) [DATST]

Synonyms: *Datura tatula*, Jamestown-weed, thorn-apple, mad-apple, stinkwort

GENERAL DESCRIPTION: A **large summer annual** with **erect branching stems** (30–150 cm tall) and distinctive **egg-shaped seed capsules covered with prickles**. The foliage has a strong **unpleasant odor**. Jimsonweed has long been known to be **toxic to all classes of livestock and to humans**. All parts of the plant are poisonous, but toxic effects on humans usually occur after seeds are ingested. Plants contain tropane alkaloids, of which the most notable are atropine, hyoscyamine, and scopolamine.

PROPAGATION / PHENOLOGY: Reproduction is **by seed**. Seedlings emerge between mid-May and mid-June and throughout the growing season if adequate moisture is available.

SEEDLING: Hypocotyls are maroon and hairy. **Cotyledons** are thick, smooth, lanceolate **(5 cm long by about 6 mm wide)**. Petioles of the cotyledons are hairy on the upper surface. The seed coat is attached to the cotyledons long after germination. **Leaves are alternate. First leaves are entire; subsequent leaves have a few irregular teeth.** Seedlings emit a strong unpleasant odor.

MATURE PLANT: Stems are smooth, green or purple, with inconspicuous hairs. **Leaves are alternate, large** (7–20 cm long), on stout petioles, oval to ovate, smooth, dark green above. Leaf **margins** resemble those of oak leaves, **coarsely and unevenly toothed**.

ROOTS AND UNDERGROUND STRUCTURES: Thick, shallow, and extensively branched **taproot**.

FLOWERS AND FRUIT: Flowers are produced from June or mid-July until frost and open in late afternoon and evening. **White to purple flowers are large and conspicuous, funnel-shaped**, 5–12.5 cm long, arising from short stalks (pedicels) solitary in the branch axils. Sepals are strongly 5-ridged, 5-toothed, and enclose the lower part of the floral tube. **Petals are fused into a 5-lobed floral tube. Fruit (capsules) are 3–5 cm long**, green when immature, **egg-shaped**, 4-celled, and **covered with stiff prickles**. Mature capsules are brown and hard, splitting into 4 segments, each containing several kidney-shaped, flattened, pitted and wrinkled, dark brown to black seeds (3 mm long).

POSTSENESCENCE CHARACTERISTICS: **Leafless stems persist after death, bearing the distinctive spiny 4-parted capsules.** Sepals form a skirt-like structure at the base of the capsule.

HABITAT: A weed of most agronomic, horticultural, and nursery crops, jimsonweed is found on most soil types but prefers nutrient-rich soils.

DISTRIBUTION: Distributed throughout most of the United States except for the Northwest and northern Great Plains; most common in the South.

SIMILAR SPECIES: The **seedlings of common cocklebur** have larger cotyledons than jimsonweed and may appear similar, but young leaves of common cocklebur are not smooth and have more pronounced teeth on the margin. Common cocklebur also lacks the distinctive odor of jimsonweed.

A. Senesac

Jimsonweed fruit

J. DiTomaso

J. Derr

Jimsonweed seedling

Jimsonweed foliage and flower

Univ. Calif. Statewide IPM Project

J. DiTomaso

Jimsonweed seeds, 3 mm

Jimsonweed seedling with cotyledons

Smooth groundcherry (*Physalis subglabrata* Mackenz. & Bush) [PHYSU]

Synonym: husk-tomato

GENERAL DESCRIPTION: **Perennial** with deeply buried **thick, fleshy rhizomes**, branched erect stems (20–90 cm tall), and a **characteristic papery, bladder-like case over the fruit**. Unripe fruit is **suspected of causing poisoning in some animals**, particularly sheep.

PROPAGATION / PHENOLOGY: Reproduction is by **seeds and rhizomes**. Seedlings emerge in warm soil in late spring or early summer.

SEEDLING: Cotyledons are smooth, green, 4–9 mm long by 1–4 mm wide. **Young leaves are alternate**, about 1.5 cm long, and have a **characteristic nightshade odor** when bruised. Emerging perennial shoots lack cotyledons and are more robust than seedlings.

MATURE PLANT: Stems are angled, slightly hairy on young growth, smooth on older tissue. **Leaves are alternate, ovate** to lanceolate, 5–7.5 cm long, pointed at the tip, long-petioled (3–5 cm), smooth or slightly hairy. **Margins** are entire or with **a few small teeth**. Stems become woody with age.

ROOTS AND UNDERGROUND STRUCTURES: Deep penetrating and spreading fibrous roots associated with **rhizomes**.

FLOWERS AND FRUIT: Flowers bloom from June through September on short recurved pedicels solitary in the axils of the branches and leaves. Sepals are fused (calyx), with 5 triangular lobes. **Petals are yellow or greenish yellow with purplish centers, fused and bell-shaped, 5-lobed**, 1.5–2.2 cm in diameter. As the fruit matures, the calyx expands to form a **papery, bladder-like casing** (3–4 cm long) **completely enclosing the small tomato-like berry. Berries are orange to red or purple** when mature and contain many seeds. Seeds are about 1.5–2 mm in diameter, flattened, circular, and yellowish.

POSTSENESCENCE CHARACTERISTICS: Erect woody stems persist well into winter. Dried fruit may also remain attached within the inflated calyx.

HABITAT: Smooth groundcherry is a weed of many cultivated agronomic, vegetable, and nursery crops. It also grows in meadows, pastures, landscapes, waste areas, and roadsides, often on coarse, gravelly soils.

DISTRIBUTION: Found throughout the eastern United States, westward to Washington, and in Utah and Texas.

SIMILAR SPECIES: **Clammy groundcherry (*Physalis heterophylla* Nees, PHYHE)** is similar but **covered with sticky (clammy) hairs**. In addition, the berries of clammy groundcherry are yellow when mature. Clammy groundcherry is also primarily a weed in the eastern United States and extends as far west as the Rocky Mountains. **See Table 17 for a comparison with weedy solanaceous species.**

Smooth groundcherry habit

J. Derr

Juvenile smooth groundcherry

J. Neal

Smooth groundcherry flower

J. Neal

Clammy groundcherry shoot with flower and fruit

J. Neal

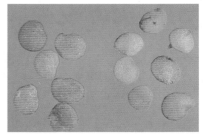

J. DiTomaso

Left, clammy groundcherry seeds, 1.8 mm; *right*, smooth groundcherry seeds, 1.5 mm

Horsenettle (*Solanum carolinense* L.) [SOLCA]

Synonyms: bull nettle, apple-of-Sodom, wild tomato, devil's tomato, devil's potato, sand briar

GENERAL DESCRIPTION: An **erect perennial** (30 cm to 1 m tall), **spreads by rhizomes and adventitous shoots from roots. Stems and leaves have conspicuous spine-like prickles.** Vegetative parts and fruit of horsenettle can **poison livestock.** All parts of the plant, except the mature fruit, contain the glycoalkaloid solanine, which is not lost upon drying. Symptoms of toxicity include gastrointestinal irritation. Reports of horsenettle poisoning in animals is rare, as the prickly vegetation deters foraging.

PROPAGATION / PHENOLOGY: Reproduction is **by seeds and creeping rhizomes** that can produce new shoots as far as 1 m away from the central plant. Rhizome fragments can also be spread by cultivation. Shoots emerge around mid-May.

SEEDLING: Short stiff hairs are present on the stem and hypocotyl. Cotyledons are oval to oblong, about 1.2 cm long, hairy on the margins, glossy green above, light green below. **Young leaves are alternate;** the first 2 are sparsely hairy on the upper surface, with unbranched and star-shaped (4–8 rayed) hairs. **Subsequent leaves are wavy or lobed, and hairy and prickly on both surfaces.**

MATURE PLANT: **Stems are erect,** angled at the nodes, somewhat branched, with **sharp, stout, yellowish or white prickles** (6–12 mm long), and star-shaped hairs. **Leaves are alternate,** 7–12 cm long and about half as wide, **egg-shaped,** with **wavy or 2–5 shallow lobes** on the margin and star-shaped hairs on both surfaces. **Prominent sharp prickles are present on the veins, midrib, and petioles.**

ROOTS AND UNDERGROUND STRUCTURES: Deep, fleshy, **spreading rhizomes.**

FLOWERS AND FRUIT: Flowers are produced in clusters on **prickly flower-stalks** (peduncles) as early as June and continuing through the growing season. **Flowers (2 cm in diameter) resemble those of potato** and consist of 5 fused hairy sepals, **5 fused white to violet petals,** and 5 stamens **with prominent bright yellow anthers** in a cone surrounding the pistil. **Fruit** are smooth, round (1–1.5 cm diameter), **yellow berries (green when immature)** containing 40–170 seeds. Berries become wrinkled late in the season. Seeds are round and flattened (2–3 mm in diameter), smooth and glossy, orange to dark or light yellow. A single plant can produce up to 5000 seeds.

POSTSENESCENCE CHARACTERISTICS: Dead stems bear persistent yellow wrinkled berries. Prominent prickles, conspicuous during the growing season, may fall off by winter.

HABITAT: Horsenettle is a weed of orchards, pastures, nursery crops, and other perennial crops. It is also weedy in conventionally tilled and reduced-tillage crops including corn, small grains, and vegetables. It is **particularly difficult to control in solanaceous crops,** such as tomato and potato. Horsenettle grows on a wide range of soil types but thrives on sandy or gravelly soils.

DISTRIBUTION: Native to the southeastern United States but has spread northward to the eastern and north-central states and into southern Canada and west to Texas.

SIMILAR SPECIES: **The groundcherries** resemble horsenettle but do not have the conspicuous prickles on the stems and leaves. The berries of groundcherry are enclosed by an inflated papery membrane (calyx). **See Table 17 for a comparison with other weedy solanaceous species.**

J. Neal

Horsenettle habit

R. Uva

Horsenettle foliage, prickles, and flowers

Horsenettle flowering shoot

J. Neal

J. Neal

Immature horsenettle from rhizome

J. DiTomaso

Horsenettle seeds, 2.8 mm

Eastern black nightshade (*Solanum ptycanthum* Dun.) [SOLPT]

Synonyms: *Solanum americanum*, deadly nightshade, poison berry, garden nightshade

GENERAL DESCRIPTION: An **erect branching summer annual** or short-lived perennial (15–60 cm tall). Vegetative parts and fruit can **poison all classes of livestock**. All parts of the plant, except the mature fruit, contain the glycoalkaloid solanine, which is not lost upon drying. Symptoms of toxicity include gastrointestinal irritation. The mature fruit have erroneously been noted as being poisonous.

PROPAGATION / PHENOLOGY: Reproduction is **by seed**. Germination occurs in late spring and continues throughout the summer if sufficient moisture is available.

SEEDLING: Hypocotyls are green, but often tinged maroon, and are covered with short hairs. Cotyledons are smooth on both surfaces, green on the upper surface and tinged maroon on the lower surface. **Young leaves are alternate, wavy**, and **tinged purplish on the underside**. Foliage and stems are generally smooth, or not obviously hairy. **Petioles and stems are purplish**.

MATURE PLANT: Stems are round and angular, smooth or only partially hairy, and branching. **Leaves are alternate**, slightly hairy, **triangular-ovate** to elliptic (2–8 cm long by 1–5.5 cm wide). **Margins** are entire or have **irregular blunt teeth**.

ROOTS AND UNDERGROUND STRUCTURES: **Slender taproot** with a branched fibrous root system.

FLOWERS AND FRUIT: Flowers are present from mid-June throughout the summer; the berries mature 4–5 weeks after flowering. **Flowers are star-shaped** (4–10 mm in diameter) **in small, drooping, lateral umbellate clusters of 5–7**. Sepals are 1.5–2 mm long, **the 5 fused petals are white or purple-tinged or with stripes. Five bright yellow anthers** form a cone surrounding the pistil. **Fruit are glossy black, spherical berries**, about 10 mm in diameter, each containing 50–110 seeds, which are spread by birds and other animals. Seeds are round, flattened, 1.5–2 mm long, yellow or nearly white.

POSTSENESCENCE CHARACTERISTICS: After frost, stems and fruit can persist until winter.

HABITAT: Eastern black nightshade is a weed of nursery crops, landscapes, and horticultural, agronomic, and many vegetable crops, particularly solanaceous species (e.g., potato and tomato). Although found on sandy, nutrient-poor disturbed sites, it thrives on moist, fertile, cultivated soils.

DISTRIBUTION: Primarily a weed of the eastern United States.

SIMILAR SPECIES: There is much confusion regarding the taxonomy of the nightshade species belonging to the *Solanum nigrum* complex. **See Table 17 for a comparison of weedy solanaceous species.** Of the 4 major weedy members of this complex, 3 are known as black nightshade: eastern black nightshade, most common east of the Rocky Mountains; **black nightshade (*Solanum nigrum* L., SOLNI)**, most common in the western states; and **American black nightshade (*Solanum americanum* Mill., SOLAM)**, common in many southern and coastal areas. The fourth species of the group is **hairy nightshade (*Solanum sarrachoides* Sendtner, SOLSA)**, which occurs throughout most of North America. Hairy nightshade has prominent hairs on the stems and leaves, and the mature fruit is greenish yellow or brownish. **Horsenettle** is a rhizomatous perennial that is easily distinguished by conspicuous spines on the stems and leaves.

Eastern black nightshade habit

Hairy nightshade stem with foliage, flowers, and fruit

Eastern black nightshade seedling

Hairy nightshade seedling

Eastern black nightshade foliage and fruit

Left, black nightshade seeds, 1.4 mm; *right*, eastern black nightshade seeds, 1.9 mm

Stinging nettle (*Urtica dioica* var. *procera* (Muhl.) Wedd.) [URTDI]

Synonyms: *Urtica gracilis, Urtica procera*, tall nettle, slender nettle

GENERAL DESCRIPTION: An **erect rhizomatous perennial** (2 m tall), usually unbranched or slightly branched near the top. Large colonies develop from **rhizomes. Leaf surfaces are bristly hairy** with fewer, but larger **stinging hairs**. Stinging nettle is a mechanical **skin irritant** rather than a contact allergen. The large hairs are tapered, elongated cells, constricted just below the tip with a bulbous base embedded in a sheathing pedestal. When the tip of the hair is broken off on contact with the skin, it acts as a hypodermic needle, injecting the toxins histamine, acetylcholine, and 5-hydroxytryptamine into the wound. Localized pain occurs rapidly, followed by a reddish swelling and prolonged itching and numbness.

PROPAGATION / PHENOLOGY: Reproduction is by **seeds and rhizomes**. Rhizomes can spread at a rate of 2.5 m a year. Cultivation can fragment rhizomes, further increasing the rate of spread. Seeds do not require a period of cold temperatures to germinate.

SEEDLING: Cotyledons are oval (1.5–4 mm long by 1 mm wide), notched at the apex, with a few short hairs on the upper surface. **Young leaves are opposite, oval, with rounded teeth** on the margin. The **upper leaf surface has short hairs and a few stinging hairs**; the underside has short hairs on the veins. Stipules at the base of the leaf senesce early. Stems are hairy.

MATURE PLANT: **Stems are 4-angled**, with **stinging hairs**, but shorter hairs may be absent. **Leaves are opposite**, 5–15 cm long, broadly egg-shaped to ovate or lanceolate, the base rounded to rarely heart-shaped, the apex sharply pointed. Blades are smooth on both surfaces, to sparingly hairy beneath. **Stinging hairs are on the lower surface of the blade. Margins are deeply toothed** (2–3.5 mm). Petioles are a quarter to two-thirds the length of the blade. Stipules at the base of the petiole are oblong to linear-lanceolate (5–12 mm long).

ROOTS AND UNDERGROUND STRUCTURES: **Extensive rhizome system** with secondary fibrous roots.

FLOWERS AND FRUIT: Flowers are produced from late May to October. Male and female flowers are separate but on the same plant (monoecious). **Both flower types are inconspicuous, greenish yellow**, in branched clusters arising from the leaf axils. The seed is enclosed within the egg-shaped fruit (achene). Achenes are white to brown, 1–1.5 mm long.

POSTSENESCENCE CHARACTERISTICS: Erect stems turn dark brown and persist through the winter.

HABITAT: A weed of landscapes, nurseries, orchards, and vegetable crops, stinging nettle is also found in pastures and roadsides, and along streams and drainage ditches, generally in lowland areas. It thrives in damp, nutrient-rich soil and does not grow well on low-fertility soil.

DISTRIBUTION: Found throughout most of the United States, except southern Florida, and southern Canada.

SIMILAR SPECIES: The introduced European variety, **Urtica dioica var. dioica**, is dioecious and less common in North America than is var. *procera*. Its branched stems are weak and tend to sprawl along the ground. Leaves and stems are commonly hairier than those of the native variety, and the stinging hairs are located on both the upper and lower leaf surfaces.

J. DiTomaso

Stinging nettle mature shoot

J. DiTomaso

Stinging nettle flower clusters
in leaf axils

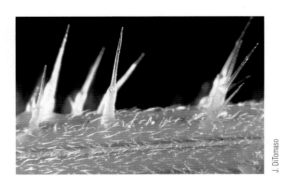

J. DiTomaso

Stinging nettle stinging hairs

J. DiTomaso

Stinging nettle seeds, 1 mm

321

Field violet (*Viola arvensis* Murr.) [VIOAR]

Synonyms: wild pansy, field pansy, hearts-ease, European field-pansy

GENERAL DESCRIPTION: Usually a **winter annual**, but a summer annual in cool, moist climates. Stems are **erect or ascending**, branching from the base (10–30 cm tall). **Plants resemble cultivated Johnny-jump-ups (*Viola tricolor* L.).**

PROPAGATION / PHENOLOGY: Reproduction is **by seed**; seeds germinate in late summer or early fall.

SEEDLING: Young plants develop as **basal rosettes**. Elongating stems are angular to cylindrical. Cotyledons are petiolated, oval, 3–5 mm long by 3–4 mm wide, blunt (or sometimes with a small notch) at the tip. **Young leaves are oval, on long petioles.** Blades are truncate at the base, blunt-pointed to rounded at the apex, with rounded teeth on the margins. **Subsequent leaves are hairy at the base and have deeply lobed stipules.**

MATURE PLANT: Stems may be branched or unbranched, angled or rounded, with short hairs at the branch angles. **Leaves are alternate**, hairy, at least on the veins of the underside, with **rounded teeth on the margin**. Leaves are **spatulate**; the blades of the lower leaves tend to be more rounded or egg-shaped, whereas the upper blades are longer and narrower. **Two large leaf-like stipules at the base of the petiole are divided into 5–9 narrow segments** with one larger central leaf-like segment. Lower leaves are 2–3.5 cm long and have smaller stipules. Upper leaves are 2–8 cm long and 1–1.5 cm wide.

ROOTS AND UNDERGROUND STRUCTURES: Fibrous root system with a wintergreen odor when crushed.

FLOWERS AND FRUIT: **Typical violet-like flowers** are produced from March to May and from September to October on long stalks (pedicels) arising from leaf axils. Flowers are 1–1.5 cm long and about 1 cm wide, **pale yellow or yellow with purple**. Petals (5) are irregular in shape; the lower is spurred and larger than the others. The fruit is a 5–10 mm long spherical, 1-celled capsule opening into 3 valves. Seeds are oval, about 1–2 mm long, yellowish brown to dark brown, and glossy.

POSTSENESCENCE CHARACTERISTICS: Plants decompose rapidly after senescence or can remain green as winter annuals.

HABITAT: Field violet is a weed of nursery crops, landscapes, and small fruits, especially strawberry. It is often found on gravelly or sandy soils. Its importance as a weed is increasing in irrigated horticultural crops.

DISTRIBUTION: Found in the northern, southeastern and western United States and in southern Canada. Increasing in importance in the Northeast.

SIMILAR SPECIES: **Pansy (*Viola tricolor* L., VIOTR) and field pansy (*Viola rafinesquii* Greene, VIORA)** have petals that are 2 and 3 times, respectively, longer than the sepals. Petals of field violet are shorter or equal to the sepal length. Unlike that of field pansy, the middle lobe of the stipules in pansy is not toothed. Plants and flowers resemble **cultivated Johnny-jump-ups**, but are more aggressive and have less-attractive floral displays.

Field violet habit

A. Senesac

R. Uva

Field violet flowering shoots

J. Neal

Field violet seedling

J. DiTomaso

Pansy habit

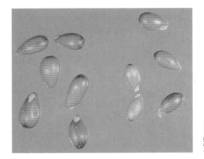

J. DiTomaso

Left, pansy seeds, 2.0 mm;
right, field violet seeds, 1.6 mm

Common blue violet (*Viola papilionacea* Pursh) [VIOPP]

Synonyms: meadow violet, hooded blue violet

GENERAL DESCRIPTION: A **low-growing** (7.5–20 cm) colony-forming **perennial** with smooth green **heart-shaped leaves** and **typical violet-like flowers**. Plants spread by short, stout, branching **rhizomes**. Leaves arise basally from a **crown** on relatively long petioles.

PROPAGATION / PHENOLOGY: Reproduction is **by seeds and rhizomes**.

SEEDLING: Not usually noticed.

MATURE PLANT: Plants are hairless, leaves (8 cm long) arise from a **basal crown. Leaf blades are heart-shaped**, pointed at the apex, with rounded teeth on the margin. **Petioles are about twice as long as the leaf blade.**

ROOTS AND UNDERGROUND STRUCTURES: **Stout, branching rhizomes** and a coarse root system.

FLOWERS AND FRUIT: **Flowers**, produced from April through June, are **usually deep purple or blue (sometimes gray, light violet, or white)**, 1.3–2 cm wide, with 5 petals. The 2 lateral petals are bearded; the lower 1 is spurred. Flowers are produced **on leafless stalks that are usually no longer than the leaves**. Fruit are 3-valved capsules (10–12 mm long) containing dark brown seeds (2 mm long).

POSTSENESCENCE CHARACTERISTICS: Foliage is not susceptible to frost and persists through the fall, but will decay under snow cover during the winter.

HABITAT: Primarily a weed of turfgrass and landscapes, blue violet, for unknown reasons, is common in the turfgrass of cemeteries. It frequently escapes from old flower gardens. It is also found in damp woods, meadows, and roadsides. Although blue violet thrives on cool, moist, shady sites, once it is established it will tolerate drought-prone soils.

DISTRIBUTION: Found throughout eastern North America.

SIMILAR SPECIES: **Dooryard violet (*Viola sororia* Willd.)**, also known as sister violet or woolly blue violet, is similar, but with hairy leaves and stems. Some taxonomists consider common blue violet to be the hairless form of *Viola sororia*. **English violet (*Viola odorata* L., VIOOD)**, can be distinguished by its wiry rhizomes and prominent creeping stoloniferous habit. The leaves are basal, heart-shaped to ovate, hairy, with 2–6 cm long blades. Flowers are white or purple and fragrant. **Field pansy** and **field violet** are 2 common winter annual weeds that can be confused with common blue violet, but they have leafy, branching, ascending to erect stems, unlike the basal leaves of common blue violet. In addition, they have spatulate leaves with long prominent stipules. Field pansy has purple or bluish white to cream-colored flower petals longer than the sepals. Field violet has pale yellow to purplish tinged petals shorter than or equal to the sepals.

Common blue violet habit in turfgrass

J. Neal

A. Senesac

Common blue violet flower

A. Senesac

Common blue violet mature crown, with seedlings around base

R. Uva

English violet, white-flowered form

Staghorn sumac (*Rhus typhina* L.) [RHUTY]

Synonyms: *Rhus hirta*, staghorn

GENERAL DESCRIPTION: A **shrub or small tree typically growing in colonies**; older plants are in the middle and smaller, younger plants radiate out on the sides. The **leaves are alternate and pinnately compound**, each with **9–31 serrate leaflets**. Twigs and petioles are densely hairy.

PROPAGATION: **Reproduction is by seeds and rhizomes.** Seeds are dispersed by birds. Once established, colonies enlarge by rhizomes and new seedlings at the margins.

FLOWERS AND FRUIT: The **red hairy fruit** are on terminal ends of the branches in cone-shaped clusters. Fruit appear in the autumn and persist into spring.

POSTSENESCENCE CHARACTERISTICS: In autumn, the foliage turns bright orange or dark red; after leaves drop the red fruit remain. The characteristically branched stems and red fruit persist through the winter.

HABITAT: Staghorn sumac is often found on poor, dry soil and in areas where other plants find conditions too difficult to survive. It readily produces new sprouts at the base of existing plants. Seedlings can grow in cracks in the pavement. Although it is often planted as an ornamental, staghorn sumac can rapidly encroach into gardens, lawns, and walkways.

DISTRIBUTION: Native to the eastern United States, ranging as far south as Tennessee.

SIMILAR SPECIES: **Dwarf sumac (*Rhus copallina* L., RHUCO)** is similar but has raised dots on the stem. The leaflets of dwarf sumac have entire margins, and the main axis (rachis) is winged between the leaflets. **Smooth sumac (*Rhus glabra* L., RHUGL)** lacks hairs on the stems and petiole. Staghorn sumac can hybridize with smooth sumac, with the hybrids possessing intermediate characteristics. **Poison-sumac (*Toxicodendron vernix* (L.) Ktze., TOXVX)** is usually found in swampy areas and has white hairless fruit, hairless stems, and entire leaf margins. Unlike the *Rhus* species, poison-sumac causes dermatitis in sensitive individuals. **Tree-of-heaven** has a similar habit and pinnately compound leaves, but unlike *Rhus* species the leaflets have only 1–2 teeth near their base.

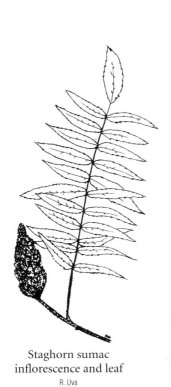

Staghorn sumac
inflorescence and leaf
R. Uva

Dormant staghorn sumac

R. Uva

Staghorn sumac foliage

R. Uva

J. DiTomaso

Left to right: staghorn sumac seeds,
4 mm; smooth sumac seeds, 3 mm;
and dwarf sumac seeds, 3 mm

Poison-ivy (*Toxicodendron radicans* (L.) Ktze.) [TOXRA]

Synonyms: *Rhus radicans*, markweed, poison creeper, three-leaved ivy, picry, mercury

GENERAL DESCRIPTION: A climbing or trailing, **deciduous woody vine** with **3 leaflets**, each about 10 cm long. Leaflet margins are toothed, lobed, or entire; leaflets vary in shape but often are egg-shaped. Leaflet stalks (petiolule) are short except on the middle leaflet. When growing as a climbing vine, poison-ivy attaches to trees or rocks by aerial roots. On older plants, aerial roots give the stems a hairy, fibrous appearance. Poison-ivy is the major cause of **allergenic dermatitis** in the eastern United States. All parts of the plant contain resinous compounds, known as urushiols, that cause inflammation of the skin, blistering, and itching. About 50–60% of Americans are sensitive to urushiols. The toxic compounds can be transmitted in smoke and by direct contact with the plant or with objects or animals exposed to the plant, including tools, pets, and clothing. The dermatitis response can occur year-round, even following contact with overwintering stems and roots. Urushiols can remain active on objects and in dead plants for over a year.

PROPAGATION: Reproduces by **seeds, creeping root stocks, and stems that root** where they contact the soil. Seeds are dispersed by birds.

FLOWERS AND FRUIT: Plants produce small yellowish green flowers on axillary panicles from May to June. Greenish to grayish **white berries** (5 mm long) lack hairs and are produced in late summer. They can persist on the plant throughout the winter.

POSTSENESCENCE CHARACTERISTICS: In autumn, leaves often turn bright red, then drop by midseason. Woody stems persist.

HABITAT: Poison-ivy can invade landscapes, disturbed sites, woodlands, and wetlands by creeping stems or seeds deposited by birds. It thrives under a variety of conditions.

DISTRIBUTION: Native and widespread throughout the midwestern, northern, and eastern United States and parts of Canada.

SIMILAR SPECIES: **Poison-oak (*Toxicodendron toxicarium* (Salisb.) Gillis, TOXQU)** is similar but grows more erect, has blunt-tipped leaf apexes, and hairs on both surfaces of the blade. Posion-oak is found only from New Jersey southward. **Virginia-creeper** is similar **but has 5 leaflets per leaf** and climbs by tendrils with terminal adhesive disks.

Poison-ivy foliage

Poison-ivy leaves
R. Uva

Poison-oak leaf (with 3 leaflets)
R. Uva

J. Neal

Poison-ivy seedling

329

Trumpetcreeper (*Campsis radicans* (L.) Seem. *ex* Bureau) [CMIRA]

Synonym: cow-itch

GENERAL DESCRIPTION: A fast-growing, **aggressive deciduous, woody vine** that either climbs on other vegetation or trails along the ground. Sometimes grown as an ornamental, it can easily escape cultivation. The **leaves** are alternate, **pinnately compound** (30 cm long), with **7–11 coarsely toothed leaflets**. Trumpetcreeper climbs with the aid of aerial roots along its stems and can produce suckers from the roots.

PROPAGATION: Reproduction is **by seeds, root sprouts, and stems that root** where they touch the ground.

FLOWERS AND FRUIT: **Orange trumpet-shaped flowers** (6–8 cm long tube-like corolla) are present from July through September and produce pod-like structures containing numerous winged seed.

POSTSENESCENCE CHARACTERISTICS: In autumn, leaves turn yellow-green, then drop. Woody vines persist.

HABITAT: Commonly found in orchards, vineyards, nursery stock, landscapes, along fence rows, and in wooded areas, trumpetcreeper can also emerge in sidewalk cracks and around foundations.

DISTRIBUTION: Native to the eastern half of the United States.

SIMILAR SPECIES: Although the compound leaves of trumpetcreeper are similar to the sumacs, the sumacs are not viny.

R. Uva

Trumpetcreeper in flower

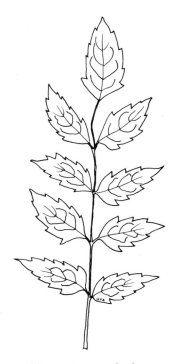

Trumpetcreeper leaf
R. Uva

J. Neal

Trumpetcreeper seedling in late spring

Japanese honeysuckle (*Lonicera japonica* Thunb.) [LONJA]

Synonym: Chinese honeysuckle

GENERAL DESCRIPTION: A twining, **climbing, or trailing vine** that is **deciduous in colder climates but semievergreen to evergreen in more southerly locations**. Leaves are opposite and simple, ovate to oblong, with entire, or sometimes lobed, margins. Both the **leaves and twigs are hairy**. Stems are woody and have a hollow pith.

PROPAGATION: Plants spread **by seeds and rapidly growing runners that root** at the nodes. Runner growth can exceed 9 m a year.

FLOWERS AND FRUIT: The **fragrant white to yellow flowers** (to 38 mm long) bloom in May. Flowers are produced in pairs attached to a short common stalk (peduncle) arising from the upper leaf axils. Fruit are black berries (6 mm in diameter) that mature in late summer but persist into autumn.

POSTSENESCENCE CHARACTERISTICS: Semi-evergreen vine. The leaves may take on a purplish tinge in autumn and may persist through mild winters. Woody stems persist.

HABITAT: A weed of perennial crops in orchards, Christmas tree plantations, nurseries, and landscapes, Japanese honeysuckle can engulf small plants and saplings. In the southeastern United States, it can displace native vegetation but is less vigorous and more easily contained in the Northeast.

DISTRIBUTION: Japanese honeysuckle is native to eastern Asia and was introduced to the United States as an ornamental in the 1800s. It has become naturalized and has spread over much of eastern, central, and western North America from Massachusetts west to California, south to Florida and Texas. It is a significant problem on the East Coast from New Jersey south.

SIMILAR SPECIES: Other weedy honeysuckles, including **Tatarian honeysuckle**, are shrubby, whereas Japanese honeysuckle is viny. In addition, Tatarian honeysuckle has red berries; the berries of Japanese honeysuckle are black.

Japanese honeysuckle flowering vines

Japanese honeysuckle flower
R. Uva

Japanese honeysuckle
stem and leaves
R. Uva

Japanese honeysuckle juvenile leaves

R. Uva

Tatarian honeysuckle (*Lonicera tatarica* L.) [LONTA]

Synonyms: bush honeysuckle, garden fly-honeysuckle

GENERAL DESCRIPTION: A **branching, deciduous shrub** (3–4 m high), whose upper branches often arch upward from spreading older branches. Stems are scaly between each season's growth. The bark is light brown to tan and splits or peels longitudinally. **Leaves of seedlings are opposite, egg-shaped, hairy**, and emerge throughout the summer. On **mature plants the leaves are opposite, egg-shaped to oblong**, simple (3–7 cm long), and **nearly hairless**, with entire margins. The stems lack hairs and have a hollow pith.

PROPAGATION: **Berries are eaten by birds, which disperse seeds** into landscape areas and nursery beds. Seeds germinate over an extended season, from midspring to midsummer. When the plant is cut down, the roots often persist and shoots resprout.

FLOWERS AND FRUIT: **Pink to white flowers** (1.5–2 cm long) bloom in pairs on a common long stalk (peduncle) arising from the leaf axils. Flowers are produced in late May, and **attractive red berries** (6 mm in diameter) are produced in late summer.

POSTSENESCENCE CHARACTERISTICS: No distinctive fall leaf color. Arching woody stems with tan peeling bark are notable from fall through spring.

HABITAT: Primarily a weed in field nurseries and landscapes, Tatarian honeysuckle is also common in roadsides, along fence rows, and hedgerows, and at the edges of woods.

DISTRIBUTION: Introduced from Eurasia to the United States as an ornamental in the late 1700s; has escaped to become naturalized over much of the eastern United States.

SIMILAR SPECIES: Tatarian honeysuckle is the only species of *Lonicera* in the northeastern states that has a hollow pith, hairless twigs, and nearly hairless leaves. **Japanese honeysuckle** is also weedy, but it is a vine with hairy leaves and twigs, a short peduncle, and black fruit.

Tatarian honeysuckle leaves and fruit

R. Uva

Tatarian honeysuckle stem,
leaves, and fruit
R. Uva

Tatarian honeysuckle seedling

J. Neal

Oriental bittersweet (*Celastrus orbiculatus* Thunb.) [CELOR]

Synonym: Asiatic bittersweet

GENERAL DESCRIPTION: An invasive **climbing deciduous woody vine**. Leaves are somewhat rounded to obovate (2–12 cm long), alternate, simple, with bluntly toothed margins.

PROPAGATION: Reproduction is **by seed**.

FLOWERS AND FRUIT: Inconspicuous greenish white flowers bloom in the spring. **Fleshy red seeds enclosed in yellow capsules** are produced during the autumn. The fruit has been sporadically **reported to be poisonous to humans**.

POSTSENESCENCE CHARACTERISTICS: Leaves turn yellow in autumn, then drop. Distinctive yellow fruit with red seeds persist to late fall or early winter.

HABITAT: Oriental bittersweet forms tangles and thickets when growing alone, but it can strangle other shrubs and small trees by girdling their stems. It is often found in landscapes, roadsides, and other uncultivated areas.

DISTRIBUTION: A native of eastern Asia, Oriental bittersweet was introduced to the United States as an ornamental in the late 1800s. It has escaped from cultivation and become naturalized over much of the northeastern states, south to Virginia.

SIMILAR SPECIES: **American bittersweet (*Celastrus scandens* L.)** is native to the United States. It has been replaced in some areas by the more aggressive Oriental bittersweet. American bittersweet has ovate to oblong-ovate leaves, whereas the leaves of Oriental bittersweet are more rounded.

Oriental bittersweet
foliage and fruit
R. Uva

Oriental bittersweet foliage

Oriental bittersweet fruit

R. Uva

J. Neal

Roundleaf greenbriar (*Smilax rotundifolia* L.) [SMIRO]

Synonyms: common greenbriar, common catbriar, bullbriar, horsebriar

GENERAL DESCRIPTION: A **woody vine** that forms thickets or climbs other vegetation by tendrils attached to the petiole. The leaves are alternate, simple, and heart-shaped or rounded (5–13 cm long), with entire margins and parallel venation. **Stems are green**, either angled or rounded, and **armed with sharp prickles**. Sharp prickles on viny foliage can entangle ankles, calves, and arms, causing considerable injury.

PROPAGATION: Plants slowly creep into new areas **by vegetative growth**, or **seeds** can be **deposited in the landscape by birds**. Seedlings emerge from spring through midsummer.

FLOWERS AND FRUIT: Greenish flowers bloom from April through August. The **berry-like fruit are bluish black**, mature in September, and may persist through the winter. Seeds are round, reddish, and 5–6 mm in diameter.

POSTSENESCENCE CHARACTERISTICS: Green, vining stems with sharp prickles are persistent.

HABITAT: Roundleaf greenbriar may form impenetrable patches around clearings, in roadsides, and in open woods. Often found along moist edges of swampy woods and in drier upland areas, it is also a common weed in landscapes, Christmas tree plantations, and orchards.

DISTRIBUTION: Native to the eastern United States, extending to Illinois, Oklahoma, Florida, and Texas.

SIMILAR SPECIES: **Cat sawbriar (*Smilax glauca* Walt., SMIGL)** has round stems with weak prickles, and the leaves are whitish on the underside. **Catbriar (*Smilax bonanox* L., SMIBN)** has 4-sided stems and bristly edged leaves. Both cat sawbriar and catbriar are found primarily on moist to dry, sandy soil.

J. Neal

Roundleaf greenbriar foilage

R. Uva

Greenbriar stem and thorns

Roundleaf greenbriar
leaf and stem
R. Uva

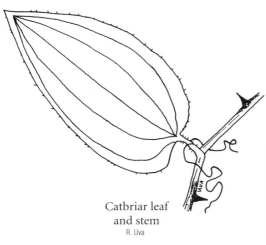

Catbriar leaf
and stem
R. Uva

J. DiTomaso

Left to right: cat sawbriar seed, 4.0 mm;
catbriar seed, 5.0 mm; and roundleaf
greenbriar seed, 5.5 mm

339

Virgin's bower (*Clematis virginiana* L.)

Synonym: clematis

GENERAL DESCRIPTION: A herbaceous to **soft-woody vine that climbs by twining petioles**. **Leaves** are opposite and **palmately compound** with 3 (sometimes 5) toothed leaflets (5 cm long). The sap of stems and leaves causes **irritant dermatitis**.

PROPAGATION: Reproduction is **by seed**.

FLOWERS AND FRUIT: The **feathery white flowers** (2.5 cm in diameter) are produced in loose clusters from July through September. The seed is enclosed within the fruit, which is a **feathery achene**, 4.5 cm long. Each flower produces a large number of achenes.

POSTSENESCENCE CHARACTERISTICS: Woody vines persist. No notable fall leaf color. Distinctive fruit persist for a short time.

HABITAT: Found in open woodlands climbing on trees and shrubs, virgin's bower also grows in woody perennial crops, along fence rows, and in landscapes. It climbs by twisting its petioles over other plants and over structures such as fences.

DISTRIBUTION: Native to the eastern United States, as far west as Kansas.

SIMILAR SPECIES: **Poison-ivy** can be distinguished because its leaves are alternate, it has broader leaflets, and it climbs by aerial roots rather than twining petioles.

R. Uva

Virgin's bower mature foliage and stem

Virgin's bower fruit

J. Neal

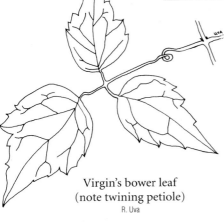

Virgin's bower leaf
(note twining petiole)
R. Uva

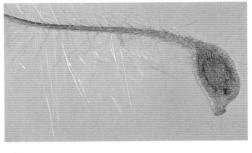

J. DiTomaso

Virgin's bower seed, 3.5 mm (not including
feathery style)

Multiflora rose (*Rosa multiflora* Thunb. *ex* Murr.) [ROSMU]

GENERAL DESCRIPTION: A rapid-growing, **prickly-stemmed shrub** (1–3 m tall) that can form thickets or scramble over other plants with its arching stems. The **compound leaves** are alternate, **subtended by large fringe-like stipules**, and are composed of 7–9 serrate leaflets (2–4 cm long). Once established, multiflora rose is difficult to control.

PROPAGATION: Reproduction is **by seeds and runners (stems), which form adventitious roots. Seeds are spread by birds and other animals** that eat the fruit. Runners from existing plants can quickly transform unmanaged areas into impenetrable thickets.

FLOWERS AND FRUIT: **White flowers** are 2.5 cm in diameter, bloom in June, and produce **clusters of red fruit** that persist into the winter.

POSTSENESCENCE CHARACTERISTICS: Woody stems with sharp prickles persist. The red fruit last into winter.

HABITAT: Multiflora rose is a common weed of pastures, rangeland, landscapes, and fence rows. It tolerates most soil conditions and is often found in uncultivated and unmowed areas, such as roadsides, rights-of-way, and fields.

DISTRIBUTION: A native of East Asia, multiflora rose was introduced into the United States in the late 1800s as a rootstock for other roses. It has escaped cultivation and is now naturalized over much of the United States, where it has become a serious weed of rangeland.

SIMILAR SPECIES: Multiflora rose can be distinguished from **other roses** by the presence of fringed stipules on the leaf petiole.

R. Uva

Multiflora rose habit

Multiflora rose stem, leaf, and fruit
(note feathery stipules at leaf base)
R. Uva

R. Uva

Multiflora rose flowering shoot

Brambles: raspberries, dewberries, blackberries (*Rubus* spp.)

GENERAL DESCRIPTION: The genus *Rubus* contains many plants of difficult taxonomy. The weedy members, sometimes referred to as brambles, include raspberries, blackberries, and the dewberries. Brambles have **upright and arching to trailing stems** (3–4 m high) arising from root buds. The **leaves are alternate and compound,** composed of 3–7 leaflets with serrate margins. Stems are red or green, with **prickles.** Individual stems generally survive for 2 years.

PROPAGATION: Brambles spread **by seeds, root sprouts, rhizomes, and stems that arch to the ground and root at the tips.** Plants can form prickly impenetrable thickets.

FLOWERS AND FRUIT: Flowers have **5 white petals** and produce **a red or black, berry-like fruit** (aggregate), actually composed of a cluster of smaller fruit (drupes). Fleshy portion of fruit dries over seed to form a pitted structure (2 mm long).

POSTSENESCENCE CHARACTERISTICS: Leaves become darker and remain for a short time in autumn. Upright prickly stems are very distinctive and persist for 2–3 years.

HABITAT: Brambles are common along fence rows and in orchards, roadsides, and other open sunny locations. Seedlings are common in mulched landscape beds.

DISTRIBUTION: Many of the brambles are native to North America, and different species occur throughout the northeastern United States.

Raspberry foliage and fruit

Bramble stem and leaf
R. Uva

Bramble seedling

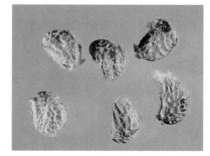

Bramble seeds, 2 mm

345

Tree-of-heaven (*Ailanthus altissima* (Mill.) Swingle) [AILAL]

GENERAL DESCRIPTION: A **large deciduous tree** (to 18 m in height), but can be **weedy as a sapling or small tree**. Grows rapidly, about 1–1.5 m per year. **Leaves are alternate and compound** (60 cm long), with 11–25 or more leaflets per leaf. **Leaflets have 1–2 teeth** near their base. The twigs are stout, with a large brown pith and conspicuous leaf scars. The **foliage has a peanut butter- or popcorn-like odor. Some people are allergic to the pollen of the male flowers.** Contact with this plant has been known to cause **dermatitis**.

PROPAGATION: After being cut down, the plant can spread **by suckers**, sprouting as far as 3.5 m from main stem. Also produces a large number of **seeds**, which can be **dispersed short distances by wind**.

FLOWERS AND FRUIT: Small, greenish yellow flowers (June) are produced in long clusters. Fruit is a single-seeded winged samara. Clusters of samaras (3–4 cm long) persist on trees long into winter. The male flowers have a popcorn-like odor, similar to that of the foliage.

POSTSENESCENCE CHARACTERISTICS: No notable fall color. Woody stems persist.

HABITAT: At one time planted along city streets, tree-of-heaven has escaped into waste areas, vacant lots, noncultivated fields, and nurseries. It survives under the harshest of urban conditions, growing along foundations, in cracks in cement, and in rubble.

DISTRIBUTION: Native to eastern Asia and introduced into North America in 1751. It has become naturalized across much of the United States.

SIMILAR SPECIES: **Staghorn sumac** also has large compound leaves, but its leaflets have toothed margins. In winter, staghorn sumac is easily distinguished by conspicuous red, cone-shaped fruit clusters at the end of the branches. **Poison-sumac** is also a small tree with large compound leaves, but the margins of its leaflets are not toothed. Also, poison sumac has white berry-like fruit.

R. Uva

Tree-of-heaven urban habit

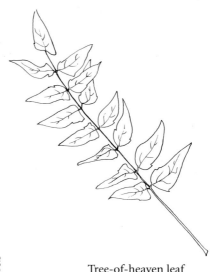

Tree-of-heaven leaf
R. Uva

J. DiTomaso

Tree-of-heaven seeds, 40 mm

R. Uva

Poison-sumac habit

J. DiTomaso

Left, poison-sumac seeds, 6 mm; *right*, staghorn sumac seeds (with seed coat), 6 mm

Bittersweet nightshade (*Solanum dulcamara* L.) [SOLDU]

Synonyms: European bittersweet, bitter nightshade, blue nightshade, woody nightshade, poison berry, climbing nightshade, scarlet berry, blue bindweed, dogwood, fellenwort

GENERAL DESCRIPTION: A **semiwoody to herbaceous perennial vine** growing to about 2–3 m tall. The foliage can twine over other plants, trail along the ground, or grow erect with arching hollow stems. **Leaves** (5–12 cm long) are petiolated, alternate, and of **2 forms. One has 2 basal lobes; the other is ovate to oval.** The margins of both leaf types are smooth. The foliage is purple-tinged and has an unpleasant odor. **Vegetative parts and fruit can poison all classes of livestock.** The plant contains the glycoalkaloid solanine, which is not lost upon drying. Symptoms of toxicity include gastrointestinal irritation. The **berries have been reported to poison children.**

PROPAGATION: Spreads **by seeds and creeping prostrate stems**, which root at the nodes.

FLOWERS AND FRUIT: **Flowers** (12–16 mm in diameter) consist of petals that are fused at the base but deeply 5-lobed, **resembling the flowers of potato. Petals are purple** to blue **with a yellow center. Fruit is a thin-skinned, oval, red berry** (8–12 mm long) containing many flat, round, yellowish seeds (2 mm in diameter).

POSTSENESCENCE CHARACTERISTICS: None of note.

HABITAT: Bittersweet nightshade is found in landscapes, nurseries, orchards, along edges of cultivated fields, and in uncultivated or wooded areas, often on moist soils.

DISTRIBUTION: Native to Eurasia, bittersweet nightshade was introduced as a cultivated ornamental. It has become naturalized over much of the United States but is most common in the eastern and north-central states.

SIMILAR SPECIES: **See Table 17 for a comparison with other weedy *Solanum* species. Eastern black nightshade** is similar to bittersweet nightshade but is an upright, branched annual with wavy leaf margins and black berries. **Oriental bittersweet** is an unrelated woody plant with unlobed leaves and reddish orange seeds in yellow capsules.

Bittersweet nightshade seedlings

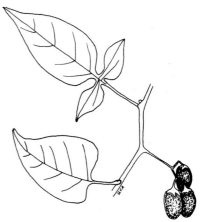

Bittersweet nightshade
leaves (2 forms) and fruit
R. Uva

Bittersweet nightshade foliage and fruit

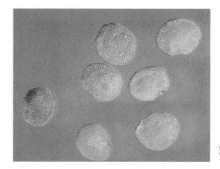

Bittersweet nightshade seeds, 2 mm

Virginia-creeper (*Parthenocissus quinquefolia* (L.) Planch.) [PRTQU]

Synonyms: woodbine, American ivy, five-leaved ivy

GENERAL DESCRIPTION: A **woody vine** that climbs on objects or vegetation or trails along the ground. The **vines climb by tendrils** that have oval **adhesive disks** at their tips. **Leaves are alternate and palmately compound, with 3–7, but usually 5, leaflets.** The leaflets are 6–12 cm long with **toothed margins**.

PROPAGATION: Plants are often **established from seeds** dropped by birds but **spread by stems**, which root when in contact with the ground.

FLOWERS AND FRUIT: Inconspicuous green-white flowers yield small blue-black berries in the autumn.

POSTSENESCENCE CHARACTERISTICS: Leaves turn deep red in the fall. Woody stems persist.

HABITAT: Valued for its fall color, Virginia-creeper is often **grown as an ornamental**. It is a common weed of landscapes, orchards, and vineyards, as well as fence rows and other noncultivated areas. It tolerates a wide range of conditions including dry, sandy sites, moist, nutrient-rich soil, shade, sun, and high salinity.

DISTRIBUTION: Native to the eastern United States.

SIMILAR SPECIES: **Poison-ivy** has compound leaves with 3 leaflets; the terminal leaflet is attached to a short stalk (petiolule). Poison-ivy climbs by aerial roots not by adhesive disks.

Virginia-creeper habit

Virginia-creeper mature foliage

Virginia-creeper stem and
palmately compound leaves
R. Uva

Virginia-creeper spring growth

351

Wild grape (*Vitis* spp.)

GENERAL DESCRIPTION: There are **several species of wild grape** that invade landscapes as **climbing, woody, deciduous vines**. The vines can form a canopy over large trees and are capable of blocking enough light to kill or significantly reduce the trees' growth. Thickets of wild grape can also grow over low shrubs and along the ground. **Leaves are alternate, simple with toothed margins, palmately veined**, rounded, often 3-lobed. Wild grapes **climb by forked tendrils** that are opposite the leaves. Stems are brown, and the **bark shreds in strips**.

PROPAGATION: Spread **by seeds**, which may be dispersed by birds or other animals. **Cut stems can readily resprout.**

FLOWERS AND FRUIT: Flowers in late spring to early summer. **Fruit are purplish black berries, smaller than cultivated grapes.** Berries are produced from August into the autumn.

POSTSENESCENCE CHARACTERISTICS: No notable fall color. Woody stems have brown bark that shreds in strips. Tendrils persist and become dark and brittle.

HABITAT: Wild grape is a common weed of orchards, vineyards, landscapes, nurseries, Christmas tree plantations, and fence rows. Some species thrive on moist, rich soils, others on sandy, dry sites.

DISTRIBUTION: Many species of wild grape are native and grow throughout eastern and central North America.

SIMILAR SPECIES: The weedy species of wild grape in the northeastern states include **summer grape (*Vitis aestivalis* Michx., VITAE), fox grape (*Vitis labrusca* L., VITLA), riverbank grape (*Vitis riparia* Michx.),** and **frost grape (*Vitis vulpina* L., VITVU). Virginia-creeper** has compound leaves, whereas the leaves of all wild grape species are simple. In addition, wild grape has conspicuous tendrils and does not climb by adhesive disks, as does Virginia-creeper.

Grape vine

Wild grape stem,
leaf, and tendril
R. Uva

Young grape vine, with lobed leaf form

353

Hardwood Seedlings

Seedlings and root sprouts of these and other hardwood trees can be troublesome weeds in landscapes, nurseries, Christmas tree plantations, orchards, and no-till crops.

Aceraceae (Maple Family)

Box elder (*Acer negundo* L.): tree to 20 m at maturity; seedlings and saplings weedy; **leaves opposite, 3–5 pinnately compound**; leaflets lanceolate to ovate or oblong, each 6–10 cm long; margins entire to coarsely toothed or lobed; twigs often green or purplish with a whitish waxy coat; paired, winged fruit (schizocarp), wings of fruit spread apart at <90° angle.

Norway maple (*Acer platanoides* L.): tree to 25 m at maturity; seedlings and saplings weedy; leaves opposite, simple, 7–12 cm long, 5–7 lobed, lower surface green, margins toothed; exudes **milky latex**; paired, winged fruit (schizocarp), wings of fruit spread apart at 180° angle.

Red maple (*Acer rubrum* L., ACRRB): tree to 35 m at maturity; seedlings weedy; leaves opposite, simple, 5–20 cm long, 3–5 lobed, lower surface gray or white, margins irregularly toothed; paired, winged fruit (schizocarp), wings of fruit spread apart at <90° angle.

Young box elder

Box elder leaf and fruit
R. Uva

Red maple
seedlings

Red maple mature leaves and fruit
R. Uva

Norway maple seedling (note milky sap on
broken petiole)

355

Fabaceae = Leguminosae (Pea or Bean Family)

Honey locust (*Gleditsia triacanthos* L.): tree commonly to 20–35 m at maturity; seedlings or root sprouts weedy in landscapes; **stems spiny**; leaves alternate (15–20 cm long), **once or twice pinnately compound**; leaflets numerous, lanceolate to oblong, about 1–2 cm long, margins faintly toothed, often appearing entire; fruit a many-seeded, twisting pod (legume), 30–45 cm long.

Black locust (*Robinia pseudoacacia* L., ROBPS): tree to 30 m at maturity; root sprouts or seedlings weedy; **leaves alternate, once compound**; leaflets 2.5–5 cm long, ovate, 6–20 per leaf; **stems with sharp spines**; fruit a 2–10 seeded pod (legume).

R. Uva

Young honey locust habit

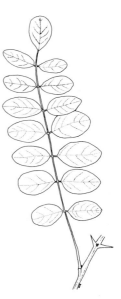
J. Neal

Black locust thorns

R. Uva

Black locust sprout

Black locust leaf and
stem (with thorns)
R. Uva

Moraceae (Mulberry Family)

White mulberry (*Morus alba* L., MORAL): tree to 15 m at maturity; saplings weedy; leaves alternate, simple, 3–7 cm long, margins toothed, **leaves both lobed and unlobed; milky sap from young twigs**; male and female flowers on separate plants (dioecious); **fruit berry-like.**

Oleaceae (Ash Family)

White ash (*Fraxinus americana* L.) and **green ash (*Fraxinus pennsylvanica* Marshall):** large tree, 18–25 m at maturity; seedlings or saplings weedy; **leaves opposite, once pinnately compound, 5–9 leaflets, usually 7**; leaflets oblong to ovate or lanceolate, 11 cm long, margins entire to toothed; fruit a single-seeded samara; buds large and brown. White ash lacks hairs on undersurface of leaf, and the wing of the samara is terminal to the seed. Green ash is hairy below, at least on midrib, and the wing of the fruit is lateral and terminal to the seed.

White mulberry in groundcover bed

J. Neal

White mulberry leaves
(2 forms)
R. Uva

White ash stem and leaf
R. Uva

359

Rosaceae (Rose Family)

Black cherry (*Prunus serotina* Ehrh.): tree to 25 m at maturity; seedlings or saplings weedy; **leaves alternate, simple, lanceolate** to oblong, 6–12 cm long, midrib on underside with white to brown hairs, margins with incurved teeth; **petiole with a pair of glands just below the leaf base**; bark aromatic; fruit a purple to black drupe.

Common chokecherry (*Prunus virginiana* L., PRNVG): similar to black cherry, but only 10 m tall at maturity; teeth on leaf margin point outward, midrib on underside of blade lacks hairs; fruit a deep red drupe.

Salicaceae (Willow Family)

Common cottonwood (*Populus deltoides* Marshall), also known as poplar: tree to 23 m at maturity; seedlings and root sprouts weedy; **leaves** alternate, simple, 8–13 cm long, **triangular**, serrate margins, flattened petioles; fruit a capsule, with **seeds surrounded by cotton-like hairs** that aid in wind dispersal.

Black cherry
stem and leaves
R. Uva

J. Neal

Wild cherry seedling

Common
cottonwood leaf
R. Uva

R. Uva

Common cottonwood seeds

J. Neal

Poplar sapling

COMPARISON TABLES

Table 8. Comparison of pigweeds and amaranths

Species	Habit	Stem and foliage	Bracts	Inflorescence
Tumble pigweed (*Amaranthus albus*)	bushy-branched, low and diffuse to erect	stems whitish; leaves small, spatulate, light green, margin wavy	2–4 times longer than sepals	flowers in short, thick, dense, axillary clusters
Prostrate pigweed (*A. blitoides*)	prostrate	stems and leaves smooth; leaves pale green	equal to length of sepals	flowers in short, thick, dense, axillary clusters
Smooth pigweed (*A. hybridus*)	erect	upper stem densely hairy; leaves dark green, margin wavy	1.5–2 times longer than sepals	flowers in lax, nodding, terminal branched spikes (some axillary flowers)
Powell amaranth (*A. powellii*)	erect	upper stem mostly smooth; leaves diamond-shaped, shiny, dark green, entire	2–3 times longer than sepals	flowers in elongated, stiff, mostly unbranched spikes (some axillary flowers)
Redroot pigweed (*A. retroflexus*)	erect	upper stem very hairy; leaf margin wavy	2 times longer than sepals	flowers in short, thick, terminal branched spikes (some axillary flowers)
Spiny amaranth (*A. spinosus*)	low and diffuse	pair of sharp spines at base of most leaves; leaves smooth, dull green	equal to length of sepals	flowers in elongated, lax, terminal and axillary spikes

Table 9. Comparison of weedy species in the carrot family (Apiaceae)

Character	Spotted waterhemlock (*Cicuta maculata*)	Poison-hemlock (*Conium maculatum*)	Wild carrot (*Daucus carota*)	Giant hogweed (*Heracleum mantegazzianum*)
Life cycle	perennial	biennial	biennial	biennial or monocarpic perennial
Height	50 cm to 2 m	60 cm to 2 m	20 cm to 1 m (rosette tolerates mowing)	2–5 m
Stems	smooth, purple-spotted	smooth, purple-spotted, ridged	bristly hairy, vertically ribbed	coarse hairy, purple-blotched, thick (4–8 cm)
Leaves	3–12 cm long, 2 times pinnately compound; leaflets 2–5 cm long	20–40 cm long, 3–4 times pinnately compound; leaflets finely cut	up to 15 cm long, many times pinnately compound, finely dissected	up to 1 m long, 1–2 times pinnately compound
Compound umbel (flower cluster)	to 12 cm wide	4–6 cm wide	8–16 cm wide	to 50 cm wide

Character	Corn chamomile (*Anthemis arvensis*)	Mayweed chamomile (*A. cotula*)	Pineapple-weed (*Matricaria matricarioides*)	Scentless chamomile (*M. perforata* Merat MATIN)
odor	pleasant chamomile odor when crushed	unpleasant pungent odor when crushed	sweet pineapple-like odor when crushed	no distinct odor
leaves	similar to *A. cotula* but slightly less finely dissected	2–3 times pinnatifid, 2–6 cm long; segments narrow	1–3 times pinnatifid, 1–5 cm long; segments short, linear or filiform	2–3 times pinnatifid, 6–7 cm long; segments linear to filiform, with acute tips
ray flowers	10–16 white flowers, 6–12 mm long	10–16 white flowers, 5–11 mm long	absent	15–35 white flowers, 10–20 mm long
receptacle	chaffy scales all over receptacle surface	chaffy scales on receptacle surface only toward the middle	receptacle naked	receptacle naked

Table 11. Comparison of sowthistles and prickly lettuce

Character	Prickly lettuce (*Lactuca serriola*)	Perennial sowthistle (*Sonchus arvensis*)	Spiny sowthistle (*S. asper*)	Annual sowthistle (*S. oleraceus*)
Life cycle	annual or biennial	perennial	annual	annual
Root system	large taproot	creeping, spreading rhizomes	taproot	short taproot
Flower head width	0.8–1.0 cm	3–5 cm	1.2–2.5 cm	1.2–2.5 cm
Ray flower color	yellow	yellow to bright yellow-orange	pale yellow	pale yellow
Achenes	5–7 longitudinal ribs on each side, long-beaked, grayish yellow to brown, 3–4 mm long	5–7 prominent longitudinal ribs on each side, wrinkled, dark brown, 3 mm long	3(4–5) prominent longitudinal ribs, smooth, light brown, 2.3 mm long	3–5 longitudinal ribs on each side, wrinkled, light brown to olive, 4 mm long
Auricles	acute (sagittate)	small and rounded	prominent and rounded	sharply acute
Leaf margin	fine prickly toothed	prickly	very prickly	weakly or sparsely prickly
Leaf midrib (underside)	stiff, sharp prickles	not prickly	not prickly	not prickly
Leaf shape	pinnatifid, with half-moon lobes	entire to deeply pinnatifid	pinnatifid or obovate and lacking lobes	pinnatifid
Leaves, stems, roots	exude milky sap when cut	exude milky sap when cut	exude milky sap when cut	exude milky sap when cut

Left to right: spiny sowthistle, perennial sowthistle, and annual sowthistle

Table 12. Comparison of bindweeds and wild buckwheat

Character	Hedge bindweed (*Calystegia sepium*)	Field bindweed (*Convolvulus arvensis*)	Wild buckwheat (*Polygonum convolvulus*)
Life cycle	perennial	perennial	annual
Leaf shape			
Ocrea	absent	absent	present
Flower	usually white, sometimes pink; petals fused into a a funnel-shaped tube 3–6 cm long	similar to hedge bindweed, but 1.2–2.5 cm long	greenish white, inconspicuous, about 4 mm long
Bracts below flower	very large, concealing the sepals	small, well below the sepals	absent

Drawings by R. Uva.

Table 13. Comparison of wild cucumber and burcucumber

Character	Wild cucumber (*Echinocystis lobata*)	Burcucumber (*Sicyos angulatus*)
Hairiness	stems rarely hairy, only nerves on upper leaf surface hairy	stems bristly, tendrils hairy, leaf hairy throughout
Flower	6 sepals and petals	5 sepals and petals
Fruit	2-celled, 4-seeded; 3–6 cm long, 3–4 cm wide; solitary at each leaf axil; fruit with weak smooth prickles, not hairy	1-celled, 1-seeded; 1–2 cm long, 0.5–1.5 cm wide; in clusters of 3 or more at each leaf axil; fruit with stiff bristles and short hairs

Table 14. Comparison of trifoliolate (3 leaflets) legumes and woodsorrel

Species	Life cycle/ growth form	Leaflet shape	Terminal leaflet stalk	Petiole length	Flower color	Flower head
Woodsorrel (*Oxalis* spp.)	erect to prostrate, annual or perennial	heart-shaped	absent	much longer than leaflets	yellow	individua flowers, r clustered head
Birdsfoot trefoil (*Lotus corniculatus*)	prostrate to suberect, perennial	elliptic to oblanceolate	absent	shorter than leaflets	yellow	4–8 flowe each 1.5 c long
Black medic (*Medicago lupulina*)	prostrate to ascending, annual or biennial	elliptic to obovate	present	shorter than leaflets	yellow	10–50 flowers, globose
Rabbitfoot clover (*Trifolium arvense*)	erect, annual	oblong	absent	shorter than leaflets	pink to white	numerou flowers, cylindrica
Hop clover (*T. aureum*)	ascending, annual	oblong to obovate	absent	shorter than leaflets	yellow	numerou flowers, globose t cylindrica
Large hop clover (*T. campestre*)	low, spreading, annual	obovate	present	usually shorter than leaflets	yellow	numerou flowers, globose
Strawberry clover (*T. fragiferum*)	creeping, perennial	obovate	absent	longer than leaflets	pink to rose	numerou flowers, globose t ovoid
Alsike (*T. hybridum*)	ascending, perennial	oval to elliptic, rounded at the apex	absent	longer than leaflets	white to pink	numerou flowers, globose
Red clover (*T. pratense*)	ascending or suberect, short-lived perennial	oval	absent	shorter than leaflets	red or magenta to pink	numerou flowers, globose
White clover (*T. repens*)	creeping, perennial	broadly elliptic to obovate, rounded at the apex	absent	longer than leaflets	white, or tinged with pink	numerou flowers, globose

R. Uva

Left to right: strawberry clover, white clover, alsike, and red clover

R. Uva

Left to right: white clover, black medic, yellow woodsorrel, and birdsfoot trefoil

R. Uva

Rabbitfoot clover flowering stem

Table 15. Comparison of broadleaf plantain and blackseed plantain

Character	Broadleaf plantain (*Plantago major*)	Blackseed plantain (*Plantago rugelii*)
Hairs on leaf blade	short, inconspicuous	mostly lacking
Leaf margin	entire or irregularly toothed	usually wavy-toothed
Petiole	seldom with red coloration at base	often with red coloration at base
Bracts subtending flowers	egg-shaped, blunt at the tip	lanceolate, gradually tapering to a very slender tip
Fruit capsule	egg- to diamond-shaped, 2.5–4 mm long, 6–20 seeded, opens by splitting around the middle	cylindrical or elliptic, 4–6 mm long, 4–10 seeded, opens by splitting well below the middle
Seeds	light to dark brown, glossy	dark brown or black, dull

Comparison of selected speedwell species

pecies	Life cycle	Leaf shape, margin, and surface	Leaf arrangement		Flower arrangement
			Lower	Upper	
eld speedwell (*Jeronica agrestis*)	annual		opposite	alternate	
orn speedwell (*J. arvensis*)	annual		opposite	alternate	
ermander speedwell (*J. chamaedrys*)	perennial		opposite	opposite	
ender speedwell (*J. filiformis*)	perennial		opposite	alternate	
ryleaf speedwell (*J. hederifolia*)	annual		opposite	alternate	
ommon speedwell (*J. officinalis* L., VEROF)	perennial		opposite	opposite	
urslane speedwell (*V. peregrina*)	annual		opposite	alternate	
ersian speedwell (*V. persica*)	annual		opposite	alternate	
hymeleaf speedwell (*V. serpyllifolia*)	perennial		opposite	alternate	

rawings by Bente Starcke King.

Table 17. Comparison of groundcherry and nightshade species

Character	Clammy groundcherry (*Physalis heterophylla*)	Smooth groundcherry (*P. subglabrata*)	Horsenettle (*Solanum carolinense*)	Bittersweet nightshade (*S. dulcamara*)	Black nightshade (*S. nigrum*)	Eastern black nightshade (*S. ptycanthum*)	Hairy nightshade (*S. sarrachoides*)
Life cycle	rhizomatous perennial, 20–90 cm tall	rhizomatous perennial, 20–90 cm tall	rhizomatous perennial, to 1 m tall	rhizomatous climbing or trailing perennial	annual, to 0.5 m tall	annual, rarely a short-lived perennial, to 1 m tall	annual, to 0.8 m tall
Stem	very hairy all over	angled, young shoots slightly hairy, older shoots smooth	armed with sharp prickles	viny, woody at the base, slightly hairy	round to angular, hairs absent or few	round to angular, hairs absent or few	round to slightly angular, many spreading hairs
Leaf surface	very hairy	smooth to slightly hairy	sharp prickles and sparsely branched hairs	hairs absent or short and few	slightly hairy	nearly lacking hairs	soft, sticky glandular hairs
Inflorescence	solitary in leaf axils	solitary in leaf axils	racemose	compound cyme	racemose	umbellate	racemose or occasionally umbellate
Flower	petals yellow or greenish yellow with purplish centers	petals yellow or greenish yellow with purplish centers	petals purple, sometimes whitish	petals blue to purple	petals white or faintly bluish	petals white or faintly bluish	petals white
Fruit	yellow, enclosed in a papery bladder-like casing	orange to red or purple, enclosed in a papery bladder-like casing	yellow	bright red	dull black, 15–60 seeds per berry	glossy dark purple to black, 50–110 seeds per berry	green, olive-green, or yellow, 10–35 seeds per berry

GLOSSARY

Abscission   The process by which fruit, flowers, or leaves are separated from a plant by the normal development of a thin layer of pithy cells produced at the base of the part to be separated.

Achene   A single-seeded, dry fruit that does not open at maturity (e.g., a sunflower seed).

Acuminate   With a long, tapering point and concave sides.

Adventitious root   A root that originates from stem or leaf tissue rather than from another root.

Alternate   Arranged singly along an axis; 1 leaf per node (Fig. 7). *Contrast* Opposite; Whorled.

Androecium   All of the stamens of the flower collectively (Fig. 2). *Contrast* Gynoecium.

Annual   *See* Summer annual; Winter annual.

Anther   The pollen-bearing portion of the stamen.

Apex   The tip of a leaf blade (Fig. 6), a root, or a stem.

Apomixis   The production of seeds without fertilization.

Appressed   Closely and flatly pressed against.

Auricle   In grasses, a small projecting lobe or appendage found where the blade meets the sheath (Fig. 1), or at the base of the blade in broadleaf plants.

Awn   A slender bristle of a grass floret.

Axil   The position between the stem and a leaf or other lateral organ.

Basal rosette   A circular cluster of leaves radiating from the stem of a plant at ground level (e.g., the leaf arrangement in dandelion). Basal rosettes result from a series of very short internodes; the leaves are not considered to be whorled. *Contrast* Whorled.

Biennial   An herbaceous plant that requires 2 years to complete its life cycle. During the first season the seed germinates and only vegetative growth follows; in the next season, after winter vernalization, flowering, seed set, and death occur (Fig. 12).

Bipinnate   Having 2 rows of lateral branches, appendages, or other parts along an axis which are themselves again divided into 2 rows along an axis (Fig. 8).

Blade   The part of a leaf above the sheath in grasses, and above the petiole in broadleaf plants (Figs. 1, 6).

Boat-shaped   *See* Prow-shaped.

Bolt   To produce erect, elongate stems from a basal rosette; often associated with winter annual or biennial species that have rapidly elongating, erect flowering stems.

Bract   A specialized leaf that is usually greatly reduced in size and is associated with flowers (Fig. 4).

Broadleaf plants   Dicots; characterized by having relatively wide leaves of various shapes. Distinguished from grasses, which are monocots and have narrow leaves with parallel veins.

Bud   An undeveloped leafy shoot or flower.

Bulb   A short, thickened, vertical underground shoot composed of modified scale-like leaves in which food is stored.

Bur   A fruiting structure covered with spines or prickles.

Calyx   The sepals of a flower collectively (Fig. 2).

Carpel   The organ that bears the juvenile seed (Fig. 2). *See also* Pistil.

Caudex   A perennial stem, below the ground or at ground level, often resembling a taproot.

Definitions are modified from Hitchcock (1950), Jones and Luchsinger (1986), Walters and Keil (1988), and Gleason and Cronquist (1991).

Chaff Small thin, dry scales on the receptacles of many of the Asteraceae (Fig. 3).

Ciliate Having a fringe of hairs.

Cleft Cut halfway to the midrib or base.

Cleistogamous flower A self-pollinating flower that produces seeds without opening; grows mostly on or under the ground.

Clump-forming (tufted) Describes a grass that grows in a compact cluster attached at the base.

Collar The outer side of a grass leaf at the juncture of the blade and sheath (Fig. 1).

Composite A member of the Asteraceae.

Composite head The dense inflorescence of the Asteraceae, usually composed of florets, a receptacle, and bracts (Fig. 3).

Compound leaf A leaf with 2 or more leaflets.

Compressed Flattened laterally, as are the sheaths and spikelets of some grasses.

Cordate Heart-shaped (Fig. 10).

Corm A thickened, short, vertical underground perennial stem in which food is stored.

Corolla The petals of a flower collectively (Fig. 2).

Corymb A flat-topped or convex flower cluster in which the outer flowers open first (Fig. 4). *Contrast* Cyme.

Cotyledon A seed leaf (Fig. 5).

Crenate Having a margin with rounded teeth (Fig. 9).

Crown The part of a perennial plant, at or just below the ground, where the stem and root join and from which new shoots are produced.

Cyathium The inflorescence of spurges (*Euphorbia* spp.); consists of cup-like bracts that contain a central female (pistillate) flower and several male (staminate) flowers.

Cyme A flat-topped or convex flower cluster in which the central flowers open first (Fig. 4). *Contrast* Corymb.

Decumbent Lying on the ground but with the tips ascending.

Decurrent With an attached wing or margin extending down the axis (e.g., the margin of a leaf extending down a stem).

Dehiscent Describes fruit that open at maturity. *Contrast* Indehiscent.

Dentate With spreading, pointed teeth (Fig. 9).

Denticulate With very small spreading, pointed teeth (Fig. 9).

Dicot *See* Dicotyledon.

Dicotyledon A plant in the class of angiosperms (Magnoliopsida) that is characterized by embryos (seedlings) with 2 cotyledons, netted leaf veins, flower parts in 4's or 5's, and cambium; broadleaf plants. *Contrast* Monocotyledon.

Dioecious Producing male and female flowers on different plants. *Contrast* Monoecious.

Disciform head A composite head composed of filiform florets (pistillated florets with very slender tubular corollas) and disk florets.

Discoid head A composite head composed of disk florets only.

Disk flower A tubular, radially symmetric flower (i.e., floret) of the Asteraceae with male and female organs (Fig. 3). *Contrast* Ligulate flower; Ray flower.

Dissected Divided into many slender segments (Fig. 10).

Divided Cut into distinct parts. A divided leaf is cut to the midrib or the base.

Drupe A fleshy fruit containing a seed enclosed in a hardened ovarian wall.

Elliptic Widest in the middle, narrowing equally toward both ends (Fig. 10).

Emarginate With a small notch at the apex.

Entire With a continuous, untoothed margin (Fig. 9).

Fibrous root A thin root arising from another root or from stem tissue.

Filament The stalk of a stamen (Fig. 2).

First leaf   In a seedling, the next leaf that grows after the cotyledons.

Floret   An individual flower of a defined flower cluster, as an individual flower of a grass spikelet or of a composite head.

Folded   Describes grass blades or grass leafbuds that are folded together lengthwise so that the upper surface is inside the fold (Fig. 1). *Contrast* Rolled.

Gemmae   In liverworts, small bud-like outgrowths that become detached and can grow into new plants.

Glabrous   Without hairs.

Glaucous   Covered with a removable powder-like waxy coating, as is commonly seen on the fruit of grape and plum.

Glume   One of a pair of bracts at the base of a grass spikelet.

Grasses   *See* Broadleaf plants.

Gynoecium   The female organs of a flower collectively (Fig. 2).

Hastate   Shaped like an arrowhead but with the basal lobes more divergent (Fig. 11).

Hypocotyl   The part of the stem below the cotyledons of a seedling (Fig. 5).

Indehiscent   Describes fruit that remain closed at maturity. *Contrast* Dehiscent.

Inflorescence   A flower cluster.

Internode   The part of a stem between 2 successive nodes.

Involucre   One or more whorls of bracts beneath a flower or inflorescence, often forming a cup-like structure (Fig. 3).

Keel   The sharp fold at the back of a compressed sheath or blade. Figs. 5 and 6 illustrate leaves of broadleaf plants.

Lacerate   Appearing to have been torn or irregularly cut.

Lanceolate   Much longer than wide; widest below the middle and tapering to both ends or rounded at the base (Fig. 10).

Landscape   A section of land whose natural features have been altered with the intention of making it more attractive, usually by the addition of a lawn, trees, and shrubs.

Lateral   On or at the sides.

Leaf   In grasses, the lateral organ of a stem, consisting of a sheath and blade. Figs. 5 and 6 illustrate leaves of broadleaf plants.

Leafbud   An emerging blade of grass (Fig. 1).

Leaflet   One subunit of a compound leaf (Fig. 8).

Legume   A several-seeded, usually dry fruit produced by members of the Fabaceae (bean family) or a closely related family; composed of a single carpel that opens down both sutures at maturity. Also, a plant in the Fabaceae or a closely related family.

Lemma   In grasses, the lower of the 2 bracts enclosing the flower.

Ligulate flower   A flower (i.e., floret) of the Asteraceae with stamens and a pistil that has a strap-shaped, 5-lobed corolla. Ligulate florets occur only in ligulate heads, never with other kinds of florets. *Contrast* Disk flower; Ray flower.

Ligulate head   A composite head composed of ligulate florets only.

Ligule   In grasses, the thin membranous appendage or a ring of hairs on the inside of a leaf at the junction of the sheath and blade (Fig. 1).

Linear   Very long and narrow, with essentially parallel sides (Fig. 10).

Lobe   A projecting segment of a leaf that is larger than a tooth but with the adjoining sinus extending less than halfway to the midrib (Fig. 9).

Lyrate   Pinnatifid, with the terminal lobe the largest and usually rounded (Fig. 10).

Membranous   Thin and flexible, membrane-like (Fig. 1).

Mericarp   An individual section of a schizocarp.

Midrib   The central vein of a leaf (Figs. 1, 6).

Midvein   *See* Midrib.

Monocarpic   Living a few years, blooming once, then dying.

Monocot   *See* Monocotyledon.

Monocotyledon   A plant in the class of angiosperms (Liliopsida) characterized by embryos (seedlings) with 1 cotyledon, parallel-veined leaves, flower parts in multiples of 3, and no secondary growth; grasses and grass-like plants such as sedges, rushes, and lilies. *Contrast* Dicotyledon.

Monoecious   Producing male and female organs in different flowers (imperfect flowers) on the same plant. *Contrast* Dioecious.

Mucronate   Describes a leaf or leaflet that terminates in a short, abrupt spur or spiny tip.

Node   A place on a stem where a leaf is or has been attached (Fig. 1).

Nutlet   A small nut. Also, a 1-seeded segment of the ovary found in members of the mint family.

Ob-   In a reverse direction.

Oblanceolate   Much longer than wide, like lanceolate, but widest above the middle and tapering to the base.

Oblong   Longer than wide, with parallel sides; more or less rectangular (Fig. 10).

Obovate   Egg-shaped and widest at the apex (Fig. 10).

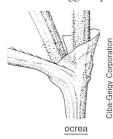

Ciba-Geigy Corporation

ocrea

Ocrea   A papery sheath that encloses the stem at the nodes; made from the fusion of 2 stipules; found in members of the Polygonaceae.

Opposite   Arranged in pairs along an axis; 2 leaves per node (Fig. 7). *Contrast* Alternate; Whorled.

Ovary   The expanded basal part of a pistil, containing the ovules.

Ovate   Egg-shaped and widest near the base (Fig. 10).

Palea   In grasses, the upper of the 2 bracts enclosing the flower.

Palmate   With 3 or more lobes, nerves, leaflets, or branches arising from a common point (Fig. 8).

Panicle   An inflorescence with a main axis and subdivided branches; may be compact and spike-like (Fig. 4).

Pappus   A modified calyx consisting of dry scales, bristles, or awns that often facilitate wind dispersal of seeds (e.g., the feathery portion of a dandelion "seed"); common in the Asteraceae and other families.

Parted   Deeply cut, usually more than halfway to the midvein or base.

Pedicel   The stalk of a single flower of a flower cluster (Fig. 4).

Peduncle   The stalk of a flower cluster or of a solitary flower (Fig. 4).

Perennial   Plants that generally live for more than 2 years (Fig. 12).

Perianth   All of the sepals and petals collectively (Fig. 2).

Petal   One of the inner floral leaves that make up the corolla; typically white or brightly colored (Fig. 2).

Petiolated   With a petiole.

Petiole   The stalk between the leaf blade and the stem (Fig. 6).

Petiolule   A stalk, similar to a petiole, attaching a leaflet to the rachis of a compound leaf.

Phyllary   One of the involucre bracts in the Asteraceae (Fig. 3).

Pinnate   With 2 rows of lateral branches, appendages, or parts along an axis (Fig. 8).

Pinnatifid   More or less deeply cut with 2 rows of lateral appendages (Fig. 10).

Pistil   The female organ of a flower, composed of stigma, style, and ovary; the pistil consists of 1 or more carpels (Fig. 2).

Prickle   A sharp outgrowth of the outermost layer of cells (epidermis) or bark.

Protonema   A thread-like growth, arising from germinating spores, that develops into small moss plants.

Prow-shaped   Shaped like the bow of a boat; common shape of *Poa* spp. leaf tips.

Pubescent   With hairs.

Raceme   An elongated inflorescence in which the stalked flowers arise from an unbranched central axis (Fig. 4).

Rachis   The main axis of a compound leaf. Also, an axis bearing flowers.

Radiate head   A composite head composed of disk and ray florets.

Ray flower   A flower (i.e., floret) of the Asteraceae that has a pistil or is neutral and has a 3-lobed strap-shaped lip (Fig. 3). *Contrast* Disk flower; Ligulate flower.

Receptacle   The basal part of the flower, representing the end of the stem (pedicel or peduncle) to which the flower parts are attached (Fig. 2). It is often greatly enlarged, as in the Asteraceae (Fig. 3).

Recurved   Bent or curved downward or backward.

Reflexed   Abruptly bent or curved downward or backward.

Reniform   Kidney-shaped (Fig. 10).

Rhizoids   Root-like filaments of liverworts and mosses.

Rhizome   A creeping underground stem (Fig. 1).

Rhombic   Diamond-shaped (Fig. 10).

Rolled   Describes a grass leafbud that is positioned as if turned on its axis over and over (Fig. 1).

Root crown   *See* Crown.

Rosette   *See* Basal rosette.

Runcinate   Sharply cleft or pinnatifid, with backward-pointing segments.

Runner   *See* Stolon.

Sagittate   Arrowhead-shaped, with the basal lobes more or less in line with the body (Fig. 11).

Samara   A winged fruit such as that of maple and ash.

Scape   A leafless peduncle arising from ground level.

Schizocarp   A fruit that splits into separate carpels (mericarps) at maturity.

Seedhead   An inflorescence bearing mature fruit (Fig. 1).

Sepal   One of the outer floral leaves that make up the calyx; typically green (Fig. 2).

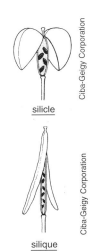

silicle

silique

Serrate   Toothed along the margin with sharp, forward-pointing teeth (Fig. 9).

Sessile   Lacking a petiole.

Sheath   In grasses, the lower part of a leaf that encloses the stem and younger leaves (Fig. 1).

Silicle   A fruit of the Brassicaceae that is similar to a silique but not much (if at all) longer than wide.

Silicula   *See* Silicle.

Siliqua   *See* Silique.

Silique   A fruit of the Brassicaceae that is an elongated capsule in which the 2 valves are deciduous from the persistent replum (frame-like placenta) to which the seeds are attached.

Simple leaf   A leaf blade that is all 1 piece; may be deeply lobed or divided.

Sinuate   With a strongly wavy margin (Fig. 9).

Spatulate   Shaped like a spatula; rounded above and narrowed to the base (Fig. 10).

Spike   An unbranched inflorescence in which the spikelets are sessile on the main axis (Fig. 4).

Spikelet   In grasses, an inflorescence consisting of 1 to many flowers and minute specialized leaves (Fig. 1).

Spike-like panicle   A panicle with compact branches hidden by the spikelets of grasses or the flowers of broadleaf plants.

Stamen   The male, or pollen-producing, part of a flower (Fig. 2).

Stigma   The part of the pistil that receives the pollen (Fig. 2).

Stipule   One of a pair of basal appendages of a leaf (Fig. 6).

Stolon   A horizontal stem at or just above the surface of the ground that gives rise to a new plant at its tip or from axillary branches (Fig. 1).

Style   The slender stalk that typically connects the stigma(s) to the ovary.

Subulate   Awl-shaped (Fig. 10).

Sucker   A shoot on a plant that arises from below ground; more precisely, a shoot arising from an adventitious bud on a root. Also, to bear suckers or shoots.

Summer annual   A plant that germinates in the spring or summer, flowers, sets seed, and dies during a single growing season (Fig. 12).

Taproot   An enlarged vertical main root.

Tepal   An undifferentiated sepal or petal.

Tiller   A shoot growing from the base of the stem of a grass plant (Fig. 1).

Trifoliate   Refers to a plant with 3 leaves; term often misused to describe a plant with trifoliolate leaves.

Trifoliolate   Refers to a compound leaf consisting of 3 leaflets (e.g., poison-ivy and most clovers) (Fig. 8).

Truncate   Appearing as if cut off transversely straight at the end.

Umbel   A cluster of flowers in which the stalks (pedicels) arise from a common point; may be simple or compound (Fig. 4).

Undulate   With a wavy margin.

Urticle   A thin-walled, 1-seeded, more or less inflated fruit.

Vein   One of the bundles of vascular tissue forming the framework of a leaf blade, particularly those that are externally visible (Fig. 6).

Whorled   Arranged in 3 or more along an axis; 3 or more leaves per node (Fig. 7). Contrast Alternate; Basal rosette; Opposite.

Winter annual   A plant that germinates in late summer to early spring, flowers, and produces seeds in mid to late spring, after which it dies (Fig. 12). Many winter annual weeds tolerate cold weather, often overwintering then flowering the following spring or summer. They generally do not thrive under hot, dry conditions.

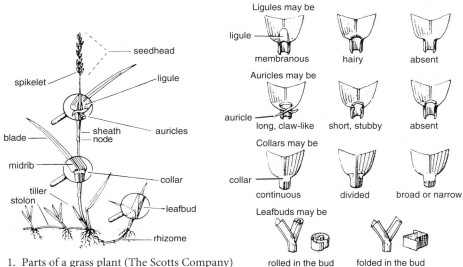

1. Parts of a grass plant (The Scotts Company)

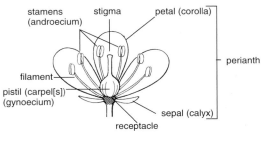

2. Parts of a flower (Ciba-Geigy Corporation)

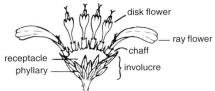

3. A composite flower (Regina O. Hughes, USDA)

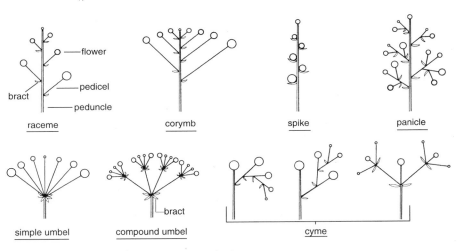

4. Inflorescence types (Ciba-Geigy Corporation)

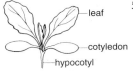

5. A dicot seedling (Ciba-Geigy Corporation)

6. A dicot leaf (Ciba-Geigy Corporation)

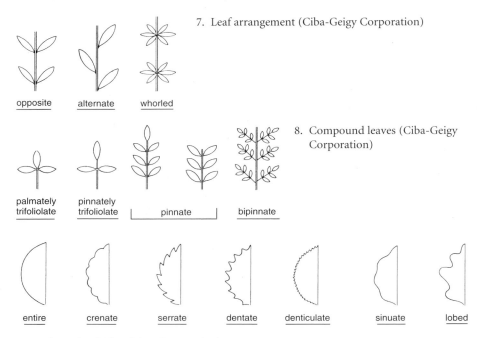

7. Leaf arrangement (Ciba-Geigy Corporation)

opposite   alternate   whorled

8. Compound leaves (Ciba-Geigy Corporation)

palmately trifoliolate   pinnately trifoliolate   pinnate   bipinnate

entire   crenate   serrate   dentate   denticulate   sinuate   lobed

9. Leaf margins (Ciba-Geigy Corporation)

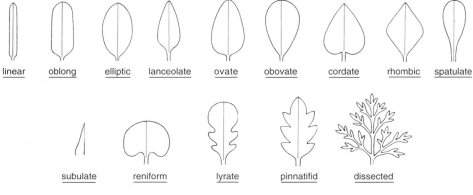

linear   oblong   elliptic   lanceolate   ovate   obovate   cordate   rhombic   spatulate

subulate   reniform   lyrate   pinnatifid   dissected

10. Leaf shapes (Ciba-Geigy Corporation)

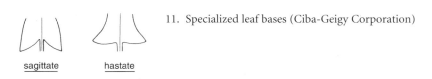

11. Specialized leaf bases (Ciba-Geigy Corporation)

sagittate   hastate

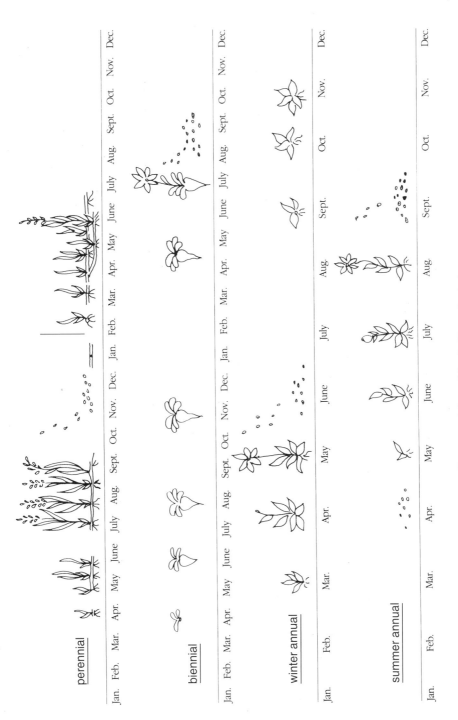

12. Life cycles (Cornell Cooperative Extension Bulletin, *Weed Control for the Home Garden*)

BIBLIOGRAPHY

Alex, J.F. 1992. Ontario weeds. Ontario Ministry of Agriculture and Food, Toronto.

Barkley, T.M. 1983. Field guide to the common weeds of Kansas. Contribution 82-547-B. Kansas Agricultural Experiment Station and Division of Biology, Kansas State University, Manhattan.

Bassett, I.J., and C.W. Crompton. 1978. The biology of Canadian weeds. 32. *Chenopodium album* L. Can. J. Plant Sci. 58: 1061–1072.

Bassett, I.J., and D.B. Munro. 1985. The biology of Canadian weeds. 67. *Solanum ptycanthum* Dun., *S. nigrum* L. and *S. sarrachoides* Sendt. Can. J. Plant Sci. 65: 401–414.

Bassett, I.J., and D.B. Munro. 1986. The biology of Canadian weeds. 78. *Solanum carolinense* L. and *S. rostratum* Dunal. Can. J. Plant Sci. 66: 977–991.

Bellinder, R.R., R.A. Kline, and D.T. Warholic. 1989. Weed control for the home vegetable garden. Information Bulletin 216. Cornell Cooperative Extension, Ithaca, N.Y.

Bhowmik, P.C., and J.D. Bandeen. 1976. The biology of Canadian weeds. 19. *Asclepias syriaca* L. Can. J. Plant Sci. 56: 579–589.

Britton, N.L., and H.A. Brown. 1913. An illustrated flora of the northern United States and Canada. Dover, New York.

Brown, L. 1976. Weeds in winter. Norton, New York.

Brown, M.L., and R.G. Brown. 1984. Herbaceous plants of Maryland. Department of Botany, University of Maryland, College Park.

Chancellor, R.J. 1966. The identification of weed seedlings of farm and garden. Blackwell Scientific, Oxford.

Cody, W.J., and V. Wagner. 1980. The biology of Canadian weeds. 49. *Equisetum arvense* L. Can. J. Plant Sci. 61: 123–133.

Cooperative Extension Service University of Georgia. Common weed seedlings of the United States and Canada. University of Georgia College of Agriculture, Athens.

Cooperative Extension University of California. 1991. Growers weed identification handbook. Publication 4030. Division of Agriculture and Natural Resources, Davis, Calif.

Crockett, L.J. 1977. Wildly successful plants. Collier Books, New York.

Dirr, M.A. 1990. Manual of woody landscape plants. 4th ed. Stipes Publishing, Champaign, Ill.

Douglas, B.J., T.A. Gordon, I.N. Morrison, and M.G. Maw. 1985. The biology of Canadian weeds. 70. *Setaria viridis* (L.) Beauv. Can. J. Plant Sci. 65: 669–690.

Doust, L.L., A. MacKinnon, and J.L. Doust. 1985. The biology of Canadian weeds. 71. *Oxalis stricta* L., *O. corniculata* L., *O. dillenii* Jacq. ssp. *dillenii* and *O. dillenii* Jacq. ssp. *filipes* (Small) Eiten. Can. J. Plant Sci. 65: 691–705.

Duncan, W.H., and M.B. Duncan. 1987. The Smithsonian guide to seaside plants of the Gulf and Atlantic Coasts from Louisiana to Massachusetts, exclusive of lower peninsular Florida. Smithsonian Institution Press, Washington, D.C.

Fernald, M.L. 1950. Gray's manual of botany. 8th ed. American Book Co., New York.

Fogg, J.M., Jr. 1956. Weeds of lawn and garden, a handbook for eastern temperate North America. University of Pennsylvania Press, Philadelphia.

Frankton, C., and G.A. Mulligan. 1970. Weeds of Canada. Publication 948. Canada Department of Agriculture, Ottawa.

Gleason, H.A. 1963. The new Britton and Brown illustrated flora of the northeastern United States and adjacent Canada. The New York Botanical Garden, Bronx, N.Y.

Gleason, H.A., and A. Cronquist. 1991. Manual of vascular plants of northeastern United States and adjacent Canada. 2nd ed. The New York Botanical Garden, Bronx, N.Y.

Häfliger, E., and H. Scholz. 1980. Grass weeds 1. Ciba-Geigy, Basel, Switzerland.

Häfliger, E., and H. Scholz. 1981. Grass weeds 2. Ciba-Geigy, Basel, Switzerland.

Häfliger, E., U. Kühn, et al. 1982. Monocot weeds 3. Ciba-Geigy, Basel, Switzerland.

Hanf, M. 1983. The arable weeds of Europe. BASF Aktiengesellschaft, Ludwigshafen.

Hitchcock, A.S. 1950. Manual of the grasses of the United States. 2nd ed. Misc. Publ. No. 200. United States Department of Agriculture, Washington, D.C.

Hulten, E. 1962. The circumpolar plants I: vascular cryptogams, conifers, monocotyledons. Almqvist & Wiksell, Stockholm.

Hume, L., J. Martinez, and K. Best. 1983. The biology of Canadian weeds. 60. *Polygonum convolvulus* L. Can. J. Plant Sci. 63: 959–971.

Jones, S.B., and A.E. Luchsinger. 1986. Plant systematics. McGraw-Hill, New York.

Kummer, A.P. 1951. Weed seedlings. University of Chicago Press, Chicago.

Liberty Hyde Bailey Hortorium. 1976. Hortus third: A concise dictionary of plants cultivated in the United States and Canada. 3rd ed. Macmillan, New York.

Lorenzi, H. 1987. Weeds of the United States and their control. Van Nostrand Reinhold, New York.

Manitoba Agriculture. 1986. Weed seedling identification guide. Manitoba Agriculture and the crop protection section of Saskatchewan Agriculture, Agdex 640.

Maun, M.A., and S.C.H. Barrett. 1986. The biology of Canadian weeds. 77. *Echinochloa crus-galli* (L.) Beauv. Can. J. Plant Sci. 66: 739–759.

Miyanishi, K., and P.B. Cavers. 1980. The biology of Canadian weeds. 40. *Portulaca oleracea* L. Can. J. Plant Sci. 60: 953–963.

Muenscher, W.C. 1987. Weeds, with a new foreword and new appendixes by Peter A. Hyypio. Cornell University Press, Ithaca, N.Y.

Mulligan, G.A., and B.E. Junkins. 1976. The biology of Canadian weeds. 17. *Cyperus esculentus* L. Can. J. Plant Sci. 56: 339–350.

Murphy, T.R. (ed.). Weeds of southern turfgrass. University of Georgia Cooperative Extension Service, Athens, Ga.

Niering, W.A., and N.C. Olmstead. 1979. The Audubon Society field guide to North American wildflowers. Alfred A. Knopf, New York.

North Central Regional Technical Committee NC-121. 1981. Weeds of the north central states. North Central Regional Res. Publ. No. 281. University of Illinois at Urbana-Champaign, College of Agriculture, Agricultural Experiment Station.

O.M. Scott & Sons. 1985. Scott's guide to the identification of dicot turf weeds. O.M. Scott & Sons, Marysville, Ohio.

O.M. Scott & Sons. 1985. Scott's guide to the identification of grasses. O.M. Scott & Sons, Marysville, Ohio.

Page, N.M., and R.E. Weaver Jr. 1975. Wild plants in the city. New York Times Book Co., New York.

Peterson, L.A. 1977. A field guide to edible wild plants of eastern and central North America. Houghton Mifflin, Boston.

Petrides, G.A. 1977. A field guide to trees and shrubs. Houghton Mifflin, Boston.

Pohl, R.W. 1978. How to know the grasses. 3rd ed. Wm. C. Brown, Dubuque, Iowa.

Puntener, W. (ed.). 1988. Dicot weeds 1. Ciba-Geigy, Basel, Switzerland.

Rice, R.P., Jr. 1992. Nursery and landscape weed control manual. Thomson, Fresno, Calif.

Schuster, R.M. 1949. The ecology and distribution of Hepaticae in central and western New York. Am. Midl. Naturalist 42(3): 513–710.

Southern Weed Science Society Weed Identification Committee. Weed identification guide. Southern Weed Science Society, Champaign, Ill.

Stucky, J.M., T.J. Monaco, and A.D. Worsham. 1981. Identifying seedling and mature weeds common in the southeastern United States. AG-208, Bulletin No. 461. North Carolina Agricultural Research Service and North Carolina Agricultural Extension Service, Raleigh.

Thompson, J.D., and R. Turkington. 1988. The biology of Canadian weeds. 82. *Holcus lanatus* L. Can. J. Plant Sci. 68: 131–147.

Tiner, R.W., Jr. 1988. Field guide to nontidal wetland identification. Maryland Department of Natural Resources, Annapolis.

Turkington R., and J.J. Burdon. 1983. The biology of Canadian weeds. 54. *Trifolium repens* L. Can. J. Plant Sci. 63: 243–266.

Turkington, R., and P.B. Cavers. 1979. The biology of Canadian weeds. 33. *Medicago lupulina* L. Can. J. Plant Sci. 59: 99–110.

Turkington, R., N.C. Kenkel, and G.D. Franko. 1980. The biology of Canadian weeds. 42. *Stellaria media* (L.) Vill. Can J. Plant Sci. 60: 981–992.

United States Department of Agriculture. 1971. Common weeds of the United States. Dover, New York.

Upadhyaya, M.K., R. Turkington, and D. McIlvride. 1986. The biology of Canadian weeds. 75. *Bromus tectorum* L. Can. J. Plant Sci. 66: 689–709.

Walters, D.R., and D.J. Keil. 1988. Vascular plant taxonomy. Kendall/Hunt, Dubuque, Iowa.

Warwick, S.I. 1979. The biology of Canadian weeds. 37. *Poa annua* L. Can. J. Plant Sci. 59: 1053–1066.

Warwick, S.I., and L.D. Black. 1983. The biology of Canadian weeds. 61. *Sorghum halepense* (L.) Pers. Can. J. Plant Sci. 63: 997–1014.

Weaver, S.E., and W.R. Riley. 1982. The biology of Canadian weeds. 53. *Convolvulus arvensis*. Can. J. Plant Sci. 62: 461–472.

Weed Science Society of America, Standardized Plant Names Subcommittee. 1989. Composite list of weeds. Rev. ed. Available from the Weed Science Society of America, 1508 West University Ave., Champaign, IL 61821–3133.

Werner, P.A., and S.D. Judith. 1976. The biology of Canadian weeds. 18. *Potentilla recta* L., *P. norvegica* L. and *P. argentea* L. Can. J. Plant Sci. 56: 591–603.

Werner, P.A., I.K. Bradbury, and R.S. Gross. 1980. The biology of Canadian weeds. 45. *Solidago canadensis* L. Can. J. Plant Sci. 60: 1393–1409.

Whitson, T.D. (ed.). 1991. Weeds of the west. Western Society of Weed Science, in cooperation with the Western U.S. Land Grant Universities Cooperative Extension Service and the University of Wyoming, Laramie.

INDEX

Page numbers in **boldface** indicate the location of the main text description. Entries without a boldface page number are synonyms.

Abutilon theophrasti, **256**, 262
Acalypha rhomboidea, **222**
   virginica, **222**, 262
Acer negundo, **354**
   platanoides, **354**
   rubrum, **354**
Achillea millefolium, 100, **106**
Agropyron repens, 52
Agrostemma githago, **190**
Agrostis stolonifera, **62**, 80
   tenuis, **80**
Ailanthus altissima, 326, **346**
Allium canadense, **30**
   vineale, **30**
alsike, 234, **236**, 266, 370
Alsine media, 202
amaranth, Powell, **94–96**, 363
   spiny, **96**, 363
Amaranthus albus, **90**, 363
   blitoides, 90, **92**, 363
   graecizans, 92
   hybridus, **94–96**, 363
   powellii, **94–96**, 363
   retroflexus, **94–96**, 363
   spinosus, **96**, 363
Ambrosia artemisiifolia, **108**, 110, 116, 154
   elatior, 108
   media, 108
   trifida, 108, **110**
Anagallis arvensis, **290**
Andropogon gerardii, **34**
   scoparius, **34**
   virginicus, **34**
Antennaria, **144**
Anthemis arvensis, 106, **112**, 128, 365
   cotula, 100, 106, **112**, 128, 365
Apocynum cannabinum, **102**
Arctium minus, **114**, 134, 166
Arenaria serpyllifolia, **202**
Artemisia vulgaris, **116**, 140, 154, 206
artichoke, Jerusalem, **146**
Arundo donax, 72, **76**
Asclepias syriaca, **102**

ash, green, **358**
   white, **358**
aster, New England, **118**, 120, 198
   white heath, **118**, 120, 198
Aster novae-angliae, **118**, 120, 198
   pilosus, **118**, 120, 198
Avena fauta, **36**
   sativa, **36**

bamboo, **278**
   Japanese, 278
Bambusa spp., 278
Barbarea vulgaris, **168**
barnyardgrass, **48**
bachelor's buttons, 126
bedstraw, catchweed, 88, **302**
   smooth, 88, **302**
beggarticks, devils, **122**
   nodding, **122**, 138
Bellis perennis, **120**, 128
bentgrass, colonial, **80**
   creeping, **62**, 80
bermudagrass, **42**, 62
Bidens bipinnta, **122**
   cernua, **122**, 138
   frondosa, **122**
bindweed, black, 276
   field, 208, **210**, 276, 368
   hedge, **208**, 210, 276, 368
birdseye pearlwort, 20, **194**, 196
birdsfoot trefoil, **228**, 230, 370
bittercress, hairy, **174**
   lesser-seeded, **174**
   smallflowered, **174**
bittersweet, American, **336**
   Oriental, **336**, 348
bittersweet nightshade, **348**, 374
blackberry, **344**
bluegrass, annual, **78**, 80
   Canada, **78**
   Kentucky, **78**, 80
   roughstalk, **80**
bluestem, big, **34**

bluestem (*cont.*)
  little, **34**
bower, virgin's, **340**
box elder, **354**
brambles, **344**
Brassica arvensis, 170
  hirta, **170**
  juncea, **170**
  kaber, 168, **170**, 180
  nigra, **170**
  rapa, **170**
briar, 338
brome, downy, **38**, 56
Bromus secalinus, **38**
  tectorum, **38**, 56
broomsedge, **34**
Brunella vulgaris, 250
bryum, silvery, **20**
Bryum argenteum, **20**
buckwheat, wild, 208, 210, **276**, 282, 368
burcucumber, **218**, 369
burdock, common, **114**, 134, 166
bur-grass, 40
butter-and-eggs, 304
buttercup, bulbous, **294**
  creeping, **294**
  tall, **294**
buttonweed, Virginia, **300**

Calystegia sepium, **208**, 210, 368
campion, bladder, 198
  white, 190, **198**
Campsis radicans, **330**
canarygrass, reed, **72**, 76
Capriola dactylon, 42
Capsella bursa-pastoris, 136, 168, **172**
Cardamine hirsuta, **174**
  oligosperma, **174**
  parviflora, **174**
Carduus arvense, 132
  nutans, **124**, 220
  vulgare, 134
carpetweed, **88**, 302
carrot, wild, **100**, 106, 364
catchfly, nightflowering, **198**
  sleepy, **198**
catchweed, 302
catbriar, **338**
catsear, common, **148**, 162
Celastrus orbiculatus, **336**, 348
  scandens, **336**
Cenchrus incertus, **40**
  longspinus, **40**
  pauciflorus, 40
Centaurea cyanus, **126**

  maculosa, **126**
  stoebe, 126
Cerastium arvense, **192**
  glomeratum, **192**
  viscosum, 192
  vulgatum, 88, **192**, 202
Chamaeplium officinale, 184
Chamaesyce maculata, 226
chamomile, corn, 106, **112**, 128, 365
  mayweed, 100, 106, **112**, 128, 365
  scentless, **365**
Chamomilla suaveolens, 152
cheat, **38**
cheatgrass, 38
cheese-weed, 260
Chenopodium album, 96, **204**, 206
cherry, black, **360**
  choke, **360**
chess, **38**
  downy, **38**
chickweed, common, 88, 192, 200, **202**, 290, 292
  field, **192**
  mouseear, 88, **192**, 202
  sticky, **192**
chicory, **130**, 162
chrysanthemum, garden, 116
  weed, 116
Chrysanthemum leucanthemum, **128**
chufa, 26
Cichorium intybus, **130**, 162
Cicuta maculata, **98**, 364
cinquefoil, common, **298**
  oldfield, 296, **298**
  rough, 296, **298**
  silvery, **298**
  sulfur, **298**
Cirsium arvense, 124, **132**, 134, 220
  lanceolatum, 134
  vulgare, 124, 132, **134**, 220
cleavers, 302
Clematis virginiana, **340**
clover, alsike, 234, **236**, 266, 370
  hop, **228**, 230, 234, 236, 266, 370
  large hop, **228**, 230, 236, 266, 370
  rabbitfoot, **234**, 266, 370
  red, 234, **236**, 266, 370
  strawberry, 234, **236**, 266, 370
  white, 234, **236**, 266, 370
cockle, corn, **190**
  purple, 190
  white, 190, 198
cocklebur, common, 110, **166**, 312
  spiny, **166**
colt's-tail, 136
Commelina communis, **24**

diffusa, **24**
erecta, **24**
Conium maculatum, **98**, 100, 364
Convolvulus arvensis, 208, **210**, 276, 368
  sepium, 208, 276
Conyza canadensis, 116, 118, **136**, 140, 178
copperleaf, rhombic, **222**
  Virginia, **222**, 262
corn, **68**
cornflower, **126**
Coronilla varia, **240**
cottonwood, common, 268, **360**
couchgrass, 42, 52
crabgrass, hairy, 46
  large, **46**, 50, 70
  silver, 50
  smooth, **46**, 50
  southern, **46**, 50
cranesbill, 244
  Carolina, 244
  smallflower, 244
creeping Charlie, 246
creeping Jenny, 292
crownvetch, trailing, **240**
cucumber, bur, **218**, 369
  wild, **218**, 369
cudweed, clammy, 120, **144**
  fragrant, 120, **144**
  low, 120, **144**
  purple, 120, **144**
Cuscuta spp., **212**
Cynanchum nigrum, **104**
  vincetoricum, **104**
Cynodon dactylon, **42**, 62
Cyperus esculentus, **26**
  rotundus, **26**
cypress, summer-, 206

Dactylis glomerata, **44**, 50, 74
daisy, English, **120**, 128
  oxeye, **128**
dallisgrass, **70**
dandelion, 130, 148, **162**
  false, 148
Datura stramonium, 166, **312**
  tatula, 312
Daucus carota, **100**, 106, 364
dayflower, Asiatic, **24**
  common, **24**
  erect, **24**
  spreading, **24**
deadnettle, purple, **248**, 250
  red, 248
  spotted, **248**
dewberry, **344**

Digitaria ciliaris, **46**
  ischaemum, **46**
  sanguinalis, **46**, 70
Diodia hirsuta, **300**
  teres, **300**
  tetragona, **300**
  virginiana, **300**
Dipsacus fullonum, **220**
  laciniatus, **220**
  sylvestris, 220
dock, broadleaf, 114, **286**
  curly, 114, **286**
dodder, **212**
dogbane, hemp, **102**
dogfennel, **140**
Duchesnea indica, **296**

Echinochloa crus-galli, **48**
Echinocystis lobata, **218**, 369
eclipta, **138**
Eclipta alba, 138
  prostrata, **138**
Eleusine indica, 44, **50**
Elytrigia repens, **52**, 54, 58, 74
Epilobium ciliatum, **254**
  hirsutum, **254**
Equisetum arvense, **22**
  hyemale, **22**
Erigeron annuus, 118, **136**
  canadensis, 136
  strigosis, 118, **136**
Erodium cicutarium, **242**
  moschatum, **242**
Erysimum officinale, 184
Eupatorium capillifolium, **140**
Euphorbia, *cyparissias*, **224**
  esula, **224**
  humistrata, 92, **226**, 234, 274, 288
  maculata, **226**, 274, 288
  nutans, **226**
  supina, **226**
eveningprimrose, common, **264**
  cutleaf, **264**

Fallopia convolvulus, 276
fescue, tall, 52, **54**
Festuca arundinacea, 52, **54**
  elatior, 54
fieldcress, yellow, **182**
filaree, redstem, **242**
  whitestem, **242**
fleabane, annual, 118, **136**
  rough, 118, **136**
foxtail, giant, 40, 66, 74, **82**
  green, 40, 66, 74, **82**

foxtail (*cont.*)
    yellow, 40, 66, 74, **82**
Fragaria virginiana, **296**
Fraxinus americana, **358**
    pennsylvanica, **358**

galinsoga, hairy, **142**, 222
    smallflower, **142**, 222
Galinsoga ciliata, **142**, 222
    parviflora, **142**, 222
    quadriradiata, 142
Galium aparine, 88, **302**
    mollugo, 88, **302**
garlic, wild, **30**
geranium, Carolina, 242, **244**
    dovefoot, **244**
    smallflower, **244**
    wild, 244
Geranium carolinianum, **244**
    molle, **244**
    pusillum, **244**
gill-over-the-ground, 246
Glechoma hederacea, **246**, 260, 310
Gleditsia triacanthos, **356**
Gnaphalium obtusifolium, 120, **144**
    purpureum, 120, **144**
    uliginosum, 120, **144**
    viscosum, 120, **144**
goat's beard, yellow, 164
goldenrod, Canada, **156**
    tall, **156**
goosegrass, 44, **50**
grape, fox, **352**
    frost, **352**
    riverbank, **352**
    summer, **352**
    wild, **352**
greenbriar, roundleaf, **338**
groundcherry, clammy, **314**, 316, 374
    smooth, **314**, 316, 374
ground ivy, **246**, 260, 310
groundsel, common, 106, **154**

hawkweed, orange, **148**
    yellow, **148**
healall, **250**, 252
Helianthus annuus, 110, **146**
    tuberosus, **146**
hemlock, poison-, **98**, 100, 364
    spotted water-, **98**, 364
henbit, 246, **248**
Heracleum mantegazzianum, **98**, 364
Hibiscus trionum, **258**
Hieracium aurantiacum, **148**
    caespitosum, 148

    pratense, **148**
hogweed, giant, **98**, 364
Holcus halepense, 86
    lanatus, 38, **56**
honeysuckle, Japanese, **332**, 334
    Tatarian, 332, **334**
horsenettle, **316**, 318, 374
horsetail, common, 22
    field, **22**
horseweed, 116, 118, **136**, 140, 178
Hypochoeris radicata, **148**, 162

Ipomoea barbigera, 214
    hederacea, 208, 210, **214–216**
    hederacea var. *integriuscula*, **216**
    hirsutula, 214
    lacunosa, 208, 210, **214–216**
    pandulata, 208, 210, **216**
    purpurea, 208, 210, **214–216**
ivy, ground, **246**, 260, 310
    poison-, **328**, 340, 350

Jamestown-weed, 312
jimsonweed, 166, **312**
Johnny-jump-ups, 322
johnsongrass, 48, 66, 84, **86**
Juncus tenuis, **28**

knapweed, spotted, **126**
knawel, 194, **196**
knotgrass, **70**
knotweed, Japanese, 268, **278**
    prostrate, 226, **274**
kochia, **206**
Kochia scoparia, **206**
kudzu, **232**

Lactuca scariola, 150
    serriola, **150**, 158, 160, 366
ladysthumb, **280**
lambsquarters, common, 96, **204**, 206
Lamium amplexicaule, 246, **248**
    maculatum, **248**
    purpureum, **248**, 250
Lappa minor, 114
Lentodon taraxacum, 162
Lepidium campestre, 168, **176**, 178
    virginicum, 136, 168, 172, 176, **178**
Leption canadense, 136
lettuce, prickly, **150**, 158, 160, 366
Leucanthemum leucanthemum, 128
    vulgare, 128
Linaria canadensis, **304**
    vulgaris, 224, **304**
liverworts, **18**

locust, black, **356**
  honey, **356**
Lolium italicum, 58
  multiflorum, 52, 54, **58**
  perenne, 52, 54, **58**
Lonicera japonica, **332**, 334
  tatarica, 332, **334**
loosestrife, purple, **254**
Lotus corniculatus, **228**, 230, 370
Lunularia cruciata, **18**
Lychnis alba, 198
  githago, 190
Lysimachia nummularia, **292**
Lythrum salicaria, **254**

mallow, common, 246, 256, **260**
  musk, **258**, 260
  Venice, **258**
Malva moschata, **258**, 260
  neglecta, 246, 256, **260**
maple, Norway, **354**
  red, **354**
Marchantia polymorpha, **18**
marestail, 136
Matricaria discoidea, 152
  matricarioides, 106, 112, **152**, 365
  perforata, **365**
  suaveolens, 152
medic, black, 228, **230**, 236, 266, 370
Medicago lupulina, 228, **230**, 236, 266, 370
Melandrium album, 198
mile-a-minute, **282**
milkweed, common, **102**
millet, domestic proso, **68**
  wild-proso, **68**
mock-strawberry, Indian, **296**
Mollugo verticillata, **88**, 302
moneywort, **292**
morningglory, bigroot, 208, 210, **216**
  ivyleaf, 208, 210, **214–216**
  pitted, 208, 210, **214–216**
  tall, 208, 210, **214–216**
Morus alba, **358**
moss, **20**, 194
mugwort, **116**, 140, 154, 206
Muhlenbergia commutata, 60
  frondosa, **60**
  mexicana, 60
  schreberi, 42, 60, **62**
muhly, wirestem, **60**
mulberry, white, **358**
mullein, common, **306**
  moth, **306**
mustard, birdsrape, **170**
  black, **170**

  Indian, **170**
  hedge, **184**
  tumble, **184**
  white, 168, **170**
  wild, **170**, 180

Nasturtium palustre, 182
Nepeta hederacea, 246
nettle, stinging, **320**
nightshade, American black, **318**
  bittersweet, **348**, 374
  black, **318**, 374
  deadly, **318**
  eastern black, **318**, 348, 374
  hairy, **318**, 374
nimblewill, 42, 60, **62**
nut-grass, yellow, 26
nutsedge, purple, **26**
  yellow, **26**

oat, cultivated, **36**
  wild, **36**
Oenothera biennis, **264**
  laciniata, **264**
  sinuata, 264
onion, wild, **30**
orchardgrass, **44**, 50, 74
Ornithogalum umbellatum, **32**
Oxalis corniculata, 230, 236, **266**, 370
  dillenii, 266
  europaea, 266
  stricta, 230, 236, **266**, 370

panicum, fall, 40, 48, 64, **66**, 82, 86
Panicum capillare, **64**, 66, 68
  dichotomiflorum, 40, 48, 64, **66**, 82, 86
  miliaceum, **68**
pansy, **322**
  field, **322**, 324
Parthenocissus quinquefolia, 328, **350**, 352
paspalum, fringeleaf, **70**
Paspalum dilatatum, **70**
  distchum, **70**
  setaceum var. *ciliatifolium*, **70**
pearlwort, birdseye, 20, **194**, 196
pennycress, field, **186**
  thoroughwort, **186**
peppercress, Virginian, 178
pepperweed, field, 168, **176**, 178
  Virginia, 136, 168, 172, 176, **178**
Persicaria pensylvanica, 280
  perfoliata, 282
Phalaris arundinacea, **72**, 76
  arundinacea var. *picta*, **72**
Pharbitis barbigera, 214

Pharbitis (cont.)
  hederacea, 214
Phleum pratense, **74**
Phragmites australis, 72, **76**
  communis, 76
  maximus, **76**
Physalis heterophylla, **314**, 316, 374
  subglabrata, **314**, 316, 374
Phytolacca americana, **268**
  decandra, **268**
pigweed, green, 94
  prostrate, 90, **92**, 363
  redroot, **94–96**, 363
  smooth, **94–96**, 363
  tumble, **90**, 363
pimpernel, scarlet, **290**
pineapple-weed, 106, 112, **152**, 365
Plantago aristata, **270**, 272
  asiatica, 272
  lanceolata, **270**, 272
  major, **272**, 372
  rugelii, **272**, 372
plantain, blackseed, **272**, 372
  bracted, **270**, 272
  broadleaf, **272**, 372
  buckhorn, **270**, 272
  English, 270
  narrow-leaved, 270
Pleuropterus zuccarinii, 278
Poa annua, **78**, 80
  annua ssp. *annua*, **78**
  annua ssp. *reptans*, **78**
  compressa, **78**
  pratensis, **78**, 80
  trivialis, **80**
poison-hemlock, **98**, 100, 364
poison-ivy, **328**, 340, 350
poison-oak, **328**
poison-sumac, 346
pokeberry, 268
pokeweed, common, **268**
Polygonum arenastrum, 274
  aviculare, 226, **274**
  caespitosum, 280
  convolvulus, 208, 210, **276**, 282, 368
  cuspidatum, 268, **278**
  monspeliense, 274
  pensylvanicum, **280**
  perfoliatum, **282**
  persicaria, **280**
poorjoe, **300**
poor man's weather-glass, 290
poplar, 360
Populus deltoides, 268, **360**
Portulaca oleracea, 92, **288**

Potentilla argentea, **298**
  canadensis, **298**
  norvegica, 296, **298**
  recta, **298**
  simplex, 296, **298**
primrose, common evening, **264**
  cutleaf evening, **264**
Prunella vulgaris, **250**
Prunus serotina, **360**
  virginiana, **360**
Pueraria lobata, **232**
  thunbergiana, 232
purslane, common, 92, **288**
pusley, Florida, **300**
pussytoes, **144**

quackgrass, **52**, 54, 58, 74
Queen Anne's lace, 100

Radicula palustris, 182
radish, wild, 168, 170, **180**
ragweed, common, **108**, 110, 116, 154
  giant, 108, **110**
ragwort, tansy, **154**
Raimannia laciniata, 264
Ranunculus acris, **294**
  bulbosus, **294**
  repens, **294**
Raphanus raphanistrum, 168, 170, **180**
raspberry, **344**
reed, common, 72, **76**
  giant, 72, **76**
Rhus copallina, **326**, 330
  glabra, **326**, 330
  hirta, 326
  radicans, 328
  toxicarium, 328
  typhina, **326**, 330, 346
  vernix, 326
ribbon-grass, **72**
Richardia scabra, **300**
Robinia pseudoacia, **356**
rocket, yellow, 168
Rorippa islandica, **182**
  palustris, 182
  sylvestris, **182**
Rosa multiflora, **342**
rose, multiflora, **342**
Rubus, **344**
Rumex acetosella, **284**
  crispus, 114, **286**
  elongatus, 286
  obtusifolius, 114, **286**
rush, slender, **28**

ryegrass, annual, 58
  Italian, 52, 54, **58**
  perennial, 52, 54, **58**

Sagina procumbens, 20, **194**, 196
salsify, meadow, **164**
  western, **164**
Salsola iberica, **90**
sandbur, field, **40**
  longspine, **40**
sandspurry, red, **194**, 196
sandwort, thymeleaf, **202**
sawbriar, cat, **338**
Schizachyrium scoparium, 34
Scleranthus annuus, 194, **196**
scouringrush, **22**
sedge, 26
Senecio jacobaca, **154**
  vulgaris, 106, **154**
Setaria faberi, 40, 66, 74, **82**
  glauca, 40, 66, 74, **82**
  lutenscens, 82
  viridis, 40, 66, 74, **82**
shattercane, **84**, 86
shepherd's-purse, 136, 168, **172**
Sicyos angulatus, **218**, 369
sida, prickly, **262**
Sida spinosa, **262**
Silene alba, **198**
  antirrhina, **198**
  latifolia, 198
  noctiflora, **198**
  vulgaris, **198**
silver thread, **20**
Sinapis arvensis, 170
Sisymbrium altissimum, **184**
  officinale, **184**
smartweed, Pennsylvania, **280**
Smilax bona-nox, **338**
  glauca, **338**
  rotundifolia, **338**
Solanum americanum, **318**
  carolinense, **316**, 318, 374
  dulcamara, **348**, 374
  nigrum, **318**, 374
  ptycanthum, **318**, 348, 374
  sarrachoides, **318**, 374
Solidago altissima, **156**
  canadensis, **156**
Sonchus arvensis, 150, **158**, 160, 366
  asper, 150, 158, **160**, 366
  oleraceus, 150, 158, **160**, 366
Sorghum bicolor, **84**, 86
  bicolor var. *drummondii*, 84
  halepense, 48, 66, 84, **86**

vulgare, 84
sorrel, red, **284**
  sheep, 284
sowthistle, annual, 150, 158, **160**, 366
  perennial, 150, **158**, 160, 366
  spiny, 150, 158, **160**, 366
spanishneedles, **122**
Specularia perfoliata, 188
speedwell, common, 88, 373
  corn, 88, 188, **308**, 310, 373
  field, 88, **310**, 373
  germander, 88, **310**, 373
  ivyleaf, 88, **308**, 373
  Persian, 88, 248, **308**, 310, 373
  purslane, 88, **308**, 373
  slender, 88, 246, **310**, 373
  thymeleaf, 88, **192**, 202, 292, 373
  wayside, 88, **308**
Spergula arvensis, **194**, 196, 200
Spergularia rubra, **194**, 196
spurge, cypress, **224**
  leafy, **224**
  nodding, **226**
  prostrate, 92, **226**, 234, 274, 288
  spotted, **226**, 274, 288
spurry, corn, **194**, 196, 200
  red sand, **194**, 196
star-of-Bethlehem, **32**
starwort, little, **200**
Stellaria graminea, **200**
  media, 88, 200, **202**, 290, 292
storksbill, common, 242
strawberry, wild, **296**
sumac, dwarf, **326**, 330
  poison-, **326**, 330, 346
  smooth, **326**, 330
  staghorn, **326**, 330, 346
summer-cypress, 206
sunflower, common, 110, **146**
swallowwort, black, **104**
  white, **104**

Taraxacum officinale, 130, 148, **162**
teasel, common, **220**
  cutleaf, **220**
thistle, bull, 124, 132, **134**, 220
  Canada, 124, **132**, 134, 220
  musk, **124**, 220
  Russian, **90**
Thlaspi arvense, **186**
  perfoliatum, **186**
thread, silver, **20**
three-seeded mercury, 222
thyme, creeping, 250, **252**
Thymus serpyllum, 250, **252**

timothy, **74**
Tithymalus esula, 224
toadflax, oldfield, **304**
   yellow, 224, **304**
Toxicodendron radicans, **328**, 340, 350
   toxicarium, **328**
   vernix, **326**, 330, 346
Tracaulon perfoliatum, **282**
Tragopogon dubius, **164**
   pratensis, **164**
tree-of-heaven, 326, **346**
trefoil, birdsfoot, **228**, 230, 370
Trifolium arvense, **234**, 266, 370
   aureum, **228**, 230, 234, 266, 370
   campestre, **228**, 230, 266, 370
   fragiferum, 234, **236**, 266, 370
   hybridum, 234, **236**, 266, 370
   pratense, 234, **236**, 266, 370
   repens, 234, **236**, 266, 370
Triodanis biflora, **188**
   perfoliata, **188**
trumpetcreeper, **330**

Urtica dioica, **320**
   gracilis, 320
   procera, 320

velvetgrass, common, 38, **56**
velvetleaf, **256**, 262
Venus' looking-glass, common, **188**
   small, **188**
Verbascum blattaria, **306**
   thapsus, **306**
Veronica agrestis, 88, **308**, 373
   arvensis, 88, 188, **308**, 373
   chamaedrys, 88, **310**, 373
   filiformis, 88, 246, **310**, 373
   hederifolia, 88, **308**, 373
   officinalis, 88, 373
   peregrina, 88, **308**, 373
   persica, 88, 248, **308**, 373
   polita, 88, **308**
   serpyllifolia, 88, **192**, 202, 292, 373
vetch, bird, **238**
   common, **238**
   four-seed, 238
   hairy, **238**
   narrowleaf, **238**
   sparrow, **238**
Vicia angustifolia, 238
   cracca, **238**
   sativa, **238**
   sativa ssp. *nigra*, **238**
   tetrasperma, **238**
   villosa, **238**
Vincetoxicum nigrum, 104
Viola arvensis, **322**
   odorata, **324**
   papilionacea, **324**
   rafinesquii, **322**
   sororia, **324**
   tricolor, **322**
violet, common blue, **324**
   dooryard, **324**
   English, **324**
   field, **322**, 324
   sister, 324
Virginia-creeper, 328, **350**, 352
virgin's bower, **340**
Vitis aestivalis, **352**
   labrusca, **352**
   riparia, **352**
   vulpina, **352**

watergrass, 48
waterhemlock, spotted, **98**, 364
willowherb, northern, **254**
willowweed, hairy, **254**
wiregrass, 42
witchgrass, **64**, 66, 68
woodbine, 350
woodsorrel, creeping, 230, 236, **266**, 370
   yellow, 230, 236, **266**, 370

Xanthium spinosum, **166**
   strumarium, 110, **166**, 312
Xanthoxalis cymosa, 266
   stricta, 266

yarrow, common, 100, **106**
yellowcress, marsh, **182**
yerba-de-tago, 138

Zea mays, **68**

ABOUT THE AUTHORS

Richard H. Uva is, at press time, a Ph.D. candidate at Cornell University. Much of the information in this book, and the way it is presented, is derived from his master's thesis. Joseph C. Neal is Associate Professor of Weed Science at North Carolina State University, Raleigh. Joseph M. DiTomaso is Associate Weed Specialist at the University of California, Davis. He and Joseph Neal were formerly on the faculty of Cornell University. Andrew F. Senesac, a key contributor to this book, is Weed Science Specialist for Cornell Cooperative Extension at the Long Island Horticultural Research Laboratory, Riverhead, N.Y. His cooperation and counsel on this project were invaluable.

Richard H. Uva

Joseph C. Neal

Joseph M. DiTomaso

Andrew F. Senesac